AF541767

UNDERSTANDING PLANT REPRODUCTION

By

Dr. Shubhrata R. Mishra

Department of Botany

Vikram University

Ujjain (M.P.)

(India)

DISCOVERY PUBLISHING HOUSE PVT. LTD.

NEW DELHI-110 002

First Published-2009

ISBN 978-81-8356-481-6

Published by:

DISCOVERY PUBLISHING HOUSE PVT. LTD.
4831/24, Ansari Road, Prahlad Street,
Darya Ganj, New Delhi-110002 (India)
Phone: 23279245 • Fax: 91-11-23253475
E-mail: dphbooks@rediffmail.com
dphtemp@indiatimes.com

Printed at:

Sachin Printers
Delhi

Preface

The present title "Understanding Plant Reproduction" has been written for those students interested in careers in diverse fields of biological sciences. It provides a structured approach to learning by covering all the important topics in a uniform, systematic format. The book has been comprehensively designed incorporating recent advances in this fast moving field. It also provides accessible information on plant reproduction in compact form for undergraduate students in biology and related life sciences. It is intelligible to the educated layman, though it deals with some complex ideas. It is an adequate text for all the requirements of students in this area. In addition, busy lecturers who require a quick reference compendium will find it useful, particularly for tutional planning. Simple, yet hopefully clear figures and tables are provided throughout the book.

The over-riding goal of this book, and indeed of the whole *Understanding series*, is to present the essential information concering plant reproduction in a compact, readily accessible form which leads itself to student learning and revision. The convergence of various approaches has generated a rich panorama of detail, the significance of which we are still attempting to unraval. The present text has been written as an introduction to this rapidly growing field.

To make the work more comprehensive and informative, the author has consulted many authoritative books, research journals, abstracts, monographs etc., so there can be no claim to originality except in the manner of treatment.

The author expresses his thanks to his friends and colleagues whose continue inspirations have initiated him to bring out this book.

The author expresses his gratitude to Mr. Wasan and staff of M/s Discovery Publishing House Pvt. Ltd. for their whole hearted co-operation in the publication of this book.

In the mean time, the author will remain sincerely responsible for any shortcomings of the book and be grateful to the readers for their suggestions and constructive criticism for the continuous betterment of the book. He takes this opportunity to appeal to the readers to send their suggestions straightaway to his Publisher.

Author

CONTENTS

1

INTRODUCTION

Asexual propagation involves reproduction from vegetative parts of plants and is possible because the vegetative organs of many plants have the capacity for regeneration. Stem cuttings have the ability to form adventitious roots. Root cuttings can regenerate a new shoot system. Leaves can regenerate new roots and new shoots. A stem and a root (or two stems) can be grafted together to form a continuous vascular connection when properly combined as a graft. New plants can start from a single cell. Cells of tobacco pith and carrot root in aseptic cultures have regenerated entire plants identical with the one from which the original cultures were made. Any living cell of the plant appears to have all the genetic information needed to regenerate the complete organism.

Reasons for Using Asexual Propagation

Asexual propagation reproduces *clones*. Such propagation involves mitotic cell division in which there is duplication (usually) of the complete chromosome system and associated cytoplasm from the parent cell to the two daughter cells. Consequently plants propagated vegetatively reproduce all the genetic information of the parent plant. This is why the unique characteristics of any single plant are perpetuated in the establishment of a *clone*.

The asexual process is, particularly important in horticulture because the genetic makeup (genotype) of most of the valuable fruit and ornamental cultivars is highly heterozygous, and the unique characteristics of such plants are immediately lost if they are propagated by seed. Asexual propagation is necessary to grow cultivars that produce no viable seeds, such as some bananas, figs, oranges, and grapes.

Propagation of some species may be easier, more rapid, and more economical by vegetative methods than by seed. Cotoneaster seed has complex dormancy conditions; leafy stem cuttings, on the other hand, root rapidly and in high percentages. Seedlings of some species grow more slowly than rooted cuttings. Some plants grown from seed have an extended *juvenile* period and during this time the plant may not only fail to produce flowers and fruit, but may exhibit other undesirable morphological features (e.g. thorniness) that are not present when propagation is by material in the adult stage. On the other hand, it may be desirable to maintain this juvenile stage indefinitely so as to facilitate propagation of difficult-to-root cuttings.

The Clone

Many fruit and ornamental cultivars are groups of plants propagated vegetatively, starting with an individual plant, usually one grown from seed, or a part of a plant, e.g., a *bud sport*. Such a group of plants taken collectively has been given the name *clone*. A *clone* can be defined as "genetically uniform material derived from a single individual and propagated exclusively by vegetative means, such as cuttings, divisions, or grafts". A discovery with any individual member of the clone, e.g., a method of propagation, a certain cultural practice, a method of disease control, or a cross-pollination requirement, applies in the same manner to all other members of that clone.

When a member plant of a certain clone requires cross-pollination to set fruit, it must be pollinated by a plant of a different clone, rather than by a different plant of the same clone, which in reality is just another part of the same plant. Many clones of horticultural interest have been discovered and perpetuated by man. The 'Bartlett' pear clone originated from seed in England about 1770 and has been maintained asexually ever since. The 'Winesap' apple clone originated similarly some 200 years ago. The original seedling tree has probably been dead for over 100 years. Buds taken from it and budded to rootstocks produced new trees having tops of the same genetic constitution as the original seedling tree.

By continuing this process of asexual propagation, thousands upon thousands of trees have since been grown whose budded tops, collectively, make up the 'Winesap' apple clone. Clones exist in nature, reproducing naturally by such structures as bulbs, rhizomes, runners, stolons and tip layers. The species *Lilium tigrinum* is said to be a single clone. Apomixis in some species of Rosaceae, Gramineae, and Compositeae makes possible the reproduction of some clones naturally by seeds.

A clone can perpetuate itself successfully in nature, sometimes better than can seed-propagated plants, as long as the environment remains reasonably constant. If the environment changes drastically, however, a clonally reproduced species will be at a disadvantage because it has no opportunity to evolve forms better adapted to the new environment. Similarly, cultivated clones have a disadvantage in that an adverse situation, such as disease or insect attack, can affect all members of the clone equally and may even destroy it. The concept of the clone, however, does not mean that all individual members are necessarily identical in all characteristics.

The actual appearance and behaviour of a plant, i.e., its *phenotype*, results from the interaction of its genes (*genotype*) with the *environment* in which the plant is growing. Consequently, within a given clone the appearance of the plants, or of fruits and flowers on different plants, may vary some what because of climate, soil, disease, and the like. In many years 'Barlett' pear trees grown in California produce round, apple shaped fruit, whereas 'Barlett' pears grown in Washington and Oregon are relatively long and narrow; this difference is believed to be due to different climatic factors. Variation in fruit shape within any one area and even within an orchard or tree may also be related to the presence, the absence, or the number of seeds within the fruit. Some plants produce leaves of different appearance when growing in shade than when growing in the sun.

Some water plants produce leaves quite different in appearance on the part of the plant submerged than on the part in the air. Within a single orchard, fruit trees of the same clone often differ to some extent because of differences in soil, water availability, rootstock, or competition from surrounding plants. Although the environment can modify the growth and appearance of individual members of a clone such changes are not permanent, since the genotype of the plants is unaffected by the environmental modifications. Further in this chapter several causes of more or less permanent changes within clones are discussed. The life of the clone is theoretically unlimited. An early belief, that has long prevailed, is that a clone deteriorates with age and can only be rejuvenated by seed propagation. Evidence now shows that modification, sometimes leading to deterioration, can indeed occur in particular clones, and must be guarded against in propagation.

The most significant factor seems to be virus infection. In fact, virtually any clone that is grown for any period of time is likely to become infected sooner or later, its success being determined by its ability to tolerate the virus. Genetic changes (mutations) may occur in the clone which, although not always degenerative in a strict sense, can produce off-type individuals that will reduce the value of the clone. An unfavourable environment may lead to progressive deterioration of a clone. For example, lack of sufficiently long post-bloom vegetative period for some bulbous plants may lead to gradual decline in vigor and productivity.

If a clone is maintained in a proper environment, and procedures are carried out whereby viruses, other pathogens, and off-type mutants are eliminated, a clone could be perpetuated indefinitely. Such procedures, described later in this chapter, are an important aspect of plant propagation. Another belief, proposed by some people, is that permanent genetic changes in the clone can be induced by the environment or by the influence of one genetically different plant on another if the two are grafted together. Although some aspects of the latter theory have not perhaps been examined critically, the prevailing belief among most scientists is that such permanent genetic changes in clonal material do not occur.

Changes in Clones Associated with Age

The growth cycle of a seedling plant involves a change from a *juvenile* phase to a *adult* phase. The two phases may be distinguished by distinctive morphological and physiological differences. The Juvenile-to-adult change may be referred to as *ontogenetic* because more or less permanent changes occur within the apical meristem as it grows, but the basic genetic information in the cells is not altered. New seedlings revert to the juvenile phase and undergo the same transition to the adult phase as did the parent. Evidence that no permanent genetic change is involved is found with nucellar seedlings, which are asexually produced by apomixis and reproduce genetically the same parent plant but only after having gone through the transitional juvenile phase. The juvenile-to-adult change is not the same as the vegetative to-reproductive change, although the two kinds of changes may be correlated. Likewise, the development of senescence is different from either of these phenomena.

The juvenile and adult phases may differ distinctly in appearance or they may show transitional development from one phase to the other. Leaf shape is a common means of identifying phase changes such as illustrated in *Acacia* and *Eucalyptus*. The juvenile phase of many plants—for example, citrus, pear, apple and honey locust—is characterized also by non flowering, excessive vigor, and thorniness; the adult phase by flowering and fruiting, reduced vigor, and thorniness.

The juvenile phase of a number of plants, of which English ivy (*Hedera helix*) is a classic example, is a trailing vine with alternate palmate leaves. The mature, flowering form is an erect or semierect shrub with entire, ovate leaves, produced oppositely around the stem.

In certain conifers, such as junipers, the juvenile forms produce needle-shaped leaves, but the adult produces scale-like leaves. Cuttings taken from juvenile parts of many perennial plants can reproduce adventitious shoots and roots easily, whereas cuttings taken from the mature phase of the same plant are much less, if at all, capable of forming adventitious roots or shoots. The ontogenetic change from juvenile to adult as the seedling grows older occurs in the somatic (vegetative)cells and results in differences in the apical meristem in separate parts of the plant at various stages of development. Prevailing evidence suggest that a plant must attain a certain size before the adult phase appears. Consequently the growing points produced in different parts of an individual plant where such ontogenetic changes are taking place may differ considerably in their ontogenetic age. This explains why a portion of an individual plant may be in the juvenile phase and another portion in the adult phase.

The phenomenon that different growing points at different parts of a plant may perpetuate particular phases (juvenile or mature) it used in propagation has been called *topophysis*. For example, buds taken from the lower, juvenile portion of seedling trees of pear, apple, citrus, or honey locust, if used in budding, will produce nursery trees that are vigorous, thorny, and slow to flower; buds from the upper portion of the same tree can be used to produce nursery trees that are less vigorous, smooth-barked, and thornless, and that flower quickly. By proper selection of propagation material from a seedling plant, it is possible to propagate leaf persistent (juvenile) or deciduous (adult) beech trees, or to propagate fungus (*Keithia thusima*)-resistant (juvenile) or fungus-susceptible (adult) forms of *Thuja plicata*.

By such selection of propagating material, the juvenile forms of many conifers can be maintained almost indefinitely; this can be done in certain vines, such as *Hedera*. Another type of topophysis occurring in some plants in that the direction of shoot growth produced by a cutting may differ, depending upon whether the cutting was taken from an upright or a lateral branch. For example, cuttings of *Araucaria*, or of coffee, taken from lateral shoots will continue to grow in a horizontal direction, whereas cuttings made from upright shoots of the same plant will develop into upright plants. Juvenile-to-adult phase changes are important in the initial establishment of a clone from a seedling plant.

Various horticultural techniques are designed to speed this transition. To attain the adult phase in the shortest time, selection of propagation wood from the upper, onto-genetically older part of the plant is desirable.

In most well-established clones, however, considerable vegetative propagation has already taken place, a flowering and fruiting pattern has become set, and the adult phase has been attained. Consequently plants propagated from material taken from different parts of most grafted or rooted plants do not exhibit such differences. However, sometimes juvenile characteristics can persist for several vegetative generations. In propagation by rooting cuttings it may be desirable to preserve the juvenile phase of the clone. This can be done to some extent by selection of propagation material, since juvenility tends to persist in the lower part of the plant, particularly in the crown and roots. Likewise, adventitious buds from roots or from heavily cut-back stems, or from "sphaeroblasts" (wart-like growths containing meristematic and conductive tissue) also tend to produce juvenile growth. The success in propagation by stooling is believed to be due to the perpetuation of the juvenile form.

Budsports

A branch which shows changes in one or more inheritable characters that can be perpetuated by asexual means in termed a *bud sport*. Bud sports can originate by any of the somatic mutations or chromosomal changes mentioned earlier. Many of these sports are chimeras and are discovered when a lateral shoot develops from a mutated area. In addition, a bud sport may result when there is a rearrangement of tissues of a chimera such that a shoot may arise from a deeper layer, either from the displacement of epidermal cells with cells of the L-II layer, or by formation of adventitious buds.

Somatic variants such as these are starting points of new clones and, if introduced as cultivars, are given names. Numerous bud sports have been discovered, and a great many more have undoubtedly gone undetected. Some have become important new clones in both fruit and ornamental species. In Florida, pink-fleshed grapefruits were found on a single branch of a tree in a grove of thousands of trees producing whitefleshed grapefruits: an obvious mutation. The seedless 'Washington Navel' orange probably arose as bud mutation of the Brazilian orange, 'Laranja Selecta'. The first citrus fruit to be patented originated in 1929 as a mutation: the red-fleshed 'Ruby' grapefruit. Mutations in apples are common, resulting in changes in fruit colour, size, and shape.

Polyploidy may give rise to "grant" sports in certain plants. Individual tetraploid grapevines occur in vineyards, growers referring to such vines with prodigious growth habits and poor fruitfulness as "bulls," "males," or "giants". Chromosome counts have shown them to be often only partial mutations, (periclinal chimeras) consisting of a single outer layer of diploid cells surrounding the mutated tetraploid inner tissues. Such giant sport canes in the grape are observed to arise at pruning wounds or near areas where a bud or shoot has been injured or killed. These mutant shoots seem to arise from deeply embedded dormant bud initials.

Spontaneous polyploidy also occurs in apples, producing giants sports. Fruits of these sports are usually larger, flatter, and more irregular in shape than those from the parent plant. Trees bearing such fruits are vigorous, with thick twigs, often having wide-angled crotches, which gives them a low, flat shape. Certain of such giant apple sports are diploid-tetraploid periclinal chimeras, with a $2n$ layer (34 chromosomes per cell), one, two, or three cell layers in thickness, over a $4n$ tetraploid (68 chromosomes per cell) interior. A certain 'Delicious' apple giant sport was found to be tetraploid in all internal tissues, but diploid in the epidermis. Many (possibly most) mutations produce sports inferior to the parent plant in one or more characteristics. If detected by the propagator, such sports are discarded. Sometimes, as in citrus, these may be propagated unknowingly and cause serious economic loss.

Graft Chimeras

While most chimeras occur naturally, they can also be established artificially by grafting. If scions are cut back severely, almost to the stock, adventitious buds may sometimes arise from the callus in the region of the graft union. Occasionally, a bud may develop which contains tissues of both stock and scion. The resulting structure is a chimera, in which the cells of the two graft components remain distinct regardless of how intermingled they become. Winkler artificially produced in Germany many graft chimeras, using species in the Solanaceae family. He prepared wedge or saddle grafts or tomato (*Lycopersicon esculentum*) on black nightshade (*Solanum nigrum*) and black nightshade on tomato, both of which are easily grafted and produce callus readily.

Winkler's grafts were made, following union, the graft was cut transversely at the junction, exposing tissues of both components. The cut surface soon became covered with a pad of callus derived from both the tomato and nightshade. From this callus, adventitious buds formed which developed into shoots. Most of these shoots had the appearance of either pure tomato or pure nightshade. Occasionally, however, shoots arose and grew normally which were different from either component. Some showed mixed characters, with half the shoot resembling tomato and the other half the nightshade. Winkler gave it the name "chimera," after the fabulous mythological monster that was part lion and part dragon. Graft chimeras in the periclinal form also developed. One was found to consist mostly of a nightshade tissue covered with a single layer of tomato epidermal cells. It bore fruit like that of the true nightshade and its seeds produced nightshade plants.

Graft chimeras among woody perennials have long been known to exist, and some have been perpetuated indefinitely by asexual methods. Probably the earliest known "authentic" chimera is one called the "bizzarria" orange. It is described as bearing a fruit which is citron on one side and orange on the other. It originated supposedly in 1644 in a garden in Florence, Italy, from a grafting operation in which a scion of sour orange (*Citrus aurantium*) was grafted on a stock of citron (*C. medica*). According to the story, the original scion failed to grow, but in the swollen callus around the graft a shoot developed bearing the unusual "bizzarria" orange were still being published 250 years after its origin, agreeing that it probably was a periclinal chimera.

Grafting medlar (*Mespilus germanica*) on a stock of the hawthorn (*Crataegus monogyna*) has led to several recorded instances of chimeras. Near Metz, France, in 1899, two adventitious shoots were found arising at the graft union of an old medlar tree. They had a different appearance from either the medlar or the hawthorn and were different from each other. They were named *Crataegomespilus asnieresi* and *Crataegomespilus dardari* and were regarded for many years as true "*graft hybrids*" believed to have resulted from a fusion of the nuclei of vegetative cells.

Both of these types, sometimes called hawmedlars, have been maintained vegetatively, grafted on the hawthorn and widely distributed to botanical gardens. It is likely, however, that these two forms are periclinal chimeras. There have been several strong proponents of the graft hybrid hypothesis. Winkler made his Solanaceae graft chimeras in the hope of gaining evidence for the graft hybrid idea. He believed that some of these unusual plant forms were true graft hybrids involving fusion of vegetative cell nuclei. Daniel is probably the most conspicuous supporter of this hypothesis and has written extensively on the subject although many of his views are not generally accepted.

2

Grafting and Budding

Grafting is the art of joining parts of plants together in such a manner that they will unite and continue their growth as one plant. The part of the graft combination which is to become the upper portion or top of the new plant is termed the *scion* (cion), and the part which is to become the lower portion or root is termed the *rootstock*, or *understock*, or sometimes the *stock*. All methods of joining plants are properly termed *grafting*, but when the scion part is a small piece of bark (and sometimes wood) containing a single bud, the operation is termed *budding*. Most of the situations discussed in this chapter affecting grafting would therefore apply equally well to budding, although the techniques involved are somewhat different.

Natural Grafting

One occasionally sees branches of trees that have become grafted together naturally following a long period of being pressed together without disturbance. The English Ivy (*Hedera helix*) forms such grafts, and detailed studies have been made of translocation in natural grafts of this species. Not so obvious but of much greater occurrence, particularly in forest stands, is the natural grafting of roots. Such grafts are most common between roots of the same tree or between roots of trees of the same species. Grafts between roots of trees of different species are rare. In the forests living stumps sometimes occur, kept alive because their roots have become grafted to those of nearly intact, living trees. The anatomy of natural grafting of aerial roots has been studies; the initial contact is established by the formation and fusion of epidermal hairs. Such natural grafting provides a means of virus transmission from an infected tree to its neighbours. This can be important in closely set orchard and nursery plantings of fruit trees, where numerous root grafts could occur and result in the slow spread of the virus throughout the planting . Natural root grafting is a potential source of error in virus indexing procedures where virus-free and virus-infected trees are grown in close proximity. The fact that natural grafting does take place throws some doubt on the assumption usually held that each tree is an independent, discrete organism.

Formation of the Graft Union

A number of detailed studies have been made of the healing of graft unions, mostly with woody plants.

Briefly, the usual sequence of events in the healing of a normal graft union is as follows:

(a) Freshly cut scion tissue capable of meristematic activity is brought into secure, intimate contact with similar freshly cut stock tissue in such a manner that the cambial regions of both are in close proximity. Temperature and humidity conditions must be such as to promote activity in the newly exposed, and surrounding, cells.

(b) The outer exposed layers of cells in the cambial region of both scion and stock produce parenchyma cells which soon intermingle and interlock; this is called *callus tissue*.

(c) Certain cells of this newly formed callus which are in line with the cambium layer of the intact scion and stock differentiate into new cambium cells.

(d) These new cambium cells produce new vascular tissue, xylem toward the inside and phloem toward the outside, thus establishing vascular connection between the scion and stock, a requisite of a successful graft union.

The healing of a graft union can be considered as the healing of a wound. Such injury to tissue as would occur if the end of a branch were split longitudinally would heal quickly if the split pieces were bound tightly together. New parenchyma cells would be produced by abundant proliferation of cells of the cambium region of both pieces, forming callus tissue. Some of the interlocking parenchyma cells differentiate into cambium cells, which subsequently produce xylem and phloem.

If between the two split pieces, one interposed a third, detached, piece which had been cut so that a large number of its cells in the cambial region could be placed in intimate contact with cells of the cambial region of the two split pieces, proliferation of cells from all cambial areas would soon result in complete healing, with the foreign, detached piece joined completely between the two original split pieces. A graft union is essentially a healed wound, with an additional, foreign, piece of tissue incorporated into the healed wound.

This added piece of tissue, the scion, will not resume its growth successfully, however, unless vascular connection has been established so that it may obtain water and mineral nutrients. In addition, the scion must have a terminal meristematic region—a bud—to resume shoot growth.

In the healing of a graft union, the parts of the graft that are originally prepared and placed in close contact do not themselves move about or grow together. The union is accomplished entirely by cells which develop *after* the actual grafting operation has been made.

In addition, it should be stressed that in a graft union *there is no intermingling of cell contents.* Cells produced by the stock and by the scion each maintain their own distinct identity.

Considering in more detail the steps involved in the healing of a graft union, we may say that the first one listed below is a preliminary step, but nevertheless, it is essential and one over which the propagator has control.

(a) Establishment of intimate contact of a considerable amount of the cambial region of both stock and scion under favourable environmental conditions.

Temperature conditions that will cause high cell activity are necessary. Usually, temperatures from 55°to 90°F (12.8° to 32°C), depending upon the species, are conductive to rapid cell growth. The grafting operation should thus take place at a time of year when such favourable temperatures can be expected and when the plant tissues, especially the cambium, are in a naturally active state. These conditions generally occur during the early spring months.

The new callus tissue arising from the cambial region is composed of thin-walled, turgid cells which can easily become desiccated and die. It is important for the production of these parenchyma cells that the humidity in the vicinity of the cambial region of the graft union be kept at a high level. This explains the necessity of thoroughly waxing the graft union or using some other method to maintain a high degree of tissue hydration.

It is important, too, that the region of the graft union be kept as free as possible from pathogenic organisms. The thin walled parenchyma cells, at relatively high humidity and temperature, will provide favourable conditions for growth of certain fungi and bacteria which are exceedingly detrimental to the successful healing of the graft union. Prompt waxing of the graft helps prevent disease infection.

It is essential that the two original graft components be held together firmly by some means, such as wrapping, tying, or nailing, or better yet, by wedging (as in the cleft or sawkerf grafts) so that the parts will not move about and dislodge the interlocking parenchyma cells after proliferation has started.

The statement is often made that for successful grafting the cambium layers of stock and scion must be "matched." Although this is desirable, it is unlikely that complete matching of the two cambium layers is, or ever can be, attained. In fact, it is only necessary that the cambial regions be close fact, it is only necessary that the cambial regions be close enough together so that the parenchyma cells from both stock and scion produced in this region can become interlocked. It is in the region of the cambium that the essential callus production is the highest. Two badly matched cambial layers may delay union or, if extremely mismatched, prevent union. In studies of grafting monocotyledonous plants, it was found that a cambium layer is not required for a successful graft union but that any meristematic tissue could be utilized for this purpose and is capable of forming a union between stock and scion.

(b) Production and interlocking of parenchyma cells (callus tissue) by both stock and scion.

During the grafting operation the cells cut and damaged by the grafting knife turn brown and die. Underneath these dead cells new parenchyma cells arise from both stock and scion, coming from the parenchyma of the phloem rays and the immature parts of the xylem. The actual cambial layer itself seems to take little or no part in this first development of the callus. In grafting scions on established stocks, the stock produces most of the callus. These parenchyma cells, comprising the spongy callus tissue, fill the space between the two original components of the graft (the scion and the stock), becoming intimately interlocked and providing some mechanical support, as well as allowing for some passage of water and nutrients from the stock into the scion. For a time, between the callus arising from the stock and that arising from the scion, there is a more or less continuous brown line consisting of the above- mentioned dead and crushed cells remaining from the grafting cuts. This line of cells is gradually resorbed, however, and disappears. At the final stage of healing the cells of the outer layer of callus become suberized. Exposed dead cells (tracheids, vessels) are sealed off with a deposit of gum.

(c) Production of a new cambium across the callus "bridge"

At the edges of the newly formed callus mass, parenchyma cells which are touching the cambial cells of the stock and scion will differentiate into new cambium cells. This cambial formation in the callus mass proceeds farther and farther inward away from the original stock and scion cambium, and on through the callus bridge, until a continuous cambial connection between stock and scion has finally formed.

(d) Formation of new xylem and phloem from the new vascular cambium in the callus bridge

The newly formed cambial sheath in the callus bridge begins typical cambial activity, laying down new xylem and phloem, along with the original vascular cambium of the stock and scion, continuing this throughout the life of the plant.

In the formation of new vascular tissues following cambial continuity, it appears that the type of cells formed by the cambium may be influenced by the cells of the stock adjacent to the cambium. For example, xylem ray cells are formed where the cambium is in contact with xylem rays of the stock, and xylem elements where they were in contact with xylem elements.

The new xylem tissue originates from the scion rather than from the stock. This is shown by "ring grafting" (where a ring of bark from a young tree is removed and replaced by a ring of bark from another tree). Researchers found that using bark rings of the 'Scugog' apple variety, which has purple xylem, subsequent xylem growth of the tree following grafting was entirely purple in colour just under the 'Scugog' ring of bark, whereas in the remainder of the tree the xylem remained white.

This production of new xylem and phloem then establishes vascular connection between the scion and the stock. Under high transpiration rates this must occur before much new shoot growth takes place from buds on the scion; otherwise, the enlarging leaf surfaces on the scion shoots will have little or no water supply to offset that lost by transpiration, and the scion will quickly become desiccated and die. Under some conditions, however, where vascular connections fail to occur, enough translocation can take place between the parenchyma cells of the callus to permit survival. In grafts of the monocot, *Vanilla* orchid, scions survived and grew for two years with only parenchyma unions.

A somewhat different developmental sequence occurs in tobacco and cotton. Here, xylem tracheary elements or phloem sieve tubes, or both, form directly by differentiation of callus into these vascular elements. A cambium layer subsequently differentiates between the two vascular elements. Apparently parenchyma cells, which make up the callus, can differentiate into tracheid-like elements with relative ease. Buds, as would occur on the scions of grafts, seem to be effective in inducing processes of dedifferentiation and subsequent redifferentiation in the tissue on which they are grafted. This bud influence has been shown by inserting a bud into a piece of *Cichorium intybus* root consisting only of old vascular parenchyma, and observing that under the influence of the bud, the old parenchyma cells redifferentiate and dedifferentiate into groups of conducting elements.

The Healing Process in T-Budding

In T-budding, the bud piece usually consists of the periderm, cortex, phloem, and often some xylem tissue to which is attached a lateral bud. In budding, this bark piece is laid against the exposed xylem of the stock.

Detailed studies of the healing process in T-budding have been made for the rose, citrus and apple.

When the bud piece is removed from the budstick, and when the flaps of bark on either side of the "T" incision, on the stock are raised, the cambium and newly formed cambial derivatives in these tissues are usually destroyed, owing to their very tender, succulent nature.

In the apple when the bark is lifted in the budding operation the separation occurs in the young, undifferentiated xylem. The entire cambial zone remains attached to the inside of the bark flaps. After the bud shield is inserted, callus is produced, which surrounds the bud shield and holds it in place. The callus originates almost entirely from the rootstock tissue, mainly from the exposed surface of the xylem cylinder. Very little callus is produced from the sides of the bud shield. Callus starts development 2 days after budding and continues rapidly for 2 to 3 weeks until all internal air pockets are filled. Following this, a continuous cambium is established between the bud and the rootstock. The callus then begins to lignify, an isolated tracheary elements appear. Lignification of the callus is completed about 12 weeks after budding.

In the rose, about 3 days after budding the terminal cells of the brôken xylem rays and adjacent cambial derivatives on the exposed surface of the stock begin to enlarge and divide, leading to the production of callus strands. In the same manner, callus strands develop from terminal cells of broken phloem rays and adjacent young secondary phloem cells on the cut surface of the inner side of the bud piece. Within 14 days the space between the stock and the bud piece is completely filled with callus, which has developed mainly from the proliferating immature secondary xylem of the stock and the immature secondary phloem of the bud piece. During the second week, short areas of cambium cells appear in this newly developed callus tissue. By the tenth day, a completed band of cambium tissue extends over the face of the stock and is joined to the uninjured cambium on either side of the bud piece.

After cambial continuity is completed, continuity of vascular tissues soon becomes established between the bud and stock. In T-budding, then, the primary union is between the surface of the phloem on the inner face of the shield and the meristematic xylem surface of the stock. A secondary type of union may occur, however, at the edges of the shield piece, as it would in chip budding.

The various stages in the healing process of the union in T-budding of citrus have been determined as follows:

Stage of Development	*Approximate Time after Budding*
1. First cell division	24 hours
2. First callus bridge	5 days
3. Differentiation :	
(a) in the callus of the bark flaps	10 days
(b) in the callus of the shield	15 days
4. First occurrence of xylem tracheids:	
(a) in the callus of the bark flaps 15 days	
(b) in the callus of the shield 20 days	
5. Lignification of the callus completed :	
(a) in the bark flaps	25 to 30 days
(b) under the shield	30 to 45 days
6. First occurrence of meristematic layers in the callus between shield and bark flaps	15 days

Factors Influencing the Healing of the Graft or Bud Union

As anyone experienced in grafting or budding knows, the results obtained in grafting are often inconsistent, an excellent percentage of "takes" occurring in some operations, whereas in others the results are very discouraging. There are a number of factors which influence the healing of graft unions.

Incompatibility

One of the symptoms of incompatibility in grafts between distantly related plants is a complete lack, or a very low percentage, of successful unions. Grafts between some plants known to be incompatible, however, will initially make a satisfactory union, even though the combination eventually fails.

Kind of Plants

Some plants are much more difficult to graft than others even when no incompatibility is involved. Difficult ones, for example, are the hickories, oaks, and beeches. Nevertheless, such plants, once successfully grafted, grow very well with a perfect graft union. In top grafting apples and pears, even the simplest techniques usually give a good percentage of successful unions, but in topgrafting certain of the stone fruits, such as peaches and apricots, much more care and attention to details are necessary. Strangely enough, topgrafting peaches to some other compatible species, such as plums or almonds, is more successful than reworking them back to peaches. Many times one method of grafting will give better results than another, or budding may be more successful than grafting, or vice versa. For example, in topworking the native black walnut (*Juglans hindsii*) to the Persian walnut (*Juglans regia*) in California, the bark graft method is more successful than the cleft graft.

Some easily grafted plants, such as the apple, form a "wound gum" plugging exposed xylem elements after the grafting operation, thus preventing excessive dessication and the death of tissues. Other plants, such as the walnut, in which graft unions heal with difficulty, form such "wound gum" very slowly, and in these desiccation and death of tissues in the area of the graft union may be extensive.

Some species, such as the Muscadine grape (*Vitis rotundifolia*), mango (*Mangifera indica*), and *Camellia reticulata*, are so difficult to propagate by the usual grafting or budding methods that "approach grafting," in which both partners of the graft are maintained for a time on their own roots, is often used. This variation among plant species and varieties in their grafting ability is probably related to their production of callus, which is essential for a successful graft union. *Camellia reticulata*, for example, is difficult to graft and is a very poor callus producer.

Temperature and Moisture Conditions During and Following Crafting

There are certain environmental requirements which must be met for callus tissue to develop.

Temperature has a pronounced effect on the production of callus tissue. In apple grafts little, if any, callus is formed below 32°F (0°C) or above about 104°F (40°C). Even around 40°F (4°C), callus development is slow and meager, and at 90°F (32°C) and higher, callus production is retarded, with cell injury becoming more apparent as the temperature increases, until death of the cells occurs at 104°F. Between 40°and 90°F, however the rate of callus formation increases directly with the temperature. In such operations as bench grafting, callusing may be allowed to proceed slowly for several months by storing the grafts at relatively low temperatures (45° to 50°F; 7° to 10°C), or if rapid callusing is desired, they may be kept at higher temperatures for a shorter time. Since excessive callusing of root graft unions may result in the formation of undersirable "callus knots" (sometimes mistaken by plant inspectors for crown gall tumors), it

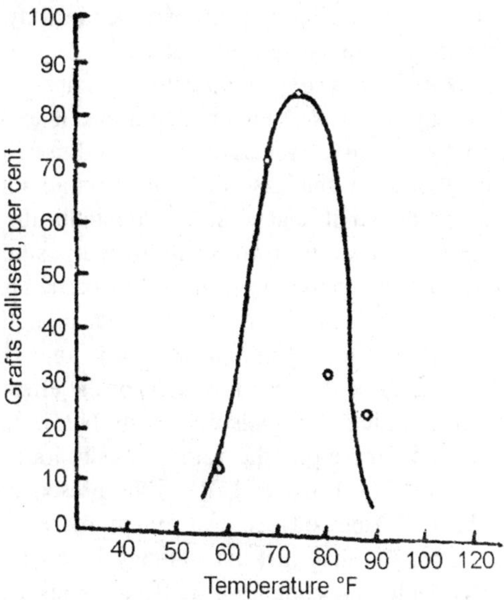

Fig. 2.1. Influence of temperature on the callusing of wheat (Juglans) grafts.

can be controlled by storing well-callused grafts at reduced temperatures to prevent further callus development.

Temperature during the healing period following grafting was found to have a pronounced effect upon the degree of successful unions obtained in whip grafting of black walnuts. Studies show clearly that a temperature in the range of 77° to 86°F (25° to 30°C) during the callusing period gives much better results than either higher or lower temperatures. This was confirmed by studies in which black walnut root grafts placed in a cool nursery cellar at 41° to 56° (5°to 13°C) for callusing failed completely to unite. Another group of grafts planted in the nursery row immediately after grafting (air temperature 41° to 72°F; (5° to 22°C) resulted in only about 3 percent growing. In a third group which was allowed to callus in a warm green house (air temperature 65° to 80°, 8° to 27°C), an average of 88 percent grew.

Following bench grafting of grapes, a temperature of 70° to 75°F (21° to 24°C) is about optimum; 85°F (29°C) or higher results in profuse formation of a soft type of callus tissue which is easily injured during the planting operations. Below 70°F, callus formation is slow, and below 60°F (5°C), it almost ceases.

Grafting operations performed late in the spring when excessively high temperatures may occur, often result in failure. Tests of walnut top grafting in California during very hot weather in May showed that whitewashing the area of the completed graft union definitely promoted healing of the union. Whitewash would reflect a considerable portion of the radiant energy of the sun rather than allow it to be absorbed, thus resulting in lower bark temperatures. In addition in these tests scions placed on the north and east sides of the stub survived much better than these on the south and west. Undoubtedly this was due to the lower temperatures resulting from their shaded position. Since the parenchyma cells comprising the important callus tissue are thin-walled and tender, with no provision for resisting desiccation, it is obvious that if they are exposed to drying air for very long, they will be killed. This was found to be the case in studies of the effect of humidity on healing of apple grafts. Air moisture levels below the saturation point inhibited callus formation, the rate of desiccation of the cells increasing as the humidity dropped. In fact, the presence of a film of water against the callusing surface was much more conductive to abundant callus formation than just maintaining the air at 100 percent relative humidity. Unless a completed graft union is kept by some means at a very high humidity level, the chances of successful healing are rather remote. With most plants, thorough waxing of the graft union, which retains the natural moisture of the tissues, is all that is necessary.

Often root grafts are not waxed but stored in a moist packing material during the callusing period. Damp peat moss is an excellent material for callusing, because it provides proper moisture and aeration.

It has been shown that oxygen is necessary at the graft union for the production of callus tissue. This would be expected, since such rapid cell division and growth is accompanied by relatively high respiration, which requires oxygen. For some plants, a lower percentage of oxygen than is found naturally in air is sufficient, but for others, healing of the graft union is better if the union is left unwaxed and placed in an enclosure of water-saturated air. This may indicate that the latter plants have a high oxygen requirement for callus formation. Waxing restricts air movement to such an extent that oxygen may become limiting, and callus tissue fails to form. This situation apparently exists in grafting the grape, in which usually the union is not covered with wax or other air excluding material.

Growth Activity of the Stock Plant

Some propagation methods, such as T-budding and bark grafting, dependent upon the bark "slipping," which means the vascular cambium cells are actively dividing, producing young thin- walled cells on each side of the cambium. These newly formed cells readily separate from one another, so the bark "slips." Initiation of such cambial activity in the spring is thought to result from swelling of the buds in warm weather, since shortly afterwards cambial activity can be detected beneath each developing bud with a wave of cambial activity progressing down the stems and trunk. This stimulus is believed to be due to increased auxin levels originating in the expanding buds.

In budding seedlings in the nursery row in late summer it is important that they have an ample supply of soil moisture just before, during, and following the budding operation. If they should lack water during this period, active growth is checked, cell division in the cambium stops, and the chances of getting the buds to unite are lessened.

There is evidence to show that callus proliferation essential for a successful graft union-occurs most readily at the time of year just before and during "bud break" in the spring, diminishing through the summer and into the winter. Increasing callus proliferation takes place again in late winter, but this is not dependent upon breaking of bud dormancy.

Plants exhibiting strong root pressure (such as the walnut) will show, at certain periods of high growth activity in the spring, excessive sap flow or "bleeding" when cuts are made preparatory to grafting. Grafts made with moisture exudation around the union will not heal, and should be made at some other stage of growth; such "bleeding" can be overcome by making slanting knife cuts around the tree through the bark and into the xylem to permit the exudation to take place below the graft union. When potted rootstock plants to be grafted (in such species as *Fagus*, *Betula*, or *Acer*) show excessive root pressure, they should be put in a cool place with reduced watering until the "bleeding" stops.

On the other hand, potted rootstock plants, such as junipers or rhododendrons, when first brought into a warm greenhouse in winter for grafting, are dormant, and grafting done then would be unsuccessful. Grafting should be delayed until the rootstock plants have been held for several weeks at 60° to 65°F (15° to 18°C) and new roots start to form; then the rootstock plant is physiologically active enough for the union to heal. When the rootstock plant is physiologically overactive (excessive root pressure and "bleeding"), or underactive (no root growth being made), some form of side graft in which the rootstock top is not at first removed, should be used. In situations in which the rootstock is neither overactive or underactive, one of the many forms of topgrafting, in which the top of the stock is completely removed at the time the graft is made, is likely to be successful.

Propagation Techniques

Even in using the standard grafting or budding methods, there are numerous possible variables which may affect the success of the operation. There are many opinions, often conflicting, about the proper techniques to use.

Sometimes the grafting technique is so poor that only a very small portion of the cambial regions of the stock and scion are brought together. Although healing occurs in this region and growth of the scion may start, when a large leaf area develops and high temperatures and high transpiration rates occur, sufficient movement of water through the limited conducting area cannot take place, and the scion subsequently dies. Other errors in grafting technique, such as poor or delayed waxing, uneven cuts, or use of desiccated scions can, of course, result in grafting failure.

Poor grafting techniques, although they may delay adequate healing for some time—weeks, or even years—do not in themselves cause any permanent incompatibility. Once the union is adequately healed, growth can proceed normally.

Virus Contamination, Insect Pests, and Diseases

Usring virus-infected propagating materials in nurseries can reduce bud "take" as well as the vigor of the resulting plant. In stone fruit propagation the use of budwood free of ring spot virus has consistently given improved percentages of "takes" over infected wood.

Topgrafting olives in California is seriously hindered in some years by attacks of the American plum borer (*Euzophera semifuneralis*), which feeds on the soft callus tissue around the graft union, result in the death of the scion. (This is easily controlled, however, by painting the completed graft, before waxing , with a 3 oz per gal, solution of 50 percent DDT in water). In England, nurserymen are often plagued with the red bud borer (*Thomasiniana oculiperda*), which eats the healing callus beneath the bud-shield in newly inserted T-buds.

Sometimes bacteria or fungi gain entrance at the wounds made in preparing the graft or bud unions. For example, it was found that a rash of failures in grafts of *Cornus florida rubra* on common *C. florida* stock was due to the presence of the fungus *Chalaropsis thielavioides*. Chemical control of such infections materially aids in promoting healing of the unions.

In South and Central American, rubber (*Hevea*) trees are propagated by a modification of the patch bud. A major cause of budding failures in these countries has been infection of the out surfaces by a fungus, *Diplodia theobromae*. Control of this infection has been obtained by fungicidal treatments.

In topgrafting mangos in Florida, control of the fungus diseases anthracnose and scab is essential for success. This is done by spraying the rootstock trees and the source of scionwood regularly with copper fungicides before grafting is attempted.

Possible Relation of Growth Substances to Healing of the Graft Union

Studies of the practical application of growth substances, particularly auxin, to tree wounds or to graft unions and their effect on promoting subsequent healing have not given consistent results; consequently such materials are not generally used for this purpose. It is known from tissue culture studies, however, that there is a definite relationship between callus production (which is essential for graft healing) and the levels of certain endogenous growth substances,

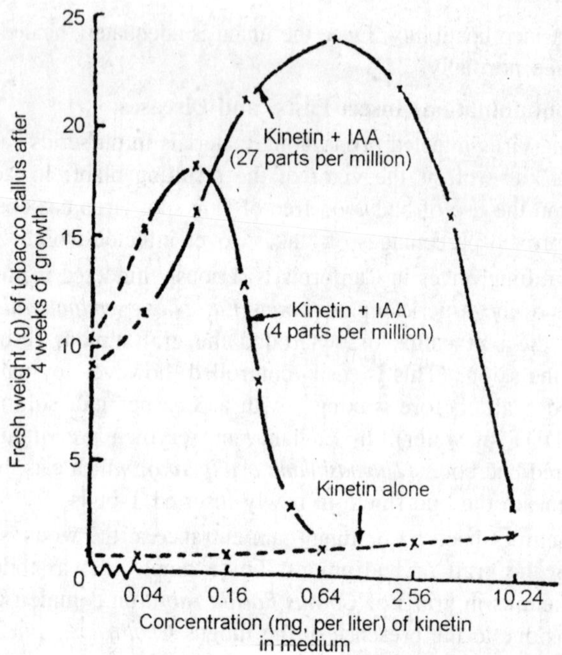

Fig. 2.2. Relationship between raltive concentration of auxin (indoleacetic acid) and kinetin upon callus production.

particularly kinetin, and auxin. The relationship between auxin (indoleacetic acid) and kinetin levels in the production of callus in tobacco segments maintained under aseptic conditions. Perhaps further studies may show some practical benefit from the use of combinations of auxin and kinetin in stimulating callus formation and subsequent healing of graft unions, thereby facilitating grafting of combinations considered to be difficult.

Polarity in Grafting

Attention to proper polarity is very important if the graft union is to be permanently successful. In all commercial grafting operations correct polarity is strictly observed. As a general rule, in grafting two pieces of stem tissue together, the morphologically proximal end of the scion should be inserted into the morphologically distal end of the stock. But in grafting a piece of stem tissue on a piece of root, as it is done in root grafting, the proximal end of the scion should be inserted into the proximal end of the root piece.

The *proximal* end of either the shoot or the root is that nearest the stem-root junction of the plant. The *distal* end of either the shoot

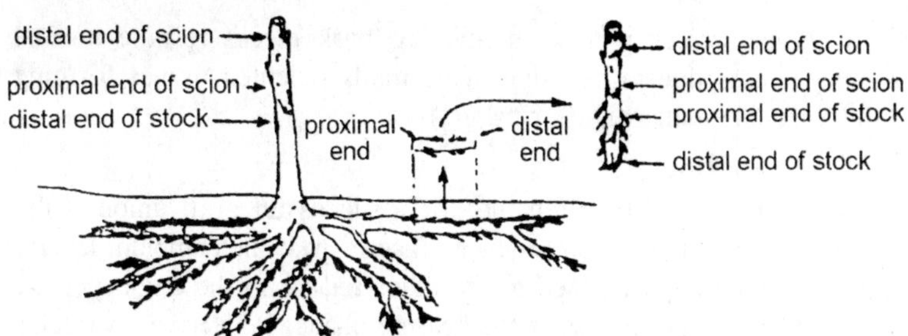

Fig. 2.3. Polarity in grafting.

or the root is that furthest from the stem-root junction of the plant and nearest the tip of the shoot or root.

Should a scion be inserted with reversed polarity— "upside down"— in bridge-grafting, for example, it is possible for the two graft unions to be successful and the scion to stay alive for a time. But, the reversed scion does not increase from its original size, whereas the scion with correct polarity enlarges normally.

In nurse-root grafting, the rootstock may be purposely grafted to the scion with reversed polarity. Union will occur, and the root will supply water and mineral nutrients to the scion. Since the scion is unable to supply necessary organic materials to the rootstock, the stock eventually dies. In this case, the graft union is purposely set well below the ground level, and the scion itself produces adventitious roots which ultimately become the entire root system of the plant.

In T-budding or patch budding, the rule for observance of correct polarity is not as exacting. Buds can be inserted with reversed polarity and still make permanently successful unions. The buds start growing downward, then the shoots recurve and start upward. In the inverted bud piece, the cambium seems capable of continued functioning and growth. However, in the vessels as well as in the fibres formed from cambial activity, there is a twisting configuration which apparently keeps translocation and water conduction oriented as in the original position.

If a complete ring of bark is removed from the trunk of a young tree, inverted, and regrafted into place, the growth of the tree will be markedly retarded. Organic materials that stimulate growth of the roots move downward through the phloem. When they reach the inverted bark piece, their movement is obstructed. Presumably, lack of these materials retards root growth subsequently dwarfing the entire tree. Such dwarfing is temporary, however; experiments have shown that within 2 years trees with such inverted bark pieces resume normal growth. This is due to a bridge of normally oriented tissues forming at the vertical seams of the ring grafts.

Limits of Grafting

Since one of the requirements for a successful graft union is the close matching of the callus- producing tissues near the cambium layers, grafting is generally confined to the dicotyledons in the angiosperms, and to the gymnosperms,. the cone-bearing plants. Both have a vascular cambium layer existing as a continuous tissue between the xylem and the phloem. In the monocotyledonous plants of the Angiospermae, which do not have a vascular cambium, grafting is more difficult and the percentage of "takes" much lower than in the dicots. There are cases of successful graft unions between the stem parts of monocots. By making use of the meristematic properties found in the intercalary tissues (located at the base of internodes), successful grafts have been obtained with various grass species as well as the large tropical monocotyledonous vanilla orchid of commerce.

Before a grafting operation is started, it should be determined that the plants to be combined are capable of uniting. There is no definite rule that can be followed exactly which will give this information. *Generally, the more closely the plants to be grafted are related botanically, the better the chances are of the graft union being successful.* This will not hold true consistently, however, since botanical classifications are based on reproductive characteristics, whereas grafting is concerned primarily with the vegetative properties of plants.

Grafting Within a Clone

A scion can be grafted back on the plant from which it came, and a scion from a plant of a given clone can be grafted to any other plant of the same clone. For example, a scion taken from an "Elberta' peach tree could be grafted successfully to any other 'Elberta' peach tree in the world.

Grafting between Clones within a Species

Almost always, different clones within a species can be grafted together without difficulty and will produce normal plants.

Grafting between Species within a Genus

For plants in different species but in the same genus, the situation is confused. In some cases grafting can be done successfully, in others it cannot. Grafting between most species in the genus *Citrus*, for example, is successfully and widely used commercially. Varieties of the almond *Prunus amydalus*), the apricot (*Prunus armeniaca*), the European plum (*Prunus domestica*), and the Japanese plum (*Prunus salicina*) all different species—are grafted commercially on the peach (*Prunus persica*), a still different species, as a rootstock. On the other hand, the almond and the apricot, both in the same genus, cannot be integrated successfully. The complexity of the situation is further illustrated by the fact that the 'Beauty' variety of Japanese plum (*Prunus salicina*) makes a good union when grafted on the almond, but another variety of *P. salicina*, 'Santa Rosa,' cannot be successfully grafted on the almond.

Compatibility between species may depend upon the particular clone or seedling used, either for stock or scion. For example, choice of the almond variety (clone) is highly important when grafting to 'Marianna 2624' plum as a rootstock, some varieties being, successful, others not. Likewise, clonal selections from different seedlings of the St.Julien plum (*Prunus insititia*), when used as rootstocks, have resulted in greatly different behaviour of the trees after top working to the same peach clone. For example, clonal selections A and C produced good peach trees with no signs of incompatibility, while trees of the same peach variety worked on selection B died within 5 years; peach trees on rootstock selection D died after 1 year.

There are some cases in which a given interspecies graft is successful, but the reciprocal combination is not. For instance, the 'Marianna plum' (*Prunus cerasifera* × *P. munsoniana* ?) on the peach (*Prunus persica*) makes an excellent graft combination, but grafts of the peach on 'Marianna plum either soon die or fail to develop normally. Although many varieties of Japanese plums (*Prunus salicina*) can be successfully grafted on the European plum (*P. domestica*), grafts of most varieties of the European plum on the Japanese are unsuccessful.

Grafting between Genera within a Family

When the plants to be grafted together are in different genera but in the same family, the chances of the union being successful become more remote. Cases can be found in which such grafts are highly successful and used commercially, but in most instances such combinations are failures.

Trifoliate orange (*Poncirus trifoliata*) is used commercially as a dwarfing stock for various species in the genus *Citrus*. The quince (*Cydonia oblonga*) has long been used as a dwarfing root stock for certain varieties of the pear (*Pyrus communis*). The reverse combination, quince on pear, though, is unsuccessful. Intergeneric grafts in the nightshade family, Solanaceae, are quite common. Tomato (*Lycopersicon esculentum*) can be grafted successfully on Jimson weed (*Datura stramonium*), tobacco (*Nicotiana tobacum*), potato (*Solanum tuberosum*), and black nightshade (*Solanum nigrum*).

Grafting between Families

Grafting such plants together is usually considered impossible, but there are reported instances in which it has been accomplished. These are with short-lived, herbaceous plants, though, for which the item involved is relatively short. Grafts, with vascular connections between the scion and stock, were successfully made, using white weet clover, *Melilotus alba* (Leguminosae), as the scion and sunflower. *Helianthus annuus* (Compositae), as the stock. Cleft grafting was used, with the scion inserted into the pith parenchyma of the stock. The scions continued growth with normal vigor for over 5 months. As far as is known, however, there are no instances in which woody perennial plants belonging to different families have been successfully and permanently grafted together.

For any successful grafting operation there are five important requirements :

(a) *The stock and scion must be compatible.* They must be capable of uniting. Usually, but not always, plants closely related, such as two apple varieties, can be grafted together. Distantly related plants, such as an oak tree and an apple tree, cannot be grafted together.

(b) *The cambial region of the scion must be in intimate contact with that of the stock.* The cut surfaces should be held together tightly by wrapping, nailing, or some other such method. Rapid healing of the graft union is necessary so that the scion may be supplied with water and nutrients from the stock by the time the buds start to open.

(c) *The grafting operation must be done at a time when the stock and scion are in the proper physiologcial stage.* Usually this means that the scion buds are dormant. For deciduous plants, dormant scion wood is often collected during the winter and kept inactive by storing at low temperature. The rootstock plant may be dormant or in active growth, depending upon the grafting method used.

(d) *Immediately after the grafting operation is completed, all cut surfaces must be carefully protected from desiccation.* This is done either by covering with grafting wax or by placing the grafts in moist material or in a covered grafting frame.

(e) *Proper care must be given the grafts for a period of time after grafting.* Shoots coming from the stock below the graft will often choke out the desired growth from the scion. Or, in some cases, shoots from the scion will grow so vigorously that they break off unless staked on tied or cut back.

METHODS OF GRAFTING

Whip, or Tongue, Grafting

This method is particularly useful for grafting relatively small material, 1/4 to 1/2 in. in diameter. It is highly successful if properly

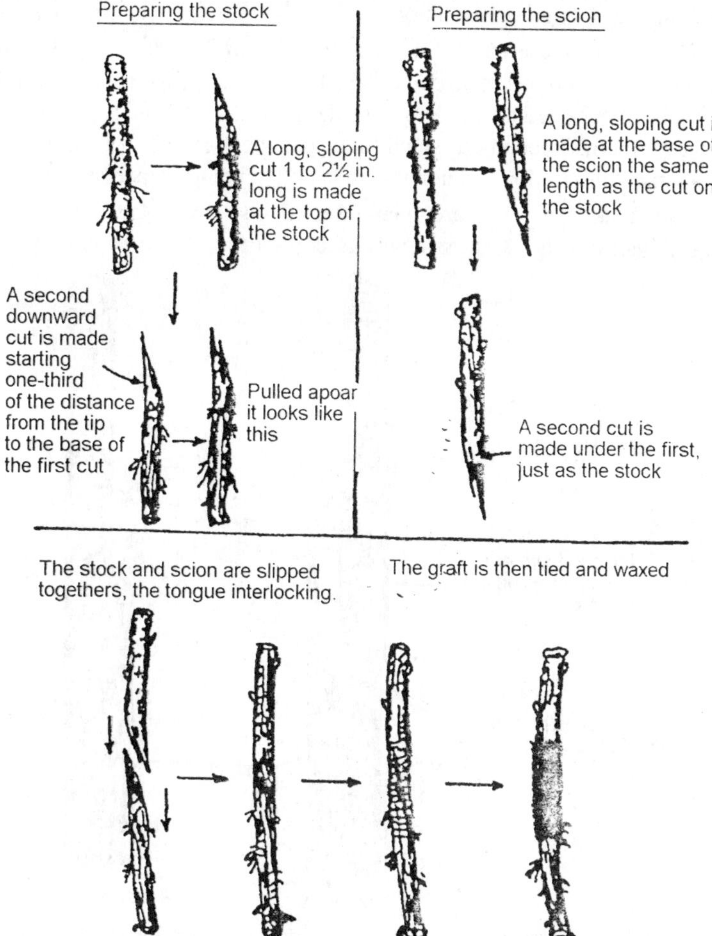

Fig. 2.4. The whip or tongue, graft.

done because there is considerable cambial contact. It heals quickly and makes a strong union. Preferably, the scion and stock should be of equal diameter. The scion should contain two or three buds with the graft made in the smooth internode area below the lower bud.

The cuts made at the top of the stock should be exactly the same as those made at the bottom of the scion. First, a long, smooth, sloping cut is made, 1 to 2½ in. long. The longer cuts are made when working with large material. This first cut should be made, preferably with one single stroke of the knife, so as to leave a very smooth surface. To do this, the knife must be sharp. Wavy, uneven cuts will not result in a satisfactory union.

On each of these cut surfaces, a reverse cut is made. It is started downward at a point about one-third of the distance from the tip and should be about one-half the length of the first cut. To obtain a smooth-fitting graft, this second cut should not just split the grain of the wood but should follow along under the first cut, tending to parrel it.

The stock and scion are then inserted into each other, with the tongues interlocking. It is extremely important that the cambium layers

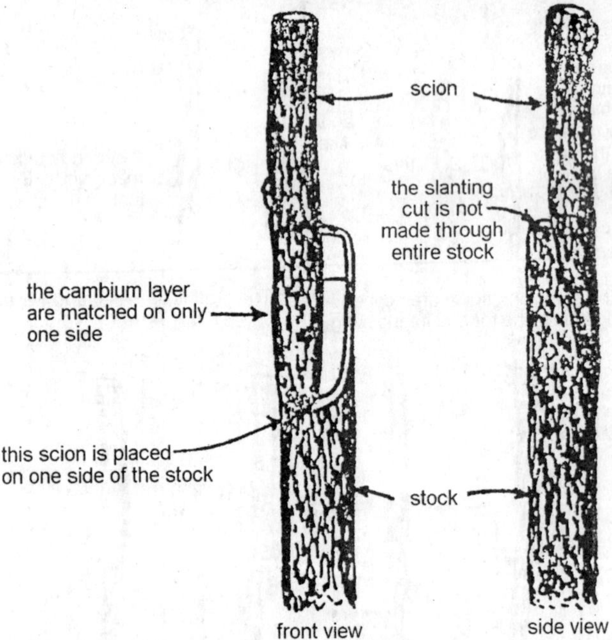

Fig. 2.5. Method of making a whip, or tongue, graft when the scion is considerably smaller than the stock.

match along at least one side, preferably along both sides. The lower tip of the scion should not overhang the stock, as there is a likelihood of the formation of large callus knots. In some species, such callus overgrowths are often mistaken for crown gall knots, which are caused by bacteria. The use of scion lårger than the stock should be avoided for the same reason. If the scion is smaller than the stock, it should be set at one side of the stock so that the cambium layers will be certain to match along that side. If the scion is considerably smaller than the stock, the first cut on the stock consists only of a slice taken off one corner.

After the scion and stock are fitted together, they should be held securely in some manner until the pieces have united. There are a number of possible ways of doing this.

(a) If the unions are very well made with a tight, snug fit, it is possible that no additional wrapping or tying is needed, but it is safer to provide some type of wrapping. If not wrapped, the grafts must be protected from drying by burying in moist sand, peat moss, or sawdust until the union has healed. Or they may be planted directely in the nursery with the union below soil level. If the whip graft is used in topworking, the exposed union must be protected in some manner.

(b) With a secure fit it may be sufficient to omit tying and merely cover the union with hot grafting wax, which will secure the pieces to some extent and give good protection against drying. This is not recommended for inexperienced grafters.

(c) A common method is to wrap the union with budding rubbers or possibly raffia or waxed string. After wrapping, the whole union can be covered with grafting wax. Waxing may be omitted if the grafts are to be protected from drying by burying in moist sand or peat moss, or if the grafts are planted immediately with the union below the soil surface. Grafts wrapped with budding rubbers and covered with soil should be inspected later, since the rubber decomposes very slowly below ground and may cause a constriction at the graft union.

(d) A practice widely used is to wrap the grafts with some type of adhesive tape. A special nurseryman's tape is available. The tape is drawn tightly around the graft union with the edges slightly overlapping. This holds the parts together very well and prevents drying, thus eliminating the need for waxing. If just one thickness of tape is used, it will decompose sufficiently fast (if the union is below ground) that no constriction of growth will develop. If used above ground, the tape should be cut after the graft has healed. The use of tight wrapping material such as this is especially recommended when difficulty is encountered with the formation of excessive callus.

(e) Plastic tapes are available for wrapping grafts. They are used just as adhesive tape, although they are not adhesive. The final turn of the tape is secured by slipping it under the previous turn. This tape has some elasticity. Also, it deteriorates more slowly below ground than above.

The whip graft can also be used in topworking young trees. The stocks in this case would be small, pencil-sized branches, well distributed around the tree. The grafts are usually tied with nurseryman's adhesive tape or with string, the latter covered with a coat of grafting wax. After the parts of the graft have united, the tying material must be cut; otherwise, the branch may be constricted as growth commences.

Splice Grafting

This method is the same as the whip, or tongue, graft except that the second or "tongue" cut is not made in either the stock or scion. A simple slanting cut of the same length and angle is made in both the stock and the scion. These are placed together and wrapped or tied as described for the whip graft. The splice graft is simple and easy to make. It is particularly useful in grafting plants that have a very pithy stem or which have wood that is not flexible enough to permit a tight fit when a tongue is made as in the whip graft.

Side Grafting

There are numerous variations of the side graft; three of the most useful are described. As the name suggests, the scion is inserted into the side of the stock, which is generally larger in diameter than the scion.

Stub Graft

This method is useful in grafting branches of trees that are too large for the whip graft yet not large enough for other methods such as the cleft or bark graft. For this type of side graft, the best stocks are branches about 1 in. in diameter. An oblique cut is made into the stock branch with a chisel or heavy knife at an angle of 20 to 30 degrees. The cut should be about 1 in. deep, and at such an angle and depth that when the branch is pulled back the cut will open slightly but will close when the pull is released.

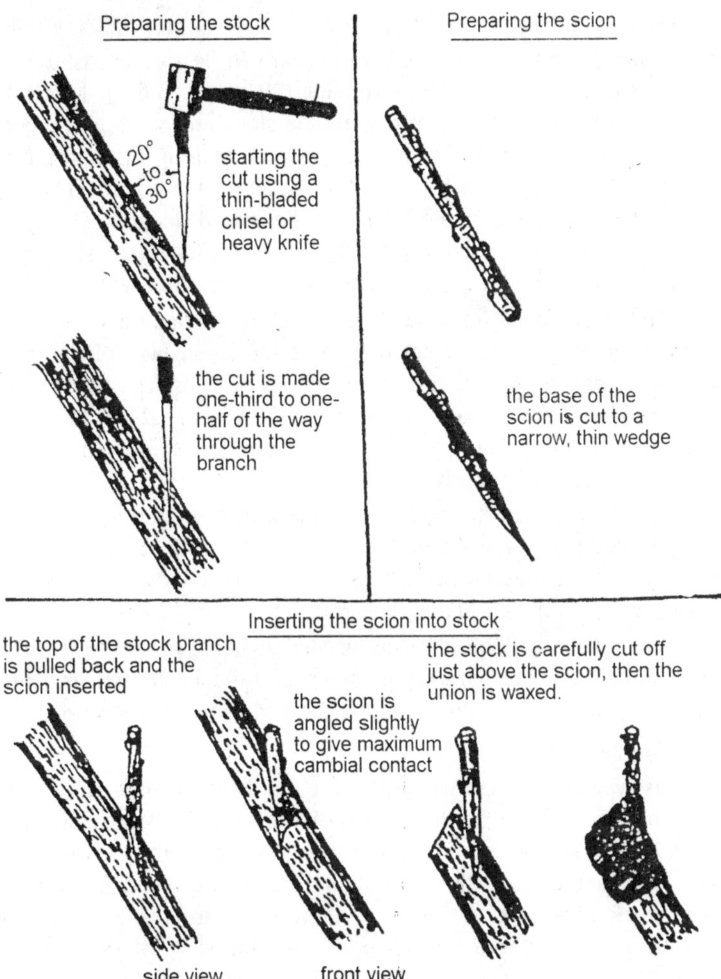

Fig. 2.6. Steps in preparing the side, or stub graft. A thinbladed chisel as illustrated here is ideal for making the cut.

The scion should contain two or three buds and be about 3 in. long and relatively thin. At the basal end of the scion, a wedge about 1 in. long is made. The cuts on both sides of the scion should be very smooth, each made by one single cut with a sharp knife. It is best to insert the scion into the stock at an angle as so as to obtain maximum contact of the cambium layers. The grafter inserts the scion into the cut while the upper part of the stock is pulled backward, using care to obtain the best cambium contact. Then the stock is released. The pressure of the stock should grip the scion tightly, making tying unnecessary, but if it is desired, the scion can be further secured by driving two small flat-headed wire nails (20 gauge, 5/8 in. long) into the stock through the scion. Wrapping the stock and scion at the point of union with nurseryman's tape may also be helpful. After the graft is completed, the stock may be cut off just above the union. This must be very carefully done or the scion may become dislodged. The entire graft union must be thoroughly covered with grafting wax, sealing all openings. The end of the scion should also be covered with wax.

Under some conditions, healing will be more rapid and certain if the stock is left intact and cut off above the scion later. In grafting citrus seedlings by use of the side grafting methods, it is a common practice to lop over the top of the stock about 6 in, above the graft. Some time later, after growth starts from the scion, the top is completely removed just above the graft.

This method may be used to provide a new branch at a position in a tree where it is particularly needed. To force the new scion into active growth, it may be necessary to prune back rather severely the top of the stock branch above the graft.

This grafting method is recommended as being particularly useful in the nursery for the purpose of spring grafting young nursery trees which were fall-budded but in which the bud failed to grow.

Side-Tongue Graft

This type of side graft is useful for small plants, especially some of the broad- and narrow-leaved evergreen species. The stock plant should have a smooth section in the stem just above the crown of the plant. The diameter of the scion should be slightly smaller than that of the stock. The cuts at the base of the scion are made just as for the whip graft. Along a smooth portion of the stem of the stock, a thin piece of bark and wood, the same length as the cut surface of the scion, is completely removed. Then a reverse cut is made downward in the cut on the stock, starting one-third of the distance from the top of the cut. This second cut in the stock should be the same length as the reverse cut in the scion. The scion is then inserted into the cut in the stock, the two tongues interlocking, and the cambium layer(s) matching.

The top of the stock is left intact for several weeks until the graft union has healed. Then it may be cut back above the scion gradually or all at once. This forces the buds on the scion into active growth.

Side-Veneer Graft (Spliced Side Graft)

This variation of side grafting is widely used, especially for grafting small potted plants, such as seedling evergreen. A shallow downward and inward cut from 1 to 1½ in. long is made in a smooth area just above the crown of the stock plant. At the base of this cut, a second short inward and downward cut is made, intersecting the first cut, so as to remove the piece of wood and bark. The scion is prepared with a long cut along one side and a very short one at the base of the scion on the opposite side. These scion cuts should be the same length and width as those made in the stock so that the cambium layers can be matched as closely as possible.

After inserting the scion, the graft is tightly wrapped with waxed or paraffined string or with ordinary budding rubbers. The graft may or may not be covered with wax, depending upon the species. A common practice in side grafting small potted plants of some of the woody ornamental species is to plunge the grafted plants into a damp medium, such as peat moss, so that it just covers the graft union. The newly grafted plants may be placed for healing in a mist propagating house or set in grafting cases. The latter are closed boxes with a transparent cover which permits retention of a high humidity around the grafted plant until the union has healed. The grafting cases are kept closed for a week or so after the grafts are put in, then gradually opened over a period of several weeks; finally, the cover is taken off completely.

After the union has healed, the stock can be cut back above the scion either in gradual steps or all at once.

Cleft Grafting

This is one of the oldest and most widely used methods of grafting, being especially adapted to topworking trees, either in the trunk of a small tree or in the scaffold branches of a larger tree. Cleft grafting is also useful for smaller plants, as in crown grafting established grape vines or camellias. In topworking trees, this method should be limited to stock branches about 1 to 4 in. in diameter and to species with fairly straight-grained wood which will split evenly. Although cleft grafting can be done any time during the dormant season, the chances for successful healing of the graft union are best if the work is done in early spring just when the buds of the stock are beginning to swell but before active growth has started. If cleft grafting is done after the tree is in active growth, it is likely that the bark of the stock will separate from the wood, causing difficulties in obtaining a good union. When this occurs, the loosened bark must be firmly nailed back in

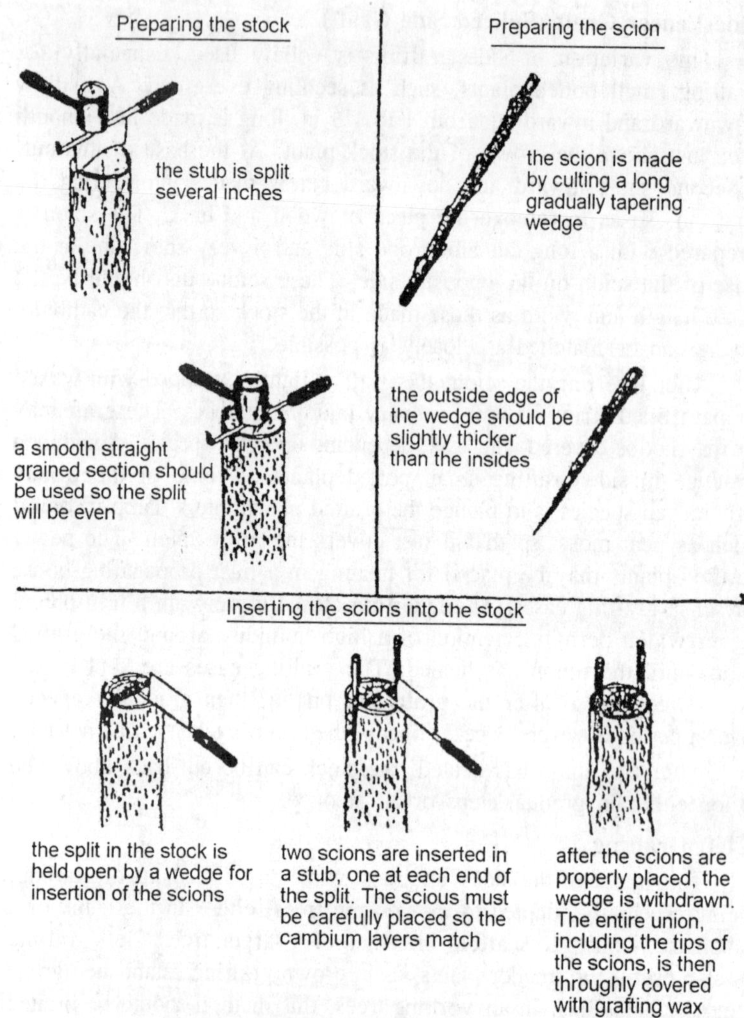

Fig. 2.7. Steps in making the cleft graft.

place. The scions should be made from dormant, 1 - year-old wood. Unless the grafting is done early in the season (when the dormant scions can be collected and used immediately), the scion wood should be collected in advance and held under refrigeration until time for use.

In sawing off the branch for this and other topworking methods, the cut should be made at right angles to the main axis of the branch. In making the cleft graft, a heavy knife, such as a butcher knife, or one of several special cleft grafting tools, is used to make a vertical split for a distance of 2 to 3 in. down the center of the stub to be grafted. This is done by pounding the knife in with a hammer or mallet. It is very important to have the branch sawed off in such a position that the end of the stub which is left is smooth, straight-grained, and free of knots, for at least 6 in. Otherwise, when the split is made it may not be straight, or the wood may split one way and the bark another. The split should be in tangential rather than radial direction is relation to the center of the tree. This permits better placement of the scions for their subsequent growth. Sometimes this cleft is made by a longitudinal saw cut rather than by splitting. After a good, straight split is made, a screwdriver, chisel, or the wedge part of the cleft-grafting tool is driven into the top of the split to hold it open.

Two scions are usually inserted, one at each side of the stock where the cambium layer is located, although in large branches, two splits are sometimes made at right angles to each other and four scions inserted. The scions should be 3 or 4 in. long and have two or three buds. The basal end of each scion should be cut into a long, gently sloping wedge—about 2 in. long. It is not necessary that the end of the wedge come to a point. The side of the wedge which is to go to the outer side of the stock should be slightly wider than the inside edge. Thus, when the scion is inserted and the tool is removed, the full pressure of the split stock will come to bear on the scions at the position where the cambium of the stock touches the cambium layer on the outer edge of the scion. Since the bark of the stock is almost always thicker than the bark of the scion, it is usually necessary for the outer surface of the scion to set slightly in from the outer surface of the stock in order to match the cambium layers.

In all types of grafting the scion must be inserted right side up. That is, the points of the buds on the scion should be pointing away from the stock. Failure to observe this means ultimate failure of the graft to grow.

The long, sloping wedge cuts at the base of the scion should be smooth, made by a single cut on each side with a very sharp knife. Both sides of the scion wedge should press, firmly against the stock for their entire length. A common mistake in cutting scions for this type of graft is to make the cut on the scion too short with too abrupt a slope, so that the only point of contact is just at the top. Shaving slightly the sides of the split in the stock will often permit a smoother contact.

After the scions are properly made and inserted, the tool is carefully withdrawn, using care not to disturb the scions. They should be held so tightly by the pressure of the stock that they cannot be pulled loose by hand. No further tying or nailing is needed unless very small stock branches have been used, in which case wrapping around the top of the stock tightly with string or waxed cloth can be done to hold the scions in place more securely.

Through waxing of the completed graft is essential. The top surface of the stub should be entirely covered, permitting the wax to work into the split in the stock. The sides of the grafted stub should be well covered with wax as far down the stub as the split has gone. The top of the scions should be waxed but not necessarily the bark or buds of the scion. Two or 3 days later all the grafts should be inspected and rewaxed where openings appear. Lack of thorough and complete waxing in this type of graft is almost certain to result in failure.

Saw-Kerf (Notch) Grafting

This can be used in place of the left graft. It is especially useful in topworking trees with branches 3 to 4 in. or more in diameter. It does not have the serious disadvantage of a deep split in the stock (as does the cleft graft), which may permit the entrance of decay-producing organisms. Sawkerf grafting can be done over a long period of time - 2 to 3 months—before growth of the stock starts in the spring. If the work is to be performed late in the season, at the time active growth is starting, it is necessary to collect the scion wood earlier and hold it under refrigeration to keep it dormant until the grafting is to be done. Curly-grained stock branches, which could not split evenly for the cleft graft, can be worked readily by the saw-kerf graft. The saw-kerf graft is somewhat more difficult for beginners to perform than most of the other types, but in the hands of experienced workers it can be done rapidly and is highly successful, especially with certain hard-to-graft species, such as the peach.

There are two types of saw-kerf grafts—deep and shallow. Usually, three scions are inserted into each stock branch. A cut with a thin-bladed, fine-toothed saw is made into the stub for each scion. This cut should extend 1 to 1½ in. toward the center of the stub and about 4 in down the side of the stub. Then, using a very sharp "round knife," the grafter widens this saw cut to fit the scion. The knife should be placed at the bottom of the saw cut and brought upward and inward to cut out thin slices of wood. Care should be taken not to get the cut in the stock too wide for use with the available scions.

The scions should be 4 or 5 in. long and contain two or three buds. The basal end of the scion is cut to a wedge shape with the outside edge of the wedge somewhat thicker than the inside edge so as to conform to the general shape of the widened saw cut as made in the stock. The wedge cut on the scions should be 1½ to 2 in. long and, as in all grafting, the cut areas should be perfectly smooth, with no wavy surfaces. The scion should be tried for a good fit as the groove in the stock is widened to the right size. It is usually easier to enlarge the cut in the stock to fit the scion rather than trying to fit the scion to the cut in the stock. After the cuts on the scion and stock are completed, the scion is tapped firmly into place. The cambium layers should cross to insure contact. Since the bark of the scion is usually thinner than that of the stock, at the correct position the scion will set slightly in from the outside of the stock. If this graft is properly made, the scion should be held very securely by tapping it into place. No further nailing or tying is necessary, but of course, as with all exposed grafts, the cut surfaces must be thoroughly waxed.

The round knife is a useful tool in making this graft. It may be adapted from a leather-worker's knife or a cook's mincing knife. The edge of the knife should be sharpened to that it is flat on one side and beveled on the other, being used so that the flat side is held against the wood in widening out the saw cut made in the stock. If a round knife of this type is not available, a large-bladed grafting knife may be substituted.

The shallow type of saw-kerf graft is made in essentially the same manner, except that the cut into the stock is quite shallow. The outer edge of the scion is considerably thicker than the inner edge. It should be cut to just fit into the opening in the stock. Care must be taken to see that the cambium layers match exactly. The scions, in this case, are held in place by nailing with flat-headed wire nails (5/8 in. long. 20 gauge). Finally, of course, the exposed cut surfaces and the end of the scions are thoroughly covered with wax.

Bark Grafting

This method is rapid, simple, readily performed by amateurs, and if properly done, gives a high percentage of "takes". It requires no special equipment and can be performed on branches ranging from 1 in. up to a foot or more in diameter. The latter size is not recommended as it is difficult to heal over such large stubs before decay-producing organisms get started. The bark graft, since it depends on the bark separating readily from the wood, can only be done after active growth of the stock has started in the spring. As dormant scions must be used, it is necessary to gather the scion wood for deciduous species during the dormant season and hold it under refrigeration until the grafting operation is done. For evergreen species, freshly collected scion wood can be used. Scions are not as securely attached to the stock as in some of the other methods and are more susceptible to wind breakage during the first year even though the healing has been satisfactory. Therefore the new shoots arising from the scions probably should be staked during the first year, or cut back to about half their length, especially in windy areas. After a few years growth, the bark graft union is as strong as the unions formed by other methods.

There are several modifications of the bark graft. Three important types are described.

Bark graft (Method No.1)

Several scions are inserted into each stub. For each scion, a vertical knife cut about 2 in, long is made at the top end of the stub through the bark to the wood. The bark is then lifted slightly along both sides of this cut, in preparation for the insertion of the scion. The scion should be of dormant wood, 4 or 5 in. long, containing two or three buds, and be ¼ to ½ in. in thickness. One cut about 2 in. long is made along one side at the base of the scion. With large scions, this cut extends about one third of the way into the scion, leaving a "shoulder' at the top. The purpose of this shoulder is to reduce the thickness of the scion to minimize the separation of bark and wood after insertion in the stock. The scion should not be cut too thin, however, or it will be mechanically weak and break off at the point of attachment to the stock. If small scions are used, no shoulder is necessary. On the side of the scion opposite the first long cut, a second shorter cut is made, thereby bringing the basal end of the scion to a wedge shape. The scion is then inserted between the bark and the wood of the stock, centered directly under the vertical cut through the bark. The longer cut on the scion is placed against the wood, and the shoulder on the scion is brought down until it rests on top of the stub. The scion is then ready to be fastened in place. A satisfactory method is to nail the scion into the wood, using two nails per scion. Flat-headed nails 5/8 to 1 in. long. of 19 or 20 gauge wire, depending on the size of the scions, are satisfactory. The bark on both sides of the scion should also be securely nailed down, or it will tend to peel back from the wood. Another method commonly used with soft-barked trees, such as the avocado, is to insert all the scions in the stub and then hold them in place by wrapping with string, adhesive tape, or waxed cloth around the stub. This is more effective than nailing in preventing the scions from blowing out but probably does not give as tight a fit. Both nailing and wrapping are advisable for maximum strength. If a wrapping material is used, it may be necessary to cut this later to prevent constriction.

In cases in which the bark of the stock is quite thick and small scions are used, it may not be necessary to make the vertical slit in the bark. The scions, cut as described before, can be pushed into place between the bark and the wood. They can then be nailed or tied securely with string or waxed cloth.

After the stub has been grafted and the scions fastened by nailing or tying, all cut surfaces, including the end of the scions, should be thoroughly covered with grafting wax.

Bark graft (Method No.2)

This type of graft is similar to method No.1, except that the scion is not inserted centered on the vertical cut in the bark of the stock. The bark is lifted only along one side of the vertical cut; the bark on the other side is not disturbed. The scion is inserted under the raised bark and held in place with two nails driven through the bark of the stock, through the scion, and into the wood of the stock. The scion is cut with a shoulder, just as described for method No.1. However, the short cut on the back of the scion, rather than being parallel to the first longer cut, is slanted to one side slightly to conform to the slope of the bark under which the scion is inserted. As in method No.1, the raised bark near the scion should be fastened securely in place with two or more nails or wrapped with tape to prevent it from peeling back. This modification of the bark graft has been widely used with good results. It has an advantage over method No.1, in that one of the edges of the scion is placed against undisturbed bark with its intact cambium cells. This tends to promote more rapid healing of the union. In method No.1, where the bark is lifted away from the scion on both sides, intact cambium cells are some distance from the scion and healing is usually slower.

Bark graft (Method No.3)

In this method, *two* knife cuts about 2 in, long are made through the bark of the stock down to the wood, rather than just one as in the other two methods. The distance between these two cuts should be exactly the same as the width of the scion. The piece of bark between the cuts should be lifted and the terminal two-thirds cut off. The scion is prepared with a smooth slanting cut along one side at the basal end. This cut should be about 2 in. long but made *without* the shoulder, in contrast to the other two methods. On the opposite side of the scion, a cut about ½ in. long is made, forming a wedge at the base of the scion. The scion should fit snugly into the opening in the bark with the longer cut inward and with the wedge at the base slipped under the flap of remaining bark. Rapid healing can be expected because both sides of the scion are touching undisturbed bark and cambium cells, which is not the case in the other two type of the bark graft.

The scion should be nailed into place with two nails, the lower nail going through the flap of bark covering the short cut on the back of the scion. If the bark along the sides of the scion should accidentally become disturbed, it must be nailed back into place.

Method No.3 is well adapted for use with thick-barked trees, such as walnuts, on which it is not feasible to insert the scion under the bark.

Approach Grafting

The distinguishing feature of approach grafting is that two independent, self-sustaining plants are grafted together. After a union has occurred, the top of the stock plant is removed above the graft and the base of the scion plant is removed below the graft. Sometimes it is necessary to sever these parts gradually rather than all at once. Approach grafting provides a means of establishing a successful union between certain plants which are difficult to graft together otherwise. It is usually performed with one or both of the plants to be grafted growing in a pot or container. Use is often made of this method by placing seedling plants growing in containers under an established plant which is to furnish the scion part of the new, grafted plant.

This type of grafting can be done at any time of the year, but healing of the union is more rapid if it is performed at a season when growth is active. As in other methods of grafting, the cut surfaces should be securely fastened together, then covered with grafting wax to prevent drying of the tissues.

Spliced Approach Graft

Preferably the two stems should be approximately the same size. At the point where the union is to occur, a slice of bark and wood 1 to 2 in. long is cut from both stems. This cut should be the same size on each so that identical cambium patterns will be made. The cuts must be perfectly smooth and as nearly flat as possible so that when they are pressed together there will be close contact of the cambium layers. The two cut surfaces are then bound tightly together with string, raffia, or nurseryman's tape. The whole union should then be covered with grafting wax. After the parts are well united, which may require considerable time in some cases, the stock above the union and the scion below the union are cut, and the graft is then completed. It may be necessary to reduce the leaf area of the scion if it is more than the root system of the stock can sustain.

Tongued Approach Graft

This is the same as the spliced approach graft except that after the first cut is made in each stem to be joined, a second cut—downward on the stock and upward on the scion—is made, thus providing a thin tongue on each piece. By interlocking these tongues a very tight, closely fitting graft union can be obtained.

Inlay Approach Graft

This method may be used if the bark of the stock plant is considerably thicker than that of the scion plant. A narrow slot, 3 or 4 in, long, is made in the bark of the stock plant by making two parallel knife cut stand removing the strip of bark between. This can only be done when the stock plant is actively growing and the bark "slipping." The slot should be exactly as wide as the scion to be inserted. The stem of the scion plant, at the point of union, should be given along, shallow cut along one side, of the same length as the slot in the stock plant and deep enough to go through the bark and slightly into the wood. This cut surface of the scion branch should be laid into the slot cut in the stock plant and held there by nailing with two or more small, flat-headed wire nails. The entire union must has healed, the stock can be cut off above the graft and the scion below the graft.

Inarching

This method is similar to approach grafting in that both stock and scion plants are on their own roots at the time of grafting; it differs in that the top of the new rootstock plant usually does not extend above the point of the graft union as it does in approach grafting. Inarching is generally considered to be a form of "repair grafting," being used in cases in which the roots of an established tree have been damaged by such things as cultivation implements, rodents, or disease. It can be used to very good advantage in saving a valuable tree or improving its root system.

Seedlings (or rooted cuttings) planted beside the older, damaged tree, or suckers arising near its base, are grafted into the trunk of the tree for the purpose of providing a new root system to supplant the damaged roots. The seedlings to be inarched into the tree should be spaced about 5 or 6 in. apart around the circumference of the tree if the damage is extensive. The tree will usually stay alive for sometime after the injury occurs unless it is very severe. A satisfactory procedure for inarching is to plant seedlings of a compatible species or variety around the tree during the dormant season. Then, as active growth commences in early spring, the grafting operation can be done.

Inarching old, weakly growing trees with strong, vigorous seedling rootstocks has on some occasions proved beneficial in promoting renewed active growth of the old trees.

The seedling plants to provide the new root system are usually considerably smaller than the tree to be rapaired. The graft union is made in a manner similar to that described for method No.3 of the bark graft. The upper end of the seedling, which should be ¼ to ½ in. thick, is given a long shallow cut along the side for 4 to 6 in. This cut should be on the side next to the trunk of the tree and made deep enough to remove some of the wood, thus exposing two strips of cambium tissue. At the end of the seedling another shorter cut, about ½ in. long, is made on the side opposite the long cut, this makes a sharp, wedge-shaped end on the seedling stem. A long slot is made in the trunk of the older tree by removing a piece of bark the exact width of the seedling and just as along as the cut surface made on the seedling. A small flap of bark is left at the upper end of the slot, under which the wedge end of the seedling is inserted. Then the seedling is nailed into the slot with four or five small, flat-headed wire nails. The nail at the top of the slot should go through the flap of bark and through the end of the seedling. If any of the bark of the tree along the sides of the seedling should accidentally be pulled loosed, it is necessary to nail it back in place. After nailing, the entire area of the graft union should be thoroughly waxed.

In inarching some species, such as the walnuts, better healing of the union takes place if the top of the seedling is retained and allowed to extend above the graft union for a period of time, finally being cut off just above .the union.

Owing to the food materials translocated from the larger tree, the seedlings grow very rapidly and soon provide a considerable number of new roots for the grafted tree. If shoots arise from the inarches, they should be suppressed by cutting off their tips. The shoots should finally be removed entirely as the union becomes well established.

Bridge Grafting

This is a form of repair grafting, and is used in cases in which the root system of the tree has not been damaged but where there is injury to the bark of the trunk. Sometimes cultivation implements, rodents, disease, the winter injury will damage a considerable trunk area, often girdling the tree completely. If the damage to the bark is extensive, the tree is almost certain to die, because the roots will be deprived of their food supply from the top of the tree. Trees of some species, such as the elm, cherry, and pecan, can heal over extensively injured areas by the development of callus tissue. But trees of most species which have had the bark of the trunk severely damaged should be bridge grafted if they are to be saved.

The bridge grafting operation is best performed in early spring just as active growth of the tree is beginning and the bark is slipping easily. The scions to be used should be taken when dormant from 1-year-old growth, ¼ to ½ in. in diameter, of the same or a compatible species, and held under refrigeration until the grafting work is to be done. In an emergency, one may successfully perform bridge grafting late in the spring, using scion wood whose buds have already started to grow. The developing buds or new shoots must be removed.

The first step in bridge grafting is to trim the wounded area back to healthy, undamaged tissue by removing dead or torn bark. Then every 2 or 3 in. around the injured section a scion is inserted, attached at both the upper and lower ends into live bark. It is important that the scions be inserted right side up. If they are put in reversed, they may make a union and stay alive for a year or two, but the scions will not grow and enlarge in diameter as they would if inserted correctly.

It is essentially the same as method No. 3 of the bank graft. Just above and below the injured area, a slot 2 to 3 in. long and exactly the width of the scion is cut in the bark of the trunk for each scion. The piece of bark is removed, with the exception of a flap about ½ in. long which is left at the end of the slot. The scions are cut to fit into these slots at each end of the wound, and long enough to bow outward slightly. This bow allows for good contact at each end and permits some swaying of the trunk in the wind without tearing the scions loose. To prepare the scions, a cut is made along both ends on the side which is to fit into the slot. The cut should be the same length as the slot and deep enough to remove some bark and wood and expose two strips of cambium tissue. Then, on the opposite side of the scion, at each end, another shorter cut, about ½ in. long, is made to form the end of the scion into a wedge shape. The ends of the scion should be inserted under the flaps of bark and nailed in place, using 3/4 in. 20 gauge flat-headed wire nails. One nail should go through the flap of bark at each end of the scion with enough additional nails to hold the scion securely.

After all the scions have been inserted, the cut surfaces must be thoroughly covered with grafting wax, particular care being taken to work the wax around the scions, especially at the graft unions. The Exposed wood of the injured section may also be covered with grafting wax to prevent the entrance of decay organisms and to prevent excessive drying out of the wood, which is important, being the path for upward movement of water and nutrients in the tree.

The buds on the scions will often push into growth if the grafts are successful. These shoots should be removed, because no branches would be desired in this position. The scions will rapidly enlarge in size and completely heal over the wound in a few years.

Bracing

The same type of graft union practiced in inarching and bridge grafting can often be used to establish a "natural" brace in young trees. This method is useful in supporting branches that may be in danger of breaking off or where there is a weak crotch. A small branch, about pencil size or a little larger, coming a foot or so above the weak crotch is grafted into the adjacent branch to be supported. It should be wrapped spirally and upward partly around the branch. In the region where the graft union is to be, the bark on the large branch is cut just under the small branch to its exact width. This should extend for a length of 6 in. or more, and the spiral piece of bark should be removed. Grafting such as this could only be done at a time of year when there is active growth and the bark is slipping easily. Early spring, just as the new growth is starting, is the preferable time.

After the slot in the bark is ready, the "scion"—the small branch-should be smoothly cut on the lower side through about a third of its thickness and for the length of the slot—6 in. or more. If the cuts are well made, the small branch should fit snugly into the slot. It is helpful to trim the end of the small branch to a wedge point by cutting it on the top side so that it can be inserted under the bark at the top end of the slot.

The next step is to nail the branch in place in the slot with small, flat-headed wire nails (5/8 or 3/4 in., 20 gauge) placed at 1- or

2-in, intervals. The graft union should then be thoroughly waxed to prevent drying. It is advisable to tie the two branches together temporarily with a strong cord to prevent shipping by the wind, which might put the graft union loose.

Grafting Classified According to Placement

Grafting may be classified according to the part of the plant on which the scion is placed- a root, the crown (the junction of the stem and root at the ground level), or various places in the top of the plant.

Root Grafting

In this class of grafting the rootstock seedling, rooted cutting, or layered plant is dug up, and the roots are used as the stock for the graft. The entire root system may be used (*whole-root graft*), or the roots may be cut up into small pieces and each piece used as a stock (*piece-root graft*). Both methods give satisfactory results. As the roots used are relatively small (¼ to ½ in. in diameter), the whip, or tongue, graft is generally used. Root grafting is usually performed indoors during the late winter or early spring. The scion wood collected previously is held in storage, while the rootstock plants are also dug in the late fall and stored under cool(40° to 50°F : 4° to 10°C) and moist conditions until the grafting is done.

The term *bench grafting* is sometimes given to this process, because it is often performed at benches by skilled grafters as a large-scale operation. A number of plants are propagated commercially by root grafting—apples, pears, grapes and such ornamentals as the wisteria and rhododendron.

In making root grafts, the root piece should be 3 to 6 in. long and the scions about the same length, containing two to four buds. After the grafts are made and properly tied they are bundled together in groups of 50 to 100 and stored for callusing in damp sand, peat moss, or other packing material. They may be placed in a cool cellar or under refrigeration at approximately 45°F (7°C) for about 2 months. The callusing period for apples can be shortened to around 30 days if the grafts are stored at a temperature of about 70°F (21°C) and at a high humidity. To use this higher callusing temperature the material should be collected in the fall and the grafts made before any cold weather has overcome the rest period of the scion buds. After the unions are well healed, the grafts must be stored at cool temperature—35° to 40°F (2° to 4°C)—to overcome the "rest period" of the buds and to hold them dormant until panting. The grafts are lined out in early spring to the nursery row directly from the low temperature storage conditions. For general callusing purposes, temperatures below rather than above 70°F (21°C) are the most satisfactory. By the proper regulation of temperature, callusing processes may be accelerated by increased temperature or retarded by decreased temperature so that, within reasonable limits, a desired degree of callus formation may be had within a given length of time. Provision should be made for adequate aeration of the callusing grafts.

As soon as the ground can be prepared in the spring, the grafts are lined out in the nursery row 4 to 6 in. apart. They should be planted before growth, of the buds or roots begins. If this starts before the grafts can be planted, they should be moved to lower temperatures (30° to 35° F; — 1° to 2°C). The grafts are usually planted deep enough so that the graft union is just below the ground level, but if roots are to arise only from the rootstock, the graft should be planted with the union well above the soil level. It is very important to prevent scion rooting where certain definite influences, such as dwarfing or disease resistance, are expected from the rootstock.

After one summer's growth, the grafts should be large enough to transplant to their permanent location. If not, the scion may be cut back to one or two buds, or headed back somewhat to force out scaffold branches, and then allowed to grow a second year. With the older root system a strong, vigorous top is obtained the second year.

Nurse-Root Grafting

Under certain conditions, it is desired to have a stem cutting of a difficult-to-root species on its own roots. One way this can be done is by making a root graft, using the plant to be grown on its own roots as the scion and a root of a compatible species as the stock. The scion may be made longer than usual and the graft planted deeply with the major portion of the scion below ground. In some cases scion-rooting is promoted by rubbing a rooting stimulant, such as idolebutyric acid into several vertical cuts made through the bark at the base of the scion, just above the graft union. This is done just before planting, and the grafts are set deeply so that most of the scion is covered with soil. After one or two seasons of growth many of the scions will have roots. The temporary nurse rootstock is then cut off and the top reduced in proportion to the root system. The rooted scion is replanted to grow on its own roots.

Scion rooting is often better if the nurse-root is buried deeply enough so that a new shoot of the current season's developing from a bud on the scion, will be rooted, rather than trying to root the older, lignified tissue of the original scion. This is essentially a form of mound layering. As the new scion shoot grows, soil is gradually mounded up around it to a height of 5 or 6 in. although the terminal leaves are at no time covered.

Several methods of handling eliminate the necessity of digging up the graft and cutting off the rootstock. The rootstock piece will eventually die if it is grafted onto the scion in an inverted position. The inverted stock piece sustains the scion until scion roots are formed, but the stock fails to receive food from the scion and eventually dies, thus leaving the scion on its own roots. In another method an incompatible rootstock is used. Hence, if the graft is planted deeply, scion roots will gradually become more important in sustaining the plant, and the incompatible rootstock will finally cease to function.

In a third method the base of the scion, just above the graft union, is bound with some type of wrapping material to eventually girdle and cut off the rootstock. Excellent results have been obtained with ordinary budding rubber strips (0.016 gauge). Budding rubbers disintegrate within a month when exposed to sun and air; when buried in the soil, they will last as long as 2 years, allowing sufficient time for the scion to become rooted. Yet, owing to the slow deterioration of the rubber below ground, the rootstock is finally girdled and cut off.

Crown Grafting

A graft union made at the rootstem transition region- the "crown" of the plant—on an established rootstock is termed a "crown graft." Several methods of grafting are commonly used in crown grafting, such as the whip, side, cleft, saw-kerf, or bark graft, depending upon the species and size of the root stock.

Crown grafting of deciduous plants is best done in late winter or early spring, shortly before new growth starts. The scions should be prepared from well-matured, dormant wood of the previous season's growth. Since the operation is performed just below, at, or just above the soil level, it is possible to cover the graft union, or even the entire scion, with soil and thus eliminate the necessity for waxing. The union should be tied securely with string or tape to hold the grafted parts together until healing takes place.

Double-Working

A double-worked tree has three parts, usually all different genetically—the rootstock, the intermediate stock, and the scion or fruiting, top. Such a tree has two graft unions, one between the rootstock and intermediate stock, and one between the intermediate stock and the scion. The intermediate stock may be less than an inch in length or extensive enough to include the trunk and secondary scaffold branches. Double-working is used for various purposes, such as (a) overcoming graft incompatibility between a desired top variety and the rootstock, (b) providing a cold or disease-resistant trunk, (c) obtaining a dwarfing effect from the use of certain intermediate stocks, or (d) obtaining the strong trunk or crotch systems of certain varieties.

A good example of double-working is the use of an intermediate stock when the 'Bartlett' pear is grafted on dwarfing quince roots. 'Bartlett' will not, generally, form a compatible union if grafted directly on quince. Cuttings of the quince may be rooted during one summer and fall-budded to a compatible stock, such as 'Old Home' pear. This grows the following summer, after which it is again fall-budded to the 'Barlett' pear, the 'Barlett' bud being inserted in the intermediate stock. The 'Barlett' top is developed the next summer, after which the double-worked nursery tree is ready to dig and set in its permanent location.

A quicker method—which also produces a straighter trunk than double-budding. Dormant 'Bartlett' pear scions are bench-grafted onto dormant 'Hardly' pear stem pieces during late winter, using the whip or tongue grafting method. These grafts are then packed in damp material: after several weeks in a cool location, they become well-callused and have united. In early spring such grafts (scion variety on the interstock) are crown-grafted in the nursery row to the rootstock—in this case, rooted quince cuttings. After one year in the nursery row, the double-worked nursery trees are ready to be dug.

Another method of double- working all at one time is by bench grafting, using the whip or tongue grafting method, but making two graft unions rather than one. The subsequent callusing and planting procedure is the same as for a simple root graft.

A method, termed "double-shield budding" has been developed both in England and Germany for double-working. Essentially, this method consists of preparing a T-bud but inserting a thin budless shield of the intermediate variety under and below the shield piece containing the bud of the variety desired for the top. However, such short "compatibility bridges" may not always produce the desired effect. It has been shown that the degree of dwarfing is proportional to the length of the interstock.

Top-Grafting (Topworking)

One of the principal uses of grafting is to change the variety of an established plant—tree, shrub, or vine. If budding is used, then the process is termed *top-budding*.

In some cases pulling out the existing trees and planting new nursery trees may be more economical than topworking. This is especially true if the existing trees are old or diseased or if the species is relatively short-lived, as is the peach. Long-lived species, such as apples and pears, are worth topworking if the tree is in a healthy condition. Also to be considered in planning for topworking is the hazard of viruses being present in the scion wood. In the peach, for example, virus diseases such as "stubby twig." "ringspot" or "necrotic leaf spot" may be introduced by infected scions into an otherwise healthy orchard. Care should be taken to obtain scion wood for top-grafting, if possible, from known virus- tested sources. Of equal significance is the possibility that the stock trees may be infected with viruses or part of a virus complex. The value of scion wood from virus-tested sources can be nullified if the stock is virus infected.

Preparation for Top-Grafting

Any of the methods of grafting described earlier in this chapter—whip, side, cleft, saw-kerf, or bark- can be used for top-grafting, which is usually done in the spring, shortly before new growth starts. The exact time depends upon the method to be used. The cleft, side, whip and saw-kerf graft can be done before the bark is slipping. The bark graft must be done when the bark is slipping, preferably just a s the buds of the stock tree are starting growth.

It is usually advisable to obtain an ample amount of good quality scion wood prior to grafting and store it under the proper conditions.

In preparing the stock tree for topworking, one must decide, for each individual tree, which and how many scaffold branches (usually three to five) should be used. If the work is done high in the tree in the smaller, secondary scaffold branches, an earlier return to bearing will result than when fewer and larger limbs are grafted lower in the tree. The branches to be grafted should be well distributed around the tree and up and down the main trunk, avoiding branches with weak, narrow crotches. All others can be removed unless one or more nurse branches are used.

Retaining *nurse branches* is a common practice in topworking deciduous trees in regions where cold winters are experienced. In localities where the winters are mild and damage of succulent growth by winter killing is slight, nurse branches are not used. For broad-leaved evergreens, such as citrus and olives, it is customary to leave nurse branches. The presence of nurse branches, especially if they are on the south and west sides of the tree, is desirable because they protect the grafted branches from sun scald; otherwise, the branches should be whitewashed to prevent this. Retaining a large scaffold branch as a nurse limb results in less vigorous growth of the scions. They are then less likely to blow out in winds or be winter- killed than the more vigorous, succulent shoots which develop from the scions where no nurse branches are retained. Also, fewer suckers and water sprouts (which must be removed) develop when nurse branches are left . The latter should be so pruned as not to interfere with the growth of the young grafts.

A practice which is often recommended, especially for older trees, is to top work them during a 2-year period, grafting perhaps two main branches on the northeast side of the tree the first year and retaining two branches on the southwest as nurse branches. The second year these are topworked.

Topworking is most successful when done on relatively young trees where the branches to be grafted are to larger than 3 or 4 in. in diameter and are relatively close to the ground. When attempting to topwork large, old trees, it is often necessary to go high up in the trees to find branches with a diameter as small as 4 in. If the grafting is done on such branches, the new top is inconveniently high for the various orchard operations, such as thinning and harvesting. The other alternative is cutting off the branches or main trunk close to the ground and inserting the scions into wood one or more feet in diameter. Although many scions can be inserted around the tree between the bark and the wood by the bark graft method and may grow well for several years, it is quite likely, that wood rot will develop in the center of the stub before the growth of the scions can heal it over. Also, some scions are not mechanically held in place very securely and may be blown out by strong winds after they reach considerable size.

It is important that the branch to be topworked be cut off in such a location that the region just below the cut is smooth and free from knots or small branches, so that there will be a satisfactory place for inserting the scions. The branches are best cut off about 9 to 12 in. from the main trunk to keep the tree headed low. The branch should not be cut off more than a few hours before the grafting is to be done.

In Preparation for Topworking (Top-Grafting)

(a) Do the work in the spring when the trees are dormant or shortly after growth starts.

(b) Select for grafting three to five well-placed scaffold branches which are not larger than about 4 in. in diameter and which are conveniently close to the ground.

(c) Retain nurse branches for broad-leaved evergreen trees and for deciduous trees where the winters are severe.

(d) Cut off the branches properly so that the bark is not torn down the trunk.

Grafting on a cool, overcast day with no wind blowing offers the most protection from drying of the cut surfaces of the scion and stock until they can be covered with grafting wax. Grafting on hot, sunny, and windy days should be avoided. During grafting, the scion wood must not dry out by being exposed to the sun. It should be kept moist and cool in some container or be wrapped in moist burlap.

The need for prompt and thorough coverage of all cuts, including the tip end of the scions, cannot be stressed too strongly. The wax should be worked into the bark of the stock, sealing all small cuts or cracks where air could penetrate in and around the cut surfaces where healing tissue is expected to develop.

Subsequent Care of Topworked Trees

After the actual top-grafting (or top-budding) operation is finished, much important work needs to be done before the topworking is successfully completed. A good grafting job can be ruined by failure to care for the trees properly.

If the grafting has been done in late spring when growth is active, trees of some species, such as the walnut, will "bleed" to a considerable extent from the grafted stub, even though it has been covered with grafting wax. This flow of sap around the scions can be so heavy as to interfere with the normal healing processes at the graft union. If this condition appears, it can often be corrected by making several slanting cuts with a knife through the bark in the trunk of the tree several feet below the grafted stubs. The bleeding will then take place at these cuts rather than around the graft union. This extensive sap flow is not particularly harmful to the tree and will usually stop within a few days. In 3 to 5 days after grafting, the trees should be carefully inspected and the graft unions rewaxed if cracks or holes appear in the wax.

A problem needling immediate attention is the prevention of sunburn on the portions of the trunk and large branches which are exposed to the direct rays of the sun by the removal of the protecting top foliage. This is especially important if the grafting has been done late in the season when not weather can be expected, and when no protecting nurse branches have been retained. The radiant energy from the sun absorbed by the dark-coloured bark can raise the temperature of the living cells below the bark to a lethal level.

It is generally advisable to whitewash the trunk, branches and scions of the grafted trees, unless the grafting is done in late winter or early spring when the days are still cold. Various cold-water paints, some made especially for this purpose, are available. The white colour reflects a considerable portion of the sun's radiant energy, thus keeping the temperature of the living tissues within safe limits. Interior, water-base house paints (both latex and acrylic) prevent sunburn for one season. Exterior paints give longer protection but are more likely to cause injury to the tree.

To Prepare Whitewash for Grafted Trees

Formula I. Quicklime, 5 lb; salt, ½ lb; sulphur, ¼ lb. Add water to the lime to start it slaking. Then add the salt and sulphur. This mixture should be prepared in a crockery or wood container. Allow to age for several days, they dilute to a consistency just thick enough to apply with a paint brush. Dilute to a thinner consistency for spray application.

Formula II. Hydrated lime, 25 lb; zinc sulphate, 2lb; water, 50gal. Add water first to a power sprayer with agitator running, then add other components. Spray mixture on trees.

One way to protect the scions from the heat of the sun when the grafting has been done late in the season is to cover the end of the grafted stub and the scions with a large paper bag, the corners of which have been cut to allow for ventilation. The bag is tied securely on the stub with heavy string. However, in a test, of various methods of protecting scions of grafted walnut trees, including the use of paper bags, whitewashing proved the best.

Another help in preventing sunburn is to retain some of the watersprouts which soon start growth along the trunk and branches of the grafted tree. They must be kept under control or they will quickly shade out the developing scions. Rather than removing the watersprouts completely, the grafter can head them back to several inches in length, and they will shade the bark underneath. An additional benefit is that the food manufactured by this leaf area will help sustain the tree until the new scions develop sufficient foliage to do so.

It should be emphasized that, especially during the first summer after topworking the sucker and water sprout growth arising from below the grafted branches must be kept pruned back so as not to interfere with the growth of the scions. If it has been customary to fertilize the trees with nitrogen, this should be withheld for a year or two after grafting, because no stimulation of growth is usually needed. If the trees have been under irrigation, their water requirement will be much less, owing to the removal of a considerable amount of leaf area when the tops were cut back for grafting.

Two to four scions are generally inserted in each stub. If all the scions grow, they should all be retained during the first year, because they will help heal over the stub. However, just one branch, from the best placed and strongest growing scion, should be retained permanently. Growth from the remaining scions should be retarded by rather severe pruning, keeping them alive to help heal the branch, but allowing the permanent scion to become the dominant one. To keep two or more scions for permanent branches at one point will undoubtedly result in a weak crotch, which will eventually break. The first year, then, the best practice is to retain all scions to help heal the stub but, by pruning, to retard the growth of all but the best one. If two shoots arise from the scion to be retained permanently, select the best of these and remove the other. After the stub has healed over, the temporary scions can be removed completely. This may be in the second or third year.

If the permanent scion grows rather vigorously, the danger arises of its becoming top heavy and breaking off during winds. This may be handled in two ways—either by retarding the growth of the permanent branch by pruning it back or by nailing a lath or other type of stick onto the tree and tying the new branch to this stick. *When tying a cord around a branch, always make a loop so that there is no chance of the branch being girdled as it grows.*

Should only one scion grow at each stub, the problem of securing adequate healing off the stub on the side opposite the living scion may prove to be serious. Healing may be helped by sawing off the stub at an angle away from the surviving scion. The cut surface of the stub can be covered with grafting wax to retard wood rotting . It may take a number of years for the single scion to heal over the stub, and it is possible that wood rotting may start before it can do so.

When none of the scions grow in a stub, there are still some possibilities for getting it topworked. One is by allowing several well-placed water sprouts arising just below the cut surface to grow, then top-budding them during the summer. Or the watersprouts may be allowed to grow so as to keep the branch alive and healthy, then the grafting operation repeated the following year, making a fresh cut a foot or so below the original cut.

If nurse branches have been used, they should be cut back and away from the scions at intervals throughout the summer so that scion shoots are always fully exposed to the sun and have sufficient space to grow. Nurse branches should be removed entirely or grafted by the second or third year.

When the top of the tree has been finally worked over to the new variety, it will grow vigorously for a few years. Good pruning practices are needed to prevent badly placed branches from developing.

Frameworking

In this method of changing the variety of fruit trees, all the main scaffold branches are retained on the tree but most of the small laterals throughout the top of the tree are replaced by a large number of scions of the replacement variety. These are inserted by the side graft method with the cuts made very close to the origin of lateral branches (about 1 in. in diameter) arising from the secondary scaffolds. Long scions having 7 or 8 buds are often used. In frame working the tree quickly returns to fruiting, but considerable labour is needed for grafting, and much aftercare is required in keeping growth from the original tree below the scions cut away so that only the replacement variety is maintained.

Herbaceous Grafting

Grafting herbaceous types of plants is used for various purposes, such as studying virus transmission, stock-scion physiology, and grafting compatibility, as well as for the commercial greenhouse production of certain cucurbitaceous crops, particularly in Europe. Usually such grafts are made while the plants are quite small, the stock being grafted shortly after seed germination. Such material is generally very soft, succulent, and susceptible to injury. In one technique a simple splice graft is used with a diagonal cut made through the seedling stock, just above the cotyledons. A piece of thin-walled polyethylene tubing of the proper size to give a snug fit is slipped over the cut end of the stock. The basal end of the scion receives a diagonal cut similar in length and angle to that given the stock. The scion is then slipped down into the plastic tubing so that the two cut surfaces make intimate contact. The tubing holds the graft in place until healing occurs—about 12 days after grafting. Then the tubing may be slipped off over the scion if there are no leaves and if the bud has not expanded; otherwise, it may be cut off with a razor blade.

In another procedure used in grafting older herbaceous stock plants, several leaves are retained below the graft union. The cleft graft is used (but with only one scion), and the graft union is bound with raffia, budding rubbers, or adhesive latex tape. To prevent drying out, the entire plant—following grafting—is covered with a supported polyethylene bag. The grafted plant is then set in the shade until the graft has healed; then the plastic cover can be removed.

A method of establishing *Vitis vinifera* grapes on phylloxera or nematode-resistant rootstocks is by "greenwood" grafting, in which the grafting is done in the spring, placing the scion taken from new growth—on a new green shoot which has developed from the rootstock plant. A simple splice graft is made with the sloping cuts 1 to 1½ in. long. The stock and scion pieces must be the same diameter. The scion has only one bud. The cuts are matched as closely as possible, and the graft union is completely covered by wrapping with a budding rubber. The graft union should be healed and the bud growing by two weeks after grafting. Since these grafts are quite fragile, they must be tied to a stake.

Nurse-Seed Grafting

Germination of some large-seeded woody species, such as the chestnut, is hypogeal ; that is, the cotyledons remain below ground in the seed coats with the shoot tip appears above ground. In a grafting procedure using certain species with seeds of this type, when the seeds have just germinated, the petioles of the cotyledons are cut off transversely just at the seed, leaving the cotyledons inside. A knife point is inserted into the seed between the cut petioles, making an opening for the scion. The scion, which is prepared from dormant wood of the previous season's growth, is cut to a wedge shape at the base, as for a cleft graft. The scion is inserted into the cut between the cotyledons so that the exposed cambium surfaces of the scion are in close contact with the cut surfaces of the cotyledons. The "seed-grafts" are then lined out in the rooting medium with the union about 1 ½ in. below the surface. A graft union takes place, and roots arise from the cut cotyledon petioles. This type of grafting is done in early spring, using properly stratified seed and dormant scion wood. Chestnuts, avocados, and camellias have been grafted successfully by this method; in fact grafted camellia plants of the desired cultivar can be obtained in the same length of time it would take for the seedlings to become large enough to graft by the conventional cleft graft method.

In a modification of the nurse-seed graft, which has worked well in propagating chestnuts, pecans, walnuts, and oaks, the actual graft union is made into the seedling hypocotyl at the point of attachment of the cotyledons. The scion is cut to a thin wedge and inserted into a split made in the hypocotyl. After insertion of the scion, the graft is wrapped firmly with rubber strips or waxed string.

Cutting-Grafts

In this type of graft, a leafy scion is grafted onto a leafy, unrooted stem piece (which is to become the rootstock), and the combination is then placed in a rooting medium under intermittent mist for simultaneous healing of the graft union and rooting of the stock. This procedure was utilized many years ago in studying stock- scion physiology in citrus. More recently it has been used in commercial propagation of various types of citrus on clonal dwarfing rootstocks. It is also of value in propagating certain conifer species that are difficult to start as cuttings.

For citrus a simple splice graft is used. The slope of the cut is at 15-deg, angle, and the union is died with a rubber band. The base of the stock is dipped into a root-promoting material, such as indolebutyric acid and then the grafts are placed under mist, or in a closed case, in flats of the rooting medium over bottom heat. After healing of the union and rooting of the stock, the grafts are allowed to harden by discontinuing the mist and bottom heat for about 2 weeks. Then the grafts are ready for planting in 1-gal. cans or other containers.

In using this method for conifers the difficult-to-root scion is grafted in early spring to the unrooted (but easily rooted) stock by a side graft. The graft union is made about 2 in. above the base of the stock. The stock and scion are both 10 to 20 in. long. The base of the stock is treated with an indolebutyric acid rooting compound, and then the combination is inserted into a flat of a well drained rooting medium, such as perlite, so that the medium covers the graft union. The flats containing the grafts are kept in a cool greenhouse under intermittent mist. About 8 weeks later the cuttings should be rooted and the graft union healed. Then the top of the stock is cut off just above the graft union, and the grafted plant is transferred to an appropriate-sized container of soil.

3

Processes of Budding

In contrast to grafting, in which the scion consists of a short detached piece of stem tissue with several buds, budding utilizes only one bud and a small section of bark, with or without wood. Budding is often termed "bud grafting", since the physiological processes involved are the same as in grafting.

The commonly used budding methods depend upon the bark "slipping". The term indicates the condition when the bark can easily separated from the wood. It denotes the period of year when the plant is in active growth, when the cambium cells are actively dividing, and newly formed tissues are easily torn as the bark is lifted from the wood. Beginning with new growth in the spring, this period should last until the plant ceases growth in the fall. However, adverse growing conditions, such as lack of water, defoliation, or low temperatures, may lead to a tightening of the bark and can seriously interfere with the budding operation. Getting the stock plants in the proper condition for budding is an important consideration. Of the commonly used methods described here, only one—the chip bud can be done when the bark is not slipping.

The budding operation, particularly T-budding, can be performed more rapidly than the simplest method of grafting, some rose budders inserting as many as 2000 or 3000 or more T-buds a day if the tying is done by helpers. If performed under the proper conditions, the percentage of successful unions in T budding is very high—90 to 100 percent. Budding is widely used in producing nursery stock of rose and fruit tree cultivars, where hundreds of thousands of individual plants are propagated each year. Therefore, for propagation operations involving

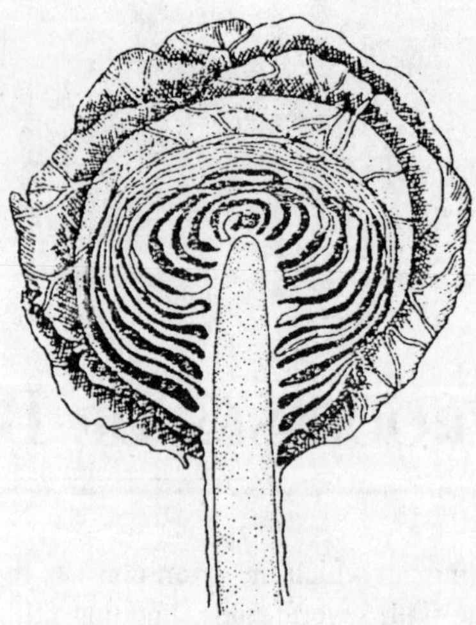

Fig. 3.1. A terminal bud of cabbage.

large numbers of plants, where speed and low mortality are essential, budding upon selected rootstocks is likely to be chosen. The use of budding is confined generally to young plants or the smaller branches of large plants where the buds can be inserted into shoots which are from $^1/_4$ to 1 in. in diameter. Topworking young trees by top-budding is quite successful. Here the buds are inserted in small, vigorously growing branches in the upper portion of the tree.

Budding may result in a stronger union, particularly during the first few years, than is obtained by some of the grafting methods, and thus the shoots are not as likely to blow out in strong winds. Budding makes more economical use of propagating wood than grafting, each bud potentially being capable of producing a new plant of the desired variety. This may be quite important if propagating wood is scarce. In addition, the techniques involved in budding are simple and can be easily performed by the amateur.

Rootstocks for Budding

In propagating nursery stock of the various fruit and ornamental species by budding, a rootstock plant is used. It should have the desired characteristics of vigor, growth habit, and disease resistance, as well as being easily propagated. This rootstock plant may be a rooted cutting, a rooted layer, or more commonly a seedling. Usually, one year's growth in the nursery row before budding is to be done is sufficient to produce a rootstock plant large enough to be budded, but seedling of slow growing species may require two seasons.

To produce nursery trees free of harmful pathogens (viruses, *fungi*, or bacteria) it is essential that the rootstock plant, as well as the budwood, be free of such organisms.

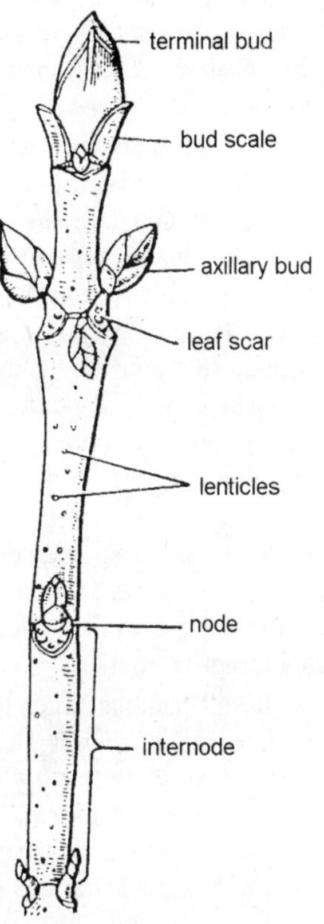

Fig. 3.2. Terminal and axillary buds.

Time of Budding—Fall, Spring, or June

The important budding methods are used at seasons of the year when the stock plant is in active growth and the cambial cells actively dividing so that the bark separates readily from the wood. It is also necessary that well-developed buds of the desired variety be available at the same time. These conditions exist for most plant species at three different times during the year. In the Northern Hemisphere, these periods are late July to early September (*fall budding*), March and April (*spring budding*), and late May and early June (*June budding*).

Fall Budding

This is the most important time of budding in the propagation of fruit tree nursery stock, although actually the budding is done mostly in late summer rather than fall. The rootstock plants are usually large enough by late summer to accommodate the bud, and the plants are still actively growing, with the bark slipping easily. Once growth has stopped and the bark adheres tightly to the wood, budding can no longer be done.

In fall budding, the budsticks, consisting of the current season's shoots, are obtained at the time of budding. They should be vigorous and should contain vegetative or leaf buds. Such shoots are sometimes termed *watersprouts*, especially if they are very vigorous. Short, slowly growing shoots on the outer portion of the tree should be avoided, because they may have chiefly flower buds rather than vegetative buds. Flower buds are usually around and plump, whereas leaf buds are smaller and pointed. Some species have mixed buds, the node containing both vegetative and flower buds. These are satisfactory for use in budding.

Every effort should be made to make sure that the trees from which the budsticks are obtained are free of any bacterial, fungus, or virus diseases. Using infected budsticks can infect every budded nursery tree with the disease.

As the budsticks are selected the leaves should be removed immediately, leaving only a short piece of the leaf stalk or petiole attached to the bud; this will aid in handling the bud later on. The budsticks should be kept from drying by wrapping in some material such as clean, moist burlap and keeping them in a cool, shady location until they are needed. The budsticks should be used promptly after cutting, although they can be stored for a short time if kept cool and moist. It is best, if possible, when a considerable amount of budding is being done, to collect the budsticks as they are being used, a day's supply at a time.

The best buds to use on the stick are usually those in the middle and basal portions. Buds on the succulent terminal portion of the shoot should be discarded. In certain species, such as the sweet cherry, buds on the basal portion of the shoots are flower buds, which of course should not be used.

In fall budding, after the buds have been inserted, there is nothing more to be done until the following spring. *Although eventually the rootstock is to be cut off above the bud, in no case should this be done immediately after the bud has been inserted.* Healing of the bud piece to the stock is greatly facilitated by the normal movement of water and nutrients up and down the stem of the rootstock. This would, of course, be stopped if the top of the rootstock were cut off above the bud.

If the budding operation is done properly, the bud piece should unite with the stock in 2 to 3 weeks, depending upon the growing conditions. If the leaf stalk or petiole drops off cleanly next to the bud, this is a good indication that the bud has united, especially if the bark piece retains its normal light brown or green colour and the bud stays plump.

The bud union has healed, in most deciduous species the bud usually does not grow or "push out" in the fall, since it is in a physiological rest period. It remains just as it is until spring, at which time the chilling winter temperatures have overcome the rest influence and the bud is ready to grow. There are some exceptions to this; for example, in fall budding of maples, roses, honey locust, and certain other plants, some of the buds may start growth in the fall. In northern areas, if

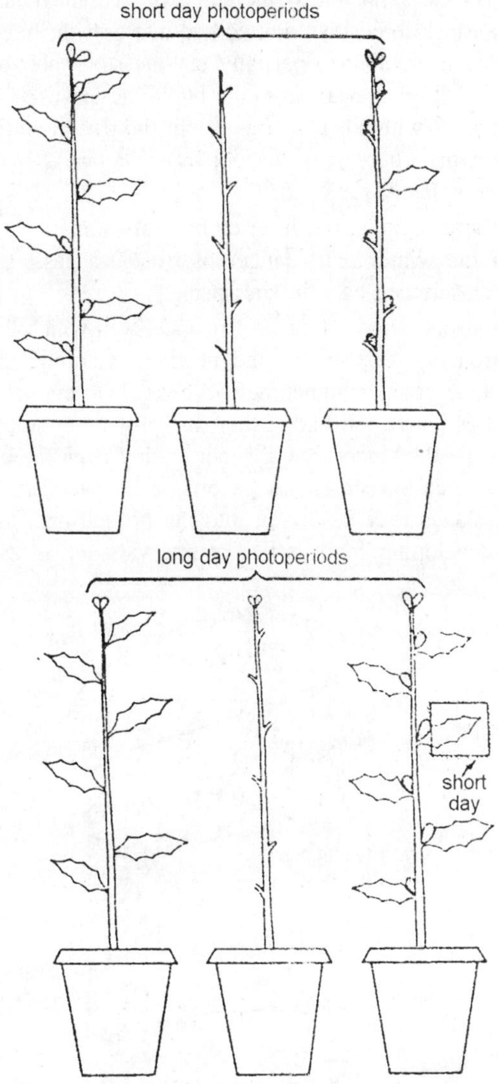

Fig. 3.3. Experiments on Xanthium plant indicate that photoperiods stimulus is perceived by leaves.

such fall-forced buds do not start early enough for the shoots to mature before cold weather starts, they are likely to be winter killed.

In the spring, just before new growth begins, the rootstock is cut off, immediately above the bud. It is desirable to make a sloping cut, slanting away from the bud. Although this cut may be waxed, it is usually not essential unless the stock is large in diameter. Cutting back the rootstock forces the inserted bud into growth. In citrus budding, it is a common practice to partially cut the stock above the bud and to lop or bend it over away from the bud. The leaves of the stock still furnish the roots with some nutrients, but the partial cutting forces the bud into growth. After the new shoot from the bud is well established, the top is completely removed.

In northern regions, fall-inserted buds are sometimes covered with soil during the winter until danger of frost has passed and are then uncovered and topped-back in late spring.

Where strong winds occur and in species in which the new shoots grow vigorously, support for the newly developing shoot may be necessary. One practice sometimes followed is to cut off the rootstock several inches above the bud, using this projecting stub as a support on which to tie the tender young shoot arising from the bud. This stub is removed after the shoot has become well established. In another procedure, stakes may be driven into the ground next to the stock to which the developing shoot is tied at intervals during its growth.

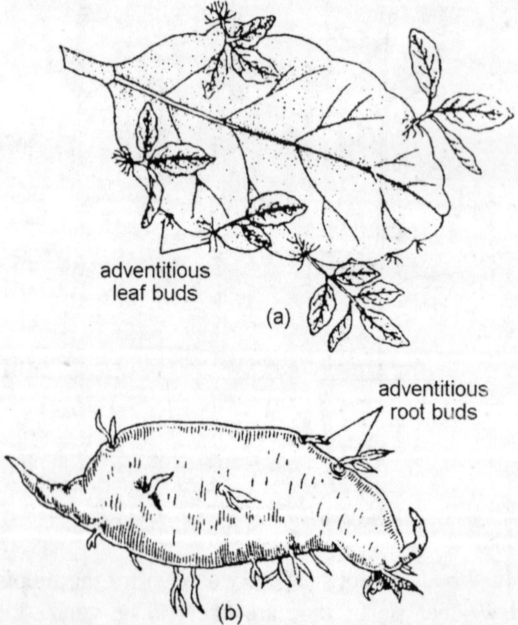

Fig. 3.4. (a) Bryophyllum–adventitious leaf buds; (b) Sweet potato–adventitious root buds.

Cutting back to force the main bud to grow also forces many latent buds on the rootstock into growth. These must be rubbed off as soon as they appear, or they will soon choke out the desired inserted bud. It may be necessary to go over the budded plants several times before these "sprouts" stop appearing. Nurserymen refer to this procedure as "suckering".

The shoot arising from the inserted bud becomes the top portion of the plant. After one season's growth in the nursery, with favourable conditions of soil, water and nutrients, temperature, and insect and disease control. Such a tree would have a 1-year-old top and a 2-or perhaps 3-year-old root, but it is still considered a "yearling" tree. If the top makes insufficient growth the first year, it can be allowed to grow a second year, and is then known as a 2-year-old tree. However, abnormally slow-growing trees should be discarded.

Spring Budding

This method is similar to fall budding except that the work takes place the following spring as soon as active growth of the rootstock begins and the bark separates easily from the wood. The period for successful spring budding is limited, and budding should be completed before the rootstocks have made much new growth.

Budsticks are chosen from the same type of shoots-in regard to vigor of growth and type of buds—that would be used in fall budding, except that they are not collected until the dormant season the following winter. The leaves would, of course, have fallen by this time, and the buds would have experienced sufficient chilling to overcome their rest period. Budwood must be collected while it is still dormant—before there is any evidence of the buds swelling. Since the buds must be dormant when they are inserted, and since the rootstocks must be in active growth, it is necessary in spring budding that the budsticks be gathered some time in advance of the time of budding and stored at temperatures (32° to 40°F; 0° to 4°C) to hold the buds dormant. The budsticks should we wrapped in bundles with damp peat moss or some similar material to prevent drying out.

In spring budding, the actual budding operation should be done just as soon as the bark on the rootstock slips easily. Then, about 2 weeks after budding, when the bud unions have healed, the top of the stock must be cut off above the bud to force the inserted bud into active growth. At the same time, latent buds on the rootstock begin to grow and should be removed. Sometimes it is helpful to permit such shoots from the rootstock to develop to some extent to prevent sunburn and help nourish the plant. They must be held in check, however, and eventually removed.

Although the new shoot from the inserted bud gets a later start in spring budding than in fall budding, spring buds will usually develop rapidly enough, if growing conditions are favourable, to make a satisfactory top by fall. Fall budding, however, is to be preferred for several reasons : the higher temperatures at that time promote more certain healing of the union, the budding season is longer, there is no necessity to store the budsticks, the inserted buds start growth earlier in the spring, and the pressure of other work is usually not so great for nurserymen in the late summer as in the spring. Spring budding is used sometimes on rootstocks which were fall-budded but on which the buds failed to take.

June Budding

June budding is used to obtain a "1-year-old" budded tree in a single growing season. Its principal characteristic is that budding is done in the early part of the growing season and the inserted bud forced into growth immediately during the same season. As a method of nursery propagation, June budding is confined to regions which have a relatively long growing season—in the U.S, this includes California and the southern states. In the propagation of fruit trees, June budding is used mostly in producing such stone fruits as peaches, nectarines, apricots, almonds, and plums. Peach seedlings are generally used as the rootstock, but almond seedlings and plum hardwood cuttings can also be used. Budding is done by the T-bud method. If seeds are planted in the fall or startified seeds as early as possible in the spring, the seedlings usually attain sufficient size (12 in.high and at least 1/8 in. in diameter) to be budded by mid-May or early June (in the Northern Hemisphere). Preferably, June budding should not be done much after mid-June, or a nursery tree of satisfactory size will not be obtained by fall. June-budded trees are not as large by the end of the growing season as those propagated by fall or spring budding but they are of sufficient size (about 3/8 in. to 5/8 in. caliper and 3 to 5ft tall) to be used commercially.

The budwood used in June budding consists of current season's growth, that is, of new shoots which have developed since growth started in the spring. By late May or early June, these shoots will usually have grown sufficiently to have a well developed bud in the axil of each leaf. At this time of year these buds will not have entered the rest period, so when they are used in budding they continue their growth on through the summer, producing the top portion of the budded seedling.

For June-budded trees handling subsequent to the actual operation of budding is some what more exacting than for fall-or spring-budded trees. The rootstocks are smaller and have less stored food than those used in fall or spring budding. The object behind the following procedures—is to keep the rootstock (and later the budded top) actively and continuously growing so as to allow no check in growth, while at the same time changing the seedling shoot to a budded top. The bud should be inserted high enough (5 to 6 in.) on the stem so that a number of leaves—at least three or four—can be retained below the bud. The method of T-budding with the "wood out" described later should be used. Healing of the inserted bud should be very rapid at this time of year, since temperatures are relatively high, and rapidly growing, succulent plant parts are used. By 4 days after budding, healing should have started, and the top of the root stock can be cut back somewhat—2 to 5 in. above the bud—leaving at least one leaf above the bud and several below it. This operation will force the inserted bud into growth and will check terminal growth from basal buds of the rootstock, which will produce additional leaf area. This continuous leaf area is necessary so that there always will be enough leaves to keep manufacturing food for the small plant. Ten days to two weeks after budding, the rootstock can be cut back to the bud, which should be starting to grow. If the budding rubber has not broken, if should be cut at this time. Other shoots arising from the rootstock should be headed back to retard their growth. After the inserted bud grows and develops a substantial leaf area, it can supply the plant with the necessary nutrients. By the time the shoot from the inserted bud has brown 8 to 12 in. high, it should have enough leaves so that all other shoots and leaves can be removed. Later inspections should be made to remove any shoots arising from the rootstock below the budded shoot.

Another method which works well is to partially cut the stock just above the bud and break it over. Nutrients are still able to pass from the top of the stock to the roots, but this partial blocking forces the inserted bud into growth.

June budding is often of considerable value to nurserymen who find that their regular supply of fall or spring-budded trees is in sufficient to meet their expected demand. By this method they can, as late as the end of June, still propagate trees to be ready by fall, provided that they have a supply of rootstock plants large enough to bud.

Methods of Budding

T-Budding (Shield Budding)

This method is known by both names, the "T-bud" designation arising from the T-like appearance of the cut in the stock, whereas the "shield bud" name is derived from the shield-like appearance of the bud piece when it is ready for insertion in the stock.

T-budding is by far the most common method of budding and is widely used by nurserymen in propagating nursery stock of most fruit tree species, roses, and many ornamental shrubs. Its use is generally limited to stocks which are about ¼ to 1 in. in diameter, with fairly thin bark, and which are actively growing so that the bark will separate readily from the wood. If the bark is so tight on the wood that it has to be forcibly pried loose, the chances of the bud healing successfully are rather remote. The operation should then be delayed until the bark is slipping easily.

The bud is inserted into the stock 2 to 10 in. above the soil level in a smooth bark surface. There are different opinions as to which is the proper side of the stock in which to insert the bud. If extreme weather conditions are likely to occur during the critical healing period just following budding, it may be desirable to place the bud on the side of the stock on which as much protection as possible may be obtained. Some believe that if the bud is placed on the windward side, there is less chance of the young shoot breaking off. Otherwise, it probably makes little difference where the bud is inserted, the convenience of the operator and the location of the smoothest bark being the controlling factors. When rows of closely planted rootstocks are budded, it is more convenient to have all the buds on the same side for later inspection and manipulations.

There are various modifications of this technique; most budders prefer to make the vertical cut first, then the horizontal crosscut at the top of the T. As the horizontal cut is made, the knife is given is given a twist to throw open the flaps of bark for insertion of the bud. It is important that neither the vertical nor horizontal cut be made longer than necessary, because this requires additional tying later to close the cuts.

After the proper cuts are made in the stock and the incision is ready to receive the bud, the shield piece is cut out of the budstick.

To remove the shield of bark containing the bud, a slicing cut is started at a point on the stem about ½ in. below the bud, continuing under and about an inch above the bud. The shield piece should be as thin as possible but still thick enough to have some rigidity. A second horizontal cut is then made ½ to ¾ in. above the bud, thus permitting the removal of the shield piece.

There are two methods of preparing the shield—with the "wood in" or with the "wood out". This refers to the little sliver of wood just under the bark of the shield piece and which will remain attached to it if the second horizontal cut is deep and goes through the bark and wood, joining the first slicing cut. Some professional budders believe it is best to remove this sliver of wood, but others retain it. In budding certain species, however, such as maples and walnuts, much better success is usually obtained with "de-wooded" buds. If it is desired to prepare the shield with the wood out, the second horizontal cut should be just deep enough to go through the bark and not through the wood. Then if the bark is slipping easily, the bark shield can be snapped loose from the wood (which still remains attached to the budstick) by pressing it against the budstick and sliding it sideways. A small core of wood comprising the vascular tissues supplying the bud is present, and this should remain in the bud, rather than adhering to the wood and leaving a hole in the bud. If the shield is pulled outward rather than being slid sideways from the wood, this core usually pulls out of the bud, eliminating the chances of success. In June budding of fruit trees, the shield piece is usually prepared with the wood out. In most other instances, however, the wood is left in. In spring budding, using dormant budwood, this silver of wood is tightly attached to the bark and cannot be removed.

The next step is the insertion of the shield piece containing the bud into the incision in the stock plant. The shield is pushed under the two raised flaps of bark until its upper horizontal cut matches the same cut on the stock. The shield should fit snugly in place, will covered by the two flaps of bark, but with the bud itself exposed.

No waxing is necessary, but the bud union must be wrapped, using materials to hold the two components firmly together until healing is completed. Rubber budding strips, especially made for wrapping, are widely used for this purpose. Their elasticity provides sufficient pressure to hold the bud securely in place. The rubber, being exposed to the sun and air, usually deteriorates, breaks, and drops off after several weeks, at which time the bud should be healed in place. If the budding rubber is covered with soil, the rate of deterioration will be much slower. This material has the advantage of eliminating cutting the wrapping ties, which can be a costly operation if thousands of plants have been budded. The rubber will expand as the rootstock grows, and thus there is little danger of constriction.

In tying the bud, the ends of the budding rubbers are held in place by inserting them under the adjacent turn. The bud itself should not be covered. The amount of tension given the budding rubber is quite important. It should not be too loose, or there will be too little pressure holding the bud in place. On the other hand, if the rubber is stretched extremely tight, it may be so thin that it will deteriorate rapidly and break too soon—before the bud union has taken place. Often the tying is done from the top down to avoid forcing the bud out through the horizontal cut.

Raffia (fiber-like leaf segments of certain *Raphia* species) has been widely used for wrapping buds. This material is soaked in water over-night before it is used so that it will be flexible. Raffia must be cut later—about 10 days after budding—to prevent constriction at the bud union at the plant grows. If such nonelastic ties are not promptly cut, the resultant constriction can have a very adverse affect on subsequent growth of the bud.

Plastic ties of polyvinyl chloride (PVC) film, 3/8 in. wide, are quite useful for budding. Such material is moisture-proof and elastic, and since it is transparent, it permits inspection of the buds after covering.

Inverted T-Budding

In localities where a great deal of rain occurs, water running down the stem of the rootstock will often enter the T-cut, soak under the bark, and cause decay of the shield piece. Under such conditions an inverted T-bud may give better results, since it is more likely to shed excess water. In citrus budding, the inverted T method is widely used, even though the conventional method also gives excellent results. In species which bleed badly during budding, such as chestnuts, the inverted T-bud allows better drainage and better healing.

The techniques of the inverted T-bud method are the same as those already described, except that the incision in the stock has the transverse cut at the bottom rather than at the top of the vertical cut, and in removing the shield piece from the budstick the knife starts above the bud and cuts downward below it. The shield is removed by making the transverse cut ½ to ¾ in. below the bud. The shield piece containing the bud is inserted into the lower part of the incision and pushed upward until the transverse cut of the shield meets that made in the stock.

It is important in using this inverted T-bud method that a normally oriented shield bud piece should not be inserted into an inverted incision in the stock. The bud would then have a reversed polarity. Although such upside down buds do live and grow, at least in some species, their use may not result in normal shoot development.

Patch Budding

The distinguishing feature of patch budding and related methods is that a rectangular patch of bark is removed completely from the stock and replaced with a patch of bark of the same size containing a bud of the variety to be propagated.

Patch budding is somewhat slower and more difficult to perform than T-budding, but it is widely and successfully used on thick-barked species, such as walnuts and pecans, in which T-budding gives poor results, presumably owing to the poor fit around the margins of the bud. Patch budding, or one of its modifications, is also extensively used in propagating various tropical species, such as the rubber tree (*Hevea brasiliensis*).

Patch budding requires that the bark of both the stock and budstick be slipping easily. It is usually done in late summer or early fall, but can also be done in the spring. In propagating nursery stock, the diameter of the root stock and the budstick should preferably be about the same, from ½ to 1 in. Although the budstick should not be much larger than about 1 in. in diameter, the patch can be inserted successfully into stocks as large as 4 in. in diameter, although adequate healing of such large stubs may be a problem.

Special knives have been devised to remove the bark pieces from the stock and the budstick. Some type of double bladed knife that will make two transverse parallel cuts 1 to 1-3/8 in. apart is necessary. These cuts, about an inch in length, are made through the bark to the wood in a smooth area of the rootstock several inches above the ground. Then the two transverse cuts are connected at each side by vertical cuts made with a single-bladed knife.

The patch of bark containing the bud is cut from the budstick in the same manner in which the bark patch is removed from the stock. Using the same two-bladed knife, the budder makes two transverse cuts through the bark, one above and one below the bud. Then two vertical cuts are made on each side of the bud so that the bark piece will be about an inch wide. The bark piece containing the bud is now ready to be removed. It is important that it be slid off sideways rather than being lifted or pulled off. There is a small core of wood,

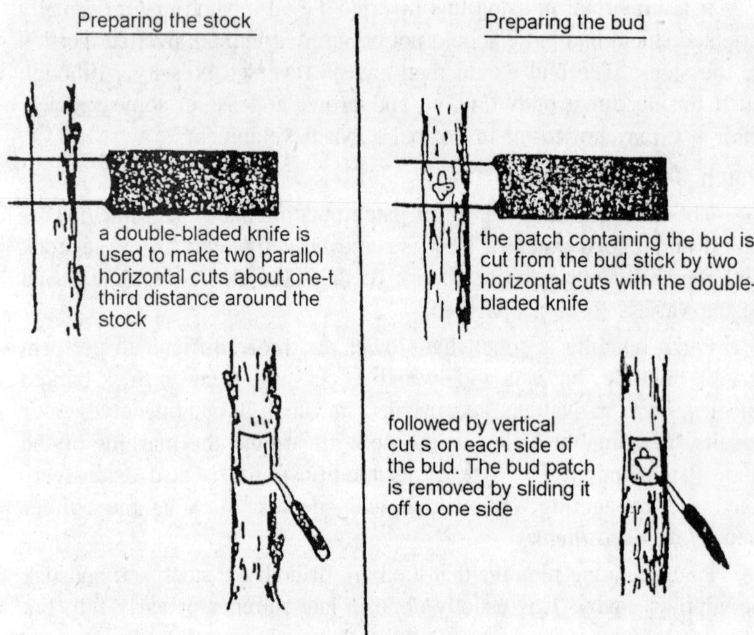

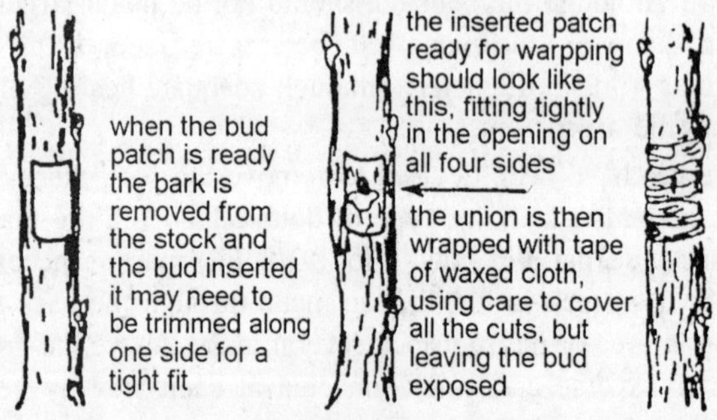

Fig. 3.5. Steps in making the patch bud.

the bud trace, which must remain inside the bud if a successful "take" is to be obtained. By sliding the bark patch to one side, this core is broken off, and it stays in the bud. If the bud patch is lifted off, this core of wood is likely to remain attached to the wood of the budstick, leaving a hold in the bud.

After the bud patch is removed from the budstick, it must be inserted immediately on the stock, which should already be prepared, needing only to have the bark piece removed. The patch from the budstick should fit snugly at the top and bottom into the opening in the stock, since both transverse cuts were made with the same knife. It is more important that the bark piece fit tightly at top and bottom than that it fit along the sides. The inserted patch is now ready to be wrapped. Often the bark of the stock will be thicker than the bark of the inserted bud patch so that, upon wrapping, it is impossible for the wrapping material to hold the bud patch tightly against the stock. In this case it is necessary that the bark of the stock be pared down around the bud patch so that it will be of the same thickness, or preferably slightly thinner, than the bark of the bud patch. Then the wrapping material will hold the bud patch tightly in place.

One type of tool, has a pair of vertical cutting blades in addition to the horizontal blades. With this, all four cuts of the rectangle are made at once. In cases in which difficulty is experienced in obtaining successful unions with the patch bud method, it may help to make the four cuts of the rectangle in the stock 1 to 3 weeks ahead of the time when the actual budding is to be done. This bark patch is not removed from the stock, however, until the patch containing the bud is ready to be inserted. When the cuts are made ahead of time, the wounding causes the callusing process to start, so that when the new bark patch is inserted, it heals very rapidly.

In wrapping the patch bud, a material should be used which not only will hold the bark tightly in place but will cover all the cut surfaces to prevent the entrance of air under the patch, with subsequent drying and death of the tissues. The bud itself mud not be covered during wrapping. The most satisfactory material is nurserymen's adhesive tape. Waxed cloth strips, are also satisfactory and have been used extensively. Another method is to tie the bud patch with heavy cotton string and cover the cut edges with grafting wax. It is important in patch budding, especially with walnuts, that the wrapping not be allowed to cause a constriction at the bud union. When the stock is rapidly growing, it is necessary to cut the tape about 10days after budding. A single vertical knife cut on the side opposite the bud is sufficient. The cut tape should not be pulled off.

Patch budding is best performed in late summer when both the seedling stock and the source of budwood are growing rapidly and their bark slipping easily. The budsticks for patch budding done at this time should have the leaf blades cut 2 to 3 weeks before they are taken from the tree. The petiole or leaf stalk is left attached to the base of the bud, but by the time the budstick is taken this petiole has dropped off or is easily removed.

Patch budding can also be done in the spring after new growth has appeared on the stocks and it has been determined that the bark is slipping. There is a problem, however, in obtaining satisfactory buds to use at this time of year, since it is necessary that the bark of the budstick separate readily from the wood. At the same time, the buds should not be starting to swell. There are two methods by which satisfactory buds can be obtained for patch budding in the spring. In one, the budsticks are selected during the dormant winter period and stored at low temperatures (about 36°F; 2°C) and wrapped in moist sphagnum or peat moss to prevent their drying out. Then, about 3 weeks before the time the spring budding is to be done, they are brought out into a warm room and set with their bases in a container of water, or they may be left packed in damp peat or sphagnum moss. The increased temperature will cause the cambium layer to become active, and soon the bark will slip sufficiently for the buds to be used. Although a few of the more terminal buds on each stick may start swelling in this time and cannot be used, there should be a number of buds in a satisfactory condition.

The second method of obtaining buds for spring patch budding is to take them directly from the tree which is the source of the budwood, but at the time the budding is to be done. If the trees are inspected carefully, it will be seen that not all of the buds start pushing at once. The terminal ones are usually more advanced than the basal ones. There is a period when the bark is slipping easily throughout the shoot containing the desired buds, but when only a few of the buds have developed so far that they cannot be used. The remaining buds, which are still dormant but upon bark that can be removed readily, may be taken and used immediately for budding. It is easier to obtain suitable buds from young trees which made vigorous shoot growth the previous year than it is from old trees. When the budding is done will be governed then by the stage of development of the buds. This will vary considerably with the species and variety being used. Stage of development of the rootstock is not as critical. Its bark must be slipping well, and the budding should be done before the stock plant has made much new growth.

Flute Budding

Flute budding is similar to patch budding, except that the patch of bark removed from the rootstock almost completely encircles it, leaving a narrow connection (about one-eighth of the circum-ference) between the upper and lower parts of the stock. In taking the bud patch from the budstick, a two-bladed knife is used, with the two transverse cuts completely encircling the budstick. A single vertical cut connects the two horizontal cuts, permitting the bud patch to be removed. In fitting this bud patch to the stock, it may be necessary to shorten its circumference by a vertical cut to remove the surplus amount of bark. If the bud patch fails to unite, the narrow connecting strip of bark on the stock keeps the top of the stock alive.

Ring or Annular Budding

By this method, a complete ring of bark is removed from the stock and a complete ring from the budstick. In order for the two to match, the size of the stock and that of the budstick should be about the same. Since the stock is completely girdled, if the bud patch fails to heal in, the stock above the ring may eventually die. This method is not as widely used as the ordinary patch bud, since it has no particular advantages and is rather cumbersome to perform.

I-Budding

In this type of budding, the bud patch is cut just as for patch budding, that is, in the form of a rectangle or square. Then, with the same parallel-bladed knife, two transverse cuts are made through the bark of the stock. These are joined at their centers by a single vertical cut to produce the figure I. The two flaps of bark can then be raised for insertion of the bud patch beneath them. It may make a better fit to slant the side edges of the bud patch. In tying the I-bud, care should be taken to see that the bud patch does not buckle upward and fail to touch the stock.

This method should be considered for use when the bark of the stock is much thicker than that of the budstick. In such cases, if the patch bud were used, considerable paring down of the bark of the stock around the patch would be necessary. This operation is not necessary in the I-bud method.

Chip Budding

This is a budding method that can be done at times when the bark is not slipping e.g., early in the spring before growth starts, or during the summer when active growth stops prematurely owing to lack of water or some other cause. It is generally used with fairly small material, ½ to 1 in. in diameter. Although chip budding is quite successful, it is not as fast or simple as T-budding and is not likely to be used if conditions are favourable for the use of T-budding. Chip budding in the fall has given consistently excellent results, however,

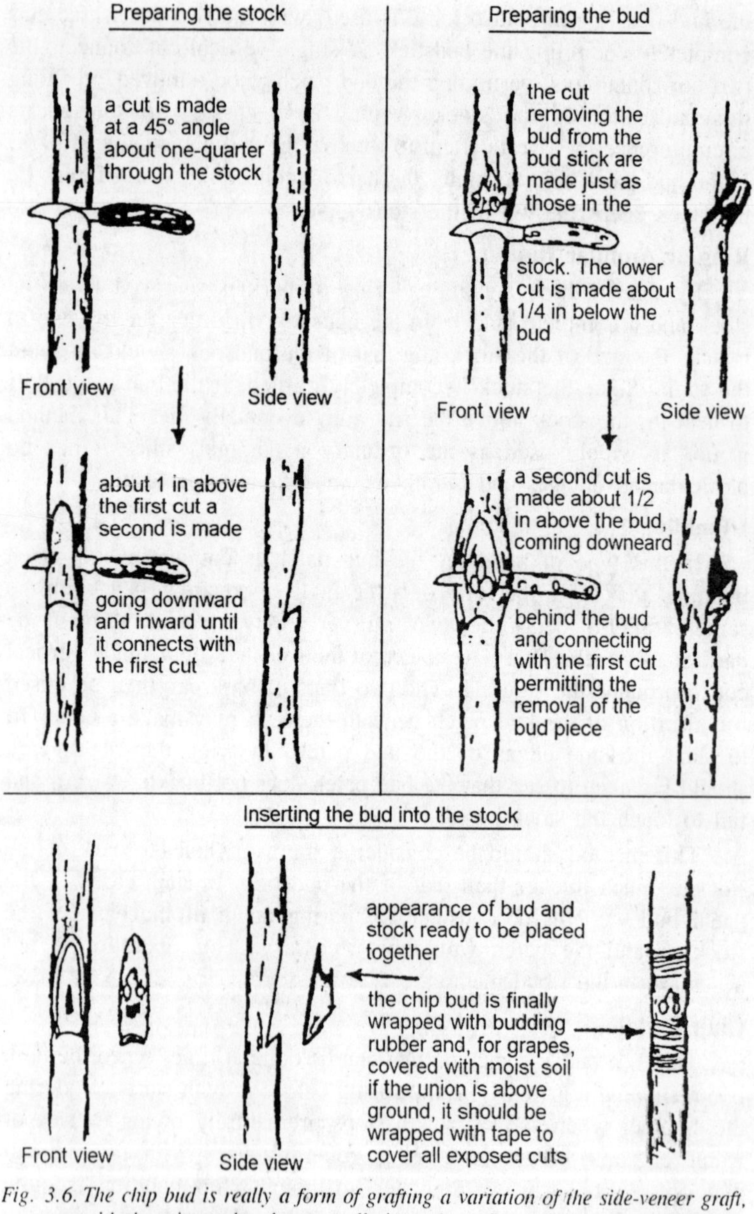

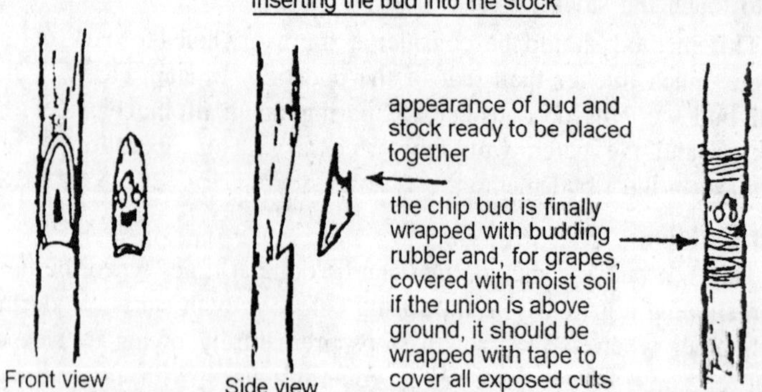

Fig. 3.6. The chip bud is really a form of grafting a variation of the side-veneer graft, with the scion reduced to a small piece of wood containing only a single bud.

in budding grape varieties or phylloxera or nematode- resistant rootstocks. It is not commonly used on deciduous tree fruit species.

A chip of bark is removed from a smooth place between nodes near the base of the stock and replaced by another chip of the same size and shape from the budstick which contains a bud of the desired variety. The chips in both stock and budstick are cut out in the same manner. The first cut is made just below the bud and down into the wood at an angle of about 45 deg. The second cut is started about ½ in. above the bud and goes inward and downward behind the bud until it intersects the fist cut. The order of making these two cuts may be reversed. The chip is removed from the stock and replaced by the one from the budstick. If they have both been cut to the same size and shape—as they should be—a good fit is obtained. It is important that the cambium layer of the bud piece be placed so as to coincide with that of the stock, preferably on both sides of the stem, but at least on one side.

There are no protective flaps of bark to prevent the bud piece from drying out, as there are in T-budding. It is very important, then, that the chip bud be wrapped to seal the cut edges as well as to hold the bud piece tightly into the stock. Nurseryman's adhesive tape works very well for this, although string can be used if all the cut edges are covered with grafting wax. If the bud is inserted into the stock close to the ground level, as it is in grape propagation, it is sufficient to wrap the bud with budding rubber and cover the whole bud union immediately with several inches of finely pulverized moist soil, which can be removed after the bud has united. Budding rubbers under the soil level are very slow to disintegrate, so they may need to be cut or removed before constriction occurs.

In chip budding, as in the other methods, the stock is not cut back above the bud until the union is completed. If the chip bud is inserted in the fall, the stock is cut back just as growth starts the next spring. If the budding is done in the spring, the stock is cut back about 10 days after the bud has been inserted.

Top-Budding

In young trees when there is an ample supply of vigorous shoots at a height of 4 to 6 ft, top-budding provides a fast and certain method of topworking. It can be used in older trees, too, if they are cut back rather severely the year before to provide a quantity of vigorous watersprout shoots fairly close to the ground.

Depending upon the size of the tree, 10 to 15 buds are placed in vigorously growing branches ¼ to ¾ in. in diameter in the upper portion of the tree—about shoulder height. Although a number of buds could be placed in a single branch, usually only one will be saved to develop into secondary branches, which will then form the permanent new top of the tree. The T-bud method is used on thin-barked species, and the patch bud on those with thick bark.

Top-budding is usually done in midsummer, as soon as well matured budwood can be obtained and while the stock tree is still in active growth with the bark slipping easily. Orchard trees generally stop growth earlier in the season than young nursery trees ; therefore the budding must be done earlier. When top-budding is done at this time of year, the buds will remain inactive until the following spring. At that time, just as vegetative growth starts, the stock branches are cut back just above the buds. This forces the buds into active growth, and they should develop into good-sized branches by the end of the summer. At the time the shoots are cut back to the buds, all other unbudded branches should be removed at the trunk. It is important that the trees be inspected carefully through the summer and any shoots removed that are arising from any but the inserted buds.

Top-budding can also be done in the spring just as the tree to be top-worked is starting active growth and the bark is slipping easily.

Double-Working by Budding

In propagating nursery trees, some of the budding methods can be used in developing double-worked trees. The intermediate stock can be budded on the rootstock; then the following year the desired variety is budded on the interstock. Although quite effective, this is a rather lengthy process, taking 3 years. It is possible, to develop a double-worked tree in one operation in 1 year by the double shield bud method. A T-bud is used, but just under and below a budless shield piece of the desired interstock is inserted.

In studies comparing the two methods of "double-shield" budding—that of Garner and that of Nicolin—it appears that the Nicolin method, with a full-length intermediate piece, is simpler and more easily done, but the results by either method are satisfactory, at least for some combinations.

Micro-Budding

This type of budding is used successfully in propagating citrus trees and probably could be utilized also for other tree and shrub species. It has been of commercial importance in the citrus districts of southeastern Australia. Micro-budding is similar to ordinary T-budding, except that the bud piece is reduced to a very small size.

The leaf petiole is cut off just above the bud, and then the bud is removed from the budstick by a flat cut just underneath the bud, with a razor-sharp knife. Only the bud itself and a small piece of wood under it are used. In the stock an inverted T-cut is made, and the micro-bud is slipped into this, right side up. The entire T-cut, including the bud, is covered with polyvinyl chloride (PVC) plastic budding tape (¾ in. in width and 0.002 in. thick). The tape is allowed to remain for 10 to 14 days for spring budding and 3 weeks for all budding, after which it is removed by cutting with a knife. By this time the buds should have healed in place; subsequent handling is the same as for conventional T-budding.

4

ASEXUAL PROPAGATION

This chapter deals with propagation by specialized vegetative structures—*bulbs*, *corms*, *tubers*, *tuberous roots*, *rhizomes*, and *pseudobulbs*. These organs are primarily modified plant parts specialized for food storage. Plants possessing them are invariably herbaceous perennials in which the shoots die down at the end of a growing season, and the plant lives over in the ground as a dormant, fleshy organ which bears buds to produce new shoots the next season. Such plants are admirably suited it withstanding periods of adverse growing conditions in their yearly growth cycle. The two principal climatic cycles for which such performance is geared are the warm cold cycle of the temperate zones and the wet-dry cycle of tropical and subtropical regions. The second function of these specialized organs is the vegetative reproduction.

BULBS

Definition and Structure

Bulbs are produced by monocotyledonous plants in which the usual plant structure is modified for storage and reproduction. A *bulb* is a specialized underground organ consisting of a short, fleshy, usually vertical stem axis (*basal plate*) bearing at its apex a growing point or a flower primordium enclosed by thick, fleshy scales.

Most of the bulb consists of *bulb scales*, which morphologically are the continuous, sheathing leaf bases. The outer bulb scales are generally fleshy and contain reserve food materials, whereas the bulb scales toward the center function less as storage organs and are more leaf-like. In the centre of the bulb, there will be either a vegetative growing point or an unexpanded flowering shoot. Growing points develop

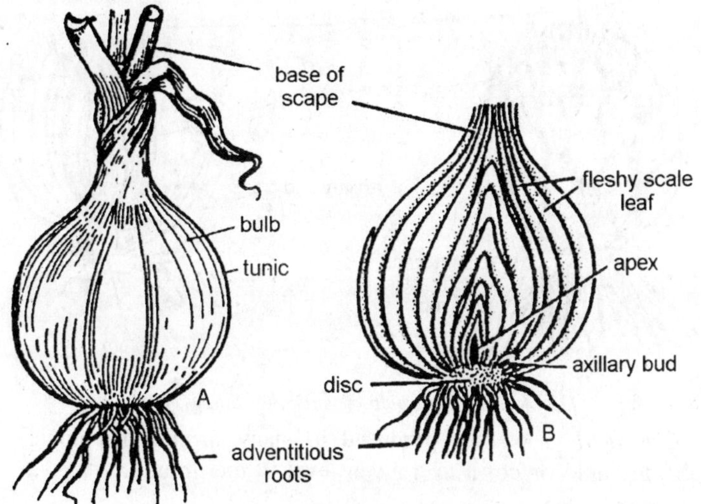

Fig. 4.1. A–Tunicated bulb of onion; B–L.S. of bulb.

in the axil of these scales to produce miniature bulbs, known as *bulblets*, which when they grow to full size are known as *offsets*. In various species of lilies, bulblets may form in the leaf axils either on the underground portion or on the aerial portion of the stem. Aerial bulblets are called *bulbils*.

There are two types of bulbs;

(a) *Tunicate (laminate)* bulbs, represented by the onion and tulip. These bulb have outer bulb scales which are dry and membranous. This covering, or *tunic*, provides protection from drying and mechanical injury to the bulb. The fleshy scales are in continuous, concentric layers, or *lamina*, so that the structure is more or less solid.

(b) *Non-tumicate (scaly)* bulbs, represented by the lilies. These bulbs do not possess the enveloping dry covering. The scales are separate and give the bulb a scaly appearance. In general, the non-tunicate bulbs are easily damaged and must be handled more carefully than the tunicate bulbs; they must be kept continuously moist because they are injured by drying.

Roots are not present on a dormant, tunicate bulb but develop adventitiously at the beginning of a growth period in a narrow band around the outside edge on the bottom of the basal plate. In the non-tunicate lily bulb, roots are produced in midsummer or later, and persist through the following year. In most lily species, roots also form on the stem above the bulb.

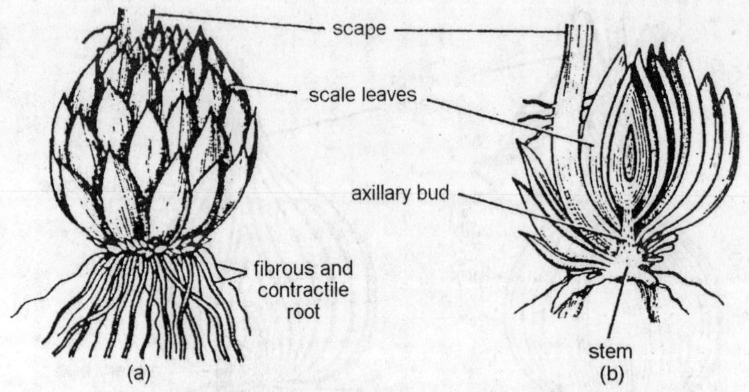

Fig. 4.2. (a) Scaly bulb of garlic; (b) L.S. of bulb.

Contractile roots are produced in many species that appear to "pull" the bulb or corm to a given level in the ground.

Growth Behaviour

An individual bulb goes through a characteristic cycle of development, beginning with its initiation as a growing point and terminating in flowering and seed production. This general developmental cycle is composed of two stages: (a) vegetative and (b) reproductive. In the vegetative stage the bulblet grows to flowering size and attains its maximum weight. The subsequent reproductive stage includes the induction of flowering, differentiation of the floral parts, elongation of the flowering shoot, and finally flowering and (sometimes) seed production. Various bulb species have specific environmental requirements for the individual phases of this cycle which determine their seasonal behaviour, environ-mental adaptions, and methods of handling. They can be grouped into classes according to their time of bloom and method of handling.

Spring-Flowering Bulbs

Important commercial crops included in this group are the tulip, daffodil, hyacinth, and bulbous iris, although other kinds are grown in gardens.

Bulb formation

The vegetative stage begins with the initiation of the bulblet on the basal plate in the axil of a bulb scale. In this initial period, which usually occupies a single growing season, the bulblet is insignificant in size, since it is present within another growing bulb and can be observed only if the bulb is dissected. Its subsequent pattern of development and the time required for the bulblet to attain flowering size are somewhat different for different species. The bulbs of the tulip and the bulbous iris, for instance, disintegrate upon flowering but leave a cluster of new bulbs and bulblets which were initiated the previous season. The largest of these may have attained flowering size at this time, but smaller ones require several additional years of growth. The flowering bulb of the daffodil, on the other hand, continues to grow from the center year by year, producing new offsets which may remain attached for several years. The hyacinth bulb also continues to grow year by year, but because the number of offsets produced is limited, artificial methods of propagation are usually used.

The size and quality of bloom is directly related to the size of the bulb and the amount of stored food. Only bulbs greater than a certain minimum size are capable of initiating flower buds. Commercial value is largely based on bulb size although the condition of the bulb and freedom from disease are also important quality factors.

The greatest increase in size and weight of the developing bulb take place in the period during and (mostly) after flowering, as long as the foliage remains in good condition. Cultural operations that encourage vegetative growth include irrigation; weed, disease, and insect control; and fertilization. Their greatest benefit, however, is to the next year's flower, because larger bulbs are produced. Conversely, adverse situations, such as poor growing conditions, removal of foliage, and premature digging of the bulb, result in smaller bulbs and inferior flower production.

Moderately low temperatures tend to prolong the vegetative period, whereas higher temperatures may cause the vegetative stage to cease and the reproductive stage to begin. Thus a shift from cool to warm conditions early in the spring, as occurs in mild climates, will shorten the vegetative period, result in smaller bulbs, and consequently produce inferior blooms the following year. Commercial bulb-producing areas for hardy spring-flowering bulbs are largely in regions of cool springs and summers, such as Holland or the Pacific North-west of the United States. The relative length of photoperiod apparently is not an important factor affecting bulb formation in most species. It has been shown, however, to be significant in some *Allium* species, such as onion and garlic.

Flowering bud formation and flowering

The beginning of the reproductive stage and the end of the vegetative stage is indicated by the drying of the foliage and the maturation of the bulb. From then on, no additional increase in size or weight of the bulb takes place. The roots disintegrate, and the bulb enters a seemingly "dormant" period. However, important internal changes take place, and in some species the vegetative growing point undergoes transition to a flowering shoot. In nature, a 1 bulb activity takes place underground during this period; in horticultural practice, the bulbs are dug, stored, and distributed during this 3-month period.

Temperature plays a key role in the progression from vegetative growth to flower bud formation. The optimum temperature—determined as the shortest time in which the bulb would flower—has been established for various developmental phase. In general, a deviation from these temperatures or an increase in the period of time at any one temperature results in an increase in the time required to bloom. Too high a temperature may prevent flower development entirely.

In the tulip, the differentiation of the flower parts takes place after the bulb becomes dormant in the summer. The optimum temperature for this process is 68°F (20°C). After 3 weeks of storage at this temperature, the optimum drops abruptly to 48°F (9°C), and remains there for 10 to 12 weeks, the lower temperatures being necessary to overcome the rest period and to stimulate the flower shoot to elongate. The optimum temperature then gradually increases as the flower shoot elongates and a flower is produced.

According to the studies from which the above information is quoted, the hyacinth has somewhat more exacting requirements. The optimum temperature immediately upon digging was quite high (90° to 95°F; 32° to 35°C) for a week or two. When the first flower primordium on the raceme had appeared, this shifted to 78°F (26°C). When the last flower primordium had appeared it had shifted to 63°F (17°C), and 3 weeks later it had shifted to F(55°F (13°C), where it remained for about 12 weeks. Maintaining the bulbs at a temperature above 86°F (30°C) or below 55°F (13°C) during this period inhibits flower bud development entirely. For the hyacinth, a storage temperature of 78°F (26°C) is generally recommended for the flower forming period. The daffodil ('King Alfred') has an optimum temperature of 62°F (17°C) for flower formation followed by a period of about 8 weeks at 48°F (19°C).

Holding the bulbs continuously at high temperatures (86° to 90°F; 30° to 32°C; or more) or at temperature near freezing will stop bulb development and can be used to increase the period required for flowering. With a shift to more optimum temperatures, flower bud development will continue unimpaired. Such storage conditions (below or above optimum) can be used when shipping bulbs from the Northern to the Southern Hemisphere.

In bulbous iris, a flower bud is not initiated within the bulb. It begins to appear when the shoot is a few inches out of the ground.

Lilies

A non-tunicate bulb, e.g., the lily exhibits certain important differences from a tunicate bulb. Different species of lily have different methods of bulb reproduction, some examples being given in the following section on propagation. After flowering, the old bulb may divide or form offsets which can be used for propagation. In the subsequent vegetative period during summer the new bulb for next year grows in size and accumulates reserve materials. Lily bulbs do not go dormant in the same manner as other bulbs, and the roots do not disintegrate. The bulb should be out of the ground as little as possible and, when it is for the purpose of propagation, should be handled carefully and kept from drying. The commercial value of the bulb depends not only on its size and weight but also on the condition of the fleshy roots and the freedom of the basal plate from decay.

In the Easter lily (*Lillium longiflorum*), transition of the growing point to a flowering shoot does not take place in the bulb, occurring after the shoot protrudes through the "nose" of the bulb. Storing the mature bulbs at 45° to 50°F (7° to 10°C) for 6 weeks and then growing them at temperatures of 60°F (16°C) or more (night) will produce blooms within 80 to 100 days. Storing the mature bulbs at room temperatures or at low (31°F; —1°C) temperatures will keep the bulbs dormant and delay flowering. In the latter case, the method of bulb storage is also important. If they dry out, they will deteriorate. If they absorb moisture from the packing material, they may decay.

Tender, Winter-Flowering Bulbs

There are a number of flowering bulbs from tropical areas whose growth cycle is geared to a wet-dry climatic cycle rather than a cycle related to cold-warm conditions.

The amaryllis (*Hippeastrum vittata*) is an example of this kind. Its bulb is perennial, growing continuously from the center, the outer scales disintegrating. New leaves are produced continuously from the center during the vegetative period extending from late winger to the following summer. In the axil of every fourth leaf (or scale) that develops, a growing point is initiated. Thus throughout the vegetative period a series of vegetative offsets are produced. By fall the leaves mature and the bulb goes dormant, during which time the bulb should be dry. In this period, the *fourth* growing point from the center and any external to it differentiate into flower buds, and the shoots begins to elongate slowly. After 2 to 3 months of dry storage, the bulbs are watered, the flowering shoots elongate rapidly, and flowering takes place in midwinter. Maximum foliage development and bulb growth are essential to produce a bulb large enough to form a flowering shoot.

Propagation

Offsets

Offsets provide a simple and reliable method for propagating many kinds of bulbs. This method is sufficiently rapid for the commercial production of tulip, daffodil, balbous iris, and grape hyacinth bulbs, but in general it is too slow for the lily, hyacinth, and amaryllis.

If undisturbed, the offsets may remain attached to the mother bulb for several years. They can also be removed at the time the bulbs are dug and replanted into beds or nursery rows to grow into flowering sized bulbs. This may require several growing seasons, depending upon the kinds of bulb and size of the offset.

Tulip

Bulb planting takes place in the fall. Two systems of planting are used : the bed system, used mostly in Europe, and the row or field system, used mostly in the United States. Beds are usually 3 ft wide and separated by 12 to 18-in. paths. The soil is removed to a depth of 4 in. the bulbs set in rows 6 in. apart, and the soil replaced. In the other system, single or double rows are placed wide enough apart to permit the use of machines. To improve drainage, two or three adjoining rows may be planted on a ridge. Bulbs are spaced one to two diameters apart, with small bulbs scattered along the row. A mulch may be applied after planting but removed the following spring before growth.

Planting stock consists of those bulbs of the minimum size for flowering (9 to 10 cm in circumference or smaller). Since the time required to produce flowering sizes varies with the size of the bulb, the planting stock is graded so that those of one size can be planted together. For instance, an 8-cm or larger bulb normally requires a single season to become of flowering size; a 5- to 7-cm bulb, two seasons; and those 5 cm or less, 3 years.

During the flowering and subsequent bulb growing period of the next spring, good growing conditions should be provided so that the size and weight of the new bulbs will be at a maximum. Foliage should not be removed until it dries or matures. Important cultural operations include removal of competing weed growth, irrigation, fungicidal sprays to control *Botrytis blight* and fertilization. It is desirable to remove the flower heads at blooming time, because they may serve as a source of *Batrytis* infection and can lower bulb weight.

Bulbs are dug in midsummer when the leaves have turned yellow or the outer coats of the bulb have become dark brown in colour. In the Pacific Northwest of the United States, where temperatures are cool and the leaves remain green for a longer period, digging may take place before the leaves dry. If the bulbs are dug too early or if warm weather causes early maturation, the bulbs may be small in size. The bulbs are dug by machine or by hand with a short-handled spade. After the loose soil is shaken from the bulbs, they are placed in trays in well—ventilated storage houses for drying, cleaning, sorting, and grading. General storage temperatures are 65° to 68°F (18° to 20°C). For early flowering, the bulbs should be held at 68°F for 3 weeks and then placed at 48°F (9°C) for 8 weeks. Later flowering will be produced by holding bulbs at 72°F (22°C) for 10 weeks. For shipment to the Southern Hemisphere, the bulbs can be held at 31°F (-1°C) until late December, when they are shifted to a higher temperature (78°F; 25.5°C).

Daffodil

Daffodil bulbs are perennial and produce a new growing point at the center every year. Offsets are produced which grow in size for several years until they break away from the original bulb, although they are still attached at the basal plate. An offset bulb, when it first separates from the mother bulb, is known as a "split," "spoon," or "slab", and can be separated from the mother bulb and planted. Within a year it become a "round", or "single-nose", bulb containing a single flower bud. One year later a new offset should be visible, enclosed within the scales of the original bulb, indicating the presence of two flower buds. At this stage the bulb is known as a "double-nose". By the next year the offsets split away, and the bulb is known as a "mother bulb". Grading of daffodil bulbs is principally by age, that is, as splits, round, double-nose, and mother bulbs. The grades marketed commercially are the round and the double-nose. The mother bulbs are used as planting stock to produce additional offsets, and only the surplus is marketed. Offsets, or splits, are replanted for additional growth.

Storage should be at 55° to 60°F (13° to 16°C) with a relative humidity of 75 percent. For earlier flowering, they can be stored at 48°F (9°C) for 8 weeks. To delay flowering, store at 72°F (22°C) for 10 weeks. For shipment from the Northern to the Southern Hemisphere, bulbs can be held at 86°F (30°C) until October, then stored at 31°F (-1°C) until late December, and then at 77°F (25°C).

Hot water treatment plus a fungicide, as formalin, for stem and bulb eelworm control is important. A three or four-hour treatment at 110°F (43°C) is used, but that temperature must be carefully maintained or the bulbs may be damaged.

Lilies

Lilies increase naturally, but except for a few species this increase is slow and of limited propagation value except in home gardens. Several methods of bulb increase are found among the different species. For instance, *Lilium concolor*, *L. hansoni*, *L. henryi* and *L. regale* increase by bulb splitting. Two to four lateral bulblets are initiated about the base of the mother bulb, which disintegrates during the process, leaving a tight cluster of new bulbs. *Lilium bulbiferum*, *L. canadense*, *L. paradalinum*, *L. parryi*, *L. superbum*, and *L. tigninum* multiply from lateral bulblets produced from the rhizome-like bulb. This is sometimes called "budding-off".

Bulblet formation on stems

The production of *underground stem bulblets* is the usual commercial method of propagating the Easter lily (*Lilium longiflorum*) and some other lily species. Flowering of the Easter lily occurs in early summer. Bulblets form and increase in size from spring through summer. Between mid August and mid- September in the Northern Hemisphere the stems are pulled from the bulbs and stacked upright in the field. Periodic sprinkling keeps the stems and bulblets from drying out. Similarly, the base of the stem can be "heeled in" the ground at an angle of 30 to 45 deg. or laid horizontally in trays at high humidity. About mid-October the bulblets are planted in the field 4 in. deep and an inch apart in double rows which are spaced 36 in apart. Here they remain for the following season. They are dug in September as yearling bulbs and again replanted, this time 6 in deep and 4 to 6 in apart in single rows. At the end of the second year, they are dug and sold as commercial bulbs.

Digging is done in September after the stem is pulled. The bulbs are graded, packed in peat moss, and shipped. Commercial bulbs have a minimum size of 7 to 10 in, in circumference. Lily bulbs must be handled carefully so they will not be injured and must be kept from drying out. The fleshy roots should also be kept in good condition. For long-term storage that will prevent flowering, the bulbs should be packed in polyethylene-lined cases containing peat moss at 30 to 50 percent moisture and stored at 31°F (-1°C). To produce flowering in the shortest period of time, they should be stored at 45° to 50°F (7° to 10°C) for 6 weeks and then grown at temperatures of 60°F (16°C) (night) or more.

Lilies are attacked by certain viruses, fungus diseases, and nematodes which can be carried in or on the bulbs. Their control during propagation is an important consideration in bulb production. Methods of control include using disease free stocks for propagation, growing plants in disease-free locations with good sanitary procedures, and treating the bulbs with fungicides. A pre-planting dip in 2 Ib of pentachloronitrobenzene (PCNB) plus 2 Ib of ferbam in 100 gal. of water has been found useful.

To obtain commercial planting stock of lilies free of *Rhizoctonia*, stem and bulb nematode, and root-lesion nematode, cure bulbs at 05°F (95°C) and 95 percent relative humidity for 1 to 2 weeks, presoak for 2 days in cool water, soak for 2 hours at 115°F (46°C) in water plus 37 percent formaldehyde diluted 1:200; aftersoak the bulbs in a fungicide such Puratized Agricultural Spray at 1:1000. Scale the bulbs, dust the dulblets with ferbam, and place in vermiculite for bulblets to form. Plant new bulblets in treated soil.

Aerial stem bulblets, commonly known as *bulbils*, are formed in the axil of the leaves of some lily species, such as *Lilium bulbiferum*, *L. sargentiae*, *L. sulphureum*, and *L. tigrinum*. Bulbils develop in the early part of the season and fall to the ground several weeks after the plant flowers. They are harvested shortly before they fall naturally and are then handled in essentially the same manner as underground stem bulblets. Increased bulbil production can be induced by disbudding as soon as the flower buds have formed. Likewise, some lily species which do not form bulbils naturally can be induced to do so by pinching out the flower buds and a week later cutting off the upper half of the stems. Species which respond to the latter procedure include *Lilium candidum*, *L. chalcedonicum*, *L. hollandicum*, *L. maculatum* and *L. testaceum*.

Stem cuttings

Lilies may be propagated as stem cuttings. The cutting is made shortly after flowering. Instead of roots and shoots forming on the cutting, as would occur in other plants, bulblets form at the axils of the leaves and then produce roots and small shoots while on the cutting.

Leaf-bud cuttings, made with a single leaf and a small heel of the old stem, may be used to propagate a number of lily species. A small bulblet will develop in the axil of the leaf. It is handled in the same manner as for the other methods described here.

Bulblet formation on scales (scaling)

An efficient method for producing lily bulbs is the technique known as *scaling*, in which individual bulb scales are separated from the mother bulb and placed in growing conditions so that adventitious bulblets from at the base of the each scale. Three to five bulblets will usually develop from each scale. This method is particularly useful for rapidly building up stocks of a new variety or to establish disease-free stocks. Almost any lily species can be propagated by scaling.

Scaling is usually done soon after flowering in midsummer, although it might be done in late fall or even in midwinter. The bulbs are dug, the outer two layers of scales are removed and the mother bulb is replanted for continued growth. It is possible to remove the scales down to the core, but this will reduce subsequent growth of the mother bulb. The scales should be kept from drying and handled so as to avoid injury. Scales with evidence of root should be discarded and the remaining ones dusted with a fungicide. Naphthaleneacetic acid will stimulate bulblet formation. Mix 1000 parts of thiram or ferbium with 1 part of naphthalene acetic acid and apply as a dust. The PCNB-thiram mixture is also an effective fungicidal treatment.

Scales can be planted directly in the field in open beds or frames, planted no more than 2½ in. deep. Somewhat better results are obtained if they are placed in trays or flats of moist sand, peat moss, sphagnum moss, or vermiculite for 6 weeks at 65° to 70°F (18° to 21°C). The scales are inserted vertically to about half their length. Small bulblets and roots should form at the base within 3 to 6 weeks. The scales are transplanted either into the open ground or into pots or flats of soil, and then planted in the field the following spring. Subsequent treatment is the same as described for underground bulblets.

Basal cuttage

The hyacinth is the principal plant propagated by this method, although others such as *Scilla* can be handled in this way. Specific methods include "scooping", "scoring", and "coring". Mature bulbs which have been dug after the foliage has died down and are 17 to 18 cm or more in circumference are used. In *scooping*, the entire basal plate is scooped out with a special curve-bladed scalpel, a round-bowled spoon, or a small-bladed knife. Adventitious bulblets develop from the base of the exposed bulb scales. Depth of cutting should be enough to destroy the main shoot. In *scoring*, three straight knife cuts are made across the base of the bulb, each deep enough to go through the basal plate and the growing point. Growing points in the axils of the bulb scales grow into bulblets. In *coring*, the growing point in the center of the bulb is removed entirely with an apple corer or a cork borer 3/8 to ½ in. in diameter. All of the growth potential is concentrated in the development of the bulblets which grow from the basal plate.

To combat decay that may develop during the later incubation period, any infected bulbs should be discarded; the tools disinfected frequently with an alcohol, formalin, or mild carbolic acid solution, and the cut bulbs dusted with a fungicide. Most important is to callus the bulbs at about 70°F (21°C) for a few days to a few days to a few weeks in dry sand or soil or in open trays, cut side up. After callusing, the bulbs are incubated in trays or flats, in dark or diffuse light, at 70° to 90°F (21° to 32°C) and high humidity for 2½ to 3 months.

The mother bulbs are planted about 4 in. deep in nursery beds in the fall. The next spring bulblets produce leaves profusely. Normally the mother bulb disintegrates during the first summer. Annual digging and replanting of the graded bulblets is required until they reach flowering sizes. Bulbs for greenhouse forcing should be 17 cm (6¾ in.) or more in circumference; bulbs for bedding should be 14 to 17cm (5½ to 6¾ in.) in circumference. On the average, a scooped bulb will produce 60 bulbets, but 4 to 5 years will be required to produce flowering sizes; a scored bulb will produce 24, requiring 3 to 4 years; and a cored bulb will produce 10, requiring 2 to 3 years.

Leaf cuttings

This method has been reported successful for blood lily (*Haemanthus*), grape hyacinth (*Muscari*), hyacinth, and *Lachenalia* although the range of species is probably wider.

Leaves are taken at a time when they are well developed and green, generally near full bloom. An entire leaf is cut from the top of the bulb and may in turn be cut into two or three pieces. Each section is placed in a rooting medium with the basal end several inches below the surface, as described for rooting cuttings. The leaves should not be allowed to dry out, and bottom heat is desirable. Within 2 to 4 weeks small bulblets form on the base of the leaf and roots develop. At this stage the bulblets are planted in soil.

Bulb cuttings

Among those plants which have been reported to respond to this method of propagation are the *Albuca*, *Chasmanthe*, *Cooperia*, *Haemanthus*, *Hippeastrum*, *Hymenocallis*, *Lycoris*, *Narcissus*, *Nerine*, *Pancratium*, *Scilla*, *Spreakelia*, and *Urceolina*.

A mature bulb is cut into a series of 8 to 10 vertical sections, each containing a part of the basal plate. These sections are further divided by sliding a knife down between each third or fourth pair of concentric scale rings and cutting through the basal plate. Each of these fractions makes up a bulb cutting consisting of a piece or basal plate and segments of three or four scales.

The bulb cuttings are planted vertically in a rooting medium, such as peat moss and sand, with just their tips showing above the surface. The subsequent technique of handling is the same as for ordinary leaf cuttings. A moderately warm temperature, slightly higher than for mature bulbs of that kind, is required. New bulblets develop from the basal plate between the bulb scales within a matter of a few weeks, along with new roots. At this time they are transferred to flats of soil to continue development.

CORMS

Definition and Structure

A *corm* is the swollen base of a stem axis enclosed by the dry, scale- like leaves. In contrast to the bulb, which is predominantly leaf scales, a corm is a solid stem structure with distinct nodes and internodes. The bulk of the corm consists of storage tissue composed of parenchyma cells. In the mature corm, the dry leaf bases persist at each of these nodes and enclose the corm. This covering, known as the *tunic*, protects it against injury and water loss. At the apex of the corm is a terminal shoot bud which will develop into the leaves and the flowering shoot. Axillary buds are produced at each of the nodes. In a large corm, several of the upper buds may develop into flowering shoots, but those nearer the base of the corm are generally inhibited from growing. However, should something prevent the main buds from growing, these lateral buds would be capable of producing a shoot.

Two types of roots are produced from the corm; a fibrous root system developing from the base of the old corm and enlarged, fleshy contractile roots developing from the base of the new corm.

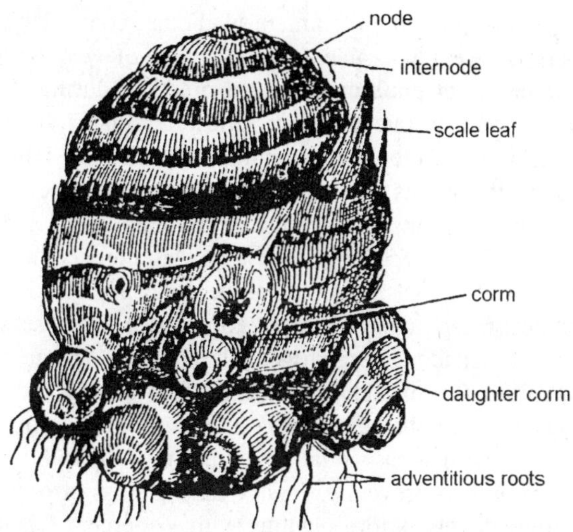

Fig. 4.3. Corm of Colocasia.

Growth Behaviour

Gladiolus and crocus are typical cormous plants. The gladiolus is a semi-hardy to tender plant which, in areas with severe winters, must be stored over winter and replanted in the spring. At the time of planting, the corm is a vegetative structure. New roots develop from the base of the corm, and one or more of the buds begin to develop leaves. Differentiation of the inflorescence takes place within a few weeks after the bud begins to grow. At the same time the base of the shoot axis thicken, and a new corm for the succeeding year begins to form above the old corm. Root-like structures bearing miniature corms or *cormels* on their tip develop from the base of the new corm. The new corm continues to enlarge, and the old corm begins to shrivel and disintegrate as its contents are utilized in flower production. After flowering, the foliage continues to manufacture food materials, which are stored in the new corm. At the end of the summer, when the foliage dries, there are one or more new corms and perhaps a great number of little cormels. The corms are dug and stored over winter until they are planted the following spring.

Propagation

New corms

Propagation of cormous plants is principally by the natural increase of new corms. Flower production in corms, as in bulbs, depends upon food materials stored in the corm the previous season, particularly during the period following bloom. In gladiolus, cool nights and long growing periods are favourable for production of very large corms. Fertilization and other good management practices during bloom have their greatest effect on the next year's flowers. Plants are left in the ground for 2 months following blooming, or until frost kills the tops. After digging, the plants are placed in trays with a screen or slat bottom arranged to allow air to circulate between them, and cured at 95°F (35°C) at 80 to 85 percent relative humidity. Then the new corms, old corms, cormels, and top can be easily separated. The corns are graded according to size, sorted to remove the diseased ones, treated with a fungicide (Spergon wettable powder), and returned to a 95°F temperature for an additional week. This process suberizes the wounds and helps combat *Fusarium* infection. The corms are then stored at 40°F (5°C) with a relative humidity of 70 to 80 percent in well-aerated rooms to prevent excessive drying. It is also desirable to treat them immediately before planting with ½ percent Lysol solution for 2 hours or with 1/8 percent solution of New Improved Ceresan for 15 minutes.

Cormels

These are miniature corms which develop between the old and the new corms. One or 2 years growth is required for them to reach flowering size. Shallow planting of the corms, only a few inches deep, results in greater production of cormels; increasing the depth of planting reduces cormel production.

Cormels are separated from the mother corms and stored over winter for planting in the spring. Dry cormels become very hard and may be slow to start growth the following spring, but if they are stored at about 40°F (5°C) in slightly moist peat moss, they will stay plump and in good condition. Soaking dry cormels in warm water for 2 to 5 days just prior to planting will hasten the onset of growth.

Disease-free cormels can be obtained by hot-water treatment. Treatment should be done between 2 and 4 months after digging. The cormels are soaked in water at air temperature for 2 days, then placed in a 1:200 dilution of commercial 37 percent fromaldehyde for 4 hours, and then immersed in a water bath at 135°F (57°C) for 30 minutes. The temperature should be maintained within 1°F, plus or minus, of this temperature. At the end of the treatment, the cormels are cooled quickly, dried immediately, and stored at 40°F (5°C) in a clean area with good air circulation. Dusting the dry cormels with a fungicide at this time is also desirable.

The cormels are planted in the field in furrows about 2 in. deep in the manner of planting large seeds. Only grass-like foliage is produced the first season. The cormel does not increase in size but produces a new corm from the base of the stem axis, in the manner described for full-sized corms. At the end of the first growing season, the beds are dug and the corms separated by size. A few of the corms may attain flowering size, but most require an additional year of growth. Size grades in gladiolus are determined by diameter. There are seven grades, the smallest 3/8 to ½ in. in diameter, the largest 2 in. or more.

Division of the corm

Large corms may be cut into sections, retaining a bud with each section. Each of these should then develop a new corm. Segments should be dusted with a fungicide because of the great likelihood of decay of the exposed surfaces.

Tubers

Definition and Structure

A *tuber* is a modified stem structure which develops below ground as a consequence of the swelling of the subapical portion of a stolon and subsequent accumulation of reserve materials.

The most notable example of a plant which produces tubers by which it is propagated is the Irish potato (*Solanum tuberosum*). The *Caladium*, grown for its striking foliage, is also propagated by tubers, as is the Jerusalem artichoke (*Helianthus tuberosus*).

A tuber has all the parts of a typical stem. The "eyes", present in regular order over the surface, represent nodes, each consisting of one or more small buds subtended by a leaf scar. The arrangement of the nodes is a spiral, beginning with the terminal bud on the end opposite the scar resulting from the attachment to the stolon. The terminal bud is at the apical end of the tuber, oriented farthest (distally) from the crown of the plant. Consequently it shows the same apical dominance as any stem.

Growth Behaviour

A tuber is a storage and propagative organ that is produced in one growing season, remains dormant during the winter, and then produces new shoots the following spring to start a new cycle. Most information on growth cycles in tubers is from studies of the potato. At the base of the main shoot adventitious roots are initiated, and lateral buds grow out horizontally to become the stolons. Continued growth of the stolon takes place during long photoperiods and is associated with the presence of auxin and a high gibberellin level. Tuberization begins with inhibition of terminal growth and the intermediate day lengths, reduced temperatures (particularly at night), good light, low mineral content, and a reduction in gibberellin levels in the plant.

Tuberization has been explained as being caused by the production of a tuber-inducing substance (perhaps a gibberellin inhibitor) that is produced in the leaves and the mother tuber. It seems to be necessary for the stolon tip to have attained a particular physiological age. Continued tuber enlargement is dependent on a continuing adequate supply of photosynthate. Conditions which favour rapid and luxurious plant growth above ground, such as an abundance of nitrogen, or high temperatures, are not conducive to tuber production. In the fall, the tops of the plants die down and the tubers are dug. At this time, the buds of potato tubers are dormant for 6 to 8 weeks. This condition must disappear before sprouting will take place.

Propagation

Division

Propagation by tubers can be done either by planting the tubers whole or by cutting them into sections, each containing a bud or eye. These small pieces of tuber to be used for propagation of the potato are commonly referred to as "seed". The weight of the tuber piece should be 1 to 2 oz to provide sufficient stored food for the new plant to become well established.

Division of tubers is done with a sharp knife shortly before planting. The cut pieces should be stored at warm (68°F; 20°C) temperatures and relatively high humidities (90 percent) for 2 to 3 days prior to planting. During this time, the cut surfaces heal (*suberization*) and the "seed" piece is effectively protected against drying and decay. Treatment of potato tubers prior to cutting for the control of *Rhizoctonia* and scab may be desirable. Caladium tubers are produced commercially in Florida. The tubers are cut into sections, usually two buds per piece. These are planted 3 to 4 in. deep, 4 to 6 in. apart in rows 18 to 24 in. apart. Harvest begins in November. After harvest, the tubers are dried in open sheds for 6 weeks or artificially dried for 48 hours. Further storage should be at a temperature not below 60°F (16°C).

Tubercles

Begonia evansiana and the cinnamon vine (*Dioscorea batatas*) produce small aerial tubers, known as *tubercles*, in the axils of the leaves. These tubercles may be removed in the fall, stored over winter, and planted in the spring.

Tuberous Roots

Definition and Structure

Certain herbaceous perennials produce thickened tuberous roots which contain large amounts of stored food. Although the appearance of such roots may vary considerably from one species to another, they have the internal and external features of a typical root. Thus they differ from the true (stem) tuber in that they lack nodes and internodes, buds are present only at the crown or stem (proximal) end, fibrous roots are commonly produced toward the opposite (distal) end. The polarity of the tuberous root is consequently the reverse of that of the true tuber.

Growth Behaviour

The sweet potato and dahlia produce swollen sections on lateral roots. In the latter case, these are borne in a cluster, each tuberous root attached to the crown of the plant. These roots are biennial. They are produced in one season, after which they go dormant as the herbaceous shoots die. The following spring, buds from the crown produce new shoots which utilize the food materials from the old root during their initial growth. The old root then disintergrates, and new roots are produced, which in turn maintain the plant through the following dormant period.

In the tuberous begonia, on the other hand, the primary taproot becomes a single enlarged tuberous root. Buds are produced at the proximal end (the crown). Fibrous roots are produced from the distal portion of the swollen root. This tuberous root is perennial and lives for a number of years, continuing to increase in size and produce additional buds from the crown. In the tuberous begonia reduced day length results in the enlargement of the tuberous root and the cessation of flowering.

Propagation

Adventitious shoots

The fleshy roots of a few species of plants such as sweet potato have the capacity to produce adventitious shoots if subjected to the proper conditions of temperature and moisture. The roots are laid in sand so that they do not touch one another and covered to a depth of about 2 in. The bed is kept moist. The temperature should be about

80°F (27°C) at the beginning and about 70° to 75°F (21° to 24°C) after sprouting has started. As the new shoots, or *slips*, come through the covering, more sand is added so that eventually the stems will be covered for 4 to 5 in. Adventitious roots develop from the base of these adventitious shoots. After the slips are well rooted, they are pulled from the parent plant and transplanted into the field. An increase in slip production takes place if sweet potato roots are cut in half and the pieces are subjected to 110°F (43°C) for about 26 hours. This treatment overcomes the apical dominance and also controls nematodes and fungus diseases.

Division

Most plants with fleshy roots must be propagated by dividing the crown so that each section bears a shoot bud. This is necessary in the dahlia, for example. The plant is dug with its cluster of roots intact, dried for a few days, and stored at 40° to 50°F (4° to 10°C) in dry sawdust, dry peat, or dry shavings. Storage in the open may result in shriveling. The cluster of roots is divided in the late winter or spring shortly before planting. In warm, moist conditions the buds begin to grow, and division can be carried out with better assurance that each section will have a bud.

The perennial tuberous root of the tuberous begonia can also be divided as long as each section has a bud. To combat decay, the cut surface should be dusted with a fungicide and each section dried for several days after cutting and before placing in a moist medium.

Vegetative propagation in such plants as these can often be better carried out with stem, leaf, or leaf-bud cuttings. The cuttings will develop tuberous roots at their base. This process can be stimulated if the stem cutting initially includes a small piece of the fleshy root.

Rhizomes

Structure

A *rhizome* is a specialized stem structure in which the main axis of the plant grows horizontally just below or on the surface of the ground. A number economically important plants, such as bamboo, sugar cane, banana and many grasses, as well as a number of ornamentals, such as *Iris* and lily-of- the-valley, have rhizome structures. Most are monocotyledons, although a few dicotyledons— for example, low bush blueberry (*Vaccinium angustifolium*)—have analogous underground stems classed as rhizomes. Many ferns and lower plant groups have rhizomes or rhizome-like structures.

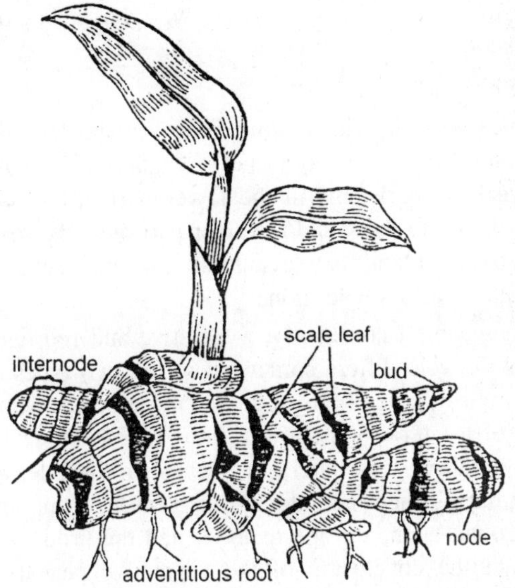

Fig. 4.4. Rhizome of ginger.

The stem appears segmented because it is composed of nodes and internodes. A leaf-like *sheath* is attached at each node; it encloses the stem and, in an expanded form, becomes the foliage leaves. When the leaves and sheaths disintegrate and scar is left at the point of attachment identifying the node and giving a segmented appearance. Adventitious roots and lateral growing points develop in the vicinity of the node. Upright-growing, above-ground shoots and flowering stems (*culms*) are produced either terminally from the rhizome tip or from lateral branches.

Two general types of rhizomes are found. The first (the (*pachymorph*) is illustrated by the *Iris*. The rhizone is thick, fleshy, and shortened in relation to length. It appears as a many-branched clump made up of short, individual sections. It is determinate; that is, each clump terminates in a flowering stalk, growth continuing only from lateral branches. The rhizome tends to be oriented horizontally with roots arising from the lower side.

The second type (the *leptomorph*) is illustrated by the lily-of-the-valley. The rhizome is slender with long internodes. It is indeterminate; that is, it grows continuously in length from the terminal apex and from lateral branch rhizomes. The stem is symmetrical and has lateral buds at most nodes, nearly all remaining dormant. This type does not produce a clump but spreads extensively over an area.

Intermediate forms between these two types also exist. These are called *mesomorphs*.

Growth Behaviour

Rhizomes grow by elongation of the growing points produced at the terminal end and on later branches. Length also increases by growth in the intercalary meristems in the lower part of the internodes. As the plant continues to grow and the older part dies, the several branches arising from one plant may eventually become separated to form individual plants of a single clone.

Rhizomes exhibit consecutive vegetative and reproductive stages, but the growth cycle differs somewhat in the two types described. In the pachymorph rhizome of *Iris*, a growth cycle begins with the initiation and growth of a lateral branch on a flowering section. The flowering stalk dies, but these new lateral branches produce leaves and grow vegetatively during the remainder of that season. Continued growth of the under ground stem, storage of food, and the production of a good flower bud at the conclusion of the vegetative period depend upon photosynthesis in the leaves. Consequently foliage should not be removed during this period. A flowering stalk is produced the following spring and no further terminal growth can take place. In general, plants with

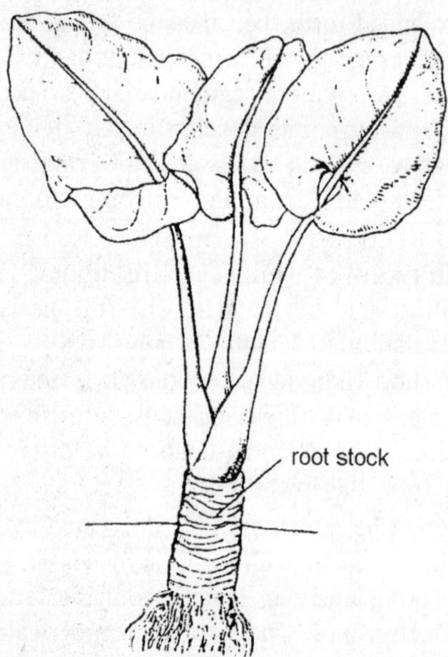

Fig. 4.5. Root stock (vertual rhizome) of Alocasia.

this structure flower in the spring and grow vegetatively during the summer and fall.

Plants with a leptomorph habit as a general rule (with exceptions) grow vegetatively during the beginning of the growth period and flower later in the same period. The length of time during which an individual rhizome remains vegetative varies with different kinds of plants. An individual branch in the lily-of-the-valley for instance, is vegetative three years before a flower bud forms. Some bamboo species remain vegetative for many years, but then they change abruptly and the entire plant produces flowers.

Propagation

Division of clumps

Clump division is the usual procedure for propagating many plants from rhizomes, but the procedure may vary some what with the two types. In pachymorph rhizomes, individual sections(or culms) are cut off at the point of attachment to the rhizome, the top is cut back, and the piece is transplanted to the new location. Leptomorph rhizomes can be handled in essentially the same way by removing a single lateral "off-shoot" from the rhizome and transplanting it. The tip of the lily-of-the-valley rhizome bearing a flower bud called a "pip" is removed along with the rooted section below and transplanted.

Division is usually carried out at the beginning of a growth period (as in early spring) or at or near the end of a growth period (i.e., in late summer or fall).

Division of rhizomes

Dividing a rhizome is done by cutting the rhizome into sections, being sure that each piece has at least one lateral bud, or "eye", it is essentially a stem cutting. Bananas, for instance, are propagated in this way. This general method works well for the leptomorph rhizomes, in which a dormant lateral growing point is present at most nodes. The rhizomes are cut or broken into pieces, and adventitious roots and new shoots develop from the nodes. Rhizomes producing turf grasses, for instance, are cut up into sections and the individual "sprigs" transplanted. New plants can be established readily by this method.

Culm cuttings

In large rhizome-bearing plants, such as bamboos, the aerial shoot, or culm, may be used as a cutting. These may be whole culm cuttings, in which the entire aerial shoot is laid horizontally in a trench. New branches arise at the nodes. A more common alternative procedure is to cut the stem into three- or four-node sections and place them vertically in the ground as for an ordinary stem cutting.

Pseudobulbs

Definition and Structure

A *pseudobulb* (literally "false bulb") is a specialized storage structure produced by many orchid species, consisting of an enlarged, fleshy section of the stem made up of one to several nodes. In general appearance the pseudobulb varies with different species of orchids, the differences being sufficiently characteristic to aid in identification.

Growth Behaviour

These pseudobulbs arise during the growing season on upright growths which develop laterally or terminally from the horizontal rhizome. Leaves and flowers from either at the terminal end or at the base of the pseudobulb, depending upon the species. During the growth period, they accumulate stored food materials and water and assist the plants in surviving the subsequent dormant period.

Propagation

Offshoots

In a few orchids, such as the *Dentrobium* species, the pseudobulb is long and jointed, being made up of many nodes. Offshoots develop at these nodes. From the base of these offshoots roots develop. The rooted offshoots are then cut from the parent plant and potted.

Division

Most important commercial species of orchids, including the *Cattleya*, *Laelia*, *Miltonia*, and *Odontoglossum*, may be propagated by dividing the rhizome into sections, the exact procedure used depending upon the particular kind of orchid. Division is done during the dormant season, preferably just before the beginning of a new period of growth. The rhizome is cut with a sharp knife back far enough from the terminal end to include four to five pseudobulbs in the new section, leaving the old rhizome section with a number of old pseudobulbs, or "back bulbs", from which the leaves have dehisced. The section is then potted, whereupon growth begins from the bases of the pseudobulbs and at the nodes.

The removal of the new section of the rhizome from the old part stimulates new growth, or "back breaks", to occur from the old parts of the rhizome. These new growths grow for a season and can be removed the following year.

An alternate procedure is to cut partly through the rhizome and leave it for 1 year. New back breaks will develop which can later be removed and potted.

Back bulbs and green bulbs

"Back Bulbs" (i.e., those without foliage) are commonly use to propagate clones of *Cymbidium*. These are removed from the plant, the cut surface is painted with a grafting compound, and they are placed in a rooting medium for a new shoots to develop. The back bulb can be repropagated and a second shoot developed from it.

"Green bulbs"(i.e., those with leaves) can also be used in *Cymbidium* propagation. Treatment with indolebutyric acid, either by soaking or by painting with a paste, has been shown to be beneficial.

By Cuttings

In propagation by cuttings, a portion of a stem, root, or leaf is cut from the parent plant, after which this plant part is placed under certain favourable environmental conditions and induced to form roots and shoots, thus producing a new independent plant which, in most cases, is identical with the parent plant.

The Importance and Advantages of Propagation by Cuttings

This is the most important method of propagating ornamental shrubs—deciduous species as well as the broad-and narrow-leaved types of evergreens. Cuttings are also used widely in commercial greenhouse propagation of many florists crops and are commonly used in propagating several fruit species. For species that can be easily propagated by cuttings, this method has numerous advantages. Many new plants can be started in a limited space from a few stock plants. It is inexpensive, rapid, and simple, and does not require the special techniques necessary in grafting or budding. There is no problem of compatibility with rootstocks or of poor graft unions. Greater uniformity is obtained by absence of the variation which sometimes appears owing to the variable seedling rootstocks of grafted plants. The parent plant is usually reproduced exactly with no genetic change. It is not always desirable, however, to produce plants on their own roots by cuttings even if it is possible to do so. It is often advantageous or necessary to use a rootstock resistant to some adverse soil condition or soil borne organism, or to utilize available dwarfing or invigorating rootstocks.

Types of Cuttings

Cuttings are almost always made from the vegetative portions of the plant, such as stems, modified stems (rhizomes, tubers, corms and bulbs), leaves, or roots. The reproductive parts of the plant are not ordinarily used, although such parts as the ovary, pedicel and petals, have been reported to form roots.

Several types of cuttings can be made; these are classified according to the part of the plant from which they are obtained:

- Stem cuttings
  - Hardwood
    - Deciduous
    - Narrow-leaved evergreen
  - Semi-hardwood
  - Softwood
  - Herbaceous
- Leaf cuttings
- Leaf bud cuttings
- Root cuttings

Many plants can be propagated by several of these different types of cuttings with satisfactory results. The type used would depend upon the individual circumstances, the least expensive and easiest usually being selected. If the particular plant being propagated will root well by hardwood stem cuttings in an outdoor nursery, this method ordinarily used, because of its simplicity and low cost. Root cuttings of some species are also satisfactory, but cutting material may be difficult to obtain in large quantities. For species more difficult to propagate, it is necessary to resort to the more expensive and elaborate facilities required for rooting the leafy types of cuttings.

In selecting cutting material it is important to use stock plants that are free from diseases, moderately vigorous and productive, and of known identity. Stock plants that are diseased or injured by frost or drought, that have been defoliated by insects or diseases, that have been stunted by excessive fruiting, or that have made rank, overly vigorous growth should be avoided.

A commendable practice for the propagator is the establishment of stock blocks as a source of propagating material, where uniform, true-to-type pathogen-free mother plants can be maintained and held under the proper nutritive condition for the best rooting of cuttings taken from them.

Stem Cuttings

This is the most important type of cutting and can be divided into four groups, according to the nature of the wood used in making the cuttings: *hardwood*, *semi-hardwood*, *softwood*, and *herbaceous*. In propagation by stem cuttings, segments of shoots containing lateral or terminal buds are obtained with the expectation that under the proper conditions adventitious roots will develop and thus produce independent plants. The type of wood, the stage of growth used in making the cuttings, the time of year in which the cuttings are taken, and several other factors can be very important in securing satisfactory rooting of some plants.

Hardwood Cuttings (Deciduous Species)

This is one of the least expansive and easiest methods of vegetative propagation. Hardwood cuttings are easy to prepare, are not readily perishable, may be shipped safely over long distances if necessary, and require no special equipment during rooting.

The cuttings are prepared during the dormant season-late fall, winter, or early spring—from wood of the previous reason's growth, although with a few species, such as the fig or olive, two-year-old or older wood is used. Hardwood cuttings are most often used in propagation of deciduous woody plants, although some broad-leaved evergreens, such as the olive can be propagated by leafless hardwood cuttings. Many deciduous ornamental shrubs are started readily by this type of cutting. Some common ones are privet, forsythia, wisteria, honeysuckle, and spiraea. Rose rootstocks, such as *Rosa multiflora* are propagated in great quantities by hardwood cuttings. A few fruit species are propagated commercially by this method— for example fig, quince, olive mulberry, grape, currant, gooseberry, pomegranate, and some plums.

The propagating material for hardwood cuttings should be taken from healthy, vigorous stock plants growing in full sunlight. The wood selected should not be from extremely rank growth with abnormally long internodes, or from small, weakly growing interior shoots. Wood of moderate size and vigor is the most desirable. The cuttings should have an ample supply of stored foods to nourish the developing roots and shoots until the new plant becomes self-sustaining.

Hardwood cuttings vary considerably in length—from 4 to 30 in. Long cuttings, when they are to be used as rootstocks for fruit trees, permit the insertion of the varietal bud into the original cutting following rooting, rather than into a smaller new shoot arising from the original cutting.

At least two nodes are included in the cutting, the basal cut is usually just below a node and the top cut ½ to 1 in. above a node.

However, in preparing stem cuttings of plants with short internodes, little attention is ordinarily given to the position of the basal cut, especially when quantities of cuttings are prepared and cut to length many at a time, by a band saw or paper cutter.

The diameter of the cuttings may range form ¼ in. to 1 or even 2 in., depending upon the species. The "mallet." the "heel", and the straight cutting are three different cuttings. The mallet includes a short section of stem of the older wood, whereas the heel cutting includes only a small piece of the older wood. The straight cutting, not including any of the older wood, is most commonly used, giving satisfactory results in most instances.

Where it is difficult to distinguish between the top and base of the cuttings, it is advisable to make all the basal cuts at a slant rather than at right angles. In large-scale operations, bundles of cutting material are cut to the desired lengths by band saws or other types of mechanical cutters rather than individually by hand.

Cuttings of the first (*Abies* sp) and pines (*Pinus* sp). are very difficult to root. In addition, there is considerable variability among the different species in these genera in regard to the ease of rooting of cuttings. As with many other plants, cuttings taken from young seedling stock plants root much more readily than those taken from older trees. Treatments with root-promoting substances particularly indolebutyric acid at relatively high concentrations, are usually beneficial increasing the speed of rooting and the percentage of cuttings rooted, and in obtaining heavier root systems.

Narrow-leaved evergreen cuttings are best taken between late fall and late winter. Rapid handling of the cuttings after the material is taken from the stock plants is important. The cuttings are best rooted in a greenhouse with relatively highlight intensity and under conditions of high humidity or very light misting but without heavy wetting of the leaves. A bottom heat temperature of 75° to 80°F (24° to 26.5°C) has given good results. Dipping the cuttings into a fungicide helps prevent disease attacks. Sand alone has given good results as a rooting medium, as has a 1:1 mixture of perlite and peat moss. Some individual cuttings take longer to root than others. The slower-rooting ones can be restuck in the rooting medium, and often will root eventually.

The type of wood to use in making the cuttings varies considerably with the particular species being-rooted. The cuttings are made 4 to 8 in. long with all the leaves removed from the lower half of the cutting. Mature terminal shoots of the previous season's growth are usually used. In some instances, such as with *Juniperus chinensis pfitzeriana*, older and heavier wood can also be used, thus resulting in a larger plant when it is rooted. On the other hand, some nurserymen use small tip cuttings, 2 to 3 in long, placed very close together in a flat for rooting. In some species, such as *Juniperus excelsa*, older growth taken from the sides and lower portion of the stock plant roots better than the more succulent tips. Cuttings of *Taxus* root best if they are taken with a piece of old wood at the base of the cutting. Such cuttings are also less subject to fungus attacks. In certain of the narrow-leaved evergreen species, some type of basal wounding is sometimes beneficial in inducing rooting.

Semi-Hardwood Cuttings

Cuttings of this type are usually made from woody, broad leaved evergreen species, but leafy summer cuttings taken from partially matured wood of deciduous plants could also be considered as semi-hard-wood. Cuttings of broad-leaved evergreen species are generally taken during the summer months from new shoots just after a flush of growth has taken place and the wood is partially matured. Many ornamental shrubs, such as camellia, pittosporum, euonymus, the evergreen azaleas, and holly are commonly propagated by semi-hardwood cuttings. A few fruit species, such as citrus and olive, can, also be started in this manner.

The cuttings are made 3 to 6 in. long with leaves retained at the upper end but removed from the lower end. If the leaves are very large, they should be reduced in size to lower the water loss and to allow closer spacing in the cutting bed. The terminal ends of the shoots are often used in making the cuttings, but the more basal parts of the stem will usually root also. The basal cut is usually just below a node. The cutting wood should be obtained in the cool, early morning hours when the stems are turgid, and kept wrapped in clean moist burlap and out of the sun at all times until the cutting are made.

It is necessary that leafy, semi-hardwood cuttings be rooted under conditions which will keep water loss from the leaves at a minimum; commercially they are usually rooted under intermittent mist sprays. Bottom heat and growth regulator treatments are also beneficial. Rooting media such as a 1:1 mixture of perlite and peat moss of perlite and vermiculite give satisfactory results.

Softwood (Greenwood) Cuttings

Cuttings prepared from the soft, succulent , new spring growth of deciduous or evergreen species may properly be classed as softwood cuttings. Many ornamental woody shrubs can be started by softwood cuttings. Typical examples are the hybrid French lilacs, forsythia, magnolia, weigela, and spiraea. Some deciduous ornamental trees such as the maples can also be started in this manner. Although fruit tree species are not commonly propagated by softwood cuttings, apple, peach, pear, plum, apricot, and cherry will root, especially under mist.

Softwood cuttings generally root easier and quicker than the other types but require more attention and equipment. This type of cutting is always made with leaves attached. They must, consequently, be handled carefully to prevent drying, and be rooted under conditions which will avoid excessive water loss from the leaves. Temperature should be maintained during rooting at 75° to 80°F (23° to 27°C) at the base and 70°F (21°C) at the leaves for most species. Softwood cuttings produce roots in 2 to 4 or 5 weeks in most cases. In general, they respond well to treatment with root-promoting substances. It is important in making softwood cuttings to obtain the proper type of cutting wood from the stock plant. This will vary greatly, however, with the species being propagated. Extremely fast-growing, soft, tender shoots generally are not desirable, as they are likely to deteriorate before rooting. At the other extreme, old, woody stems are slow to root in most cases.

The best cutting material has some degree of flexibility, but is mature enough to break when bent sharply. Weak, thin, interior shoots should be avoided as well as vigorous, abnormally thick, or heavy ones. Average growth from portions of the plant in full light is the most desirable to use. Some of the best cutting material is the lateral or side branches of the stock plant. Heading back the main shoots will usually force out numerous lateral shoots from which cuttings can be made. Softwood cuttings ordinarily are 3 to 5 in. long with two or more nodes. The basal cut is usually made just below a node. The leaves on the lower portion of the cutting are removed, but those at the upper portion are retained. If the upper leaves are very large, they should be reduced in size to lower the transpiration rate and to use less space in the propagating bed, although for the best rooting it is desirable to retain the maximum leaf area that is possible without wilting. All flower buds should be removed. In some large nurseries where quantities of cuttings are prepared, bundles of cutting material are rapidly chopped into uniform lengths by paper cutters.

The cutting material is best gathered in the early part of the day and should be kept moist, cool, and turgid at all times by wrapping in damp, clean burlap or placing in large polyethylene bags (kept out of the sun). Laying the cutting material or prepared cuttings in the sun for even a few minutes will cause serious damage. Soaking the cutting material or cuttings in water to keep them fresh is undesirable.

Herbaceous Cuttings

This type of leafy cutting is made from such succulent, herbaceous greenhouse plants as geraniums, chrysanthemums, coleus, and carnations. They are 3 to 5 in. long with leaves retained at the upper end. Most florists crops are propagated by herbaceous cuttings. They are rooted under the same conditions as softwood cuttings, requiring high humidity. Bottom heat is also helpful. Under proper conditions, rooting is rapid and in high percentages. Although root-promoting substances are not required, they are often used to gain uniformity in rooting and development of heavier root systems. Herbaceous cuttings of some plants that exude a sticky sap, such as the geranium, pineapple, or cactus, do better if the basal ends are allowed to dry for a few hours in the air before they are inserted in the rooting medium. This allows the wounded tissues to dry, which tends to prevent the entrance of decay organisms.

Leaf Cuttings

In this type of cutting, the leaf blade or leaf blade and petiole, are utilized in starting a new plant. In most cases, adventitious roots and an adventitious shoot form at the base of the leaf. Rarely does the original leaf becomes apart of the new plants. One type of propagation by leaf cuttings is illustrated by *Sansevieria*. These leaf pieces are inserted three-fourths of their length into sand, and after a period of time a new plant forms at the base of the leaf piece. The original leaf cutting does not become a part of the new plant. The variegated form of *Sansevieria*, *S. trifasciata laurenti*, is an example of a periclinal chimera which will not reproduce true to type from leaf cuttings; to retain its characteristics, it must be propagated by division of the original plants.

In starting plants with thick, fleshy leaves, such as *Begoniarex*, by leaf cuttings, the large veins are cut on the undersurface of the mature leaf, which is then laid flat on the surface of the propagating medium. The leaf is pinned or held down in some manner, with the natural upper surface of the leaf exposed. After a period of time under humid conditions, new plants will form at the point where each vein was cut. The old leaf blade will gradually disintegrate.

Another method, sometimes used with the fibrous-rooted begonias, is to cut large, well-matured leaves into triangular sections each containing a piece of a large vein. The thin outer edge of the leaf is discarded. These leaf pieces are then inserted upright in sand with the pointed end down. The new plant develops from the large vein at the base of the leaf piece. The original leaf dies, not becoming a part of the new plant.

The African violet (*Saintpaulia*) is typical of leaf cuttings which can be made of an entire leaf (leaf blade plus petiole), the leaf blade only, or just a portion of the leaf blade. The new plant forms at the base of the petiole or midrib of the leaf blade.

Leaf cuttings should be rooted under the same conditions of high humidity that are used for softwood or herbaceous cuttings. Root-promoting chemicals are usually helpful.

Leaf-Bud Cuttings

This type of cutting consists of a leaf blade, petiole, and a short piece of the stem with the attached axillary bud. Such cuttings are of particular value for species that are able to initiate roots but not shoots from detached leaves. In such cases, the axillary bud at the base of the petiole provides for the essential shoot formation. A number of plant species such as the black raspberry (*Rubus occidentalis*), blackberry, boysenberry, lemon, camellia, and rhododendron can be readily started by leaf-bud cuttings, as well as many tropical shrubs and most herbaceous green-house plants usually started by stem cuttings. Red raspberries (*Rubus idaeus*) apparently do not reproduce by leaf-bud cuttings. This method is particularly valuable when propagating material is scarce, because it will produce at least twice at many new plants from the same amount of stock material as can be started by stem cuttings. Each node can be used as a cutting. Leaf-bud cuttings should only be made from material having well-developed buds and healthy, actively growing leaves.

Treatment of the cut surfaces with one of the root-promoting substances may stimulate root production. The cuttings should be inserted in the rooting medium with the bud as soon as the plants become well established with good root development they can be transplanted to their permanent location.

Plants with Large Roots, Propagated Out-of-Doors

Root cuttings of this type are made 2 to 6 in. long. They are tied in bundles, care being used to keep the same ends together to avoid planting upside down later. The cuttings are then packed in boxes of damp sand, sawdust, or peat moss for about 3 weeks. During this storage period the cuttings should be kept cool, about 40°F (45°C). They should be planted 2 to 3 in apart in a well-prepared nursery soil with the tops of the cuttings level with, or just below the top of the soil.

Root Promoting Substances

Herbaceous Plants

Cuttings of most plants of this type have shown a definite increase in rooting when treated with growth regulators. The chief effect has been to speed the rate of rooting and to produce heavier clumps of roots. Plants which have shown good response include chrysanthemums, geraniums, carnations, begonias, poinsettias, English ivy, and African violets. Cuttings of most varieties of such herbaceous plants usually root so easily under proper care without growth-regulator treatments, however, that it is debatable whether their use is justified.

Broad-Leaved Evergreens

Propagation of this type of plant, by softwood or semi-hardwood cuttings, is often considerbly improved by growth regulator treatments, provided that the other necessary requirements of rooting are satisfied. The citrus species—orange, lemon, and grapefruit—as well as the olive are evergreen tree fruits that respond well to treatment. A great many ornamentals in this group have also given good response, including camellia, holly, rhododendron, box, daphne, euonymus, gardenia, oleander, escallonia, pittosporum, and pyracantha.

Narrow-Leaved Evergreens

For most species, if the cuttings are taken at the right time of year, and the proper material and concentration used, improved rooting can be expected to result from the use of root-promoting chemicals. Species found to respond to treatments include fir, juniper, spruce, pine, yew, aborvitae, and hemlock.

Deciduous Plants

Cuttings may be made of this type of plant either as hardwood cuttings during the dormant season or as softwood cuttings during the active growing period. Experience has shown a response to growth-regulator treatments with both types of cuttings. Plants of this type that have responded to treatments include the apple, pear, peach, plum, cherry, walnut, filbert, maple, birch, beech, and mulberry.

Environmental Conditions for Rooting Leafy Cuttings

For the successful rooting of leafy cuttings, the essential environmental requirements are proper temperature (65° to 75°F: 18° to 27°C), an atmosphere conductive to low water loss from the leaves; ample light; and a clean, moist, well-aerated, and well-drained rooting medium. There are many possible types of equipment that are satisfactory for providing these conditions-from a simple glass jar placed over a few cuttings stuck in sand to elaborate greenhouse benches with automatic mist control and automatically controlled electric soil cables below the cuttings. Probably one of the simplest devices, which is entirely satisfactory for rooting a limited number of cuttings, is an ordinary wooden box half-filled with the rooting medium, with a pane of glass or a sheet of polyethylene film over the top. If this is placed in a heated room in the winger near a window, cuttings of many species can be rooted in it. Such a box can also be used successfully in the summer for rooting cuttings of some plants, if placed out-of-doors in the shade. Cuttings of many plants can be rooted successfully with only artificial light, if placed under an ordinary large fluorescent lamp fixture. In commercial operations, large-scale rooting of leafy cuttings is done in hotbeds, cold frames, or beds in greenhouses or plastic houses. In these structures, proper environmental conditions can be established and maintained.

Sanitation

Most commercial propagators recognize the value of maintaining strict sanitary procedures during all stages of making and rooting leafy cuttings. It is much easier to prevent attacks of disease organisms than to try to stop them. Losses could be considerable from a disease attack where hundreds of thousands of cuttings might become involved.

During the preparation of facilities for rooting the cuttings and while making and inserting them in the rooting medium, the following procedures, if observed closely, will aid considerably in preventing losses from attacks by noxious organisms.

Propagating benches in the greenhouse should be washed thoroughly with water and sprayed with a copper naphthenate solution (1 part to 5 parts paint thinner). (*Caution* : Creosote and certain phenolic materials used as wood preservatives give off fumes which are toxic to plants, and should not be used.) Flats for rooting the cuttings should be thoroughly washed, filled with the rooting medium, and then sterilized by steam or methyl bromide. The work benches where the cuttings are to be prepared should be washed thoroughly with water and sprayed with a Clorox (1 part to 4 parts water)solution or a formaldehyde (1 qt 38 per cent formaldehyde to 5 gal, of water)solution. Tools used in preparing the cuttings should be dipped in such solutions several times daily.

The cutting material itself should be free of insects and disease organisms. As the cutting material is gathered, it can be placed on and wrapped in large sheets of clean, washed black polyethylene. When full these are protected from the sun and brought into the propagating room as soon as possible. The cutting material can be placed on a large raised wire rack and washed thoroughly with water. Mist nozzles should be placed over this rack to keep the material fresh while the cuttings are being prepared. After the cuttings are made, they may be soaked for about 10 minutes in a mild fungicide, such as Morsodren (1tsp per 5 gal, of water). Following this, the cuttings are allowed to drain in a wire rack and are then treated with a root-promoting compound just before they are stuck into the propagating medium.

Efforts to conduct propagating operations under clean, sterilized conditions are of no avail, however, unless all components are included—the cuttings themselves, the flats, the rooting medium, the area where the cuttings are prepared, the tools used in making the cuttings, and the rooting bench. Keep the watering house nozzle off the floor where it could pick up and later distribute harmful organisms.

Preparing the Rooting Frame and inserting the Cuttings

The frames or benches should preferably be raised or, if on the ground, equipped with drainage tile, so there is never any question of perfect drainage of excess water.

The frames or flats should be deep enough so that about 4 in. of rooting medium can be used. The depth should be enough so that an average-length cutting—3 to 5 inch can be inserted up to half its total length, with the end of the cutting still an inch or more above the bottom of the frame. The rooting medium should be watered thoroughly before the cuttings are inserted, which should be as soon as possible after they are prepared. It is very important that the cuttings be protected from drying at all stages during their preparation and insertion. After a section of the rooting bench or a flat is filled with cuttings, it should be well watered to settle the rooting medium around the cuttings.

Care of Cuttings During Rooting

Hardwood stem cuttings or root cuttings started out-of-doors in the nursery require only the usual care given to other crop plants, such as adequate soil moisture, freedom from weed competition, and insect and disease control. The best results with most species are likely to be obtained if the nursery is established in full sun where shading and root competition from large trees or shrubbery do not occur.

Leafy softwood or semi-hardwood stem cuttings and leaf-bud or leaf cuttings being rooted under high humidity require close attention throughout the rooting period. The temperature should be controlled carefully. The cuttings must not be allowed to show wilting for any length of time. Glass-covered frames, exposed even for a few hours to strong sunlight, will build up excessively high and injurious temperatures, owing to the heat accumulating under the glass. Such equipment should always be protected by cloth screens, whitewash on the glass, or some other method of reducing the light intensity.

If bottom heat is provided, thermometers should be inserted in the rooting medium to the level of the base of the cutting and checked at frequent intervals, especially at first. A temperature of 65° to 75°F (18° to 24°C) is desirable. Excessively high temperatures in the rooting medium even for a short time are likely to result in death of the cuttings.

It is very important to maintain humidity conditions as high as possible in rooting leafy cuttings to reduce water loss from the leaves to a minimum. Syringing the leaves with a spray nozzle at frequent intervals is a common practice especially during hot weather. Although more time consuming, several light sprinklings with water each day are better than heavy soakings at less frequent intervals. A nozzle should be used that breaks the water into a fine spray. A drop of the humidity to a low level with a consequent pronounced wilting of the cuttings, if prolonged for any length of time, may so injure the cuttings that rooting will not occur, even though high-humidity conditions are subsequently resumed. However most commercial nursery operations use intermittent-mist propagating beds to overcome such problems.

Although high humidity in the propagating frame is important while roots are forming, it is also necessary that adequate drainage be provided so that excess water can escape and not cause the rooting medium to become soggy and waterlogged. When peat or sphagnum moss is used as a component of the rooting medium, it is especially important to see that it does not become excessively wet. It is also necessary to maintain sanitary conditions in the propagating frame. Leaves that drop should be removed promptly, as well as any obviously dead cuttings. Organisms find ideal conditions in a humid, closed propagating frame with low light intensity and, if not controlled, can destroy thousands of cuttings overnight.

Disease problems under mist propagation conditions have not been serious. Probably the frequent washing of the leaves by the aerated water removes spores before they are able to germinate. The greater light intensity and air movement also decrease the incidence of diseases. If insects, such as red spiders, aphids, or mealy bugs, appear on the leaves of the cuttings, immediate control measures are necessary.

Handling Cuttings After Rooting

Hardwood Cuttings

Rooted hardwood cuttings in the nursery row are usually dug during the dormant season after the leaves have dropped. With fast growing species, the cuttings may be sufficiently large to dig after one season's growth. Slower growing species may require 2 or even 3 years to become large enough to transplant.

The digging should take place on cool, cloudy days, when there is no wind. If possible, digging should not be done when the soil is wet, especially if it has a high clay content. Most of the soil should drop readily from the roots after the plants are removed. After the plants are dug, they should be quickly heeled-in in a convenient location or else replanted immediately in their permanent location, "Heeling-in" is to place dug, barerooted deciduous nursery plants close together in trenches with the roots well covered. This is a temporary provision for holding the young plants until they can be set out in their permanent location.

Commercial nurseries often store quantities of deciduous plants for several months in cool, dark rooms with the roots protected by damp wood shavings, shingle two, or some similar material. Nursery stock to be kept for extended periods should be held under refrigerated conditions at 32° to 35°F (0° to 2°C).

If only a few plants are to be removed from the nursery row, they can be dug with shovels, but in large-scale nursery operations some type of mechanical digger is generally used. This digger "undercuts" the plants. A sharp U-shaped, blade travels 1 to 2 ft below the soil surface under the nursery row, cutting through the roots. Sometimes a horizontal "lifting" blade is attached to, and travels behind, the cutting blade. This slightly lifts the plants out of the soil, making them easy to pull by hand.

Unless very small, plants of evergreen species usually cannot be successfully handled bare-root, as is done with dormant and leafless deciduous plants. The presence of leaves on evergreen plants requires the continuous contact of the roots with soil. Therefore, large, salable plants of broad-or narrow-leaved evergreens, and occasionally deciduous plants, are either grown in containers or dug and sold "balled and burlapped." By the latter method, the plants are removed from the soil by carefully digging a trench around each individual. The soil mass around the roots is sometimes tapered at top and bottom, resulting in a half of soil in which the roots are embedded. It is important that the soil be at the proper moisture level—not too wet and not too dry—otherwise it will fall apart. The ball is tipped gently onto a large square of burlap, which is then pulled tightly and sewed in place with heavy twine. If properly done, this adequately holds the soil to the roots, and the plant can then be moved safely of considerable distances and replanted successfully.

To properly prepare field-grown nursery stock for transplanting, either by hand "ball and burlapping" or by machine digging prior root pruning is necessary. This is to produce a compact, fibrous root system and should be started when the young plants (*liners*) are first set in the field. Long or curled and twisted roots should be cut back to a few inches from the crown of the liner. Root pruning the second year should also be done, either by a tractor-powered U-blade cutter for large-scale operations, or with a sharp shovel where only a few plants are involved. This procedure helps confine the roots to the soil mass which will be taken with the plant during the digging and balling operation.

The production of balled and burlapped nursery stock is gradually being replaced, especially in areas with mild winters, by the production of plants in containers primarily because of the lower labour costs involved and the greater opportunities for mechanization.

Softwood, Herbaceous, Semi-Hardwood, Leaf-Bud, Leaf Cuttings

Cuttings such as these, rooted with leaves attached and under conditions of high humidity, require considerable care in being removed from the rooting medium. After rooting has started, the humidity should be lowered and ventilation of the bed provide. They should be dug as soon as a substantial root system with secondary roots has formed. Many propagators have experienced rapid rooting of cuttings only to have them die when they are dug and potted. Sometimes this trouble may be overcome by leaving the cuttings in the rooting bed longer, until after the first-formed primary roots have branched to develop a dense, fibrous secondary root system to which the rooting medium clings in a ball.

Most of the rooting media used contain little or no mineral nutrients available to the plants, hence the cuttings are dependent upon the nutrients already stored in the stems and leaves at the time the cuttings were made. This is generally sufficient to maintain the cuttings during the period of root formation. With some species, however, it may be helpful to water the cuttings with a nutrient solution about 10 days before they are to be removed, especially if digging has been delayed until a secondary root system has developed.

If for any reason the cuttings are to be kept for a prolonged period in the rooting medium, they should be watered several times with a nutrient solution.

In digging, the cuttings should be lifted gently from the rooting medium with a trowel or some similar device, taking care not to break off the roots. It is desirable for the cuttings to be lifted out with a mass of the rooting medium still adhering to the roots. This can be done if some material such as peat moss or vermiculite is included in the rooting medium. The cuttings are ready for potting when most of the roots are 1 to 2 in. long.

The rooted cuttings should be watered thoroughly shortly after potting. It is very important that potted cuttings be moved gradually from the protected conditions under which they were rooted (high humidity, low light intensity) to out-of-door conditions (low humidity, high light-intensity, and wind). It is often best to leave the cuttings for several days after they have been potted under the same conditions in which they were rooted. If they were rooted in mist, they must be given especially close attention and moved gradually to the dryer atmosphere. Before pacing the rooted cuttings in full sun, they should be hardened-off for 12 or 2 weeks in a cold frame or lathhouse or under some partial protection from the sun.

Cold Storage of Rooted and Unrooted Leafy Cuttings

Sometimes it may be convenient to take cuttings at certain times, such as when nursery plants are being sheared and shaped, for later rooting. This was done experimentally with the Kurume type of azaleas overwintered in a cold greenhouse. Softwood cuttings were taken in the spring and held in polyethylene bags at temperatures form 31° to 40°F (–0.5° to 4.5°C) for up to 10 weeks, with subsequent rooting equal to that from unstored cuttings. Unrooted carnation cuttings have long been stored commercially for subsequent rooting. In test on the effects of storage on subsequent performance of the plants, it was found that cuttings rooted after stored at 33°F (0.5°C) gave better results than those stored after rooting. In some situations cuttings may be rooted in late summer or early fall for planting outdoors the following spring.

Several studies have shown that it is possible to hold rooted cuttings of some species in polyethylene bags for prolonged periods under cold storage temperatures of 35° to 40°F (1.5° to 4.5°C). In one test, rooted cuttings of certain plants were safely stored for about 5 months at temperatures of 34° to 39°F (1° to 4°C) when placed in polyethylene bags. Packing material around the roots was of no advantage. Other studies on cold storage of rooted cuttings of 31 different species for 6 months at two temperatures (32° and 40°F) showed better survival with many of the species at 32° than at 40°, although no difference was noted with other species. With some species, dusting prior to storage with 5 per cent Captan increased survival, but in others this made no difference. Apparently some species survive cold-storage treatments much better than others.

By Layering

Layering is the development of roots on a stem while it is still attached to the parent plant. The rooted stem is then detached to become a new plant growing on its own roots. A layered stem is known as a *layer*. This may be a natural means of reproduction, as in black raspberries and trailing blackberries, or it may be induced by the "artificial" methods described in this chapter.

Factors Affecting the Propagation of Plants by Layering

Root Formation during layering is stimulated by various stem treatments which cause an interruption in the downward translocation of organic materials—carbohydrates, auxin, and other growth factors—from the leaves and growing shoot tips. These materials accumulate near the point of treatment, and rooting occurs in this general area even though the stem is still attached to the parent plant.

Water and minerals are supplied to the layered shoot, because the stem is not severed and the xylem, remains intact. Thus layering does not depend upon the length of time during which a severed shoot (cutting) can be maintained before rooting occurs. This is an important reason for layering being more successful with many plants than propagation by cuttings.

Etiolation is another means by which the internal conditions of the developing shoot can be modified during layering to stimulate rooting. It is accomplished in mound or trench layering by covering the newly developing shoot as it grows so that the basal part of the layered shoot is not exposed to the light. This apparently accounts in large measure for the success with which shy-rooting plants are rooted by these two methods.

Applying root-promoting substances, such as indolebutyric acid, during layering is sometimes beneficial, as it is with cuttings, although the method of application may be somewhat different. Applying the material to girdling cuts as a powder, in lanolin or as a solution in 50 percent alcohol can be utilized effectively.

Root formation on layers depends upon continuous moisture, good aeration, and moderate temperatures in the rooting zone. These conditions are best provided by a rooting medium such as sawdust. Prolonged dry spells and compact, heavy soils hinder root development, particularly during the initial stages of rooting. The addition of granulated peat moss to the soil mounded around apple and quince stock plants has promoted rooting. Excessively high temperatures in the upper layers of soil during the spring and summer may reduce the moisture content and cause compaction, not only inhibiting but rooting injuring the shoots as well.

Characteristics and Uses of Layering

The principal advantage of layering is the success with which plants can be rooted by this method. Many clones which will not root easily by cuttings can be propagated by layering, enabling the plant to be established on its own roots. Most methods of layering are relatively simple to perform and can be practiced out-of-doors in the nursery or garden. When small numbers of plants are involved, layering can give a high degree of success with somewhat less skill, effort, and equipment than is necessary with cuttings. With those few kinds of plants in which layering occurs naturally, it is a simple and economical method of propagation.

In some cases, a larger plant can be produced in a shorter time than it would if started as a cutting. However, since transplanting becomes increasingly difficult as the size of the layer increases, special precautions are necessary to establish successfully the larger plant on its own roots.

On the other hand, layering is an expensive method of propagation and does not lend itself to the large-scale techniques of mechanization used in modern nurseries. Part of the increased cost of propagation is due to the additional hand labour required. A layered plant requires a certain amount of individual attention, depending upon the particular method in use, even though the operations involved are in themselves simple. Also, the number of salable plants from a given number of stock plants is smaller than with cuttings, buds, or scions. The methods tend to be cumbersome, and the stock plants take up a considerable area which is difficult to cultivate and maintain free of weeds.

Layering is usually limited by American nurserymen to those plants which propagate naturally in this manner—e.g., black raspberry, trailing blackberries, and those plants too difficult or impossible to propagate by other methods, yet of sufficient value to justify the cost. For instance, the filbert (*Corylus* sp), Muscadine grape (*Vitis rotundifolia*), and litchi (*Litchi chinensis*) are propagated commercially in this manner. Layering is used in propagating certain clonal rootstocks, such as the Malling apple stocks which are not easily rooted as cuttings or which require special equipment, such as mist installations.

Some ornamental trees and shrubs are propagated by layering particularly in Europe. Established blocks of plants to be used for layering (known as *stool beds*) have been in production for many years in some cases, and nurserymen are skilled in their management.

Layering is perhaps best utilized by the amateur horticulturist who wishes to propagate a relatively small number of plants, or by specialists involved with reproducing certain kinds of plants. In these cases, expense per plant and the individual attention necessary would not be factors in the choice of method.

Procedures in Layering

Tip Layering

In tip layering, rooting takes place near the tip of the current season's shoot which is bent to the ground. The shoot tip begins to grow downward into the soil but recurves to produce a sharp bend in the stem, from which roots develop. This natural method of reproduction is characteristic of trailing blackberries, dewberries, and black and purple raspberries.

Stems of these plants are biennial in that the canes are vegetative during the first year, fruitful the second, and pruned out after fruiting. "Summer topping" new canes by pinching off 3 to 4 in of the tip after growth of 18 to 30 in. encourages lateral shoot production. This will increase the number of potential tip layers, and also next year's fruit

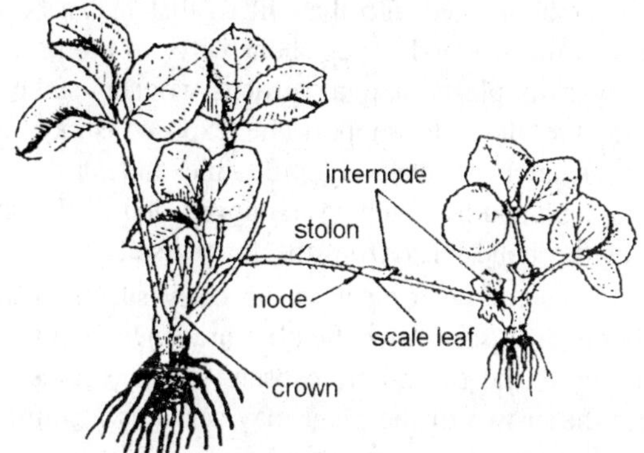

Fig. 4.6. A stolon.

crop. By late summer, the canes begin to arch over, and their tips assume a characteristic appearance in that the terminal ends become elongated and the leaves small and curled to give a "rat-tail" appearance. The best time for layering is when only part of the lateral tips have attained this appearance. If the operation is done too soon, the shoots may continue to grow instead of forming a terminal bud. If it is done too late, the root system will be small.

The tips are preferably layered by hand, a spade or trowel being used to make a hold 3 to 4 in. deep. The end of the shoot is inserted into the hole and covered with soil. For large scale operations, a shallow furrow may be plowed along the row into which the tips are placed. Rooting takes place rapidly, and the plants are ready for digging by the end of the same season. The rooted tip consists of a terminal bud, a large mass of roots, and 6 to 8 in. of the old cane to serve as a "handle" and to mark the location of the new plant. Since the tip layers are tender, easily injured and subject to drying out, digging should be done preferably just before replanting.

Rooted tip layers are planted in the late fall or early spring. New canes develop rapidly during the first season.

Simple Layering

Simple layering is performed by bending a branch to the ground and covering it partially with soil or rooting medium, but leaving the terminal end exposed. The end of the branch is sharply bent to an upright position about 6 to 12 in. back from the tip. The sharp bending of the shoot may be all that is necessary to induce rooting, although additional benefit may be gained by twisting to loosen the bark. Cutting or notching the underside of the stem is often practiced. The bent part of the shoot is next inserted into the soil so that it can be covered to a depth of 3 to 6 in. A wooden peg, bent wire, or stone may be used to hold the layer in place, and a vertical wooden stake should be inserted beside the layer to support the exposed shoot and hold it upright. If the branch is relatively inflexible and hard to bend, the tension may be lessened by notching the upper side of the shoot on the highest part of the bend back from the layer itself.

The usual time for layering is in the early spring, and dormant, 1-year-old shoots are used. Low, flexible branches of the plant which can be bent easily to the ground are chosen. In some cases, the suckers produced near the crown of the plant may serve as a source of shoots for layering. Layering could also be delayed until later in the growing season after the current season's shoots have attained sufficient length and become hardened. This timing would be used, perhaps, with some broad leaved evergreens such as *Rhododendron* and *Magnolia*. As a general rule, shoots older than one year are not satisfactory for layering.

Shoots layered in the spring will usually be adequately rooted by the end of the first growing season and can be removed either in the fall or in the next spring before growth starts. Mature shoots layered in summer should be left through the winter and either removed the next spring before growth begins or left until the end of the second growing season. When the rooted layer is removed from the parent plant, it is treated essentially in the same way as a rooted cutting of

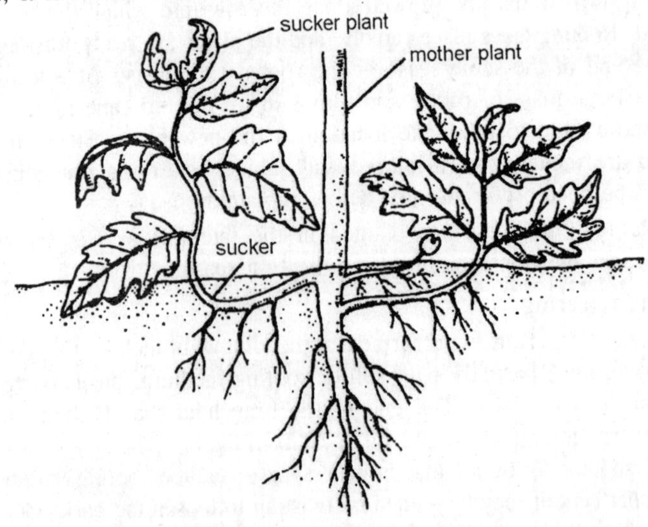

Fig. 4.7. A sucker of Chrysenthemum.

the same plant. Evergreen plants should be potted and kept humid and cool for a time. It should be possible to plant a well-rooted layer of a dormant deciduous plant directly into a nursery row or permanent location if the top is reduced to a size corresponding to the root system. Rooted layers removed in the fall can be planted in a cold frame or shaded greenhouse in a peat-sand mixture. Although defoliation may occur, root activity often continues for several weeks, and by spring the root system may be well developed.

A supply of rooted layers can be produced over a period of years by establishing a stool bed composed of stock plants far enough apart to allow room for all shoots to be layered. This procedure has been used commercially to propagate certain hard-to-root shrubs.

Compound or Serpentine Layering

Compound layering is essentially the same as simple layering, except that the branch is alternately covered and exposed along its length. Generally, the stem is injured or girdled at the lower part of the stem and covered in the same manner as for simple layering. Roots develop at each of these buried sections. The exposed part of the stem should have at least one bud to develop a new shoot. After rooting takes place or at the end of the growing season, the branch is cut in sections made up of the new shoot and the portion containing roots. Several new plants are thus possible from a single branch. This method is used for propagating plants which have long, flexible shoots, such as Muscadine grape. Ornamental vines, such as *Wisteria* and *Clematis*, can also be rooted this way, although such efforts are generally limited to use by amateurs rather than by commercial propagators.

Fig. 4.8. Compound layering of a Philodendron vine.

Air Layering

In air layering, roots form on the aerial part of a plant after the stem is girdled or slit at an angle and enclosed in a moist rooting medium at the point of injury. This method has been used for more than a thousand years, being known in various parts of the world as *Chinese layerage*, *pot layerage*, *circumposition*, *marcottage*, and *gootee*.

The principal limiting factor in air layering has been the difficulty in keeping the rooting medium properly moistened. The ancient Chinese gootee or marcottage method consists of plastering a ball of clay or other soil mixture about the ring or girdle, which is then covered with moss or fiber to hold it together. Above the gootee is a receptacle of water (perhaps a bamboo joint) from which extends a string leading to and wrapped about the gootee to keep it continuously moist. Various modifications of this technique have been made, but all require that the operation be carried out in greenhouses or in regions of high humidity. Enclosures used to surround the rooting medium have included metal or wooden boxes, split flower pots, paper cones, and rubber sheeting. Wrapping with moss alone may be adequate if the humidity is sufficiently high and daily syringing is practiced. These devices have been replaced to a large extent by sheets of polyethylene film, which have the properties of high permeability to gases (carbon dioxide and oxygen), low transmission of water vapour, and sufficient durability to withstand weathering for long periods. By this means it is possible to keep the enclosed rooting medium damp from the plant's natural moisture for long periods of time without continuous attention. Not all plastic films have the same degree of the necessary characteristics; only *polyethylene* film should be used.

Air layering is used to propagate a number of tropical and subtropical trees and shrubs. In Florida, the litchi and the Persian lime (*Citrus aurantifolia*) are propagated commercially by this method. With polyethylene film for wrapping the layers, it is possible to extend the method of air layering out-of-door plants from the tropics to the temperature zones. However, its greatest application is for the amateur horticulturist or the propagator of selected plants for cultural or for scientific purposes rather than for the commercial nurseryman. Air layers are made in the spring on wood of the previous season's growth or, in some cases, in the late summer with partially hardened shoots. Wood older than one year can be used in some cases, but rooting is less satisfactory and the larger plants produced are somewhat more difficult to handle after rooting. With tropical greenhouse plants, layering should be done after several leaves have developed during a period of growth.

The first step in air layering is to girdle or cut the bark of the stem at a point 60 to 12 in. or more from the tip end. A strip of bark

½ to 1 in. wide, depending upon the kind of plant, is completely removed from around the stem. Scraping the exposed surface to insure complete removal of the phloem and cambium is desirable to retard healing. Another procedure is to make a slanting cut about 2 in. long up and to the center of the stem, keeping the two surfaces apart by sphagnum or a piece of wood. Application of a root promoting material, such as indolebutyric acid to the exposed stem, especially to the upper edges or between the two exposed surfaces of a cut, may be beneficial. About two handfuls of only *slightly* moistened sphagnum moss are placed around the stem to enclose the cut surfaces. If the moisture content of the sphagnum moss is too high, decay of the stem tissues will occur.

A piece of polyethylene film 8 to 10 in. square is wrapped carefully about the branch so that the sphagnum moss is completely covered. The ends of the sheet should be folded (as in wrapping meat) with the fold placed on the lower side. The two ends must be twisted to make sure that no water can seep inside. Adhesive tape, such as electrician's waterproof tape, serves well to wrap the ends; the winding should be started well above the end of the plastic film to enclose the ends, particularly the upper one, securely. Budding rubbers and florist's ties are other materials which can be used for this purpose.

The time for removal of the layer from the parent plant is best determined by observing root formation through the transparent film. In some plants, rooting occurs in 2 to 3 months or less. Layers made in spring or early summer are best left until the shoots become dormant in the fall, and are removed at that time. Holly, lilac, *Azalea*, and *Magnolia* should be left for two seasons. In general, it is desirable to remove the layer at a time when it is not actively growing. The period between the removal of the rooted layer from the plant and establishment on its own roots is very critical, and the plant may be lost at that time even though it rooted well. The root system at this time is small in proportion to the top and is incapable of supporting the plant without special precautions. The difficulties of transplanting increase in proportion to the size of the top. Severe pruning usually is advisable to bring the top more in line with the size of the roots, but it may not be imperative if the following precautions are followed. The rooted layer should be potted into a suitable container and placed under cool, humid conditions, such as an enclosed frame, where the plants can be frequently syringed. If this operation is done in the fall, a sufficiently large root system may develop by spring to permit successful growth in the open. Placing the rooted layers under mist for several weeks, followed by gradual hardening-off, is probably the most satisfactory procedure.

Mound (Stool) Layering

Mound or stool layering involves cutting a plant back to the ground during the dormant season and mounding soil or other media around the base of the newly developing shoots in the spring to encourage roots to form on them. Covering with soil keeps the shoots etiolated and encourages root formation. Plants with stiff branches that do not bend easily and which are capable of producing an abundance of shoots from the crown year after year are particularly adapted to this method. Plants commonly propagated in this manner include the clonal apple stocks, certain Mazzard cherry stocks, currants, and gooseberries.

A stool bed can remain in use for 15 to 20 years; therefore it should be on loose, fertile, well-drained soil and established 1 year before the operations begin. The mother plants should be set 12 to 15 in. apart in the row, but the spacing between rows varies under different conditions and types of nursery equipment. Width between rows should be sufficient to allow for cultivation and hilling operations during spring and summer. In England 3½-ft rows are recommended, but in New York a minimum of 8 ft was found desirable. Planting in a shallow trench will permit the shoots to arise from the crown at a low level. Plants are cut back to 15 to 18 in. from the ground and left to grow unchecked for a season, the space between the rows being kept cultivated.

Before new growth starts the next spring, all plants are cut back to an inch above the ground level. Two to five new shoots usually develop from the crown the second year, more in later years. When these shoots have grown 3 to 5 in., loose soil or sawdust is drawn up around each shoot to one-half of its height. When the shoots have grown to a total height of 8 to 10 in., a second hilling operation takes place. Additional rooting medium is again added, to be mounded around the bases of the shoots but not to more than half their total height. In England, with a spacing of 3½ ft between the rows, a ridging plow is drawn between the rows so that two ridges of soil are produced about 15 in. apart. Each row of plants will thus have a ridge on each side. The trench made by the plow is kept cultivated, and the loose soil is shoveled around and between the shoots. The shoots arise close together and, to prevent crowding, should be spread apart by placing a shovelful of soil in the middle of a cluster of shoots. A third and final hilling operation is made in midsummer when the shoots have developed to a total length of approximately 18 in. The base of the shoots will then have been covered with soil to a depth of 6 to 8 in. In the Pacific North west of the United States, sawdust is used almost exclusively as a rooting medium in mound layering. A depression is left in the center of the mound to facilitate water penetration.

Layered shoots of easily propagated plants should have rooted sufficiently by the end of the growing season to be separated from the parent stool for lining out in the nursery row. This operation should not be too early in mild climates, since much root extension takes place during moist autumn months. In severe climates, the operation should be delayed until danger of winter injury is past; after removing the layers, the mother plant must be re-covered by several inches of soil. The rooted layers are cut as close to their base as possible to keep the height of the stool plant low. After the cutting away of the shoots, the mother stool remains exposed until new shoots again reach a height of 3 to 5 in., and the operation is underway again. Shoots which do not root or which root poorly often can be cut off at the same time as the well-rooted ones and treated as hardwood cuttings ready for planting in the nursery row.

Several points which are important to the proper utilization of a stool bed should be kept in mind. To prolong the life of the stool bed and to maintain the plants in a vigorous condition, good fertility should be maintained by annual fertilizer application. Disease, insects, and weeds must be controlled. Supplementary overhead irrigation is essential in some areas to maintain proper moisture conditions in the rooting zone. Soil must be added around the base of the shoots while they are still soft and succulent, not delayed until the shoots have hardened. With more difficult plants, such as certain plum varieties, it is best to add soil before the shoot begin to grow so as to induce etiolation at their bases. Girdling the bases of the shoots by wiring about 6 weeks after they begin to grow will stimulate rooting in many plants. To gradually rejuvenate old stool beds, new layers may be planted in spaces between old ones.

Trench Layering

Trench layering consists of growing a plant or a branch of a plant in a horizontal position in the base of a trench and filling in soil around the new shoots as they develop. Roots develop from the bases of these new shoots.

The first step in this procedure involves the establishment of the mother bed which, as in mound layering, can be used over a period of years. Rooted layers or 1-year-old nursery-budded or grafted trees are planted 18 to 30 in. apart at an angle of 30 to 45 deg. down a row. The rows should be 4 to 5 ft apart—wide enough to allow for cultivation and to draw soil up around the plants to a height of 6 in. The plants are then cut back to a uniform length-18 to 24 in.-and left to grow one season. In some cases- in layering walnuts, for instance—the plants are planted horizontally in the trench and the developing shoots layered the first year.

Before the beginning of growth in the spring, the parent layers are bent over and laid flat on the bottom of a trench dug along the row, about 2 in. deep and wide enough to receive the entire layer. Weak lateral branches are cut to ½ in. in length and strong laterals merely tipped back. Wooden pegs may be used to hold the mother layer in place. Short lengths of wire bent to form a U, or a longer single wire rolled on the end and set at an angle, will be useful to hold down the small shoots. It is important that all parts of the shoot be completely flat on the floor of the trench.

Before the buds swell, the entire layer is covered with 1 to 2 in. of fine soil or other rooting medium such as peat moss, sawdust, or wood shavings. Another inch of medium is added when the developing shoots have pushed through the first soil layer but before their leaves have expanded. Several more additions of soil are made the first 2 or 3 weeks of the growing season to ensure the etiolation of the basal 2 to 3 in. of the shoot. When the shoots have grown an additional 3 to 4 in. soil is again added to half the height of the exposed shoot. Further additions are made at intervals until the bases of the shoots are finally covered to a depth of 6 to 8 in. by midsummer. Roots form on the base of the current season's shoot.

At the end of the growing season after the plants have become dormant—or the next spring—the soil is removed from around the layered shoots, and rooted layers are cut off from the original layered stock as close to the base as possible. Unrooted shoots can be left to be pegged down the nexy year to fill in gaps or to rejuvenate an old bed. New shoots may arise from adventitious buds along the old original layer under ground. However, some of the vigorous shoots growing from the mother plant can be pegged down each year to produce a new supply of rooted layers.

Trench layering is primarily a nursery method for propagating particular fruit tree rootstocks difficult to propagate by other methods. It could also be practiced on established shrubs or trees by bending long, flexible shoots or vines to the ground under the same conditions as is done in simple layering. The shoot is covered along its entire length, but the tip is left exposed. New shoots which develop from the buds along the stem grow upward through the soil, with roots forming at their base. This latter procedure is sometimes known as *continuous layering*.

Plant Modifications Suitable for Natural Layering

Some plants exhibit modifications of their vegetative structure or method of growth which lead to their natural vegetative increase. Those listed below could be considered natural forms of layering and often can be utilized for propagation.

Runners

A *runner* is a specialized stem which develops from the axil of a leaf at the crown of a plant, grows horizontally along the ground, and forms a new plant at one of the nodes. The strawberry is a typical plant propagated in this way. Other plants propagated by runners include bugle (*Ajuga*) and the strawberry geranium (*Saxifraga sarmentose*). Plants of these species grow as a typical rosette or crown.

In most strawberry varieties, runner formation is related to the length of day, runners being produced under day lengths of 12 to 14 hours or more. New plants are produced at alternate nodes. These take root but remain attached to the mother plant for some time. New runners may in turn be produced by the daughter plants. The connecting stems die in the late fall and winter, and each daughter plant becomes separate from the others. In propagating by runners, the rooted daughter plants are dug when they have become well rooted, and then transplanted to the desired locations.

Stolons

Stolon is a term used to describe various types of horizontally growing stems that produce adventitious roots when in contact with the soil. Specifically these are prostrate or sprawling stems, as found in *Cornus stolonifera*, for instance. The underground stem of the potato that terminates in the tuber is a stolon. The term is sometimes used to describe the tip layers of black raspberry and blackberry or the runners of strawberry. In such plants, the stolon could be treated as a naturally occurring rooted layer, cut from the parent plant and transplanted.

Offsets

An *offset* is a characteristic type of lateral shoot or branch which develops from the base of the main stem in certain plants. This term is applied generally to a shortened, thickened stem of rosette-like appearance. Many bulbs reproduce by producing typical offset bulblets from their base. The term offset (or *offshoot*, as is sometimes used) also applies to lateral branches arising on stems of monocotyledons. The date palm produces lateral shoots from the base of the plant by which it is propagated. The pineapple is also propagated by offsets, although in commercial culture these are termed ratoons, suckers, or slips, depending upon the location on the plant where they are produced. Lateral shoots arising from rhizomes, as in the banana or orchid, are also offsets or offshoots.

Offsets are removed by cutting them close to the main stem with a sharp knife. If it is well rooted, the offset can be potted as is done with any rooted cutting. If insufficient roots are present, the shoot is placed in a favourable rooting medium and treated as a leafy stem cutting.

In cases in which offset development is meager, cutting off the main rosette may stimulate the development of offsets from the old stem just as removing the terminal bud stimulates lateral shoots in any other type of plant. For instance, in *Echeveria* the main stem may elongate so that the plant becomes a fleshy rosette borne on top of a fleshy, bare stem. The rosette, with a short piece of stem, may be removed and rooted, and new offsets will develop from buds at the base. It is desirable that this operation be carried out while the stem is somewhat soft and succulent, rather than allowing it to become hard and woody. Offshoots of the date palm do not root readily if separated from the parent plant. They are usually layered for a year prior to removing.

Suckers

A *sucker* is a shoot which arises on a plant from below ground. The most precise use of this term is to designate a shoot which arises from an adventitious bud on a root. However, in practice, shoots which arise from the vicinity of the crown are also referred to as suckers even though originating from stem tissue. Nurserymen generally designate any shoot produced from the rootstock below the bud union of a budded tree as a sucker and refer to the operation of removing them as "suckering". In contrast, a shoot arising from a latent bud of a stem several years old, as, for instance, on the trunk or main branches, should be termed a *watersprout*.

The tendency to "sucker" is a characteristic possessed by some plants and not by others. The ability of a plant to sucker and the ability of a plant to grow from root cuttings are closely related. In such cases, however, nurserymen prefer to use root cuttings rather than depend on naturally produced suckers. Since suckers arise from adventitious buds, they may show juvenile characteristics.

Suckers are dug out and cut from the parent plant. In some cases part of the old root may be retained, although most new roots arise from the base of the sucker. It is important to dig the sucker out rather than pull it, to avoid injury to its base. Suckers are treated essentially as a rooted layer or as a cutting, in case few or no roots have formed. They are usually dug during the dormant season.

Crowns

The term *crown* as generally used in horticulture designates that part of a plant at the surface of the ground from which new shoots are produced. In trees or shrubs with a single trunk, the crown is principally a points of location near the ground surface marking the general transition zone between stem and root. In herbaceous perennials, the crown is the part of the plant from which new shoots arise annually. The crown of many herbaceous perennials consists of many branches, each being the base of the current season's stem, which originated from the base of the preceding year's branch. These new shoots are stimulated to grow from the base of the old stem as it dies back after blooming. Adventitious roots develop along the base of the new shoots. These new shoots eventually flower either the same year they are produced or the following year. As a result of the annual production of new shoots and the drying back of old shoots, the crown may become extensive within a period of a relatively few years.

In certain plants for example, the strawberry or the African violet (*Saintpaulla*)—the stem is a short and thickened structure from which the leaves are produced in a rosette-like arrangement. The entire body of the plant is often referred to as the crown. Lateral shoots or offsets are produced from the base of the crown. An old plant may be composed of a number of "crowns" or "crown divisions" which have been produced in this manner.

Multibranched woody shrubs may develop extensive crowns. Although an individual woody stem may persist for a number of years, new, vigorous shoots are continuously produced from the crown, and eventually crowd out the older shoots. If left undisturbed, such shrubs develop into extensive thickets. Under normal handling, the older shoots are regularly removed by pruning to give way to the younger, more vigorous shoots.

Division of the crown is an important method of propagation for herbaceous perennials, and to some extent for woody shrubs, because of its simplicity and reliability. Such characteristics make this method particularly useful to the amateur or professional gardener who is generally interested in only a modest increase of a particular plant. Many herbaceous perennials must be divided every 2 to 3 years to prevent the plants from becoming over-crowded.

Crowns of outdoor herbaceous perennials are usually divided in the spring just before growth begins or in late summer or autumn at the end of the growing season. As a general rule, those plants which bloom in the spring and summer and produce new growth after blooming should be divided in the fall. Those which bloom in summer and fall and make little or no new growth until spring should be divided in early spring. Potted plants are divided when they become too large for the particular container in which they are growing.

In crown division, plants are dug and cut into sections with a knife. In herbaceous perennials such as the Shasta daisy or aster, where an abundance of new rooted offshoots are produced from the crown, each may be broken from the old crown and planted separately, the older part of the plant clump being discarded. If a large clump is desired, then a section of the old crown bearing a number of new shoots from its base may be used. In the case of plants in which the crown consists of a number of rosettes or offsets, as occurs in the African violet, division should be made between each of the rosettes, but roots should be present on each section.

Shrubs may be divided in the same manner with a shovel or hatchet. Such an operation should be carried out at a time when the plant is dormant. The top should be cut back and the roots trimmed at the time of divisions, and each section planted as a new shrub.

5

REGENERATION OF PLANTS

It is possible to regenerate whole plants from protoplasts, single cells and small pieces of plant tissue because plant cells are totipotent. Totipotency means that plant cells can be induced through appropriate culture conditions to develop along a 'programmed' pathway leading to the formation of an entire new plant. The regenerated plant is identical to the donor plant from which the cells were derived. Plant regeneration by tissue culture is now an essential and fundamental procedure for biotechnology and plant breeding, and is used commercially for the asexual propagation of many horticultural and agricultural plants.

One of the remarkable expressions of totipotency is the unique capacity of plants to produce normal embryos from single cells in somatic tissues or callus in culture. The process is known as *somatic embryogenesis* and the embryos formed can be cultured *in vitro* to regenerate an entire new plant. Somatic embryogenesis was first described in carrot callus cells more than 40 years ago. Since then protocols and procedures for somatic embryogenesis have been developed for several species and these are used both for the regeneration of plants and as a research model to study early morphogenetic and regulatory events in plant embryogenesis.

In addition to somatic embryogenesis, regeneration can be accomplished through other developmental pathways. In the simplest case, small pieces of tissue (known as *explants*) are excised from mature plants and under sterile conditions transferred to an appropriate nutrient culture medium. Through manipulation of the concentrations of added phytohormones in the culture medium, formation of a desired organ is induced (organogenesis).Typically, shoot development (caulogenesis) is induced on media formulated for the purpose. The shoots that differentiate are then transferred to a rooting medium for root development (rhizogenesis) leading to the formation of plantlets and entire plants.

Regeneration via Somatic Embryogenesis

Plants commonly reproduce through the development of zygotic embryos. Zygotic embryos develop from zygotes that are formed as a result of the events of fertilization within the embryo sac of the ovule. Through an orderly progression of cell divisions and differentiation, the embryo is formed and matures. The transition from zygote to embryo is known as *zygotic embryogenesis* and is the starting point of the life cycle of the plant. Further growth and development of the mature embryo is suspended as it becomes desiccated in the mature seed, but growth resumes during germination to form the emerging seedling. During embryogenesis, the pattern elements of the plant body are established including the shoot apical meristem and the root apical meristem. Almost the entire plant body is produced post-embryonically from these apical meristems.

In plants, embryogenesis is not strictly dependent on fertilization. In many plant species, embryos can originate asexually either naturally through apomixis in the seed or they can be induced in tissue culture. Apomitic embryos may be derived from unfertilized eggs or from the somatic tissue of the ovule and are genetically identical to the maternal parent.

Asexual embryos can also be induced to form *in vitro* from a single cell, or a group of cells originating from a wide range of gametophytic and somatic tissues. Androgenic embryo's develop from *in vitro* cultured microspores (immature pollen grains), and somatic embryos are induced from somatic tissue in culture. In both cases, the manipulation of the concentration of plant hormones and growth regulators in the culture medium and/or the application of a stress treatment is required for embryo induction. The nature of the donor tissue and the induction treatment together determines whether embryos develop directly from single cells or indirectly via callus tissue.

The process of development of embryos from somatic cells or tissues is called *somatic embryogenesis*. The development of somatic embryos closely resembles that of zygotic embryos. All the plants derived by somatic embryogenesis from a particular tissue culture are genetically alike. Consequently, micropropagation through somatic embryogenesis is an efficient method of producing large numbers of identical elite or transgenic plants.

Somatic embryos are induced from cultured callus cells by manipulation of the culture conditions. In carrot, this is a simple procedure and consists of the following:

1. The establishment of a callus cell line from explants of hypocotyl tissue excised from individual seedlings, grown under sterile conditions;
2. Transfer of cells to low auxin medium;
3. Dilution of cells to a low density.

Not all cells in a culture are capable of forming embryos. Embryogenic competence resides within a subpopulation of the culture called proembryogenic cell masses (PEMs). The cells of PEMs are small with a dense cytoplasm and are full of starch grains. In contrast, non-embryogenic callus cells are large and highly vacuolated. These characteristics can be used to enrich the population of embryogenic cells in a culture through selecting the PEMs out from the culture by sieving or density gradient fractionation.

Somatic embryos pass through the same sequence of characteristic morphological stages as zygotic but lack a desiccation phase and grow directly into plantlets. The first recognizable stage is the globular stage, in which the embryo is spherical. In zygotic embryogenesis, the globular embryo is attached to the maternal tissue by the suspensor. The globular stage 4 somatic embryos grows from PEMs within 5-7 days after the cultures have been transferred to a low auxin medium. In contrast to embryos developing in liquid culture, embryos grown on a solid medium may develop a small suspensor-like region. After 2-3 days of isodiametric growth, the globular stage changes to bilaterally symmetrical growth to form an oblong structure. This is the beginning of the heart stage, which is characterized by the expansion of the two cotyledons. The heart stage is followed by the torpedo stage clearly marked by the elongation of the hypocotyl and the beginning of radicle formation. Approximately 18-21 days after induction, plantlets are discernible. These plantlets have green cotyledons, elongated hypocotyls and radicles with clearly developed root hairs. These plantlets can then be transferred to solid media to complete the regeneration of whole plants.

Control of Embryogenesis

The embryogenic competence of a culture is at its highest when the culture is relatively young, i.e. up to a year after its initiation.

However, cultures that have been repeatedly subcultured and maintained in an undifferentiated state at high auxin concentrations for many years may progressively lose their embryogenic capacity.

Auxin is the most important growth regulator involved in both the induction of somatic embryogenesis and the proper morphogenic development of the embryo. Carrot cell cultures require the auxin analogue 2,4-D for embryogenic competence, but the continuous presence of this auxin blocks further development beyond the PEM stage and in some cell lines up to but not beyond the globular stage. It follows that removal of this block by shifting the culture to low auxin or to auxin-free media induces embryogenesis. As embryogenesis proceeds, the developing embryos begin to synthesize their own auxins. Furthermore, the polar transport of auxin is necessary for normal morphogenesis beyond the globular stage. In addition to added auxins, other exogenous molecules are implicated in somatic embryogenesis. These include proteins that are secreted into the culture medium such as endochitinases and arabinogalactan (AGPs) proteins.

Details of the molecular events that occur during the induction and progress of somatic embryogenesis are largely lacking. However, many attempts are being made to identify specific genes that control early events in embryogenesis. These genes would be useful as research tools to study in detail the transition of somatic cells into embryogenesis. Furthermore, these genes and/or their products could find application as specific markers suitable for the manual or automated separation of embryogenic from non-embryogenic cells in mixed cell populations. So far, the majority of genes identified appear to control basic developmental processes and are not restricted to the embryo. However, more recently, a gene has been identified that is expressed in small cell populations of carrot cultures during the initiation of embryogenesis. This gene, a somatic embryogenesis kinase encodes a Leu-rich repeat (LRR) transmembrane receptor-like kinase (RLK). DcSERK is expressed in early somatic embryos and in globular zygotic embryos. DcSERK and its *Arabidopsis* analogue AtSERK 1 are thought to be part of a signalling pathway that switch on an embryogenesis development programme.

Regeneration via Organogenesis

For many species, it is possible to regenerate plants from meristematic tissues. For example, the formation of multiple shoots can be induced from shoot tip and axillary bud explants by using tissue culture media with defined phytohormone concentrations and/or combinations. The many shoots that are formed can be separated and grown on a suitable rooting medium to produce plantlets.

In some species, it is also possible to regenerate plants directly by organogenesis from explants of adventive and non-meristematic tissue or indirectly through callus tissue. As a general principle, the regeneration is induced by variations in auxin/cytokinin ratio.

The regeneration of plants from tissue explants by organogenesis is extensively used commercially for the micropropagation of economically important plants. Typically, this procedure consists of four stages:

(i) *Initiation stage*. A selected explant (a piece of tissue) is excised from a selected donor plant, surface sterilized and transferred to a solid culture medium to establish an aseptic culture.

(ii) *Multiplication stage*. A growing explant is induced to produce vegetative shoots by transfer to a medium containing cytokinin

(iii) *Rooting* or *pre-plant stage*. The differentiated shoots are induced to produce adventitious roots by shifting to a medium that contains an auxin. For easily rooted plants, an auxin is usually not necessary and many commercial protocols omit this step.

(iv) *Acclimatization*. Growing, rooted shoots are removed from tissue culture medium and placed in soil. These plantlets are developed under carefully controlled conditions where they, are gradually acclimatized to conditions such as low humidity as tissue-cultured plants are extremely susceptible to wilting.

PROCEDURE

A general protocol is presented for the regeneration of viable seedlings from callus of both monocots and dicots, using transfer from a high-auxin, callus-inducing medium to a hormone-free medium. In our laboratory, we grow callus in Petri dishes, then initially transfer embryos to culture tubes (Universal bottles or plastic equivalents) before moving growing seedlings on into larger vessels. A protocol for *Arabidopsis* regeneration based on the method of Mather and Koncz (1998) is also presented. This is a commonly used method for transformed plants in which shoots are initialed fast, followed by roots. In our hands, we expect to obtain viable plants about 3 months after callus initiation using this type of method. In addition, we briefly summarize a method for clonal propogation of gymnosperm trees. Techniques based on this have been successfully commercialized for the bulk production of clonal trees.

PROTOCOL

Embryogenesis from Callus in a Dicot (e.g. Carrot) or Monocot (Cereals, Rice)

Equipment

Binocular microscope

Growth cabinet (25°C.16 h tight, 8 h dark).

Materials and reagents (sterile)

Embryogenic cultures growing on (Dicot) MS medium plus 2-5 mg l^{-1} 2,4-D, 0.6 mg l^{-1} kinetin and 2% sucrose (Monocot) MS medium plus 0.5 mg l^{-1} 2,4-D and 3% sucrose (3-6 weeks old, then subcultured every 4 weeks).

Ethanol 95%

Liquid MS medium 150 ml

Petri dishes containing MS medium minus hormones + 0.8% agar + 2% sucrose

Universal tubes or similar containing slopes of MS agar without hormones + 2% sucrose + 0.8% agar

Kilner jars or plasticware containing MS agar without 2,4-D or cytokinin + 2% sucrose

Plasticware or pots with translucent covers containing sterile potting compost

Sterile dissecting instruments.

Procedure

1. Remove 0.5-1.0 cm^2 pieces of callus to the surface of the MS agar without hormones.
2. Incubate in 16 h light : 8 h dark at 25°C.
3. Embryos visible first as green areas will begin to form after 2 weeks on the surface of the callus. Under the dissecting microscope, globular, heart-shaped and torpedo-shaped embryos will be seen.
4. Carefully remove the embryos and subculture them onto MS agar in the absence of hormones in Universal tubes until a viable seedling is formed.
5. Subculture seedlings to Kilner jars or equivalent plasticware until four to five leaves are formed.
6. Wash the roots in fungicide (e.g. Benomyl, 0.02%) and transfer to sterile potting compost in a humid container. Gradually reduce humidity until the seedling is fully acclimated.

Plant Regeneration by Organogenesis

Equipment

Binocular microscope

Orbital incubator at 120 rpm, 25°C, 16 h light : 8 h dark

Incubator or growth room 25°C, 16 h light: 8 h dark

Microfuge

Universal tubes

Kilner jars

Sterile forceps, scalpel, scissors

9-cm Petri dishes.

Materials and reagents

10% sodium hypochlorite with 0.1% detergent (Tween,Triton)

Sterile distilled water

0.5 MS medium, 0.8% agar (pH 5.8) (in 9 cm Petri dishes)

MS medium with 3% sucrose (pH 5.8)

0.5 MS medium with 0.5% sucrose and 0.8% agar (in Kilner jar or equivalent)

Callus medium: MS medium with 3% sucrose (pH 5.8) + 2,4-D, 0.5 mg l^{-1}; IAA, 2.0 mg l^{-1}; IPAR, 0.5 mg l^{-1}; NAA, 0.5 mg l^{-1}; 0.8% agar (in 9 cm Petri dishes)

Shoot medium: MS medium with 3% sucrose (pH 5.8) + IPAR, 2.0 mg l^{-1}; NAA, 0.05 mg l^{-1}; 0.8% agar (in 9 cm Petri dishes and Universal tubes or Kilner jars or similar plasticware)

Root medium: MS medium with 3% sucrose (pH 5.8) + IAA, 1.0 mg l^{-1}; IBA, 0.2 mg l^{-1}; IPAR, 0.2 mg l^{-1}; 0.8% agar (in Universal tubes or Kilner jars or similar plasticware).

Procedure

1. Surface-sterilize 0.1 g seeds in sodium hypochlorite in an Eppendorf tube for 15 min with shaking.
2. Pellet by brief centrifugation, pour off the supernatant and wash 5 × with sterile distilled water.
3. Germinate the seeds In Petri dishes containing 0.5 × MS medium 0.8% agar in 16 h light : 8 h dark at 25°C.
4. After 1 week, place seedlings in 250 ml flask with 35 ml of MS medium with 3% sucrose and no agar. Cap and place on orbital shaker at 120 rpm, 16 h light : 8 h dark 25°C for 15-20 days (this gives a proliferation of root material).

5. Harvest the roots by cutting them from the seedlings.
6. Place on callus medium in a Petri dish and incubate at 25°C.
7. When callus forms (2-3 weeks) transfer to shoot medium in a Petri dish and incubate for 2 weeks until shoots form.
8. Transfer to shoot medium in a Universal tube or similar.
9. When 4-6 leaves have formed, transfer to root medium in a Universal tube or Kilner jar or plastic equivalent until roots form.
10. Finally, allow to form smali seedlings in a larger Kilner jar or equivalent on 0.5 MS medium 0.8% agar and 0.5% sucrose.

Somatic Embryogenesis of Norway Spruce using a Suspension Culture Step

Equipment

Orbital incubator (150 rpm 20-25°C)

Conical flasks (250 ml)

Aluminium foil caps (sterile)

Universal tubes or similar plasticware

Fine nylon mesh sterile

9 cm filter paper (sterile)

9 cm Petri dishes

Desiccator containing saturated ammonium nitrate (yields a relative humidity of 63%).

Materials and reagents

Maintenance medium: 0.5 strength Litvay's medium with L-glutamine, 250 mg l^{-1}; casein hydrolysate, 500 mg l^{-1}; 2,4-D, 2 mg l^{-1}; benzyladenine 1 mg l^{-1}; sucrose 1%

Wash medium: 0.5 strength Litvay's medium with L-glutamine, 250 mg l^{-1}; casein hydrolysate, 500 mg l^{-1}; sucrose 3%

Development medium: 0.5 strength Litvay's medium with L-glutamine, 250 mg l^{-1}; casein hydrolysate, 500 mg l^{-1}; sucrose 3%, PEG 4000, 7.5%, ABA 4 μm; agar 0.8%

Plantlet conversion medium: 0.5 strength Litvay's medium with L-glutamine, 250 mg l^{-1}; casein hydrolysate, 500 mg l^{-1}; sucrose 2%; agar 0.6%

Procedure

1. Select white, translucent embryogenic tissue from the callus.
2. Subculture to fresh plates, every 2-4 weeks for two to four subcultures.

3. Transfer rapidly growing embryogenic callus to a 250 ml conical flask containing 20-50 ml of maintenance medium. Incubate on orbital incubator at 150 rpm.
4. Replace medium every week by allowing cells to settle and withdrawing spent medium.
5. After 4-6 weeks, remove an aliquot of suspension to 50 ml of fresh maintenance medium.
6. Repeat, reducing the amount of inoculum weekly (usually to 10 ml in 50 ml of medium) until an embryogenic suspension appears (test different volumes of inoculum in several flasks and choose the one giving most embryogenic activity).
7. Sieve the cell suspension in a fine nylon mesh. Transfer 10 g sieved cells to 50 ml of wash medium in a 250 ml flask.
8. Swirl constantly and pipette onto filter paper supports floating on the surface of development medium in Petri dishes.
9. Transfer the filter paper to fresh development medium every 2-4 weeks. Maintain for 6-8 weeks. By this stage, embryos at the cotyledonary stage will have developed.
10. Transfer filter paper supports with embryos to empty sterile Petri dishes in a desiccator at 63% relative humidity for 2 weeks.
11. After desiccation, embryos may be stored at –20°C or transferred to plantlet conversion medium while still on the filter paper support. They should be maintained under low light for 1-2 days.
12. Select individual embryos and place on plantlet conversion medium in Universal tubes or similar for 4-6 weeks.
13. Wash roots free of medium and place in sterile soil in pots or trays with translucent covers. Maintain a high relative humidity for the first week.

6

VEGETATIVE REPRODUCTION

In the filamentous fungi the basic unit of structure is the hypha. When massed together the hyphae form a mycelium. The individual hyphae are tube-like structures which exhibit polarised growth and may produce branches at sub-apical sites. In effect hyphal growth ,involves two components, an increase in volume which results from extension of the tip and an increase in protoplasmic contents. These involve a complex interaction of biosynthesis of macromolecules and their subsequent organisation into recognisable physical structures. The latter aspect of growth occurs over long distances within an individual hypha. In recent years fungal hyphae have been the subject of broad investigation in regard to their ultrastructure, biochemistry and physiology and it is now possible to devise models relating these features to the growth process.

HYPHAL CYTOLOGY

Light microscope studies, some of the earliest reports appearing in the latter part of last century, provided a lot of fundamental information about the fungal hypha which has stood the test of time and still remains central in our thinking on hyphal growth. Of particular interest were the reports an apical growth of hyphae and the discovery of the Spitzenkorper, a zone at the extreme apex of septate fungi that can be stained with iron-haemotoxylin. More sophisticated methods, e.g. autoradiography, fluorescence microscopy and phase contrast microscopy, have confirmed these early descriptions. The Spitzenkorper appears to be associated with active growth because it is not present in non-growing hyphpae. Another feature of growing hyphae, just resolvable by phase contrast microscopy in good preparations particularly

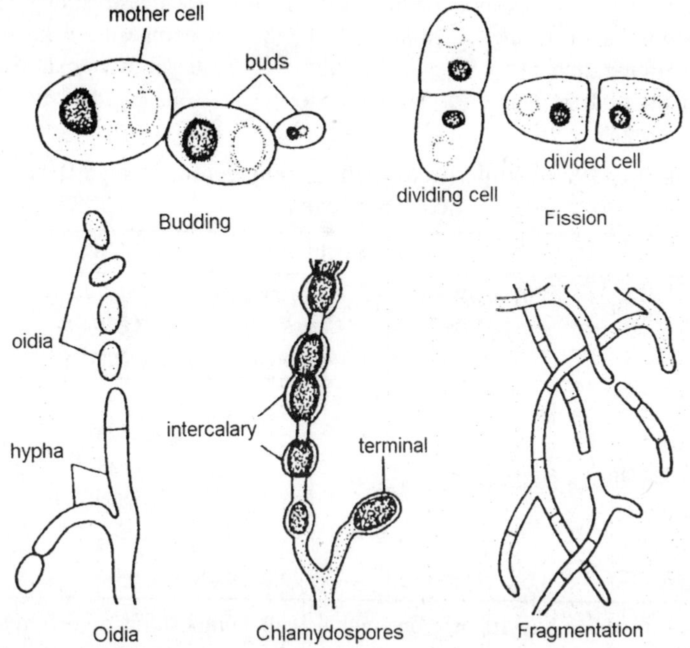

Fig. 6.1. Different types of vegetative reproduction in fungi.

of the large hyphae of Zygomycetes, is the presence of small particles which can be seen migrating towards the hyphal apex.

The tip region involved in increasing hyphal volume is known as the extension zone. The length of this zone has been determined in various ways including observations on the displacement of markers placed on hyphae and more recently by the use of optical brightener compounds, manufactured for incorporation into detergents, which bind to the extension zone of hypha of many fungi.

Hyphal Ultrastructure

Many of the early observations made by light microscopy, e.g. the Spitzenkorper and movement of particles, have been further resolved by the use of electron microscopy. However, since the proliferation of the fungal hypha involves the syntheses of new components of the rigid hyphal wall the following discussion will start with this component of the hypha.

Composition and Architecture of the Hyphal Wall

The boundary of the fungal hypha is the rigid cell wall. The analysis of the chemical composition of the wall involves a detailed procedure and preparation of the material prior to investigation. An unknown factor is the possibility of changes in composition during these preparative procedures. Once the wall material is prepared a protocol for fractionation is used and the result from an analysis are given in table 6.1.

Table 6.1. Wall composition of fungi representative of different taxonomic groups.

	% Composition		
	Phycomycete Phytophthora heveae	*Ascomycete Chaetomium globosum*	*Basidiomycete Agaricus bisporus*
Cellulose	36	—	—
Chitin	—	13.9	43
α-1,3-glucan	—	—	14
β-1,3-glucan	54	54.1	27
Lipid	2.5	3	1.5
Protein	4.6-6.7	29	16

From the many reports on hyphal wall composition of different fungal species several basic features arises. Typically the walls are comprised of polysaccharides (75–80 per cent on a dry weight basis), protein, lipid, and melanin. A variety of polysaccharides occur–the homopolymers β-1,3-glucan, β-1,4-glucan, α-1,3, glucan, chitin, chitosan, and a variety of heteropolymers which are made up from mannose, galactose, fucose and xylose. Of these different polymers the β-1,3-glucan is found more broadly across the various taxonomic groups of fungi. The analyses of wall composition of the many fungi investigated has revealed the interesting situation shown in table 6.2 where there is a relationship between the nature of the two major polymers present and the different taxonomic groups.

Examining of the organisation of the various polymers in the fungal wall. Using a combination of biochemical and chemical techniques in association with electron microscopic observations, has shown the wall to be a highly structured entity. Of the two major polymers present in the wall, one occurs in microfibrillar form making up a skeletal network and the other is a matrix material that form a filling for the spaces of the network. Additional polysaccharide polymers occur in either of these forms and in some. Ascomycetes another network comprised of glycoprotein is also found. In thin sections viewed with the electron

Table 6.2. Cell wall composition and fungal taxonomy.

Major polymers	*Taxonomic group*
Cellulose-β-1,3-glucan	Oomycetes
Cellulose-chitin	Hyphochytridiomycetes
Chitin-chitosan	Zygomycetes
Chitin-β-glucan	Chytridiomycetes
	Euascomycetes
	Homobasidromycetes
Mannan-β-glucan	Hemiascomycetes
Chitin-mannan	Heterobasidiomycetes

microscope, the wall is seen to be made up of two or more layers. In every case the microfibrillar skeletal material forms the inner layer adjacent to the plasma membrane, with the amorphous matrix, and other material when present, as the outer layers. Differences are found, however, between the wall structure in the apical extension zone and in the sub-apical region. The wall of the extension zone is called the primary wall and is comprised almost entirely of the microfibrillar wall component but may have some amorphous component. In the sub-apical region the secondary wall is deposited on the outer surface of the primary wall and involves the thickening of existing microfibrils, the addition of new ones and the formation of the amorphous and other wall components.

The hyphal wall can be removed by digestion in a mixture of the enzymes specific for the major polysaccharide components. If this digestion is done in an osmotically stabilised medium the cytoplasmic contents of the hyphae are then released as discrete units termed protoplasts. Protoplasts have proved useful for studies on wall biogenesis in fungi because when incubated in an osmotically stabilised growth medium they regenerate a new wall and revert to the normal hyphal form.

Septa

Septa of crosswalls occurring irregularly along the length of a hypha are a feature of all fungal groups. The septa are produced in the apical region in what appears to be controlled manner. With certain exceptions, the septa found in representative species of particular taxonomic groups are characteristic for the group. The simplest type is that which forms a total barrier across the hypha but more common are septa with pores. These pores are central in location, unless the septum is multiperforate. In many fungi with porous septa, each pore has a characteristic structure. The Woronin body–a membrane bounded, electron-dense proteinaceous structure– always remains adjacent to the pore despite cytoplasmic streaming. In species lacking the Woronin body, a proteinaceous crystal is found. Both structures are thought to have the same function, namely to block the pores of septa in older regions of the hyphae.

The septa of Basidiomycete fungi, except the rust and smut fungi, are more complex. They have a central pore but the margin of this is swollen and is known as the *dolipore*. On each side of the pore is a hemispherical cap of perforated membrane which is thought to be formed from an extension of the endoplasmic reticulum.

The chemical composition of the septa is unknown except for two species, *Neurospora crassa* and *Schizophyllum commune*. In the former microfibrils of chitin are found in septa of young (one day old) mycelium but as time passes both sides of the septum are covered with an amorphous proteinaceous material. The β-1,3-glucan and glycoprotein components of the hyphal wall are not found in the septum. In *Schizophyllum commune* the septa contain chitin and a β-glucan, both of which are also found in the hyphal wall. The α-glucan found in the wall is absent from the septa. Dissolution of the septa in this and other Basidiomycetes is an important feature of reproductive development.

Protoplast

Ultrastructural observations on the fungal hypha have revealed an interesting picture of organisation. The apical region of a hypha may be conveniently sub-divided into two zones; the tip or apical zone, characterised by the presence of vesicles and ribosomes, and the sub-apical zone in which the organelles characteristic of a heterotrophic eukaryote are found. The presence of vesicles at the tip zone is of particular interest and has led to the formulation of models explaning their involvement in wall formation and hence hyphal growth. The small particles seen by light microscopy have been interpreted as vesicles and the organisation of the latter at the apex provide an understanding of the nature of the Spitzenkorper. The vesicles fall into two groups on the basis of size. The smaller ones, termed microvesicles, have shown to contain chitin synthase in several fungi, and their involvement in wall synthesis must therefore be presumed.

The arrangement of vesicle in the tip zone is a variable feature with different patterns being characteristic for the different taxonomic

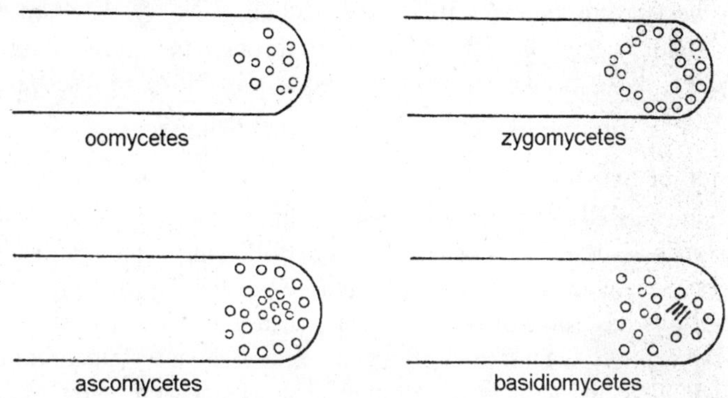

Fig. 6.2. Diagrammatic representation of the organization in hyphal apices of fungi from different taxonomic groups.

groups. In the Oomycetes both sizes of vesicles are found distributed in a random fashion. In electron micrographs, however, the larger one is seen to contain electron opaque, granular material whereas the microvesicles have more uniform contents. The sub-apical zone of these fungi is characterised by large numbers of dictyosomes frequently seen in association with cytoplasmic vesicles. Some micrographs have shown the vesicles to occur in lines between the dictyosomes and the apex, strongly suggesting a relationship between the two organelles and events in the tip zone. In representatives of other taxonomic groups the organisation of the apical vesicles shows more order. In the Zygomycetes the larger vesicles form a distinct layer beneath the plasma membrane giving the appearance of a hemispherical cap. The microvesicles occur randomly in the region behind this cap. The microvesicles in the apical zone of Ascomycete fungi occur as a spherical cluster surrounded by the large vesicles and the complete cluster is located just behind the apical wall. The Basidiomycete arrangement is somewhat smaller with a spherical arrangement of large vesicles surrounding a vesicle free zone which includes a dense core of unidentifiable structure. The vesicular arrangements seen in the tip zones of these fungi are probably the Spitzenkorpes described from light micrographs.

Vesicles are also seen in the sub-apical zones of the hyphae of fungi. Regions of cytoplasm occur that are free or ribosomes and in these, membranous structures corresponding to the cisternae of golgi bodies are present, associated with vesicles. In the sub-apical region vesicles also occur intermingled with the other organelles, nuclei, mitochondria, endomembrane components and ribosomes. Involvement of the vesicles in events at the apex, including the synthesis of the hyphal wall, necessitate their transport through the mass of other organelles, but a mechanism for this process remains to be discovered.

Biosynthesis of Cell Wall Polymers

Location of Synthesis

As mentioned previously the existence of an apical region of hyphal extension was described many years ago following light microscope observations. Substantial experimental evidence confirming these observations has come from investigations in which hyphae were fed with radioactive sugars, e.g. ^{14}C glucose, ^{14}C N-acetylglucosamine, and then subjected to autoradiography. The sugars were shown to be rapidly incorporated into polymer such as chitin and glucan at the extreme apex. When a pulse feeding of isotopic sugar is followed by a so-called cold chase, i.e. replacement of the isotope by the normal sugar, autoradiographs reveal that the area of wall just behind the apex has become labelled, but the apical zone itself is free of label. Quantification of the autoradiographs can be achieved by counts of the silver grains.

The grain density is highest at the extreme apex faling sharply at a distance of 10–15 μm behind the apex. The conclusion of these observations is that de novo wall formation occurs at the apex, but some sub-apical wall deposition cannot be ruled out. In the autoradiographs referred to above, a low but uniform number of silver grains can be seen in the wall of sub-apical regions. This incorporation is believed to reside in the microfibrils which increase in size. In *Neurospora crassa* the glycoprotein reticulum of the wall is laid down in the sub-apical zone and not at the tip. The dominance of the apex is relation to the deposition of wall polymers can be overcome experimentally, e.g. by growth in the presence of cycloheximide or by osmotic shock, and under these conditions radioactive substrates are incorporated uniformly throughout the wall. The effect of these treatments therefore is to overrule the mechanism that controls apical wall synthesis.

Biochemical aspects of Wall Synthesis

Of all the wall polymers described in the filamentous fungi, the biosynthesis of chitin is the most extensively documented. The enzyme involved in the final stage of polymer formation is chitin synthase which catalyses the reaction

$$\text{UDP—N acetylglucosamine} + (\text{N-acetylglucosamine})_n \xrightarrow{Mg^{2+}} \text{UDP} + \text{chitin}$$

The supply of UDP – N-acetylglucosamine, which is necessary for continued synthesis, is from a pathway starting with fructose-6-phosphate and glutamine as precursors. The complete pathway has not been followed in a single organism but there are descriptions of the four enzymes involved from different fungi.

The cytoplasmic location of chitin synthase has not been fully established although there is strong evidence to support a membrane site. In cell homogenates the highest levels of chitin synthase are found in the microsomal fraction which is rich in membrane. In the intact hypha the functional site of enzyme is assumed to be on the outer surface of the plasma membrane. Evidence for this view stems from several experimental sources, in autoradiographs viewed with an electron microscope silver grains were found on the membrane surface and in the wall, and never in the cytoplasm, and protoplasts isolated from hyphae by digestion of the walls are able to synthesise new wall material and revert to the normal morphology. Recent studies on the yeast form of *Mucor rouxii* showed that microfibrils of chitin could be produced *in vitro*. The preparation of chitin synthase used took the form of particles obtained by a detailed purification procedure. The particles, called chitosomes, were subsequently shown to be microvesicular structures, 40–70 nm in diameter. During microfibril synthesis the chitosomes undergo a transformation such that when the microfibril is formed the shell of the membrane is shed. The *in vivo* function of the chitosome, which has since been described in several other fungi, is presumed to be that of conveyor of chitin synthase to the cell surface where the chitin polymer is normally synthesised.

Data on glucan synthesis in growing hyphae is more limited. In Neurospora crassa where a β-1,3-glucanis present as an amorphous component in the wall, a β-1,3-glucan synthase has been found in cell wall preparations. Also in *Phytopthora cinnamomi*, which has a β-1,3, β-1,6-glucan fibrillar wall component, a synthase was also found in the wall fraction, that catalysed the synthesis of the polymer from UDP-glucose. When the fungus was grown under conditions of high glucose concentration, thus reducing the level of protease in the hyphae, a membrane bound enzyme was also found that catalysed the formation of a polymer which contained only β-1,3-linkages. A synthase system associated with the formation of the wall β-1,4-glucan has been found in *Saprolegnia monoica*, an Oomycete fungus. The enzyme has been detected in fractions containing wall and microsomal material and more recently in vesicles believed to originate from the golgi system.

Model for Wall Growth

A proposed model for wall growth involves both wall lytic enzymes as well as synthases. The lytic enzymes are believed to function by cleaving the existing wall polymers to allow extension and insertion of new material. Evidence for the significance of these enzymes is claimed firstly from experiments on the bursting of hyphal tips and secondly from studies on the release of sugars from walls during incubation. Bursting of hyphal tips can be obtained by treatment with various chemicals which have been suggested increase the activity of those lytic enzymes located in the walls. This idea has been challenged by the suggestion that the treatments caused changes in the wall matrix materials, these changes in turn led to bursting. Evidence for wall lytic enzymes from a second group of experiments is more convincing. Up to 3 per cent of the polymers were found to be released from

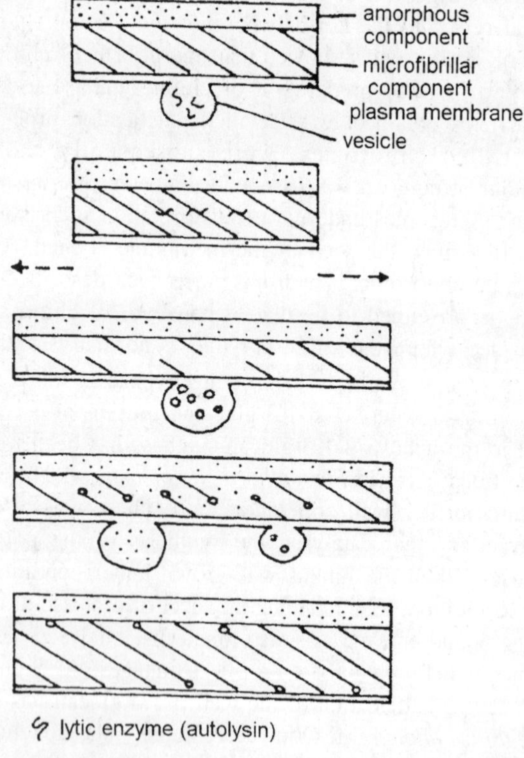

Fig. 6.3. Model of cell wall growth in fungi.

walls of *Asperegillus nidulans*, in the form of glucose, N-acetylglucosamine, mannose and galactose. In further experiments using isotopically labelled walls it was shown that the release of sugars was preferentially from the newly formed wall at the apex rather than from sub-apical regions. More recent studies on the same fungus revealed the presence of six autolytic enzymes (autolysins) that hydrolysed chitin, laminarin, α-glucoside, β-glucoside, protein and β-N-acetylglucosaminide respectively. These enzymes were found bound to the wall fraction and inthesoluble protein of the cytoplasmic fraction of cell homogenates. The attachment of the wall bound enzymes was mediated by lipids. The cytoplasmic vesicles in the hyphae are assumed to function again as carriers of these enzymes but confirmation of this and the role of the autolysin in wall formation and hyphal growth must await further research. Despite this evidence for the existence of wall-bound lytic enzymes direct information relating to their involvement in hyphal growth is lacking.

Whatever the precise details of the system, the synthesis of the hyphal wall clearly demands the secretion of a variety of materials at the surface of the plasma membrane in the region of the growing tip. Transport of these compounds is an obvious role for the vesicles described earlier in this chapter. Cytochemical data suggests that some of the vesicles may be carriers of carbohydrate material and recently there have been interesting reports that the microvesicles are carriers of chitin synthase as described earlier. Discharge of the vesicles contents will occur following fusion of the vesicle with the plasma membrane the latter event also provides a mechanism for membrane growth which is also a necessary part of hyphal extension.

The mechanism for vesicle transportation is not known, but two hypotheses have been proposed, both of which are based on reports of a gradient in membrane potential of some 100 mV in the apical zone, 7 nm long, in *Neurospora crassa* hyphae. The first hypothesis proposes that this gradient could generate enough current for the electro-phonetic movement of vesicles through the apical zone. The second view is based on the assumption that the gradient is a function of a decrease in the number of potassium pumps (ATP-ase dependent) in the membrane towards the hyphal tip. A consequence of this would be an osmotic flow forwards to the tip which could carry the vesicles.

Control of Localized Synthesis

The previous discussion has stressed that wall synthesis is localised at the hyphal apex, so how is this localisation controlled? In several

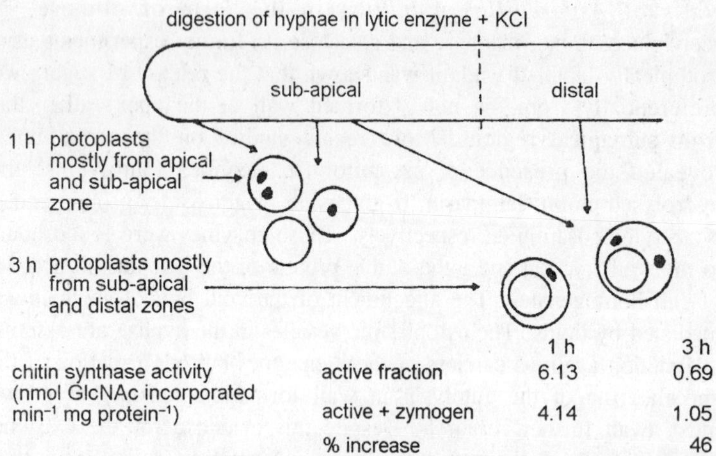

chitin synthase activity (nmol GlcNAc incorporated min^{-1} mg $protein^{-1}$)		1 h	3 h
	active fraction	6.13	0.69
	active + zymogen	4.14	1.05
	% increase		46

Fig. 6.4. Chitin synthase activities in hyphal protoplasts from Aspergillus nidulans.

fungi there is now evidence for the existence of an active and a zymogen form of chitin synthase (a similar situation to that described for the yeast *Saccharomyces cerevisiae*) and that the latter form can be activated by protease enzymes found in the hyphae. The significance of these two components in relation to the mechanism of control remains unknown. An attempt to understand their distribution within the hyphal organisation was made using the technique of protoplast isolation as a fractionation system. Protoplasts released from hyphae of *Aspergillus nidulans* during the first hour of wall digestion are predominantly from the apical tips. In the subsequent time period th ecytoplasm from sub-apical and distal zones is also released as protoplasts. Comparison of active and zymogen chitin synthase in the different preparations showed that protoplasts released in the first hour had a high level of active chitin synthase but no zymogen, and the protoplasts released later had a much reduced level of the active enzyme and higher amounts of the zymogen.

From the limited data available a possible working hypothesis would suggest that chitin synthase is released at the apex following fusion of the chitosomes with the plasma membrane. The chitin synthase, which is probably synthesised in zymogen form, is activated either in the chitosome prior to fusion, or on the membrane surface following fusion. As the hyphal tip advances the newly inserted membrane and the newly formed wall become lateral to it. In this position the majority of the enzyme molecules would become inactivated either reversibly or irreversibly.

The presence of inactivated enzyme in the lateral regions of the hyphae is one conclusion drawn from experiments on *Aspergillus nidulans* in which hyphae were either treated with cycloheximide or subjected to osmotic shock. In both instances the treated hyphae were pulse labelled with radioactive carbohydrate and examined by autoradiography. In this case the hyphae had a uniform distribution of silver grains over their whole length and not the restricted location as referred to previously. The changed pattern of incorporation and therefore presumed wall synthesis could be an expression of the reactivation of zymogen, however, an alternative explanation cannot be ruled out at this stage. This suggests that the cycloheximide treatment or osmotic shock disrupts the normal mechanism of vesicle transportation and discharged at the apex resulting in a random discharge over the whole hyphal surface, cannot be ruled out at this stage.

Branch initiation is also an important part of the model; in the case of a reversible inactivation situation the enzyme molecules would be reactivated. If the enzyme is inactivated irreversibly then the insertion of new active enzyme molecules would be required to initiate growth of a branch. Additional control of chitin synthase can be effected through N-acetylglucosamine, known to be an activator of the enzyme *in vitro*. In the hyphae this molecule would be released at localised sites following lysis of chitin by wall bound enzymes. If this lysis occurs only at the apex this would enhance the rate of synthase activity at this region.

Hyphal Growth and the Duplicatoin Cycle

In the unicellular bacteria and yeasts the events of growth and division are integrated, forming the cell cycle. It is now believed that similar integration of growth and nuclear division occurs in the apical compartment of hyphal fungi but owing to the absence of cell separation the term duplication cycle is used to describe these events. Some diversity exists in relation to the organisation of the apical compartment in different fungi. In some species the compartment is uninucleate, e.g. the *Phycomycete Basidiobolus ranarum*, and in the monokaryotic mycelium of many Basidiomycetes. In the dikaryotic mycelium of these latter fungi each hyphal compartment has two nuclei. In coenocytic species, e.g. *Aspergillus nidulans*, there are many nuclei present, in some instances up to 90. In all cases a regular sequence of events can be identified. Following septation the apical compartment elongates as a result of growth at the tip. In the species with uni- and binucleate compartments the nucleus(i) is seen to remain in a constant position

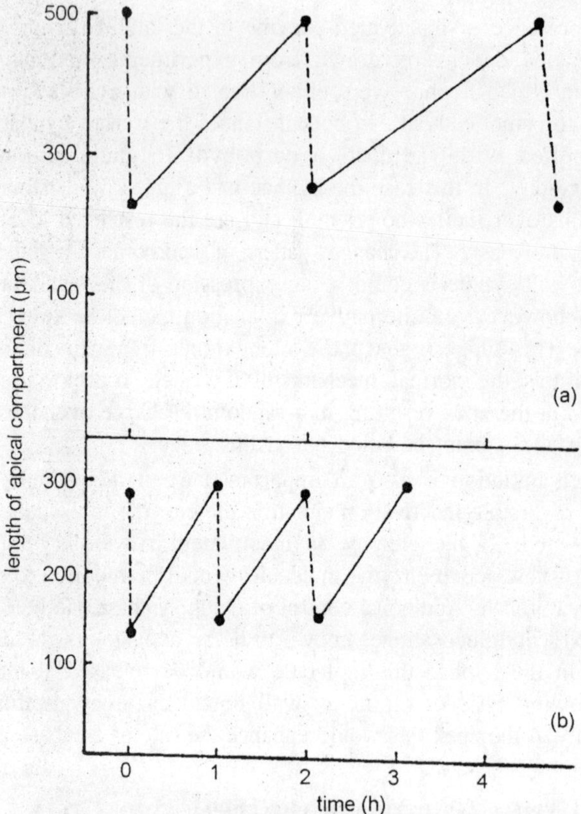

Fig. 6.5. The duplication cycle showing growth and septation of the apical compartment of fungal hypha in (a) Aspergillus nidulans and (b) the dikaryotic mycelium of Schizophyllum commune.

relative to the tip and consequently must migrate at a rate equivalent to the rate of tip growth. When the apical compartment reaches a critical size nuclear division occurs followed by septation. The timing of these events is regular indicating a cyclic nature. The situation in coenocytic fungi is identical, with certain minor modifications. Nuclear division is not completely synchronous and where a large number of nuclei are involved the division event may last for up to 20 minutes, until each nucleus has divided. Septation is also different in coenocytes. The formation of several septa divides the compartment into an apical segment and a number of other segments each of variable size and nuclear number. In all cases the apical compartment is reduced to half its length at septation thus maintaining constancy in size.

An essential feature of the duplication cycle is the as yet unexplained relationship between the volume of cytoplasm and the DNA content of the apical compartment. As the cytoplasm attains a doubling in volume, division of the nucleus or nuclei and septation occur, thus restoring the nuclear-cytoplasmic ration. The observed events suggest that a positive control system is operating.

It has been proposed that a cytoplasmic factor is involved, similar to that suggested for bacteria. If such a factor is produced during the interphase period, at a rate proportional to the rate of increase of the cytoplasm, then mitosis would be induced when a critical level is attained. The apical cells of hyphae in a mycelium show no synchrony in respect of their duplication cycles, which suggests that if such a cytoplasmic factor is involved its effect is very restricted to individual apices. This would suggest that cytoplasmic mixing is very restricted even in those fungi in which the septa have pores.

Our understanding of the duplication cycle will hopefully improve in future years through the study of mutants. Several temperature sensitive mutants have been isolated in *Aspergillus nidulans* that have blocks in nuclear division and in septation. The nuclear division mutatns fall into several groups including those blocked at the stage of DNA synthesis and others blocked during mitosis. Investigations on these strains may tell us more about the control of nuclear division in the fungal hypha and the relationship between this event and septation.

Hyphal Branching

Branch formation is a feature of all fungal hyphae which allows the organism to rapidly colonise a particular substratum. A variety of patterns of branching are seen and the frequency of branch formation is variable–both aspects are subject to environmental and genetic control of apical or sub-apical hyphal compartments. In the former instance the septa are believed to be involved in branch formation, acting as a barrier to the flow of vesicles towards the hyphal apes. Fusion of the vesicles with the plasma membrane, as is also believed to occur at the apex, results in the discharge of their contents. This initiates changes in the hyphal wall and branch formation. Where branches arise independently of septa then the location is presumed to be random and is determined only by the sites at which vesicles accumulate. The stimulus for such accumulationis unknown. On occassions the hyphal apex is seen to branch dichotomously, this could alsobe an expression of vesicle accumulation. In this case a greater supply is required than is normally needed to maintain the normal polarised growth.

DIMORPHISM

As mentioned in the previous chapter some fungal species grow in two or more morphological forms, i.e. they exhibit dimorphism. In the majority of cases the forms are distinct, yeast-like and mycelial. It is of interest that many of the species involved are pathogenic. The transformation from one form to the other is influenced by specific environmental conditions. These are diverse and may be nutritional, e.g. in *Candida albicans*, or physical factors, e.g. temperature in *Paracoccidiodes brasilieusis*, or the gaseous environment, e.g. in *Mucor rouxii*.

The morphological switch from a dividing or budding cell to a cell growing by elongation is presumed to be related to changes in the cell wall. However, examination of the cell wall composition of the three fungi mentioned above reveals major differences between each example and underlies the fact that a single mechanism cannot explain dimorphism in all fungi.

Research on *Paracoccidiodes brasiliensis* and *Candida albicans* has centred on the cell wall and in the former there is good evidence to suggest that a switch in wall biogenesis is the basis for the morphological change. Analysis of walls from the yeast and mycelial forms has shown significant differences in composition and structure. In the yeast form the major polymer is an α-glucan with chitin and in the mycelial form a β-glucan and a galacto mannan are the major components. What remains to be discovered is the nature of the underlying control mechanism which influences the pathway of wall synthesis and how this is affected by a temperature change. A much simpler change in the cell wall has been proposed for *Candida albicans* which involves the disulphide component of the wall protein. It is suggested that growth in the yeast form is maintained by high levels of sulphydryl residues in the protein, mediated by a $NADH_2$ dependent protein disulphide reductase.

The availability of the hydrogen donor stems from an excess generated during carbon metabolism. The experimental evidence for this proposal resides in the demonstration of the presence of the reductase enzyme, however, other causes for the dimorphic change cannot be ruled out and further study of this organism is necessary.

The biochemical basis of dimorphism in *Mucor rouxii* and related species appears to be different from the fungi described previously. The problem has been actively researched in recent years and whilst several mechanisms have been proposed one hypothesis implicated cAMP as the endogeneous initiator of the dimorphic switch from the yeast to hyphal form.

Yeast cells growing in CO_2 and shifted to an aerobic environment switch to the mycelial form and a simultaneous decrease in the intracellular level of cAMP (about 3–4 fold) was found. Supportive evidence also came from the observation that the lipid derivative dibutyryl cAMP transformed hyphal cells growing in air, to the yeast environment of 100 per cent CO_2 have high levels of cAMP. Other evidence does not support an involvement of cAMP. In cultures in which the growth form is controlled by the flow rate of gaseous nitrogen into the culture both yeast and hyphal cells have similar levels of cAMP and the additon of dibutyryl cAMP to hyphal cultures failed to bring about the transformation as reported previously. It can only be concluded, at this time at least, that the dimorphic switch is not linked, in an obligatory way, to the intracellular concentration of cAMP.

Another explanation for the phenomenon was sought in the relationship between the yeat form and a high rate fermentative metabolism based on growth on hexose. In this respect the yeast form of *Mucor rouxii* contrasts with *Saccharomyces cerevisiae* because fermentative metabolism in the former does not repress mitochondrial development. Mucor species cultured aerobically in the presence of high concentrations of glucose are fermentative and take the yeast form.

It could be argued that the importance of hexose for the yeast pattern of development is an indication that the enzymes of carbon catabolsim are some significance in the morphogenetic switch, however, differences in metabolic patterns between the yeast and mycelial form under certain environmental conditions do not necessarily occur under another set of conditions. One case in point relates to the utilisation of the glycolytic and the pentose phosphate papthways.

In aerobically grown yeast cells 14 per cent of the glucose is metabolised through the pentose phosphate cycle compared to 28 per cent in the mycelial form. Comparison of yeast and mycelium under anaerobic conditions revealed that the balance of carbon metabolism through the two pathways was the same for both growth forms. Several other reports have been made of differences between enzyems produced in the two growth forms, e.g. isoenzymic forms of pyruvate kinase, but in no case so far described has a clear cut correlation between specific enzymes and a particular morphological type been shown.

The two patterns of development in dimorphic fungi are clearly the phenotypic expression of different parts of the genome. Attempts to unravel molecular differences that are associated with morphogenetic switches have been few, and mostly with the dimorphic species of Mucor. The RNA polymerases of the two growth forms have been found to be similar so differences might therefore be expected at the translational level. The switch from yeast to hyphal form is accopanied by a noticeable increase in the rate of protein synthesis but the nature of the newly formed proteins still requires elucidation.

7

FLOWER

The present and the following two chapters deal with the angiospermous flower and the structures derived from it, the fruit and the seed. The phylogeny and morphologic nature of the flower and its parts are subjects of much discussion in the literature. The old classical theory homologizes the flower with a shoot, that is, it regards the flower as an entity consisting of an axis (*receptacle*) and foliar appendages (floral parts, or organs). The axis is relatively short and has determinate growth. The floral parts are divided into sterile and fertile, or reproductive. Megasporogenesis and microsporogenesis are carried out on separate floral organs, which may occur on the same or different flowers.

The floral parts concerned with megasporogenesis constitute, collectively, the *gynoecium* (from the Greek words meaning woman and house). The basic unit of the gynoecium is the *carpel* (in Greek, fruit), which is commonly regarded as a megasporophyll. One or more carpels may enter into the composition of a gynoecium. *Pistil* (in Latin, pestle) is another term referring to the megasporangial part of the flower. The pistil may consist of one carpel (simple pistil) or of several (compound pistil). If the gynoecium is composed of a single carpel or of several united carpels, the pistil and the gynoecium refer to the same entity. If the gynoecium consists of more then one separate carpel, it also consists of more than one separate pistil. The abandonment of the term pistil has been advocated but it continues to be useful. Some authors substitute *ovary* for pistil, but this word denotes only the lower part of the pistil. The other parts are the *style* and the *stigma*.

The carpels enclose the *ovule* or *ovules* (in Greek, egg) borne on the *placenta* (in Latin, cake, or flat plate). The *nucellus*, which is the central part of the ovule, is usually interpreted as the megasporangium. The functioning megaspore germinates within the megasporangium and gives rise to the female gametophyte, the *embryo sac*. Because of this developmental sequence, the gynoecium is commonly referred to as the female part of the flower.

The floral parts forming the microspores are called, collectively, the *androecium* (from the Greek words meaning man and house). The individual units of the androecium are the *stamens* (in Latin, filament). Classically, the stamen is interpreted as a microsporophyll, and the part of the stamen called *pollen sac*, as the microsporangium. The pollen sacs are contained within the *anther* (based on the Greek word for flowering). A microspore develops into the male gametophyte, the *pollen grain* (pollen from the Latin, fine flour). Since gametogenesis occurs in the anther the androecium is referred to as the male part of the flower.

The sterile parts of the flower are the *petals* (in Greek, flower leaves), collectively called the *corolla* (in Latin, small crown), and the *sepals* (in Greek, a covering) composing the calyx (in Greek, a cup). The calyx and the corolla constitute the *perianth* (from Greek words, about and flower). If the perianth is not differentiated into sepals and petals, the individual members of the perianth are called *tepals* (from the Latin *tepalum*, an anagram of *petalum*). Flowers commonly have nectarines borne on their various parts. Some of these are modified stamens, or staminodes.

The literature dealing with the question of morphologic nature of the flower is extensive and has been more or less comprehensively reviewed. Most of the proponents of the concept interpreting the flower as a modified shoot assume that the floral organs are appendicular structures in the same sense as leaves, both kinds of appendages possibly having undergone parallel evolutionary development. Emphasis is thus placed upon unity of types of structures; that is, foliage leaves and floral organs are both regarded as leaf-like appendages or phyllomes. Discussions on the nature of the flower frequently refer to the concept of leaves as derivatives of branches. The floral organs, though resembling leaves in extant angiosperms, evolved from cauline assemblages similar to those that gave rise to the foliages leaves. From such an aspect, the question to be asked is not how the leaf became a floral organ but how this organ evolved from a branch system.

Apparently plants bore ovules before the leaves–as we know them now–were in existence.

Sepals and petals are basically leaf-like in external form. They may intergrade with one another and with the small bracts (bracteoles) subtending the flower. In some flowers, however, the petals intergrade with the stamens through structures bearing characters of both. Moreover, frequently stamens and petals differ from other floral parts in having a single vascular trace. These features are used to suggest that in some taxa the petals have evolved from the stamens.

The specialized types of stamens, characterized by a distinct differentiation into a filament and an anther, appear rather unlike the leaves, but in many Ranales the stamens are wide, leaf-like structures with no differentiation of a filament. This form is the basis for the view that primitively the stamen may have been leaf-like. The fascicled types of stamens (Malvaceae, Guttiferae, and other dicotyledons), on the other hand, are thought to indicate an origin from primitive dichotomous branch systems–systems of telomes–bearing terminal sporangia. Still another theory proposes that stamens originated from the *gonophyll*, a leaf-like structure bearing fertile branches. Through condensations and deletions the gonophyll gave rise to the modern stamen either through a line with fascicled stamens or through one in which the stamen is laminar.

The classical concept of the carpel interprets it as a leaf-like appendage. By folding and fusion of margins and by unions with one another the carpels are assumed to have evolved into pistils.

The German literature deals extensively with the question regarding the type of a leaf to which the carpel may be compared. The postulate has been advanced that many carpels have the same growth form as a peltate leaf, that is, a leaf in which the stalk is attached to the lower surface of the blade. The degree of peltation is considered to be variable and absent in some forms. Peltation is recognized in stamens and perianth parts as well.

The concept of the carpel as a sporophyll bearing sporangia is frequently criticized because not all gynoecia of angiosperms can be interpreted by reference to it. Some authors consider that the ontogeny of the carpel makes it quite distinct from leaves; others find that the vascular anatomy of many flowers suggests an independence between carpellary and placental vascular traces. The inconsistencies in the sporophyll concept of the carpel are proposed to be resolved by the gonophyll theory. According to this theory, the basic component of the gynoecium is a leaf with an epiphyllous fertile branch, the two together comprising the gonophyll. Evolutionary modifications have resulted in a close association of the fertile branch–the placental axis bearing the ovules–with the laminar part of the gonophyll. If the floral parts are ultimately derived from branch systems, the flower is a condensed and highly modified inflorescence and the term flower covers reproductive structures of angiosperms in various stages of condensation. This interpretation modifies the term flower to one referring to a biological unit rather than to a morphological one and makes it applicable not only to single flowers but also to more or less condensed inflorescences.

STRUCTURE

Arrangement of Flower Parts

The apical meristem of the flower usually ceases its activity after the reproductive structures have been initiated, an expression of the determinate type of growth. In certain groups of angiosperms considered to be primitive the determinate growth is less pronounced than in the more advanced families. In the primitive groups, the activity of the apical meristem is prolonged and therefore the number of floral parts is relatively large and indefinite. Moreover, these parts occur on a rather elongated axis, with sepals, petals, stamens, and carpels succeeding each other acropetally in the order named. The similarity between such a flower and a vegetative shoot is not difficult to visualize, especially if the flower parts are arranged helically.

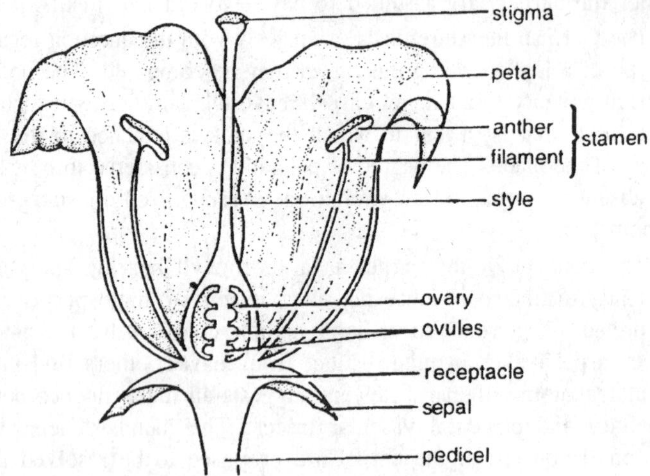

Fig. 7.1. Longitudinal section of a typical flower.

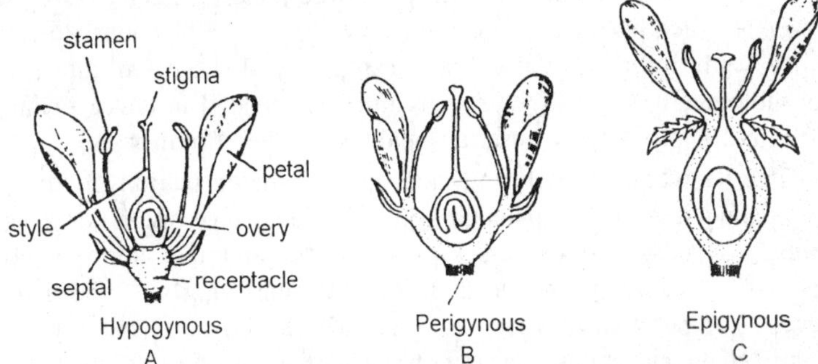

Fig. 2.2. Relative position of floral parts on the thalamus: A, hypogynous flower; B, perigynous flower.

In the more highly specialized flower types the growth period is shorter and the number of floral parts is smaller and more definite. Moreover, the shortening of the period of activity of the apical meristem is associated with a development of distinguishing characteristics that obscure or even efface the evidences of similarity between a flower and a vegetative shoot. Such characteristics are: whorled (or cyclic) instead of helical arrangement of parts; cohesion of parts within one whorl; adnation of parts of two or more different whorls; loss of parts; zygomorphy (bilateral symmetry) instead of actinomorphy (radial symmetry); and epigyny (inferior ovary) instead of hypogyny (superior ovary). The words synsepalous, sympetalous, and syncarpous are used to characterize flowers with united sepals, petals, and carpels, respectively. If the gynoecium occupies a position similar to that in

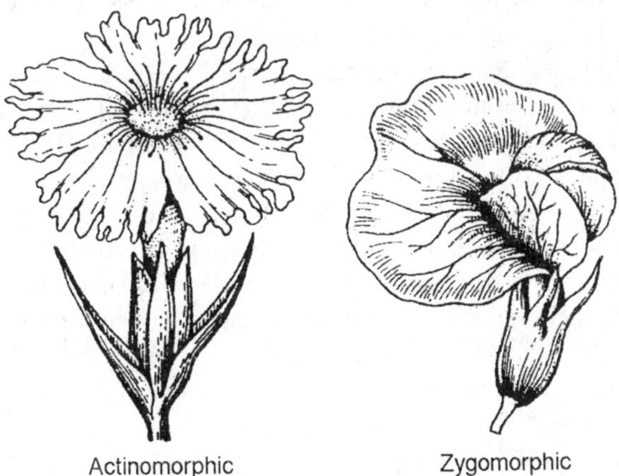

Fig. 7.3. Symmetry of flower.

an epigynous flower but is not adnate to the noncarpellary tissue, the flower is called perigynous and the ovary superior. Epigynous flowers (those with inferior ovaries) are especially difficult to interpret morphologically because the gynoecium is imbedded in noncarpellary tissue and appears to be inserted below the other floral parts.

The flowers of different degrees of specialization form an intergrading series of morphologic types. The degree of fusion of sepals, petals, stamens, and carpels varies widely, and the union is not necessarily equally pronounced in the different whorls of the same flower. The perianth may not be differentiated into calyx and corolla, or the sepals and petals may intergrade with each other. Transitional forms may also occur between the petals and the stamens. The flower may lack certain parts. If it lacks either the gynoecium or the androecium, it is called unisexual.

Vascular System

Investigations on the vascular system of the flower occupy a prominent place in the literature on the anatomy of the flower. A commonly accepted postulate is that the vascular system is conservative and, therefore, might be expected to reveal at least some of the evolutionary changes that have been obliterated in the external form. Thus, the vascular anatomy of the flower has been frequently studied to find explanations of the morphology of flowers, to obtain additional data for establishing taxonomic relations, and to construct evolutionary schemes.

The vascular system of relatively unspecialized flowers with superior ovaries is comparable to that of a vegetative shoot in which strands diverge into the lateral organs from an axial system of bundles. Many authors draw a complete parallel between the patterns of vascularization in the shoot and the flower, and apply the concepts of stele, traces, and gaps with reference to both structures. If the receptacle is elongated, the floral parts may be arranged according to a phyllotactic pattern correlated with an orderly arrangement and interconnection of vascular traces. But the shortness of internodes characteristic of so many flowers, the union of parts, the epigynous condition, and various other modifications in the interrelations of floral parts make the vascular system of flowers less regular than that of vegetative shoots and obscure the relation between the vascular system of the axis and that of the floral organs.

In a hypognous flower with relatively little fusion of parts, the vascular system may be readily depicted in terms of traces to the various floral appendages. The pedicel shows a cylindrical vascular region enclosing a pith and delimited on the outside by the cortex. In the receptacle or torus (the part of the axis bearing the floral parts), at the level of attachment of sepals, traces diverge into these appendages. Each sepal frequently has as many traces as a foliage leaf of the same plant. Above this level, traces diverge into the corolla, one or more to each petal in dicotyledons, one to many to each tepal in the monocotyledons.

Still higher, the traces to the stamens become discernible, predominantly one to each stamen, and finally is found the carpellary supply. The frequent number is three traces to each carpel, one median and two lateral, but more than three traces have been recorded. Small branches of carpellary vascular bundles, often derived from the laterals, connect the carpellary system with the ovules. The placental bundles may also be branches from the dorsal bundles, as in some Ranales, or be independent from the carpellary traces. The vascular system is prolonged into the style.

Some of the common modifications in the arrangement of the vascular system are associated with the fusion of floral parts. In many flowers the lateral bundles of the adjacent carpels are fused with each other. Similar fusions occur in other floral organs. The reduction in the numbers of traces and bundles may also occur if some of them do not develop.

The vascular system of epigynous flowers shows additional complications related to the apparently basal position of the gynoecium. The vascularization of such flowers has been frequently studied with the result that some authors have developed rather definite ideas on the nature of the noncarpellary tissue enclosing the gynoecium. In most epigynous flowers this tissue is interpreted as appendicular in origin, composed of the bases of sepals, petals, and stamens that underwent a concrescence during the evolution of the flower. The vascular system is thought to reflect this structure in that the bundles pertaining to members of different whorls are variously fused but all show the usual orientation of xylem and phloem. In some epigynous flowers (Calycanthaceae, Santalaceae, and probably Juglandaceae), however, the ovary is said to be partially enclosed in receptacular tissue. The vascular bundles are prolonged from the axis to the level below the insertion of floral parts, other than the carpels, where traces to these parts diverge. The main bundles, instead of ending here, continue farther from the periphery in a downward direction–with a corresponding inverse position of the xylem and the phloem–and at lower levels give branches to the carpels. This orientation of the vascular system is interpreted as a result of an invagination of the axis (actually intercalary growth of the tissue enclosing the gynoecium).

In general, the vascular elements in the bundles of the flower are comparable to those in foliage leaves. The tissues are mostly primary, although some secondary growth may occur later, during fruit development, particularly in the pedicel. The vascular system of the sepals, the petals, and the carpels is more or less elaborately ramified. Stamens rarely show a branched vascular system. In general character the venation of the perianth parts of monocotyledons and dicotyledons shows distinctive characteristics similar to those in the foliage leaves of these two groups of plants. Perianth parts of many flowers exhibit an open venation.

Sepal and Petal

The sepal and the petal are essentially leaf-like in form and anatomy but generally simpler in detailed structure than a foliage leaf. They consist of ground parenchyma, often called mesophyll, a vascular system permeating the ground tissue, and epidermal layers on the abaxial and adaxial sides. Crystal-containing cells, idioblasts, and laticifers may occur in the ground tissue or in association with the vascular elements. The sepals of Geraniaceae have a thick-walled hypodermis with a druse in each cell. The sepals are commonly green. The chloroplast distribution in the sepals depends on their position. If the sepals are upright and are closely applied to the petals, most chloroplasts are on the abaxial side; if the sepals are recurved, the chloroplasts are most abundant on the adaxial side. The mesophyll is rarely differentiated into palisade and spongy parenchyma. Commonly it is simple in structure and consists of approximately isodiametric cells loosely arranged into a lacunose tissue. The epidermis of the sepals shows a deposition of cutin and a development of stomata and trichomes similar to those on the foliage leaves. The vascular system resembles that in the leaves but is less elaborate.

Petals show a wider variety of shapes than the sepals and are usually distinguished from the sepals by their color. The vascular system may consist of one or several large veins and a system of small veinlets. The patterns formed by these veinlets vary greatly. Commonly the veinlets are dichotomously branched. The mesophyll is few cells in thickness, except in flowers with fleshy corollas. The tissue is parenchymatic with the cells either closely packed or loosely arranged.

The epidermis of petals shows certain peculiarities in the shape of cells and in the structure of cuticle. The anticlinal cell walls may be straight or wavy or may bear internal ridges. The undulation and ridging vary widely in degree of expression in different plants. In some the anticlinal walls are only slightly wavy; in others the undulations are so deep that the cells are star-like in shape as seen from the surface. The ridges, which arise through a localized centripetal growth of cell walls, may appear as small buttons in sectional views, or as long bars, straight or bent, solid or hollow. The degree of waviness or ridging may vary in the same petal. For instance, the anticlinal walls are usually straight at the base of the petal and along the veins, even if they are wavy elsewhere. Frequently, the undulate walls are restricted to or are more pronounced on the lower side.

Intercellular spaces may develop in the epidermis in connection with the differentiation of ridges. In some species the two wall layers composing a ridge split apart and the space between the two layers becomes filled with air. These spaces are open toward the interior of the petal but appear to be closed with the cuticle on the exterior. Ridged walls occur mainly in the dicotyledons, although they have been found in some members of the Liliaceae also.

The tangential walls of the epidermis may be horizontal or convex to various degrees. The inner tangential wall is commonly slightly convex over the entire extent. The outer wall is often strongly convex, or it may bear one or more capitate or cone-shaped papillae (*Viola*, *Nasturtium*). The papillose structure is more common in the adaxial epidermis than in the abaxial and does not develop at the base of the petals. Various trichomes may occur on the petals, usually similar to those found on the leaves of the same plants. The stomata which occur on the petals either resemble those on the foliage leaves or are incompletely differentiated.

The cuticle of the corolla is rarely smooth. Commonly it is striated, and the lines form various patterns in different plants. The development of these patterns has been suggested as resulting from two phenomena; first, a temporarily excessive production of cutin and the consequent increase in surface and folding of the cuticle; second, a stretching of the cuticle and a reorientation of the initial folds by cell extension. Cuticular patterns formed by folds were seen also at the ultrastructural level.

The color of petals is caused by the presence of chromoplasts or pigments in the cell sap. The pigment color is usually modified by acids and other components of the cell sap. Starch is often formed in young petals. Volatile oils imparting the characteristic fragrance to the flowers commonly occur in the epidermal cells of the petals, sometimes in parts of flowers differentiated as osmophors.

Stamen

The well-known type of stamen, with a single-veined filament bearing at the upper end a two-lobed, four-loculed anther, is phylogenetically an advanced structure. As was mentioned before, among the Ranales leaf-like stamens are found. In the least modified form, such stamens have three veins and bear the microsporangia on the abaxial surface between the midvein and the lateral veins. The reduction of the three veins to one is apparently a concomitant of the reduction

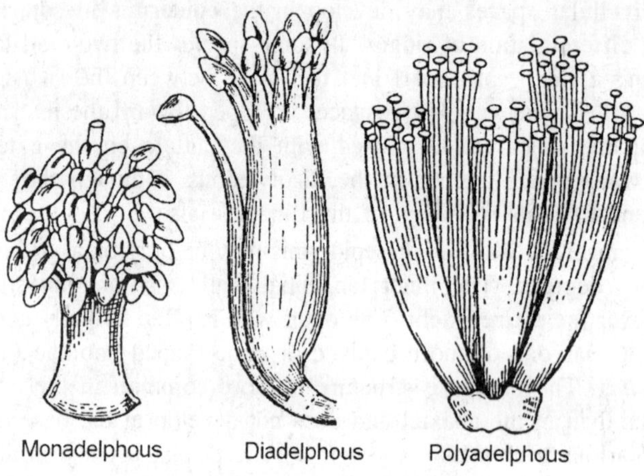

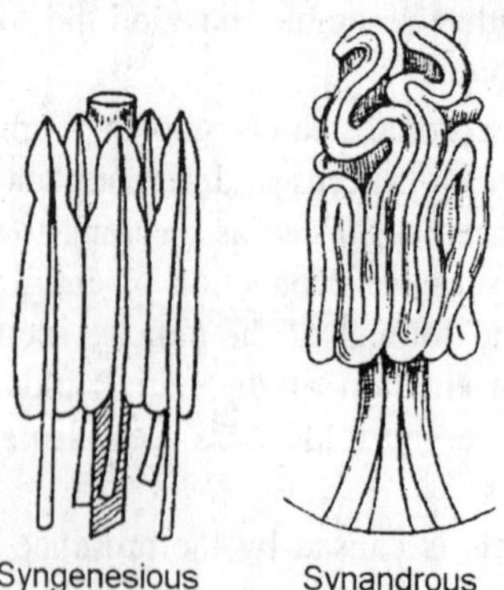

Fig. 7.4. Cohesion of stamens.

in width of the sporophyll, and particularly of the modification of the base of the sporophyll into a filament. The presence of a single vascular bundle is the prevailing condition in angiosperms. An extensive survey has shown that 95 per cent of angiosperms have a single vascular bundle in the stamen. This strand traverses the filament and may end at the base of the anther or may be prolonged into the tissue between the anther lobes, the so-called connective, terminating blindly near the apex. The vascular bundle is not connected by any vascular elements with the sporogenous tissue, but if the ground parenchyma of the anther develops secondary thickenings the cells in the vicinity of the sporogenous tissue remain thin walled and there are also vertical bands of similar thin-walled cells interpolated between the vascular strand and the anther lobes. The vascular bundle of the anther may be amphicribral in dicotyledons, but is reported to be collateral in monocotyledons. The anthers vary in shape and number of locules.

The ground tissue of the filament is vacuolated parenchyma without a prominent intercellular-space system. If often contains pigments in the vacuoles. The epidermis is cutinized, bears trichomes in some species, and may have stomata, possibly permanently open as in hydathodes. The ground tissue of the anther and the connective is also parenchymatic but is highly specialized in the vicinity of the sporogenous cells. This specialized tissue forms the wall layers or the parietal layers of the microsporangia (anther locules, or pollen sacs).

Anther wall

The wall layers vary in number and are established through a series of divisions parallel to the periphery of the anther locule. The parietal layers facing the epidermis are ontogenetically related to the sporogenous tissue. Both the parietal cells and the pollen mother cells arise from the same initial cells, the archesporial cells. The wall layers occurring internally to the pollen sacs, however, arise from the ground tissue in contact with the archesporial cells.

The outermost wall layer, the *endothecium* (from the Greek words for inner and case), is located beneath the epidermis. In anthers that open at maturity by longitudinal slits, the endothecium commonly develops secondary thickenings as the stamen approaches maturity. These thickenings occur on the anticlinal and the inner tangential cell walls. In the anticlinal walls the secondary thickenings frequently have the form of strips or ridges oriented perpendicularly to the epidermal layer. The cell walls facing the sporogenous tissue may have uniform or irregular thickenings. Because of these thickenings the endothecium is often called the fibrous layer. The pattern of the thickening is variable and may be useful in taxonomic studies. The endothecium also may have uniformly thick walls. The protoplasts either disappear as the cell layer completes its development, or they remain alive until the pollen is shed. Wall thickenings similar to those in the endothecium may develop rather generally throughout the ground parenchyma of the anther.

The innermost of the parietal layers is the *tapetum* (from the Greek, carpet). The tapetal cells are characterized by densely staining protoplasts and prominent nuclei. The nuclei show various behavior in different plants. In some, they do not divide after all the tapetal cells have been formed; in others, one or more nuclear divisions occur without being followed by cytokinesis so that the cells become bi- or multinucleate (*Lactuca*, *Taraxacum*). Sometimes the nuclear divisions are not carried to completion: the chromosomes divide but do not form separate nuclei. Such behavior results in polyploidy of the tapetal nuclei. In general, tapetal cells become richer in chromatic material. This occurs through either multiplication of nuclei, restitution of nuclei during various stages of mitosis, or endopolyploidy. The tapetal layer attains its maximal development at the tetrad stage in microspore formation. In some angiosperms the tapetum remains as a discrete layer–apparently functioning as a secretory tissue–until the pollen is mature. In many others, however, the cell walls disintegrate and the cells assume the appearance of plasmodial masses. The latter gradually disintegrate as the pollen develops.

The tapetum is apparently concerned with the nutrition of the pollen mother cells and young microspores. Ultrastructural studies suggest that the material of the outer pollen wall (exine) is synthesized in the tapetum. But autoradiographic methods have failed to show any relation between the DNA of the tapetal nuclei and that of the microspores.

The parietal layers intervening between the endothecium and the tapetum frequently are crushed and destroyed so that, after the maturation of the pollen and the disintegration of the tapetum, the anther locule is bordered on the outside only by the epidermis and the endothecium.

In many plants the release of the pollen occurs through dehiscence (from the Greek, to yawn), that is, spontaneous opening of the anther. The opening, or *stomium*, may be a longitudinal slit located between the two pollen locules of each half of the anther. Before the dehiscence, the partition between the two locules of the same anther lobe may break down. After this event, only one cell layer, the epidermis, separates the locule from the outside in the region of dehiscence. This part of the epidermis consists of particularly small cells and is easily broken when the pollen is mature. Another common type of stomium is oriented transversely near the apex of the anther lobe. When such a stomium is formed, the apex of each anther lobe separates like a cap and leaves a pore (poricidal dehiscence; many Ericaceae, *Solanum*). Pores may also be formed laterally. It has been suggested that the long, slit-like stomium is a more primitive character than one shaped like a pore. In species of *Senna*, the anther is provided with lateral sutures that do not serve as stomia. The epidermal cells along these sutures divide and apparently serve as plugs. Dehiscence occurs at the sterile tip of the anther where short linear stomia are present. The tissue located between these stomia and the pollen sacs breaks down and the pollen emerges through the stomium. In some plants, anthers do not dehisce but open by an irregular breaking and exfoliating of tissue fragments.

Pollen

The development of the sporogenous tissue in the anther involves certain characteristic phenomena of wall formation. The cells that eventually undergo meiosis, the pollen mother cells, are closely packed in their early stages of development. During meiosis these cells usually separate from one another, and the protoplasts round off and become enclosed in a thick gelatinous wall that has been identified as callose. This wall is designated as the pollen mother cell wall or special wall. The megaspore mother cells may assume a distinctive arrangement in the pollen sac. In Gramineae and Cyperaceae, for example, they appear, in transactions of the anthers, like sectors of a circle. As is well known, normal meiosis results in the formation of four nuclei, the microspore nuclei. Each nuclear division may be followed immediately by cytokinesis (successive formation of walls), or the four protoplasts may be walled off simultaneously at the end of meiosis (simultaneous formation of walls). The first type of division is particularly common in monocotyledons, the second in dicotyledons. The simultaneous wall formation may occur by development of cell plates or by furrowing.

The first wall delimiting the microspore protoplasts from each other is of the same material, callose, as the special wall around the entire tetrad of microspores. Later, each microspore forms its own wall, the *sporoderm*.

According to a submicroscopic study of *Tradescantia* anthers, mature pollen grains have abundant mitochondria, dictyosomes, and endoplasmic reticulum; in the earlier stages these entities are not fully differentiated. In younger cells leucoplasts with starch are present; later the plastids become scarce. The number of nuclei in the mature pollen grains is of taxonomic significance and is also associated with certain physiological characteristics of the grains.

The sporoderm is usually described as consisting of two layers, the *exine* (outer wall) and the *intine* (inner wall). The exine is differentiated into a sculptured *ektexine*, or *sexine*, and a nonsculptured *endexine*, or *nexine*. Some workers recognize a third layer, the *medine*, located between the exine and the intine. The exine consists mainly of a lipoidal substance *sporopollenin*, which is less soluble than cutin or suberin. The research on the structure of walls of pollen grains and spores is highly technical and is designated by a special term, *palynology*.

Most pollen grains are *aperturate*, that is, provided with pores or furrows (colpi, sing, colpa). These apertures are not actual openings but places where the exine is very thin and the intine well developed. The pollen tube emerges through the aperture during the germination of the pollen grain apparently by pushing aside the intine. The apertures are also regarded as the flexible parts of the sporoderm that permit the change in shape and size of the pollen grain caused by varying water content. The number of apertures varies from one to many.

As seen from the surface, the exine of many species has spines, depressions, arcolations (division into distinct spaces), and other types of ornamentations. These external markings and the shape of the pollen grains are characteristics that may be utilized in taxonomic studies. Ultrastructurally the ektexine often shows a porous structure.

The intine varies in thickness and in a given species is more or less thickened in the aperture region. It has no ornamentations. The intine consists mainly of polyuronides or a mixture of polyuronides and polysaccharides but its inner part contains also cellulose. In conifers the outer intine is reported to contain callose.

When the pollen tube emerges from the pollen grain it grows by addition of wall material at its apex. The pollen tube wall contains cellulose and is cutinized. It has also been described as having an outer lamella of pectin and an inner lamella of a mixture of callose and cellulose. The cytoplasm accumulates at the tip of the tube and may completely disappear from its basal part. In such instances, the older parts of the elongating pollen tube are successively sealed off by plugs of callose. Accumulation of callose is intensified under conditions of incompatibility, possibly in relation to the reduced growth rate of the pollen tube. In plants forming no plugs of callose (*Fagopyrum esculentum*) the whole tube probably has a thin layer of cytoplasm in addition to the accumulation at the apex. Cytoplasmic streaming has been observed in pollen tubes, even in parts sealed off by the callose plugs.

Carpel

Relation to the gynoecium

Whatever may be the phylogenetic origin of the carpel, in many extant angiosperms with superior ovaries it resembles a leaf. As mentioned before, the carpels may or may not be united with other carpels. If the carpels are free, the gynoecium is apocarpous, if they are united the gynoecium is syncarpous. An apocarpous gynoecium may have a single carpel (*Prunus*, *Leguminosae*).

The carpel of an apocarpous gynoecium appears as a leaf-like folded structure, differentiated, in the specialized condition, into a basal fertile part, the ovary, and an upper sterile part, the style. According to an older concept, the folded carpel has infolded or involuted margins, that is, margins turned toward the interior of the folded carpel, and these margins bear the placentae that give rise to the ovules. A later view, based on studies of the woody Ranales, states that in the primitive form the carpel is a conduplicately (from the Latin, doubling) folded structure, that is, a structure folded lengthwise without involution of margins. Such a carpel shows laminar placentation; the ovules are borne not on the margins but on the inner (ventral) surface, more or less distant from the margins, and may be vascularized by connection with the dorsal bundle rather than the ventral. The apparent involution and marginal placentation are thought to have resulted from phylogenetic change in the ontogeny of the carpel, a decrease in the extension of its folded adaxial part. An argument offered in opposition to the concept of conduplicate carpel states that the surfaces coming in contact in the folded carpel are not ventral but marginal. The evidence on the phylogenetic reduction of the adaxial margins does not support this argument.

The interpretation of the phylogenetic differentiation of the dicotyledonous carpel into ovary, style, and stigma has been consequentially developed with reference to the carpel of the woody Ranales. The unspecialized carpel is a styleless, unsealed, conduplicate leaf-like structure with laminar placentation. The stigmatic tissue occurs on the free margins of the carpel, on its inner surface, and at times also on the outer surface. Successive phylogenetic stages involve closure of the carpel, reduction in the number of ovules and their restriction to the lower part of the carpel (the ovary), and differentiation of the upper part into the style with a stigma localized on its apex. The closure of the carpel occurs through a growing together (concrescence) of the ventral surfaces along the margins that are in contact with each other. The concrescence is ontogenetic and may leave a conspicuous suture; or the union may be so complete that the evidence of a suture is partly or entirely obliterated.

The evolutionary changes in the structure of the gynoecium of the angiospermous flower also involve various manners of union of carpels of the same flower. The carpels may become joined by their margins to the receptacle, or they may grow together laterally in a folded closed condition, or they may become laterally united in a folded open condition. The union of carpels may occur during their ontogeny or they may grow as a unit structure and are then interpreted as congenitally fused, that is, fused from their inception.

The manner of union of carpels is related to differences in internal structure, such as number of locules in the ovary and the arrangement of placentae, the placentation. Each carpel typically has two placentae. If the carpel has a congenitally united lower part, the placentae may fuse in this part and the placental region then has the shape of a U. In syncarpous gynoecia, the junction of carpels in a folded condition may result in an ovary with as many locules as there are carpels and with the placentae arranged around a central column of tissue (*axile placentation*). If the carpels are united with each other in an open condition, the ovary is usually not divided into locules and the ovules are borne on the ovary wall or on extensions from it (*parietal placentation*). The parietal placentation is considered to have evolved from the axile.

Various deviations from the basic structures of the ovary just described are encountered in different angiosperms. Division of the ovary into compartments may occur in other ways than by the folding of carpels. The placentae may be borne upon a central column of tissue not connected by partitions with the ovary wall (*free central placentation*), or may occur at the very base of a unilocular ovary (*basal placentation*). The free central placentation apparently results or has resulted from disappearance of partitions in terms of either ontogeny or phylogeny. Syncarpy and apocarpy may be present in the same pistil if the carpels are joined only at the base. The type of syncarpy may also vary in different parts of the pistil since the individual carpels may have a congenitally united lower part and an open upper part; the type of concrescence of carpels may be different in the two parts.

The controversial views on the nature of the carpel are reflected in the interpretation of the placenta. According to one of the common concepts, the column of tissue bearing the ovules in ovaries with axile or free central placentation may be entirely carpellary or partly axial and partly carpellary. Presence of vascular tissue other than that of the carpels in the central column is one of the evidences used to identify the axial nature of the central tissue. In both situations the placentae would be part of the carpels. When the ovules are borne on the carpels the species is said to be *phyllosporous*. The opposite view, chiefly concerning species with central and basal placentations, considers that the placentae and ovules may be cauline structures. When the ovules are borne on cauline tissue the species is designated as *stachyosporous*.

The structure of inferior ovaries also presents problems of interpretation, especially with regard to the questions whether any carpellary tissue lines the lower part of the ovarian cavity and whether the extracarpellary tissue is axial (receptacular) or appendicular (floral tube). As was mentioned before, the use of vascular anatomy has led to the concept that the cup (hypanthium) of extracarpellary tissue is appendicular in some plants, receptacular in others. Some authors, however, see no distinction between the inferior ovaries and prefer to consider the cup as uniformly receptacular.

The ovary wall is not highly differentiated before and during anthesis (time when fertilization takes place in the flower). It consists largely of parenchyma and vascular tissue and bears a cuticularized epidermis on the outer surface. In the Compositae, calcium oxalate crystals occurring in the cells of the ovary wall were found to differ according to species. The ovary wall undergoes more or less profound changes during the development of the fruit and then may show marked specializations.

Style and stigma

The development of the style occurred as a concomitant of sterilization of the apical part of the carpel. In an apocarpous gynoecium each carpel usually has one simple style. In syncarpous gynoecia the styles of the component carpels may be variously united with each other. The carpels may be united only at their bases, leaving the styles free, or partly so. In highly modified flowers the carpels are united from base to apex and form a gynoecium with a single ovary, style, and stigma. If the styles are free, the stylar portions derived from the individual carpels are often called style branches, a designation giving an erroneous concept of the structure of the compound style; the branches are morphologically entire styles. The term *stylode* has been proposed as a replacement for stylar branch.

The style and the stigma have structural and physiological peculiarities that make possible the germination of the pollen and the growth of the pollen tube from the stigma to the ovules. On the stigma the protoderm differentiates into a glandular epidermis with cells rich in cytoplasm, often papillate in shape, and covered with a cuticle. This epidermis excretes a sugary liquid. Thus, the stigma resembles a nectary in structure and function. The cells beneath the epidermis may be as rich in cytoplasm as the epidermis, and then they constitute a part of the glandular tissue. In many plants, the stigmatic epidermal cells develop into short, densely crowded hairs (cherry, bean) or into long, branched hairs (grasses and other wind-pollinated plants).

An outstanding feature of the organization of the carpel is that the stigma is connected with the inferior of the ovary by a tissue

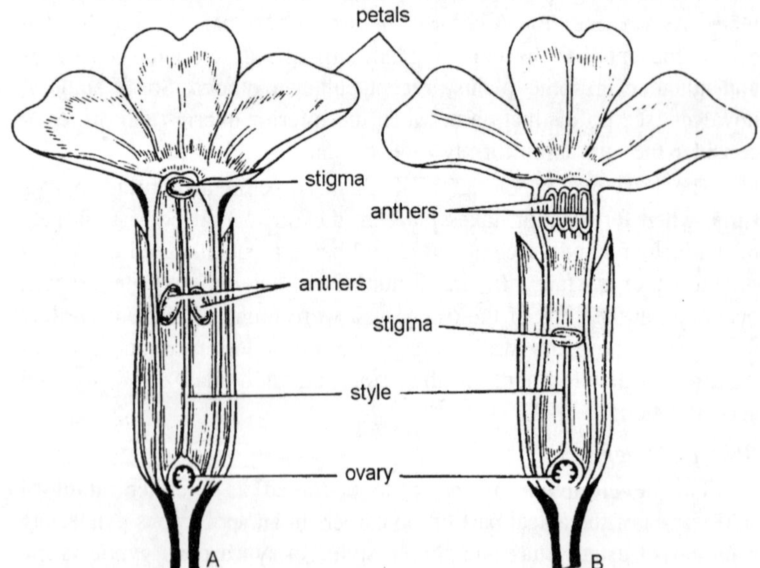

Fig. 7.5. Heterostyly: A, long styled flower; B, short styled flower.

cytologically similar to the glandular stigmatic tissue. This tissue is interpreted as a medium facilitating the progress of the pollen tube through the style and supplying the developing pollen tube with food. It is commonly called conducting tissue, a term easily confused with that referring to the vascular tissue. The terms transmitting tissue and pollen-transmitting tracts serve as substitutes. In the following discussion this tissue is referred to as *stigmatoid tissue* on the basis of its apparent cytologic and physiologic similarity to the tissue of the stigma.

The carpels of the more primitive dicotyledons do not show a differentiation into stigmatic and stigmatoid tissues, for, as was stated previously, the surfaces of the flaring margins and the inner surface of the open carpel are lined with stigmatic glandular hairs. With the increase in specialization of the carpels, characterized by their gradual closure and the development of the style, the stigma proper became restricted to a part of the style, but the continuity of the stigmatic tissue with the placentae was maintained. The internal glandular surfaces became modified into pollen-transmitting, or stigmatoid, tissue.

In relation to the variation in degree of concrescence of carpels and in methods of growth of the styles, the styles may be open or solid in both the apocarpous and the syncarpous gynoecia. The open styles are described as having a canal. In a syncarpous gynoecium the compound style may have one common canal (*Viola*, *Erythronium*), or each component style may have its own canal (*Lilium*, *Citrus*). The stigmatoid tissue lining the stylar canal resembles the glandular tissue of the stigma and may be papillose. In some plants starch has been observed in this tissue, and a cuticle has been identified on the surface exposed to the canal. The stigmatoid tissue may line the entire canal, or it may be restricted to localized parts in the form of one or more longitudinal bands. In many plants the stigmatoid tissue is several cells in thickness and if, at the same time, it is distributed in longitudinal bands, one can speak of strands of stigmatoid tissue. Stigmatoid tissue occurs on the placenta within the ovary and in some species on the funiculus of the ovule as well. In certain plants the stigmatoid tissue is brought close to the micropyle by a placental proliferation in the form of a small protuberance, the *obturator*. Developmental studies on the styles of *Datura* and *Cucurbita* have shown that the multilayered stigmatoid tissue lining the stylar canals and placentae in these plants originates from the epidermis by periclinal divisions.

In most angiosperms the styles are solid; that is, they have no canals. The stigmatoid tissue is present, nevertheless, usually in the form of strands of considerably elongated cells staining deeply with cytoplasmic stains. If the gynoecium with a single solid style is syncarpous, the stigmatoid tissue of the style forms several strands. Commonly the stigmatoid tissue has a course independent from that of the vascular bundles, but it may be associated with the bundles (*Zea*).

Syncarpous gynoecia may have openings that enable a pollen grain germinating on a stigma of one of the styloids or any part of the stigma of a single style to reach any part of the ovary rather than only the one to which a given stigma or part of stigma is related. The opening (*compitum*) may consist of a canal pore, or split in the septum between locules. In unilocular ovaries with parietal placentation the crossing over of the pollen tube may occur in the style itself. Some syncarpous gynoecia have no compital structure and, therefore, function like apocarpous gynoecia with regard to pollination.

With regard to the possible factors that might direct the growth of pollen toward the ovule, some workers stress the evidence that there is a chemotactic attraction between the pollen tube and the tissues of the stigma and of the ovule; others consider that the structure of the stigmatoid tissue and its distribution in the pistil are sufficient to account for the direction of growth of the pollen tube. The presence of pollen tubes in or on the stigmatoid tissue has been repeatedly ascertained in various plants.

The relation of the pollen tube to the stigmatoid tissue is somewhat different in styles with and without open canals. In the former, the pollen tubes may have an entirely superficial course. After the germination of the pollen grain on the stigma the pollen tube grows among the papillae or hairs or on the surface of the nonpapillate cells. The course in the stylar canal is essentially the same as on the stigma. Frequently the cuticle disappears in the stylar canal before pollination, and the walls of the glandular tissue become swollen and soft. The pollen tube may also penetrate the lining of the stylar canal to somewhat deeper layers and proceed there by growing between cells.

If the style is solid, the pollen tube usually passes through the stigmatoid tissues by intercellular growth. Reports that pollen tubes penetrate the cells themselves are not well substantiated. In grasses, the pollen tube may take an intercellular course on the stigma itself. As was mentioned previously, the grass stigma commonly bears long hairs. These may be multicellular columns, both vertically and horizontally. The pollen tube penetrates into the interior of the column of cells and proceeds from there into the stigmatoid tissue of the style. After the pollen tube reaches the ovarian cavity, it follows the stigmatoid tissue lining the ovary wall and the placenta and eventually comes in contact with the ovule.

The intercellular growth of the pollen tube appears to involve a digestion of the intercellular substance. In agreement with this assumption pollen tubes give a positive reaction for an enzyme capable of digesting pectic substances. The stigmatoid tissue, however, appears to undergo a partial weakening in its structure before the pollen tube passes through it. Its walls assume a swollen aspect (the tissue resembles collenchyma in this state), and the connection between cells is loosened, as demonstrated by the ease with which the tissue may be macerated. In fact, the walls appear as though they have been converted into a mucilage. When the pollen tube passes through the stigmatoid tissue, it occupies the space formerly filled with cell wall material. The protoplasts of the stigmatoid tissue may also become exhausted and sometimes even shrivel and die. Because of these relationships the entry of pollen tubes, even if these are very numerous, does not cause the expansion of the stigmatoid tissue. The pollen tubes may be said to replace some of the stigmatoid tissue.

The exhaustion of the protoplasts of the stigmatoid tissue by the pollen tube indicates an effect of chemical nature. In studies on Gramineae the pollen was found to have an effect on the stigmatic tissue after a short period of contact, that is, even before germination: the cells of the stigma showed increased stainability of nuclei.

The stigmatoid tissue and the vascular bundles constitute the most specialized parts of the style. The ground tissue is parenchymatic, and the outer epidermis shows no peculiar features. It bears a cuticle and may have stomata.

Ovule

The ovule developing from the placenta of the ovary is the seat of formation of the megaspores (or macrospores) and of the development of the embryo sac (female gametophyte) from a megaspore. Sporogenesis, the development of the embryo sac, and the many variations in the details of these phenomena, have been the subject of numerous investigations and are not reviewed here. Concomitant with the development of the embryo from the fertilized egg, and of the endosperm from the product of the triple fusion (two polar nuclei and one sperm nucleus), the ovule develops into a seed. Histologically, the ovule is rather simple as compared with the resulting seed.

Commonly the ovule is differentiated into the following morphologic parts: the *nucellus* (from the Latin, small kernel), a central body of tissue containing some vegetative and some sporogenous cells; one or two *integuments* (from the Latin, covering) enclosing the nucellus; the *funiculus* (from the Latin, rope), the stalk by means of which the ovule is attached to the placenta. The size of the nucellus, the number of integuments, and the shape of the ovule are important distinguishing characteristics of ovules in different groups of angiosperms. If the nucellar apex points away from the funiculus, the ovule is termed *atropous* (synonym of *orthotropous*; a, not; *tropos*, turned, in Greek), that is, not turned. If the ovule is completely inverted so that the nucellar apex is turned toward the funiculus, it is called *anatropous*. Between these two extreme forms of ovules, there are several variously named intermediate ones with various degrees of curvature.

The ovule primordium arises from the placenta as a conical protuberance with a rounded apex. The first sporogeneous cell (archesporial cell) becomes evident, in the still undifferentiated protuberance, by its size and often also by denser appearance of its cytoplasm. This cell occurs beneath the protoderm at the apex of the primordium. Slightly below the apex the inner integument (or the single integument) is initiated by periclinal divisions in the protoderm. It arises as a ring-like welt and grows upward. With the appearance of the integument, the nucellus of the primordium becomes delimited as the part enveloped by the integument. The latter grows faster than the nucellus and encloses it partially or completely. Usually a narrow, canal-like opening remains at the top of the integument. This is the *micropyle*. The outer integument, if such develops at all, arises in the protoderm slightly below the inner integument and develops in a manner similar to that of the inner. It frequently does not reach the apex of the ovule in its upward growth. In the anatropous and other curved ovules the growth of the integuments is asymmetrical, being more pronounced on the side of the ovule which eventually becomes convex.

There is no agreement on the morphologic nature of the ovule and its parts. Some workers consider the ovule a foliar structure, others an axial. The nucellus is commonly regarded as the megasporangium, but the interpretation of the homology of the integuments constitutes a major morphologic problem.

The nucellus, the integuments, and the funiculus cannot be sharply delimited from one another either morphologically or cytologically. The nucellus is usually clearly outlined above the level where the integuments originate. From this level upward the nucellus and the integument (or integuments) have each their distinct epidermal layers. Below this level, that is, at the base of the nucellus, the nucellus and the integuments are confluent with the funiculus. The region of the ovule where all its parts merge with one another is called the *chalaza*.

The ovules of certain plants show considerable deviations from the structure just outlined. Some have no integuments, and others have more than two. The nucellus may be entirely confluent with the integuments, a condition supposedly different from that interpreted as absence of integument. Ovules may have other than the integuments, such as the *aril* (*Euonymus europ* from the funiculus, and the *caruncle* (*Ricinus*), an integument protuberance near the micropyle. In some plants the integument completely overgrows the nucellus that no micropyle remain; in other the integuments do not reach the apex of the nucellus.

The nucellus varies in size in different groups of plants. It may be so small that it comprises little more than an epidermis and the sporogenous tissue enclosed by it. In other plants a more or less massive vegetative tissue envelops the sporogenous tissue. The integuments also show variations in thickness. The thinnest integument is two cells thick; that is, it consists only of two epidermal layers. Sometimes the micropylar end is somewhat thicker in the two-layered integuments. Most angiosperms have two-layered integuments, although some dicotyledonous families have integuments of three and more layers. In relation to the size of nucelli the ovules are classified into *crassinucellate* (*crassus*, thick in Latin) and *tenuinucellate* (*tenuis*, slender in Latin). Crassinucellate ovules with two integuments are considered to be more primitive than the tenuinucellate with a single integument.

The ovules have a vascular system connected with that of the placenta. The presence of integumentary bundles is sometimes considered a primitive characteristic, but such bundles occur in the more specialized as well as in the less specialized angiosperms, and therefore their phylogenetic significance is uncertain. Most commonly there is a single strand ending in the chalaza with no prolongations into the integuments. In some species the bundle extends beyond the chalaza as a single strand or is variously branched. Such an intraovular system occurs in the integument. If two integuments are present, vascular tissue may be found in both integuments or only in the outer. Rarely does vascular tissue occur in the nucellus. The vascular tissue is primary and appears to be in a functioning state during the maturation of the seed.

The distribution of cuticles in the ovules deserves special mention because of their prominence and physiologic importance in the seed that develops from the ovule. The cuticles of the ovules and seeds are called by various names: cuticles, suberized membranes, semipermeable membranes, and fatty membranes. They are here referred to as cuticles in keeping with the most prevalent designation. Cuticles are reported to be present in ovules in relatively early stages of development.

The entire surface of the ovule primordium bears a cuticle. After the development of the integuments three cuticular layers may be distinguished: the outer, on the outside of the outer integument and the funiculus; the median, double in nature, between the two integuments; the inner, also double in nature, between the inner integument and the nucellus. In ovules with a single integument the median cuticle is absent. If the nucellus is small and its vegetative tissue is disorganized during the development of the embryo sac, the cuticle of the micropylar part of the nucellus may also be dissolved.

Parts of the ovule are disorganized during the development of the embryo sac, and the resulting materials are presumably utilized by the growing female gemetophyte. The vegetative tissue of the nucellus is partly or entirely resorbed. In the latter instance the embryo sac comes in contact with the inner epidermis of the integument. Large nucelli may be partially retained, and in some plant groups they form a storage tissue (*perisperm*) in the seed (Centrospermae). The nucellar epidermis is sometimes highly resistant and may proliferate into a nucellar cap with relatively thick walls (*Allium*). The integuments undergo certain histologic changes or are disorganized to varying degrees. Particularly common is the differentiation of the inner epidermis of the integument into the so-called nutritive jacket or *integumentary tapetum* consisting of deeply staining cells elongated perpendicularly with reference to the surface of the embryo sac. Such differentiation is characteristic of families in which the nucellus is early disorganized and the integument comes in contact with the embryo sac (Sympetalae). The physiologic significance of the integumentary tapetum is not agreed upon, and it might be variable. Some connection with the nutrition of the embryo is suggested by the disintegration of the ovule tissue located next to the tapetum and the persistence of the tapetum until the contents of the embryo sac complete their development.

Origin and Development

The change from vegetative to reproductive activity in the apical meristem follows a sequence that is determined by the nature of the plant. Herbaceous annuals pass, during one season, through an uninterrupted sequence of vegetative growth, floral initiation, and floral development. Woody species, at least in the North Temperate zone, commonly initiate the flowers in one season and complete their development during the next. The degree of differentiation that the flowers attain before the end of the first season is highly variable. Floral initiation is affected by external factors, but only the limits of reactivity of the plant to a given environment, for example, characteristic responses to length of day and produce flowers under specific combinations of these two factors.

Flowers arise at the apex of the main shoot, or on lateral branches, or on both. The lateral branches may form further branches of various orders before producing flowers. In different angiosperms the grouping of the flowers, called inflorescences, are highly variable and bear special names. The formation of all types of inflorescences involves, in the activity of a given apical meristem, a cessation of the vegetative stage and the initiation of the reproductive stage. Frequently, the first visible sign of determination of the flowering stage is the enhanced development of axillary buds. In species with cymose inflorescences a change from alternate, five-ranked arrangement of leaves to the single-ranked arrangement of floral primordia occurs at the beginning of the reproductive stage.

Organogenesis

Much can be learned about floral development by comparing flowers in different stages of development in material dissected under magnifications of moderate degrees. Payer (1857) employed this method in his classic comparative study of organ development in flowers, and in modern times it has been applied with particular success to investigations of floral differentiation in the Gramineae. A correlation of the observations on dissected material with those on flowers sectioned with a microtome gives a rather comprehensive picture of the main phenomena in the development of the specific form of flowers and their parts.

Depending on the structure of the flower, the parts may appear in acropetal order at successively higher levels like the leaves on a vegetative shoot (*Ranunculus*), or the parts of a given kind may arise at the same level or nearly so (*Capsella*). In the former instance the floral parts are arranged helically; in the latter they are in whorls (cycles). If the parts arise in a helical sequence, the helices of the various parts are usually not continuous with one another. The calyx

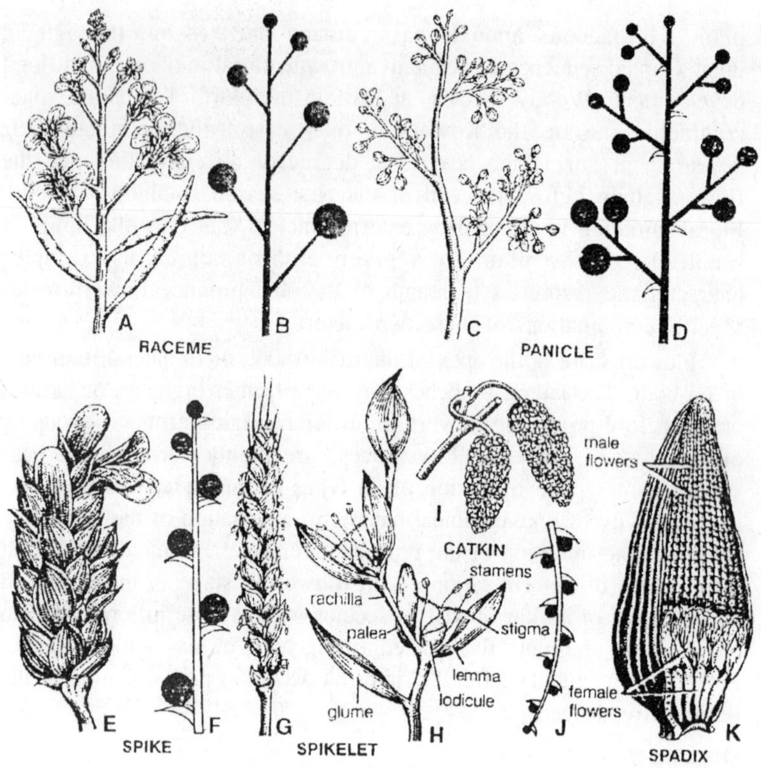

Fig. 7.6. Racemose inflorescence: A-B, raceme of brassica; C-D. panicle of Rhus; E-F. spike of Adhatoda; G-H. spikelet of Triticum; I-J. catkin of Morus; K. spadix of Musa. B, D, F H and J are diagrammatic representations.

members, however, may appear along helices that are continuation of those of the foliage leaves. The flower parts either arise in a continuous acropetal sequence of sepals, petals, stamens, and carpels, or else this sequence is more or less modified. In *Capsella*, for example, the stamen and carpel primordia appear before those of the petals. There may be a difference in the rhythm of development of floral parts. In Papaverceae, for example, the sepals arise considerably in advance of the other parts. Petals, stamens, and carpels appear in rapid succession and overlap one another in timing of their origin.

The successive formation of the different floral parts–as contrasted with that of similar parts during vegetative growth–apparently is governed by complex determination phenomena involving, among other mechanisms, those of hormonal balances. Surgical experimentation with developing flowers of *Primula* indicates that the flower passes through a succession of physiological states which permit and regulate the formation of each organ in turn.

As was mentioned previously, the floral parts may remain discrete at maturity, or they may become variously united within the whorls and between whorls. Three developmental patterns may bring about the union of parts: (1) the whorl arises as a unit structure; that is, the parts of the whorl show congenital unity; (2) the parts of a whorl or of adjacent whorls become joined during ontogeny; (3) the union of parts results from a combination of the two phenomena, the ontogenetic and congenital unions. The calyx and corolla tubes in *Datura*, for example, arise by ontogenetic fusion. Those of *Frasera* are congenitally united, for they are formed by intercalary growth of a ring of tissue at the base of the primordia of calyx and corolla. In *Vinca*, however, the corolla tube consists of two parts, one formed by intercalary growth of receptacular tissue at the base of the petals, the other resulting from the union of the bases of the initially free petals.

The development of an initially open carpel into a closed structure involves a clearly expressed ontogenetic union of carpel margins. The lower part of the carpel, however, may have a sac-like seamless form from the inception of the primordium. The formation of syncarpous gynoecia is associated with congenital and ontogenetic union in varying proportions. There may be also an ontogenetic union between the carpels and the stamens. On the other hand, the perianth parts and the stamens may originate together from unit primorida and become distinct during later growth.

The features discussed above may be elucidated by means of specific examples of floral development. The flower of *Allium cepa* (onion) is relatively unspecialized in having an undifferentiated perianth of free parts and a superior ovary. Its carpels are united, however. The six-parted perianth consists of two whorls of tepals, an outer and an inner. The six stamens occur in the axils of the six perianth members. The three carpels are united into a gynoecium with a three-loculed ovary and an axile placentation. The style is thin and has a slightly three-lobed stigma. An individual flower is a globose protuberance before the flower parts appear. The outer three tepals arise first. The stamens in the axils of these tepals arise simultaneously with the tepals and from the same primordia. The outer tepals and the associated stamens arise in a clockwise direction. The inner tepals and the stamens subtended by them also arise together, but in a counter-clockwise direction. With further growth, the tepals overarch the stamens. When this stage is reached, the carpels are initiated. They occur within the inner staminal whorl in alternation with its members. At first they project over the surface of the receptacle in the form of three horseshoe-shaped welts of meristematic tissue. Then they grow upward and toward the center where their margins meet and fuse. The compound style is formed by apical growth of the three carpels, the three parts uniting completely. The base of the style eventually appears deeply imbedded in the center of the ovary because the carpels bulge upward during the differentiation of the ovules. The ovules are initiated before the carpel margins fuse. They are anatropous and have two integuments.

The flower of *Lactuca sativa* (lettuce) may be used to illustrate the growth of a highly specialized flower, one with an inferior ovary (epigynous flower) and a zygomorphic sympetalous corolla. Lettuce belongs to the Compositae in which the flowers occur in capitate (head-like) inflorescences. The individual flowers arise acropetally on the flattened receptacle, so that the outermost flowers of the head are the oldest, the innermost the youngest. In an individual flower, the petal lobes appear first, as five protuberances on the margin of the floral primordium. However, immediately after their appearance they are thrust upward by intercalary growth of a ring of tissue upon which the corolla is inserted. As a result of this growth the central part of the flower primordium becomes cup-shaped. The stamens, which are initiated after the corolla, seem to be inserted below the corolla, but actually they occur closer to the center or apex of the flower than the other floral parts. The pappus, which is interpreted sometimes as a set of epidermal trichomes, sometimes as the calyx, appears almost at the same time as the stamens. It arises below and opposite the stamens on the outer surface of the rim of the cup-like primordium which higher up bears the corolla and the stamens.

In its further growth the corolla develops as a tubular structure with a unilateral strap-shaped prolongation (zygomorphic ligulate corolla). Two stages may be distinguished in the growth of the corolla tube. First, intercalary growth above the insertion of the stamens forms the upper part of the corolla tube. Second, intercalary growth below the insertion of the stamens forms the lower part of the tube in which the bases of the corolla and of the stamens are congenitally fused (epipetalous stamens). The second stage occurs comparatively late in the development of the flower. In the Compositae with actinomorphic tubular corollas the growth of the upper part of the corolla is uniform throughout. In zygomorphic corollas, as in lettuce, the upper part grows asymmetrically. The free parts of the stamens elongate also, and each becomes differentiated into a filament and an anther.

The carpels develop at the morphologically highest position of the flower, that is, within the cavity of the cup-like primordium. The two carpels become visible as two protuberances located seemingly below the stamens. These two carpel units overarch the ovarian cavity and become prolonged above into a solid compound style with a two-parted stigma. In Compositae the cup enclosing the ovary is commonly interpreted as consisting of adnate bases of the floral whorls joined to the carpel bases; in other words, the ovary is enclosed by the floral tube.

The development of an inflorescence and flower of a representative of the Gramineae may be illustrated by reference to the study on *Triticum* and *Avena*. The wheat inflorescence is a spike and consists of several groups of flowers, each referred to as a spikelet. The spikelets are attached directly to the main axis, the rachis. A spikelet of a grass consists of a short axis, the rachilla, bearing several chaff-like, two-ranked (distichous), overlapping bracts (commonly called glumes). The two lowermost bracts bear no flowers in their axils and are called empty glumes. Above the empty glumes are others that subtend flowers, usually referred to as florets. The wheat spikelet has four to six florets, each subtended by two bracts: the lower or abaxial called the *lemma*, and the upper or adaxial, called the *palea*. The reproductive parts of a grass floret consist of three stamens with thread-like filaments and rather large anthers, and a single, unilocular pistil with a short style and two feathery stigmas. At the base of the ovary and opposite the palea are two lodicules, small scales involved in the opening of the bracts during anthesis.

The reproductive stage of a wheat plant begins while the plant is still in the rosette stage. The initiation of reproductive stage is quickly followed by a sudden and vigorous elongation of the shoot, the subsequent culm. The addition of leaf primordia ceases, and even the further development of the existing leaf buttresses is stopped. Some of the younger buttresses may be obliterated as the apex expands in length and width. Whereas the foliage leaf primordia arise as single ridges gradually encircling the shoot axis, the spikelet development is initiated by the appearance of double ridges. The spikelet proper differentiates from the upper of the paired ridges. A spikelet is interpreted as an axillary bud, and the lower ridge as the subtending leaf. The first spikelets differentiate in the middle of the spike, and differentiation then progresses acropetally and basipetally. Within the individual spikelet differentiation is acropetal, the parts appear in the sequence of empty glumes, first flower, second flower, and so forth. Within an individual floret the parts arise in a close overlapping sequence: lemma, palea, lodicules, stamens, and gynoecium.

The primordia of the lemma, palea, and lodicules are ridge-like; that is, they resemble leaf primordia. The stamen primordia, on the other hand, are rounded like bud primordia, one of the features that is used to interpret the stamen as a cauline structure.

The gynoecium occupies the apex of the floral meristem. A crescent-shaped ridge, which is highest on the side toward the lemma, arises just below the apex. The apical mound itself constitutes the ovule primordium. The ridge grows entirely around the ovule primordium and initiates two styles on two sides of its margin. Continued upward growth of the margins below the styles brings about the closure of the ovarian cavity. The stigmatic hairs are the last parts of the gynoecium to develop. Thus, the grass gynoecium arises as a unit and does not reveal, ontogenetically, the three-carpellate origin usually ascribed to the gynoecium of Gramineae. The same method of origin and growth of the gynoecium has been observed in various other Gramineae and in Cyperaceae, except that in the latter some species have three styles. The apical position of the ovule is used for interpreting it as an axial structure, but the opinions on the number of carpels are divided. The carpellary part, or ovary wall, of the gynoecium is considered to be leaf-like in its method of origin and growth.

The rhythm of development of a flower as a whole has certain distinguishing characteristics that are closely correlated with the important phenomena of mitosis and meiosis occurring during the formation of spores and gametes. The sequence of formation of floral parts is more rapid than that of the foliage leaves so that the ontogeny of the flower may have an explosive character. Morphologic observations and studies on comparative weights of developing flowers and their parts show that these parts may have divergent rates of growth after they are initiated. The petals, for example, may appear before the stamens but may develop more slowly. Sometimes the principal period of growth of the petals occurs only after the stamens complete their growth. Both the petals and the stamens may accelerate their growth rate shortly before anthesis. The remarkable speed with which the stamens may attain their final length is well illustrated by the rate of elongation of 2.5 mm per minute observed in the growing anther filaments of rye. The stamens may lag behind the gynoecium in development at first, then rapidly attain the final length which brings the anther into a most favorable position for release of pollen. The ovary usually enlarges uniformly like a vegetative organ. Sometimes, however, the enlargement slows down before fertilization, and if fertilization fails to take place, the gynoecium dies. Comparative studies on floral parts show that the reproductive parts constitute a relatively large mass of the flower as a whole.

Histogenesis

Research on histogenesis of floral parts is used extensively for the interpretation of the morphologic nature of the flower and in comparative taxonomic studies. The sepals and petals originate, like the foliage leaves, from periclinal divisions in one or more subsurface layers of the apical meristem. Such origin of the perianth parts is apparently common in both the dicotyledons and the monocotyledons. In their upward growth, the perianth parts show apical activity of short duration followed by some intercalary growth. Marginal activity followed by intercalary growth is responsible for the increase in width of the perianth primordia. In *Vinca* the marginal meristem of the petals is more active than that of the sepals and is involved in the formation of the upper part of the floral tube which arises through the ontogenetic fusion of the corolla lobes.

Some workers find that the stamens are initiated just like the members of the perianth. Others report that the stamens have a deeper origin than the perianth parts and are, therefore, axial structures.

After their initiation the stamens undergo apical growth of short duration, followed by intercalary growth. If the stamen filament is flattened, it shows marginal growth; otherwise such growth is suppressed. The anthers have a special form of marginal activity which produces the characteristic two-lobed, four-loculed structure, rather than a flat blade. With regard to the gynoecium, frequently the origin of the placentae and ovules are considered to be distinctive from that of the carpel. Some authors find that the carpel resembles a leaf in the manner it originates from the apical meristem, whereas the placenta or the single, basally attached ovule is initiated like an axial structure. Others postulate that the primary ontogenetic relation of the ovule is with the carpel and that the method of growth, which is obviously correlated with the future form of an entity, is hardly a safe criterion of homology. Still another view has been advanced on the basis of developmental relations in cytochimeras of *Datura*. All parts of the gynoecium, carpels, placentae, and ovules are cauline in nature because they arise in the third layer of the apical meristem, whereas the foliage leaves are initiated in the second. In their future growth, the carpels undergo apical and marginal growth.

Histologic studies have revealed the manner of ontogenetic union of flower parts. As was mentioned previously, the union of perianth parts or of the carpels may be congenital, or it may occur, partly or entirely, during ontogeny. The ontogenetic union is brought about by fusion of the margins of parts that come in contact with each other during growth. In the petals of *Vinca* such union occurs through apposition of two epidermal layers, with the line of union eventually becoming obscured. Evidence of the fusion of perianth parts is thoroughly obliterated if divisions, periclinal and others, occur in the apposed epidermal layers. The degree of union of carpels also varies from a rather loose one to a thorough interlocking of the epidermal cells, accompanied by divisions in these cells and a complete effacement of the suture. In dicotyledons the carpels of syncarpous gynoecia are generally more firmly joined than in monocotyledons.

Vascular Development

Information on vascular development in the flower is meager. Some consideration has been given the question of the direction of differentiation of procambium. The assumption that there is an acropetal differentiation of procambium in the flower and a basipetal differentiation in the vegetative shoot has been used in support of the concept that the flower is a unique structure and not comparable to the shoot. Later research has shown that there is no such simple and straightforward difference between the flower and the shoot. Acropetal differentiation of procambium is common in the vegetative shoot in a wide variety of plants. In the flowers, both acropetal and basipetal differentiation of procambium have been reported.

According to the classic study of Trecul (1881), the xylem in the flower follows a pattern of differentiation similar to that in the shoot; that is, it appears in one or more loci and then progresses bidirectionally toward the distal and the proximal parts of the flower. In *Perilla* vascular differentiation appears to be speeded up when the reproductive stage is induced.

Abscission

The abscission of floral parts has been less intensively investigated than that of the leaves, but the basic phenomena appear to be similar in the separation of all these structures. Abscission of parts or of entire structures occurs at various stages in the reproductive process. The completion of flowering may be followed by the shedding of parts of flowers, of entire flowers, or of inflorescences. Particularly common is the shedding of petals. The petals may fall without previous wilting (*Canna*, *Aquilegia*, *Cydonia*, *Rosa*, *Geranium*, *Linum*). They also abscise in a wilted or dried state, either close to the level of their insertion (*Lilium*, *Tulipa*, most Cruciferae, *Cucurbita*), or a short distance above the insertion, with the basal part remaining attached to the flower (*Althaea*, *Datura*, *Nicotiana*). If the petals are not shed at the end of flowering, they remain temporarily or permanently attached to the fruit in the dry state (*Agapanthus*, *Hypericum*, *Convallaria*). In some monocotyledons the perianth becomes green and persists in the fruit (*Veratrum*, *Eucomis*, *Paris*).

Petals are often constricted in the abscission zone. Usually no cell division precedes abscission, and the separation layer is poorly differentiated. The cells in this layer remain small, little vacuolated, and closely packed. They may contain chloroplasts or chromoplasts, and also raphides. The cells are roundish or polygonal in outline, occasionally tabular, with their long diameters oriented transversely with reference to the long axis of the petal. If the petal is much constricted, collenchyma may be present beneath the epidermis. Apparently the separation results from a softening of the middle lamella. Cell division may occur in the separation layer. The protection of the scar seems to involve an impregnation of the walls with fatty substances without the deposition of a suberin lamella or formation of cork. Sepals, staminal filaments, and styles may abscise after flowering in essentially the same manner as the petals.

The abscission of entire flowers is characteristic of plants with unisexual flowers. The staminal flowers are regularly abscised after the pollen is shed. These flowers may fall singly (Cucurbitaceae) or as entire inflorescences (catkins of the Amentiferae). If fertilization does not take place, carpellate and bisexual flowers may drop also (*Solanum tuberosum*, *Nicotiana tabacum*, *Lycopersicon esculentum*). Floral abscission can be induced artificially by various treatments. The separation layer in pedicels of flowers is, in some species, preformed during development. Surface grooves are sometimes present in pedicels but do not necessarily coincide with the abscission zone.

8

POLLINATION

The fertilization of the egg and the subsequent development of the seed can occur only if pollen grains have previously been deposited upon the stigma. *Pollination*, the transfer of pollen from the anther to the stigma, should be distinguished from fertilization, which is the fusion of the male and female gametes. Pollination is of two types.

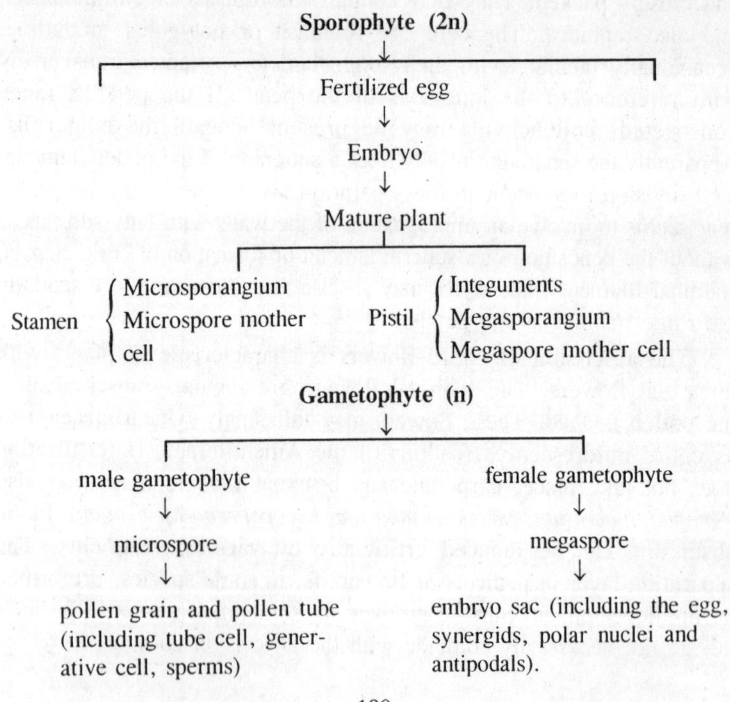

Self-pollination is the pollination of a stigma by pollen from the same flower or from another flower of the same plant. *Cross-pollination* involves the transfer of pollen from the anther of a flower of one plant to the stigma of a flower of another plant of the same or related species. The chief agents of pollination are wind and insects, but birds, snails, other small animals, and even water may carry pollen from one flower to another.

Self-pollination occurs in many plants. Among the economically important self-pollinated plants are oats, wheat, barley and rice, peas and beans, soybean, flax, cotton, and tobacco. Cross-pollination, however, is more common than self-pollination, and it probable occurs, at least occasionally, in most of the self-pollinated species.

Cross-pollination brings about a more diverse combination of hereditary units of the two parents. This results in increased variability in the offspring and greater adaptability to new environments—conditions of evolutionary advantage to the species. A more immediate effect of cross-pollination in many species is the production of more seeds or greater vigor in the offspring. A very large number of flowering plants have adaptations which prevent or reduce self-pollination. These many adaptations are usually related to pollination by insects. Prominent among them are modifications of the flower which make cross-pollination by insects possible and in some cases essential if seeds are to be formed.

So numerous and varied are these adaptations to cross-pollination that ignorance of them has caused serious difficulties when new plants have been introduced. An example of this is afforded by the history of Smyrna fig production in California. Large numbers of cuttings were introduced from Asia Minor about 1880. These grew well, but the fruits dropped from the tree before maturity. The realization that pollination is brought about by a tiny was resulted in the introduction of the insect, after which the industry flourished. Information on pollination is also needed by the plant breeder when he attempts to produce varieties of greater usefulness to man.

Insect Pollination

A large proportion of flowering plants are insect pollinated. The insects are chiefly bees, wasps, butterflies, and moths, but beetles, flies, and other kinds also frequent flowers. Insect-pollinated flowers are usually brightly coloured or scented, sometimes both. Their pollen is heavy or sticky and is not readily carried by wind. Many such

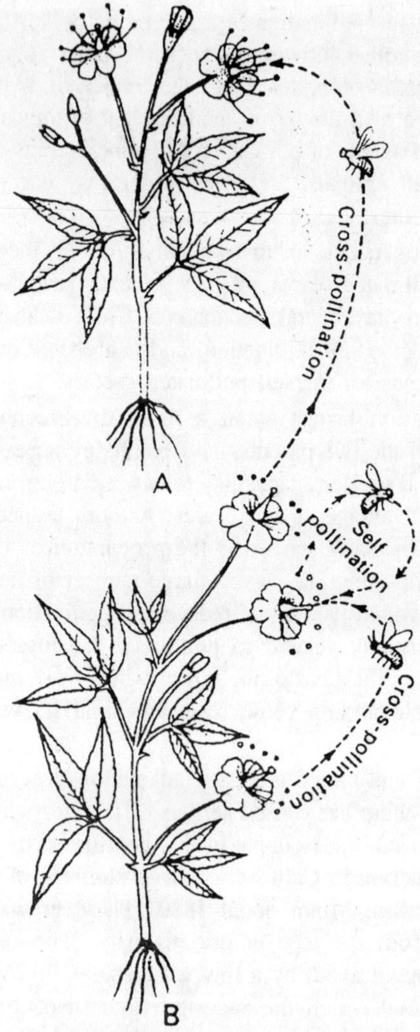

Fig. 8.1. Summary of self pollination and cross pollination.

flowers are provided with *nectaries*, specialized tissues or organs which secrete nectar, a fluid with a sugar content varying from 4 to 65 per cent. This nectar is the raw material from which honey is made. Nectaries vary greatly in form and location and may be associated with any of the floral organs. Nectar may be secreted by the surface of the receptacle, by the walls of spurlike projections of the perianth, or by hairs on the petals or ovary.

In many flowers the nectary consists of a ring around the base of the ovary. In some, the stamens or petals have become reduced and modified into nectaries. Numerous experiments, especially on the honey bee, have confirmed the general belief that insects are attracted to flowers by colour or scent. The sense of smell of the honey bee seems to be about as sensitive as that of man, but that of other insects, especially moths, is more powerful, and they may detect odors at considerable distances. Honey bees, although partly colour blind, can distinguish colours. They are colour blind to red, which they cannot distinguish yellow, blue or dark grey. They can identify blue, but not such shades of blue as purple and violet. They also distinguish yellow, blue-green, and ultraviolet. Red flowers are usually pollinated by butterflies, which are not colourblind to red, or occasionally by hummingbirds.

Bees and other insects visit flowers to gather pollen or nectar as food for themselves or their progeny. Pollination is incidental to these activities. Pollen will usually be found adhering to the mouthparts, head, legs, and body hairs of a bee after it has visited a flower. If the bee when visits another flower, some of the pollen may adhere to the stigma, resulting in cross-pollination. Insect pollination is of the greatest importance from the standpoint of plant evolution and reproduction. It is of economic importance also, for many kinds of plants used directly by man or as food for domestic animals depend upon insect pollination. They include more than fifty kinds of crop plants in this country, among them apple and pear, the Smyrna fig, melon and cucumber, avocado, cabbage, buckwheat, alfalfa, and many clovers. In the absence of certain insects, such plants yield neither seed nor fruit.

Floral Adaptations Favouring Cross-pollination

In many plants with perfect flowers, the stamens and pistils mature at different times. This, of course, favours cross-pollination. Such a flower is said to be *dichogamous*. Dichogamy manifests itself in two ways. In the most common, the anthers ripen before the stigma matures before the pollen sacs of the stamens open. The anthers of Jacob's-ladder (*Polemonium caeruleum*), a garden ornamental, shed their pollen before the stigma of the same flower is ready to receive it; the three lobes of the stigma are folded together at this stage. After the pollen is shed, the lobes spread apart and may be pollinated by pollen from younger flowers. Flowers with pistils and stamens maturing at different times are extremely common, and most families of flowering plants have some species in which this condition is present. The interval

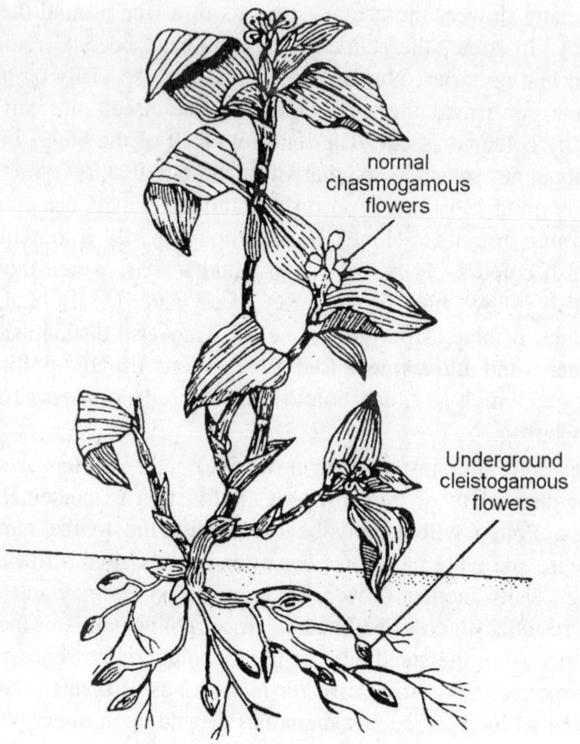

Fig. 8.2. Cleistogamous flowers of Commelina.

between the maturation of the stamens and the time when the stigma is receptive varies from an hour or so to several days. The most complex example of dichogamy is found in the avocado, widely used as a food plant in the tropics and cultivated in the warmer parts of the United States.

The approximately one hundred varieties of the avocado fall into two groups, termed class A and class B varieties. The flowers of class A varieties are functionally female in the morning and male in the afternoon. That is, in the morning the stigma is receptive but no pollen is shed, whereas in the afternoon the stigma has withered and the anthers open to discharge pollen. The flowers of class B varieties are male in the morning and female in the afternoon. During the morning, therefore, the stigmas of class A flowers are pollinated by insects which carry pollen from class B flowers. The reverse is true in the afternoon, when the stigmas of class B varieties are pollinated by pollen from anthers of class A varieties. This information on pollination in the avocado, obtained by several botanists in 1921-1926, is the basis of the recommen-dation that a grove of avocado trees should contain varieties of both class A and class B, to ensure cross-pollination. This is especially necessary in Florida. In other regions, irregularities in the time of blooming render such interplanting unnecessary, and the trees of a single variety may set fruit.

Even self-pollination, however, can be brought about only with the aid of bees, for the pollen of avocado is heavy and sticky and adapted to dispersal by insects. Insects which rove or climb over the floral parts pollinate many kinds of flowers which have no special structural adaptations to insect visitors. These visits take place by chance, and the insects bring about cross-pollination only occasionally. However, the flowers of many plants are so constructed that they are visited by one kind or at most a few kinds of insects. These insects regularly visit flowers of the same species, so that pollen is frequently carried from the anthers of one flower to the stigma of another.

Such flowers have numerous adaptations which favour cross-pollination and which make self pollination unlikely or impossible. The stigma is commonly placed so that it is brushed by an insect visiting the flower by does not receive pollen from the anthers of the same flower. This condition commonly results when the elongated style projects well above the anthers. In many flowers there is a close relationship between the depth of the corolla tube and the length of the sucking mouth parts of the insects which usually visit them. The nectar at the base of the corolla tube may be so deep that only a butterfly or moth with long tubular mouth parts can reach it. This is the case with a number of strongly scented white or nearly white flowers which open in the evening. Soapwort (*saponaria*), some species of tobacco, and the Jimson weed (*Datura*), which has a corolla tube 3 inches long, are pollinated only by night-flying hawkmoths.

The red clover is pollinated only by bees whose mouth parts are of sufficient length to reach the nectary at the back of the flower. Flowers with a short corolla tube or exposed nectar are likely to be visited by a variety of insects, including flies. Cross-pollination is also promoted in plants in which the length of the style differs in plants of the same species (*heterostyly*). In one kind of plant all the flowers have short styles and the anthers are above the stigma. In the other kind, the flowers all have long styles, and the anthers are located below the stigma. The mouth parts of an insect, thrust into a short-styled flower, come in contact with the anthers and become covered

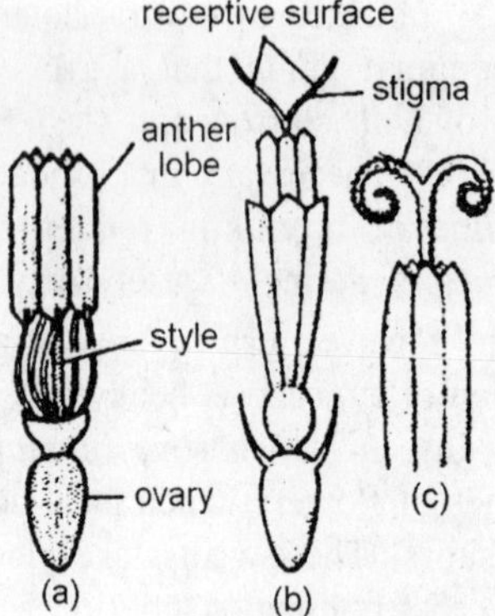

Fig. 8.3. (a) Protandrous flower of Sunflower with mature anthers but immature stigma, hidden within the anther tube; (b) Maturing and expanding bifid stigma showing receptive surface; C–Curving back of stigmatic lobes if cross pollination fails.

with pollen. If the insect should now enter a long styled flower, the pollen is deposited upon the stigma, which is located at approximately the same level as the anthers in the short-styled flower. Similarly, the pollen adhering to an insect which has visited a long-styled flower will be deposited upon the stigma of a short-styled flower, which is at the same level in the corolla as the anthers of the long-styled flower.

Self-pollination is not precluded by this structure, for pollen may fall from the anthers of a short-styled flower onto the stigma. In the long-styled flowers, self-pollination may occur because of the elongation of the corolla tube toward the end of the flowering period. In this final growth, the ring of anthers is brought to the level of the stigma. Heterostyly is very common. It is found in a large number of plant families, including the pinks, St.-John's-worts, heaths, wood sorrels,

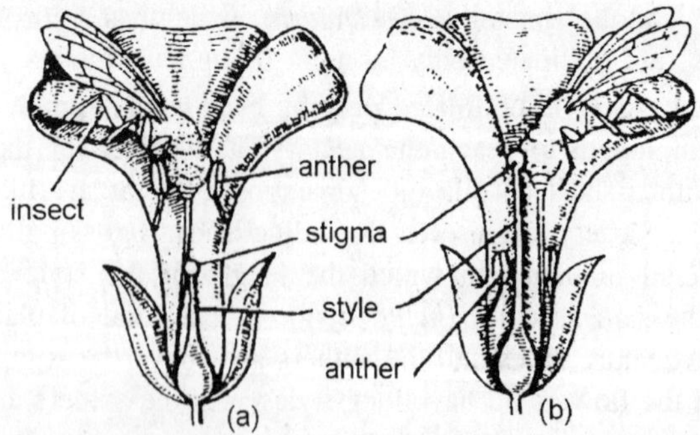

Fig. 8.4. Primula. (a) Short style and highly placed anthers; (b) Long style and lower anther.

gentians, poppies, pigweeds, and many others. Innumerable variations in pollination mechanisms and adaptation of flowers to insect visitors are known. Two final examples illustrate how complex the relation between flowers and insects have become.

Pollination in Salvia

The salvias (sages) have a pollination mechanism whereby a sudden movement of the filaments results in the transfer of pollen to an insect visitor. This mechanism is best known in *Salvia pratensis*, a cultivated ornamental herb with blue flowers. The flower is irregular, with a strongly developed upper and lower lip. Nectar is secreted by a ring of glands by the base of the ovary. Only two stamens are found, concealed under the upper lip.

Each filament is jointed near the base and is prolonged downward into a shell-shaped expansion which connects with a similar expansion from the other filament to form a plate which closes the mouth of the corolla tube. When a bee pushes into the flower to obtain nectar, its mouth parts encounter this plate, which is then pushed upward and backward, causing the filaments and their anthers to tip forward. The anthers then come in contact with the back of the bee, which is dusted with pollen. When the insect withdraws, the filaments return to their former position. The stigma, located above the anthers, now matures;

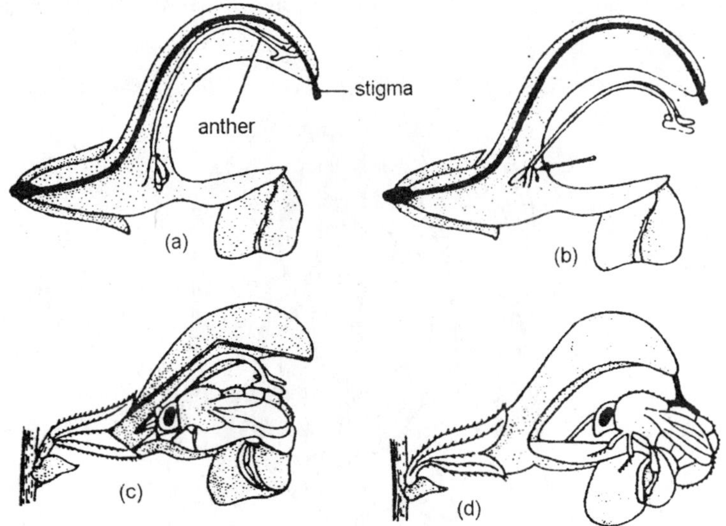

Fig. 8.5. Pollination in Salvia. (a), (b) L.S. of flower showing immature pistil and mature stamens; (c) A bee coming with pollen; (d) A flower with mature stigma.

it grows downward and the lobes open. If the bee then visits an older flower, it brushes against the downwardly directed lobes of the stigma, to which the pollen is transferred. Pollination of the stigma by pollen from the same flower is, of course, impossible.

Pollination in Yucca

The relationship between the Pronuba moth and the pollination of the flowers of the yucca plant is so extraordinary as to be unbelievable if it had not been verified repeatedly by qualified investigators since its discovery in 1892. The yuccas are a group of some thirty species of lilly-like plants with long, sword-like leaves. They are popularly called Spanish bayonet or Spanish dagger. Most the native to the arid parts of the Southwest and Mexico; some are cultivated as ornamentals. In the early summer the plant sends up a tall, coarse flower stalk bearing numerous large, white, drooping, bell-shaped flowers. The stamens, six in number, are much shorter than the pistil and also arch away from it, so that self-pollination is impossible. The style is short, and the stigma is three-lobed, with a deep chamber lying between the lobes. In the evening after the flowers open, the silvery white Pronuba moths, about 5/8 inch long, appear in the vicinity.

The moths may come from a distance, attracted by the wind borne fragrance. Both male and female Pronuba moths take no food and live only 2 to 5 days after mating. The males and females meet within the

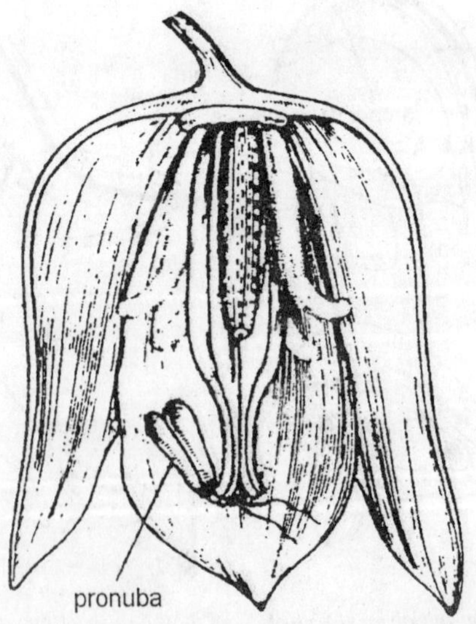

Fig. 8.6. A mature Yacca flower with pronuba moth pollinating the flower.

flower and mate. The female, then places herself at the top of a stamen, where she scrapes pollen from the anther by means of highly modified mouth parts. Visits to several stamens produce a large amount of pollen, which is kneaded into a ball held just under the moth's head. The female then flies to another plant and, after boring a hole in the soft tissues of the ovary, deposits an eggs in the vicinity of the ovules. As soon as the egg is laid, the female moves to the top of the pistil and pushes a portion of her load of pollen into the stigmatic chamber, pressing it down firmly with several vigorous thrusts. Another egg is then deposited within the same ovary, and again a portion of the pollen mass is forced into the stigmatic chamber.

The depositing of each egg is followed by pollination, until about five eggs have been laid. The egg hatches into a larva, which feeds upon the seeds which have developed from the ovules. The larva matures in about a month, bores a hole in the wall of the mature ovary (capsule), and drops to the soil, where it burrows to a depth of several inches. Here it spends the winter and spring in a tough cocoon. When the yucca flowers again, the insect appears above the ground as a winged adult and the cycle is repeated.

The pollen which the female Pronuba has placed upon the stigma serves as a supply of food for the larva when it emerges from the egg. Without pollination, the ovules would not develop into seeds with their stores of readily available food. The yucca, in turn, would be unable to reproduce without the Pronuba. Each larva eats relatively few seeds, perhaps eighteen to twenty-five, and the several hundred sound seeds which remain in each fruit allow reproduction to continue. It is difficult to avoid the conclusion that the moth behaves intelligently and purposefully in this curious relationship, perceiving in advance that her labours result in food for her young.

A more rational point of view regards this relationship as the result of a long evolutionary development, in the course of which the floral structure and the mouth parts of the insect have all become modified from a simpler condition. In whatever manner the flower and the insect became mutually adapted, it is now certain that without one there could not be the other.

Self-sterility

In many plants with perfect flowers, fertilization and seed formation follow self-pollination. This condition is known as *self-fertility*. In other plants with perfect flowers, fertilization does not occur when the stigma is pollinated by pollen of the same flower. Even pollen

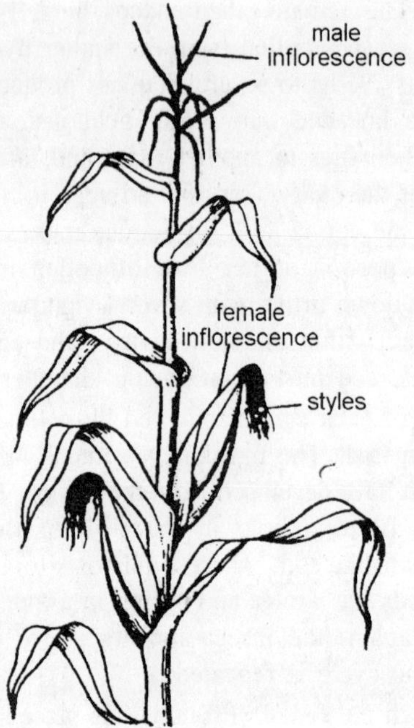

Fig. 8.7. Maize cob showing long silky style and stigma for catching pollen grains.

from another flower of the same plant or from flowers of other plants of like hereditary constitution will not result in fertilization. This condition of physiological incompatibility is known as *self-sterility*. Many species which show the phenomenon of self-sterility can be arranged in groups of individuals which fail to set seed when pollinated by other individuals of other groups. Several hundred such species, wild and cultivated, are known, and the list is probably far from complete.

Most cases of self sterility are due to the slow rate of pollen-tube growth when the flower is pollinated by pollen from flowers of like heredity. The rate of pollen-tube growth is determined by certain genes. If the pollen tubes carry the same sterility genes as the style, the rate of growth is so slow that the flower withers and falls away before fertilization takes place. If the genes of the style are suitably different from those of the pollen tube, the tube grows rapidly and fertilization follows. In most ornamental plants self-sterility is of little significance because these plants are grown for their flowers of foliage. But self-sterility in such plants as red clover, apples, pears, cherries, and plums, which are cultivated for their seeds or fruits, is another matter.

Some varieties of apples set fruits well if self-pollinated or pollinated by pollen from flowers of other trees of the same variety. Most apple varieties are self-sterile, and commercial orchards are therefore planted with at least two varieties whose pollen is effective in cross pollination and whose blooming periods overlap. Certain combinations of varieties are unsuccessful, and the grower must have a list of the varieties which are compatible when crossed. The varieties are set out in the orchard so that several rows of one variety alternate with rows of another. Bees bring about cross-pollination. Frequently hives are rented from beekeepers and places in the orchard during the period of bloom. Even many of the self-pollinated varieties set a better crop when crossed with another variety.

The existence of self-sterility in cultivated fruits has been known since the latter part of the nineteenth century, but even today large apple orchards of one variety are sometimes planted, with the result that little or no fruit is produced. This can be overcome, however, either by grafting other varieties to established trees or by placing bouquets of apple flowers of another variety in the orchard during the pollinating period. Pears and plums, like apples, include some self-sterile varieties. Sweet cherries are self-stertile, but sour cherries, nectarines, and peaches are not. A practical knowledge of these aspects of pollination may mean success or failure to the grower of fruit trees.

Insects that Visit Flowers

The chief flower-visiting insects are beetles (Coleoptera), flies (Diptera), bees and wasps (Hymenoptera), butterflies and moths (Lepidoptera). In connection with the pollination of flowers, the important differences to be noticed between these insects are the size of the body, the length of the tongue (proboscis), the time of year at which each kind is most plentiful, and their habits—*e.g.,* whether they collect pollen or nector or both, whether they fly by day or in the evening. By carefully studying the structure of a flower, and nothing such points as the time of flowering, the order in which the anthers and stigmas mature, the relative positions of anthers and stigmas in the open flower and any changes in position that may occur, we can often tell what kind of insect is capable of effecting cross-pollination, and whether or not self-pollination is possible. Most flies and beetles have very short tongues, usually less than 3 mm. long. Most of the larger and longer-tongued flies, *e.g.,* gadflies, "cleggs," and horseflies do not visit flowers; but there are some, chiefly hover-lies and bee-flies, with tongues sometimes as long as 12 mm., which are regular flower-visitors. Flowers may be arranged in various biological group or classes according to their adaptations for insect-visitation:

Flowers adapted for short-tongued insects

These may be (*a*) flowers in which the necter is freely exposed on the surface, *e.g.*, Umbelliferae, Rutaceae, etc. : (*b*) flowers with a very short tube, *e.g.*, moschatel, bedstraw, enchanter's nightshade; (*c*) shallow open flowers such as stonecrop and saxifrages. Such flowers are visited by the shorter-tongued bettles and flies.

Flowers with partially-concealed nectar

This group includes flowers in which the nectar can be reached only by insects with tongues at least 3 mm. in length, and which are therefore visited by the longer-tongued beetles and flies, as well as by insects of higher type. The nectar may be slightly concealed by the stamens, *e.g.*, *Ranunculus* and Myrtaceae; by the erect stiff sepals, as in the smaller Cruciferae; by the formation of a shallow calyx-tube, as in many Rosaceae; by a short corolla tube, *e.g.*, the shorter-tubed Compositae, etc.

Flowers with fully-concealed nectar

This type of flower differs only in degree from the last. Here the nectar can only be reached by insects having tongues about 6 mm. long, including the longest-tongued flies (chiefly hover-flies), the shorter-tongued bees, and wasps. The concealment of the nectar is effected by a further deepening of the flower, owing to the formation of a calyx-tube, to the calyx being gamosepalous or the corolla gamopetalous, or to other causes. Examples of these medium-tubed flowers are seen in some Rosaceae, Solanaceae, Scro-phulariaceae, etc.

Long-tubed flowers

When the flower-tube becomes longer, all the shorter-tongued insects are more or less completely excluded, and the flower is adapted for, and chiefly visited by, the larger bees, butterflies and moths. Many flowers belonging to the Amaryllidaceae, Iridaceae, Orchidaceae and Scitamineae, in which the perianth nearly always forms a long tube, come under this type. Flowers like those of Papilionateae, *Antirrhinum*, and *Calceolaria*, can only be opened by large bees, and only the longest-tongued bees can reach the nectar in such flowers as *Aconitum* and *Delphinium*.

Humble and hive-bees have the most perfect mechanism (the "pollen-baskets" on the hind-legs) for collecting pollen to mix with nectar and feed their broods. Humble-bees have longer tongues than hive-bees, and are particularly skilful in finding the way to well-concealed honey.

Blue, purple, and red colours are often associated with flowers visited by bees (especially blue and purple) and butterflies (especially red), while flowers visited by other insects are usually white, yellow, or variegated; but there are far too many exceptions to allow of a general rule.

Birds, especially small honey suckers and humming birds, may be active as pollinators. Flowers may be visited by both insects and birds, but bird-pollinated flowers generally show brilliant colour contrasts. Examples are afforded by *Strelitzia regina*, many species of *Protea*, *Salvia* species, *Loranthus aphyllus*, and some *Acacia* species.

Butterfly-and moth-flowers

When the flower-tube (or at any rate the level of the nectar) is more than about 12 mm. (about half an inch) deep, the nectar is beyond the reach of bees, though they may visit the flower for pollen, or the humble-bee may bite through the tube (calyx or corolla) and thus rob the flower of its nectar. Butterflies may visit many flowers which are adapted for bees, most butterflies and moths having tongues of about the same length as, or a little longer than, those of bees.

Some moths, however, have far longer tongues (30 mm. or more in British species), which are (an in butterflies) carried coiled up in a spiral under the head when flying. These moths can reach nectar when it is at the bottom or a very long tube, as in *Lonicera*, which is visited chiefly by the night-flying privet hawk-moth, and the white convolvulus, which is pollinated by another species of hawk-moth (*Sphinx convolvuli*, tongue 80 mm long). Other flowers pollinated by night-flying moths are *Oenothera*, *Nicotiana*, *Ligustrum* and *Cereus*. Moth-pollinated flowers are generally white or pale-coloured, sweetly scented, and open in the evening, usually remaining closed and almost scentless during the day.

Examples of Floral Mechanism

In the garden pansy (*Viola altaica*) the authers of the five stamens are firmly joined by hairs on their edges, and the two anterior stamens bear processes, functioning as nectar-glands, which pass down into the spur of the anterior petal. A space or chamber ("pollen-box") is enclosed above the ovary, at the base of the style, by the five membranous scales borne on top of the authers. The stigma, which projects beyond the auther-scales, is dilated and hollow. It has a tuft of hairs on each side, and below there is an opening into it, the lower edge of which is protected by a lip or flap (the "scraper").

The flowers are pendulous, and hence the pollen, which is shed on the inner faces of the anthers, and is dry and loose, not sticky as in most entomophilous flowers, falls into the "pollen-box," from which it can escape only through the opening between the scales of the two anterior anthers.

The flowers are pollinated by long-tongued bees (and butterflies). When the insect enters the flower, pollen obtained from another flower may be deposited on the stigma, and cross-pollination thus effected. Pushing down into the spur of the anterior petal to reach the nectar, the insect receives a supply of pollen which has escaped from the "pollen-box". The "scraper" prevents this pollen being deposited on the stigma as the insect retires. The conspicuously coloured centre of the flower, and the honey-guides on the lateral and spur petals serve to attract desirable insects. The entrance of small undesirable visitors is hindered by the hairs on the lateral petals and on the sides of the stigma, by the hairs lining the entrance and cavity of the spur, and by the length of the spur itself.

In *Salvia* (sage), one of the Labiatae, an interesting mechanism is found. The corolla is bilabiate. The conspicuous lower lip attracts insects, and acts as a landing-place. The arched upper lip protects the stamens and style. These are only two stamens, the other two, characteristic of the Labiatae, being represented in the sage by staminodes. The two stamens have a peculiar structure. Each has a short filament, jointed to a long curved connective. In some types of *Salvia* each end of the connective bears a half-anther, but in other types (*e.g.,* garden sage) the lower end of the connective is barren and flattened and the upper part of the connective is longer than the lower, the whole forming a delicate lever.

A bee on entering the flower pushes against the *united* lower ends of the two connectives in seeking the nectar, and causes the curved connectives to swing on the filaments as on hinges, so that the two fertile anther-lobes (*a*) come down and strike on the bee's back, dusting it with pollen. As the bee retires, the stamens return to their former place under the corollahood. The flowers are protandrous. As the flower gets older the style curves down, and the stigma is so placed that it is touched by a bee entering the flower at this stage.

Wind Pollination

In many ways the simplest form of pollination, and probably the most primitive, is pollination by wind. The flowers of wind-pollinated plants are usually small and inconspicuous. Devoid of bright colours and nectar, they are commonly grouped in dense clusters. The perianth is often reduced or lacking. The stamens may protrude prominently from the flower, suspended by long filaments. The stigmas are frequently large and branched. The pollen grains are small, light, and dry, and are commonly produced in larger quantities than in insect-pollinated flowers.

Wind pollination is found both in woody plants and herbs. Among wind-pollinated woody plants are the conifers, the poplars, oaks, ashes, elms, birches, hickories, and sycamore. In many woody plants the staminate and sometimes the pistillate flowers are grouped into drooping clusters called catkins. The wind-pollinated herbaceous plants include pigweeds, sorrels, docks, plantains, nettles, meadow rue, hops grasses, rushes, and sedges. Some species may be either wind or insect pollinated. The small flowers of willows, for example, are brightly coloured and provided with nectaries. But if the pollen is not removed by insects, it may be carried away by wind. Many maples, too, are both wind and insect pollinated.

Hay Fever

Large numbers of people are aware, to their sorrow, that numerous wild and cultivated plants are wind pollinated. These people are sensitive or susceptible to the pollen of such plants, a condition known are *allergy*. The same pollen is harmless to other individuals. The allergy to plant pollens is popularly called hay fever. In order to cause hay fever, the pollen of any given plant must have three important characteristics : it must be produced in considerable amounts; it must be buoyant, so that it floats readily in the air; and it must be toxic to allergic people.

Thus, although nearly all hay fever is produced by wind-pollinated plants, all pollen carried by the wind does not cause hay fever. The cattails shed large amounts of pollen, as do the conifers, yet except for a few species of conifers these plants do not cause hay fever, for their pollen is not toxic. The goldenrods, cosmos, roses, and sunflowers are popularly believed to be important sources of hay-fever pollen. The pollen is toxic to some people, but these plants are insect pollinated. Their pollen is heavy and is not readily carried by the wind. Only intimate contact, such as handling roses or golden-rod, will produced in an allergic person symptoms of the disease. Usually these plants are only minor offenders in causing hay fever.

Pollination Seasons

Whether or not a sensitized person will develop hay fever depends upon the kind and amount of pollen in the air. This in turn depends, except for such atmospheric conditions as rain and wind, upon the plant species which occur in a given region. The time of year when the symptoms of hay fever appear is related to the flowering period of these plants. Three hay-fever seasons are recognized in many parts of the United States. But there is great local variation in the distribution of the plants which cause hay fever and in the pollination periods of these plants.

Early spring (March to May)

The usual cause of hay fever in this period is tree pollens. Among the trees concerned are the box elder, the elms, poplars, birches, oaks, hickories, ashes and sycamore.

Late spring and Early summer (May to July)

Grasses are the most important hay-fever plants during this period. Among the more important species are Kentucky blue grass, red top, orchard grass, timothy, sweet vernal grass, and Bermuda grass.

Late summer and fall (August to September)

The ragweeds are outstanding pollen producers during this season. The plants of significance in hay fever, the pollination periods of such plants, and the quantity of pollen in the air can be determined by pollen surveys for a specific region. Atmospheric pollen counts are made by exposing to the air microscope slides covered with petroleum jelly. The pollen which adheres to the slide is stained and studied under a high powered microscope and it identified by surface features, which vary widely in pollen grains of different species. Newspapers sometimes publish daily pollen counts for the information of hay-fever victims.

Contrivances and Conditions Favouring Cross-pollination

There are in flowers many arrangements and mechanism which ensure cross-pollination. Usually such arrangements and mechanism merely give chances in favour of cross-pollination without precluding the possibility of self-pollination. Sometimes, however, they make self-pollination difficult, or altogether impossible.

In plants with unisexual flowers, of course, cross-pollination is absolutely necessary if seed is to be produced. We have this condition in its extreme form in dioecious plants, e.g., *Salix* (willow). There are a few plants, also, in which cross pollination must take place if seed is to be produced, because the plants are *self-sterile*, *i.e.*, the flower cannot be fertilized by its own microspores; this occurs in some specimens of *Passiflora* (passion-flower), or *Lobella*, and of *Abutlion*.

In some flowers, again, self-pollination may be rendered unlikely or difficult owing to the relative position of anthers and stigma. A condition of much more general occurrance is that known as Dichogamy. This is a condition in which the anthers and stigma in hermaphrodite flowers come to maturity at different times, and which, when completely developed, entirely prevents self-pollination.

There are two form of dichogamy : (*a*) protandry, in which the anthers ripen first, so that when the microspores are shed the stigma of the same flower is not ready to receive them; in their case, if the microspores are not to be wasted, they must be transferred to an older flower; (*b*) protogyny, in which the stigma ripens first; here the microspores must be transferred to a younger flower. Protandrous flowers are much more common than protogynous. Examples of the former are found in Compositae, Labiatae, Umbelliferae, Solanaceae, etc., of the latter in *Plantago*, *Luzula*, some Scrophulariaceae, Ranunculaceae, etc. Wind-pollinated flowers are more often protogynous than protandrous, but many are unisexual.

Anemophilous and entomophilous flowers have each special characters of their own, so that as a rule we can distinguish them at a glance. In *anemophilous flowers*, the microspores are usually dry and smooth, and produced in great abundance, as much must be wasted; the flowers are small and inconspicuous; there is no nectar or perfume; and frequently the stigmas are branched and feathery, to catch the microspores. In many trees which are wind-pollinated the flowers appear in spring before the leaves, so that the microspores have free access to the flowers.

In most herbaceous plants with wind-pollinated flowers, the latter are carried up on a long stem, well above the leaves, so as to expose them as freely as possible to the wind (*e.g.*, *Plantago*, Chenopodiaceae, grasses, etc.) Much greater variety of adaptation is shown by *entomophilous flowers*. As a rule they have large, conspicuous, or highly-coloured corollas, or are arranged in conspicuous inflorescences; they usually secrete nectar and give out perfume. The microspores are usually rough and sticky, and often not produced in any great abundance, as they are more sure of transference. The bright corollas, the perfume and nectar serve to attract insects which visit the flower in search of food. A nectarless but otherwise insect-attracting flower is sometimes called a "pollen-flower." Examples are found in *Papaver*, *Rosa*, *Helianthemum*, *Anemone*, *Clematis*, *Hypericum*, *Ulex*, *Cutisus*, *Ulmaria*. These flowers are visited by pollen-feeding insects.

Many entomophilous flowers are further characterized by the presence of ingenious mechanical devices, which guide and control the movements of the insect and turn them to the best account. Thus, in many cases the corolla is so constructed that the insect must alight on the flower or enter it in a special way (e.g., Labiatae, Papilionatae); the same result may be attained by the secretion of nectar into special receptacles or spurs (e.g., in *Viola*). Often the insect, on entering a flower, pushes against special processes or outgrowths which move the stamens and bring the anthers in contact with its body (e.g., *Salvia*, sage); or the stamens may be jerked, and the microspores scattered over the insect's body. In some flowers the stamens move in response to touch by a visiting insect. This is seen in *Centaurea jacea* where the filaments contract and pull the tube formed by the syngenesious anthers backwards over the style, and the microspores are thus swept out and exposed. Curvature movements of stamens in response to a shock stimulus are seen in a number of Families such as Berberidaceae, Tiliaceae, Cactaceae and Cistaceae. Also sensitive stigma may close over the deposited microspores as in Scrophulariaceae. Frequently spots or lines of a conspicuous colour are developed on the corolla; these have been called "honey-guides," as they are believed to afford insects guidance in seeking out the nectar. The general result of all these devices is that the insect receives pollen on a special part of its body, and when it enters another flower the pollen is deposited on the stigma.

In many protandrous flowers this is secured by the style bending over so that the stigma is in the position formerly occupied by the stamens. A special, but at the same time simple, arrangement for ensuring cross-pollination by insects in known as heterostyly. It is seen in primrose. Here there are two types of flower, borne on different plants. One kind (thrum-eyed) has long stamens (with anthers in the throat of the corolla tube) and a short style; the other (pin-eyed) has a long style and short stamens; thus in the two types the positions of anthers and stigma are reversed.

Pollination is effected by transference between these two forms and not between two flowers of the same form. This is the dimorphic form of heterostyly. In purple loosestrife (*Lythrum*) there are three types of flower combining two positions for the stamens and one for the stigma. Such flowers are said to be trimorphic. Trimorphism is also seen in species of *Oxalis* and dimorphism in *Turnera* and species of *Jasminum*.

Special Arrangements for Self-pollination

In studying floral mechanisms we are too apt to forget that self-pollination occurs regularly in most flowers were it is not precluded by dioecism, complete dichogamy, or self-sterility. Many annual plants are commonly self-pollinated (*e.g.*, groundsel, chick-weed). They have small flowers, often without nectar or smell, and are either homogamous, that is, their anthers and stigmas mature at the same time, or so slightly dichogamous that self-pollination is secure. Even in flowers evidently adapted for cross-pollination, if this fails, there is commonly the possibility of self-pollination. Many of them are distinctly dichogamous, but not completely so, there being usually a short period during which self-pollination becomes possible. To effect this there are sometimes special contrivances such as the curling back of the stigmas to reach the pollen on the anthers or style (*e.g..*, Compositae, Campanulaceae). A very special adaptation for self-pollination is the production of cleistogamous flowers. There are closed flowers produced later in the year by certain plants which had previously produced entomophillous flowers, *e.g.*, *Viola odorata*, *Oxalis acetosella*, *Lamium amplexicaule* (one of the dendnettles), etc. *Commelina benghalensis* also may produce cleistogamous flowers on leafless shoots.

The cleistogamous flower is small and inconspicuous. The calyx remains closed, and the stamens and pistil are developed within it. In *Viola odorata* the self-pollinating cleistogamous flowers have five very small petals and five stamens, but in the dog violet there are only two (anterior) stamens. The anthers produce few microspores, and do not open; the microspores germinate inside the anther, and the pollen-tubes grow through the anther-wall and the style to reach the ovules. The formation of these flowers is partly dependent on shade; they are always shaded by the leaves of the plant itself. If a plant is kept in feeble light, it will usually produce only cleistogamous flowers.

Essential Organs and Their Functions

The main function of the flower is the production of seeds, and for the setting of the seeds two distinct processes are necessary. They are the transference of the pollen-grains from the anthers to the stigma (pollination), and a fusion of a bit of the protoplasm of the pollen-grain with a portion of the protoplasm within the ovule (fertilization). We know that the parts of the flower direct concerned in these processes are its essential organs, the stamens and the pistil. For the clear understanding of these two processes, a knowledge of the essential organs is necessary. The stamens are the parts intended to produce the pollen-grains. A stamen usually consists of a filament and an anther, but it is the anther alone that is of importance. The filament is only a stalk supporting the anther, and we have many instances in which the filaments are absent, the stamens being reduced to mere anthers.

To study the structural details, the stamens of Tribulus may be sued, as it is typical of the anthers of a good number of plants. A transverse section this anther reveals two distinct lobes with two cavities in each, filled with pollen. But the lobes of an old anther present only a single cavity, as the two cavities get fused. The anther lobes are held together by the connective, which is traversed by a vascular bundle. The wall of the anther consists of two layers of cells, an outer layer or the epidermis and an inner layer in which the cells have special thickenings (and hence called fibrous cells). This differentiation in the cells of the wall of the anther is intended to facilitate its dehiscence. The outer wall of the cells of the epidermis bulges slightly outwards and there is protoplasm within these cells. Until the maturity of the anther these cells remain in a turgid condition. The pollen grains take some time to develop and until they are fully formed they need protection. So the wall of the anther remains intact and does not burst, till the pollen is ripe enough for shedding. As long as the epidermal cells are turgid they exert pressure on the fibrous cells laying below the epidermis. As the anther approaches maturity the epidermal cells begin to lose water gradually. This means the gradual lessening of the pressure on the fibrous cells and, as soon as they are freed from it, they tend to expand and assume their natural size.

The removal of compression on the fibrous cells leads to the curling of the anther wall. This, of course, causes the wall to break in some place where it is weak. The pollen-grain of *Tribulus terrestris* is round and it is only a bit of protoplasm enclosed by a cell wall in which, two distinct layers, anther cutinised and an inner cellulose layer, can be distinguished. The outer layer is thickened in a peculiar manner. The inner layer is smooth and uniformly thick. There is a great deal of variation in size and form, and the sculpturing of the outer layer in the case of the pollen-grains, according to the species of the plant. Those of very showy flowers are in many cases provided with spiny or other kinds of projections, or the outer layer may be sticky. In a few cases, we find some spots in the wall formed beforehand for the coming out of the pollen-tube. Some pollen-grains have special lids also, as in the case of Cucurbita.

The free end of the style or the stigma is the part intended for the reception of the pollen. It has to catch the pollen-grains and retain them, and also to assist them to germinate. The surface of the stigma is usually rough due either to papillae or hairs, and a sticky juice containing some sugar is also secreted by it. Both these conditions are useful in retaining the pollen-grains on the stigma. Sometimes the stigma becomes very much branched and is consequently plumose, as in the case of grasses. It is said that the pollen grains are safeguarded from the attacks of bacteria, by the stigmas secreting some substance detrimental to their growth.

A stigma is not always receptive; it becomes receptive as soon as the flower opens and generally continues to be so far sometime, this period varying with the kind of the plant. The sugary juice secreted by the stigma seems to be necessary to stimulate the pollen-grains to germinate. It is only when the stigma is receptive that we find the sugary juice, and if it is absent it is an indication that the stigma is not receptive.

The ovule which develops into seed after fertilization lies within the ovary. It does not develop into a seed unless a bit of protoplasm from the pollen-grain finds its way into the interior of the ovule and mixes with a definite part of the ovule. When the ovule is fully formed and ready to receive the bit of protoplasm from the end of the pollen tube, it consists of a large cell, called the *embryo-sac*, amidst a mass of cells. This mass is covered, except at the top, by two membranes called *micropyle*. The embryo-sac at this stage possesses two groups of nuclei one at the top of the sac close to the micropyle, one nucleus is slightly larger than the others, and this is called the *egg-cell*. The other two cells seem to be helpful in directing the contents of the pollen-tube to the embryo-sac. The three cells at the other or far end of the embryo-sac do not seem to take any part in the formation of seed. Within the embryo-sac, midway between the two groups of nuclei, lies a single large nucleus, which is called the nucleus of the embryo-sac, or the *secondary nucleus*.

The pollen-grain, deposited on the stigma, emits a tube and this comes to the top of the embryo-sac finding its way through the style and the micropyle. At the end of the pollen-tube we find two nuclei, and both of them get into the interior of the embryo-sac and one fuses with the embryo-cell and the other with secondary nucleus. This fusion of the nuclei of the pollen-grain with those of the ovule is really the process of fertilization. It is only after this fusion that the egg-cell is capable of division and development into the young embryo plant that we find in seed. The secondary nucleus divides and gives rise to the endosperm, after the fusion of the nucleii. Now it is obvious, that, for the production of offsprings, the fusion of the male and female cells is essential even in the case of plants, as it is in the case of animals. Further the offsprings are likely to be better in quality when the sex cells uniting together are from different plants.

The pollen-grains of a good many of the flowering plants have no power of spontaneous movement. So they have to depend upon some external agency for the pollination of their flowers. Even in the case of plants with bisexual flowers, extraneous aid is necessary for pollination. The transfer of pollen to the stigma from the anthers of the same flower, as well as from the anthers of a different flower on the same plant, is called *self-pollination*. Pollination of the stigma of a flower with the pollen from flowers of a different plant is called *cross-pollination*.

As a matter of fact, self-pollination occurs in several plants, especially annuals. In some cases flowers are self-pollinated regularly, and such flowers are usually small and inconspicuous without smell or honey. As examples for this, we may mention the Chenopodiums. We have also certain plants wherein self-pollination is made impossible in the earlier stages, but later, just before fading, this become possible. For instance, in the flowers of *Hibiscus micranthus* and *Abutilon indicum* the style branches project a little above the anthers just when the flowers open, and so the pollen cannot reach the stigma. It is evident that pollen from a different flower has to be brought and deposited on the stigmas by some agency, either wind or insects. If the stigmas fail to receive foreign pollen, they bend down so as to come near the anthers in the same flower, to be at least self-pollinated. In both these flowers, the petals close and press on the style branches and thus assist them in coming near the anthers. In some flowers, as in *Evolvulus alsinoides*, the style lies bent away from the anthers just, at first, but later it changes its position, so as to bring the stigma nearer the anthers to make self-pollination possible.

The flowers of *Mirabilis jalapa* are also adapted for self-pollination, when cross-pollination fails to occur. These flowers open towards the evening the emit a very strong scent. Just then, both the stamens and the stigma are far exerted, the stigma alone projecting above the stamens. Usually two species of moths visit these flowers and if they are not visited by any insect, the stigma manages to get self-pollinated either by the elongation of the stamens or by the slight bending of the style, so as to reach the anthers.

The flowers of some Compositae are specially interesting in that they have special adaptations in their floral mechanism to secure self-pollination, should cross-pollination fail to take place. For example, in the plant *Tridax procumbens*, a weed found everywhere, the heads have bisexual flowers in the central portion of the disc and the ray flowers are all female. The stamens are epipetalous and the anthers are adherent, so as to form a tube. The style is bifid and the branches are pressed together, in such a manner that the receptive surfaces are in contact and so not exposed. At first, when the flowers are in contact and so not exposed. At first, when the flowers are unopened, the style is short, but, as soon as the flowers begin to open, the anthers dehisce and the style elongates. So the pollen, lying in the anther tube, gets pushed out and remains at the top of the anther tube. The tip of the style may also carry a small amount of pollen, besides what may adhere to the hairs of the style branches on the outer surface. The style grows and after projecting a little above the anther tube, the branches separate and diverge, exposing the receptive surface. The stigmas thus exposed remain receptive for sometime so that cross-pollination may occur. If the stigmas fail to receive pollen by insect visits, the style branches diverge still more and even curl round, so that the receptive surface may come in contact with the pollen adhereing to the lower surface of the style branches, or with the pollen lying at the top of the anther tube. Self-pollination is thus ensured, if cross-pollination has not already taken place.

Instead of this makeshift arrangement to secure self-pollination, when cross-pollination is a matter of some difficulty, some plants produce two distinct sets of flowers, one adapted for cross-pollination and the other for self-pollination. In *Commelina benghalensis* we have a plant of this sort. The beautiful blue flowers are regularly cross-fertilized and the underground or law-lying inconspicuous flowers that remain as buds without opening are self-fertilized. These inconspicuous flowers are called *cleistogamous* flowers.

Charles Darwin, the great English naturalist, has proved by a series of experiments with different plants that cross-pollination is more advantageous to a plant than self-pollination. If we examine flowers of a number of wild plants growing in a place, we find in them numerous contrivances favouring cross-pollination to the exclusion of self-pollination. Recent workers in the field of plant-breeding have also established beyond doubt, that cross-pollination is not only more advantageous to the plant than self-pollination, but it also confers on plants certain racial advantages.

A most perfect arrangement to ensure cross-pollination is to have the essential organs on separate flowers. We find a host of plants in which the flowers are unisexual. In some plants, as in Cucurbita and Ricinus, we find both male and female flowers on the same plant (monoecious), in others, as in *Cephalandra indica* and in some palms, the male and female flowers are found on different plants and not on the same individual (dioecious).

Bisexual flowers become adapted for cross-pollination to the exclusion of self-pollination, by having the essential organs active at different times. The stigmas may nature and become receptive prior to the anthers. In Cumbu spikes (*Pennisetum typhoideum*), the stigmas protrude from the spikelets and become receptive, while the anthers are still within the glumes. Such flowers are called *protogynous*. The female sexual organs in the protogynous flowers are ready for fertilization long before the anthers are ripe in the same flower, and, therefore the flowers have to be pollinated only by the pollen of older flowers. There are also plants wherein the stamens shed their pollen prior to the receptivity of the stigmas. The flowers are then termed *protandrous*. Protandry seems to be more common than protogyny. Flowers of several Compositae, Malvaceae and *Andropogon*, *Sorghum* are protandrous. Pollination in this case is effected by the pollen from younger flowers.

In very many plants self-pollen is sterile, as in the case of many leguminous plants. The pollen in the flowers of certain orchids is said to act as a poison, if it falls on the stigma of the same flower. There are also instances in which the pollen from the same flower fails to fertilize, if foreign pollen falls on the stigma, soon after self-pollination. This means that foreign pollen is prepotent over self-pollen.

Another very effective arrangement promoting cross-pollination exists in the flowers of several species of Jasminum. The corolla in all cases is tubular and the stamens are epipetalous. In some flowers the style is short reaching only hair the length of the tube, whereas the anthers are at or near the throat of the corolla. On the same plant we also find flowers in which the styles are longer and coming up to the throat of the corolla, while the stamens remain within the tube about midway.

In the case of land plants it is obvious that for cross-pollination some extraneous aid is necessary, because of the fixity in position of these plants and of the absence of spontaneous movement on the part of the pollen-grains. The agents usually active in this work are wind and insects and, in rare cases, water. Plants depending upon insects for fertilization are very many and those pollinated by wind are not inconsiderable.

When plants depend upon wind for pollination, the stigmas have to wait for the pollen that may be wafted by the wind, and this is purely a matter of chance. Therefore, we should expect to find certain conditions specially favourable to this process in these plants. In the first place, large quantities of pollen should be available to ensure pollination. Winds may carry large quantities of pollen, but the pollen likely to fall on the stigmas can only be proportionately very inconsiderable. And, therefore, the flowers that are to be wind-pollinated should stand out far above the foliage leaves, so that the pollen may not be hindered from reaching the flowers. This is exactly what we find in the case of wind fertilized plants. For instance in grasses which are wind-pollinated the inflorescence rises far above the level of the foliage; in the case of trees dependent on wind for pollination, flowers appear, in most cases, at a time when the leaves have all fallen. As an example we may mention the tree, *Odina Wodier*.

The abundance of pollen is secured either by increase in the number of male flowers. Sometimes the anthers become larger and produce plenty of pollen. To give a vivid idea of the abundance of pollen produced by this class of plants, we may mention the male spikes of Pandanus. A single plant is capable of producing a very large quantity of pollen. It rate sized *Zea mays* plant produces about 50,000,000 pollen grains. The pollen produced by these plants should also be adapted for being carried by the wind. So these grains are smooth, light and dry. The anthers are in most cases versatile, an arrangement best suited for the shaking out of the pollen very readily.

The stigmas also have certain adaptations so as to enable them to catch the stray pollen floating in the air. They are branched and plumose, thus getting a large amount of surface. All grasses and sedges, some Amaranths, Ricinus, Pandanus and Odina are wind-pollinated. From this we see that wind-pollination involves the expenditure of a large amount of energy. As the pollen grains are composed almost wholly of protoplasm, a material most difficult to manufacture, this enormous production of pollen-grains cannot but be a drain on the resources of the plant. But this is necessary for ensuring pollination.

We have now to consider plants that are pollinated by insects. For successful cross-pollination flowers should be visited regularly and systematically by insects. Casual and erratic visits, or indiscriminateness in the choice of flowers for visits are not likely to be beneficial. Insects should have some inducement to visit the flowers. Flowers, as we know., produce pollen and honey, and both these substances are sufficient inducements to attract the insects and also ensure their visits. By the mere secretion of honey in the flowers the insects cannot be allured. To ensure their visits, it is absolutely necessary that the place where honey is secreted should be made known to them. The colours of flowers are meant to show them the place where honey may be obtained.

The infinite variety in colour and form of the flowers, as well as the different scents, is intended to attract the insect. In many plants the petals or the corollas are large and coloured so as to be very conspicuous. If the flowers are small, they are rendered conspicuous by being massed together. Sometimes instead of the petals, bracts play the same part, as in Bougainvillaea. Stamens also partake in this work, in Neptunia and Dichrostachys. There are also instances of flowers wherein the calyx becomes highly coloured, while the corolla is absent. The brightly coloured part in the flowers of Mirabilis and Boerhaavia is the calyx. Even when the petals are present the sepals become coloured like the petals, and were have such examples in Cassia and Caesalpinia.

The colour and the scent of the flowers are no doubt quite sufficient to attract the attention of the insects, but to ensure the regular visitation of insects this is not enough. Something more substantial should be offered to them to induce them to frequent the flowers very regularly. The pollen serves as food, or as material for building the hives for some insects such as the bees. Further, nectar or honey is also secreted in several flowers. Insects such as moths and butterflies live mostly on nectar. As both these substances, honey and pollen, serve as food for these insects, they come to the flowers.

Insects that visit the flowers are bees, butterflies, moths and flies. All these insects have sucking apparatus, which in the case of flies are sort and in moths and butter-flies they are very long and coiled like a spring. Bees take in honey and also gather pollen; moths, butterflies and flies drink only honey. As stated above, these insects visit the flowers, because they get food in the form of honey or pollen. Therefore, the secretion of nectar or honey is essential to ensure their visit. In the case of insect-pollinated flowers, pollen need not be abundant. So, in these flowers, stamens are generally fewer in number. Further, the grains have usually a rough surface which often also becomes sticky. Stigmas need not have a large amount of surface as in the case of wind-pollinated flowers. The special adaptations in these flowers are so perfect that pollination is a certainty.

The nectar or honey is secreted usually by a disc at the base of the ovary. There are also instances of petals and sepals having nectaries either as glands, or as special pouches, sacs or spurs. The position of the nectary and the arrangement of the other parts of the flower are such as to make it impossible for the insects to get at the honey, without at the same time effecting pollination. It must also be remembered that, is the visit of the insect is to be of use in pollination, it is absolutely necessary that the part of the body of the insect which comes in contact with the anthers should also come in contact with the stigma ; otherwise pollination will not take place.

In flowers in which the corolla is regular and shallow any insect can get at the honey and effect pollination. For instance, in the Tribulus flower there are honey glands at the base of the stamens and between the petals; the coralla is shallow and the stamens stand erect and so any insect, a bee, or butterfly or a fly can get at the honey. In trying to get at the honey the lower portion, or the sides of the insect must necessarily get dusted with the pollen, and as the stigma is also of the same height as the stamens it must also touch the same part of the body of the insect.

Flowers having long tubular corollas like those of Vinca and Jasminum, or papilionaceous corollas like those of Phseolus, Indigofera and Vigna are not meant to be visited by all kinds of insects. Only butterflies and bees are able to get at the honey and in their manoenvres in search of honey they cannot help pollinating the flowers. Other insects cannot get at the honey and so they do not visit these flowers. Colour of the petals through intended to show off well by contrast, is probably not capable of attracting insects as well as the scent of flowers and the smell of honey.

The Mirabilis flower affords an example in support of this statement. This flower is visited by one or two species of the hawk moths; and there are several varieties of Mirabilis and in all of them the flowers open towards the evening and emit a strong scent. Sometime after sunset the flowers that are white, light yellow or cream-coloured alone can be seen and the magenta coloured flowers cannot be seen. Yet the moth visits both the white and red flowers with equal ease. Insects cannot see the colour from a distance, their range of vision in this respect being limited to within a few feet. Again they are able to see some colours better than others. Bees are said to perceive blues better than yellow. Scarlet does not seem to attract them. Many of the insects visiting the flowers are usually busy with only one kind of flower at a time.

For instance the common Carpenter bee was seen while sucking honey from *Bauhinia tomentosa* flowers. For over quarter of an hour it continued to hover about the same flowers, although there were several other flowers close by, that are usually visited by these bees. On another occassion this bee was thus visiting only the flowers of *Dolichos Lablab*. Having considered the question of pollination in a general way, we shall now deal with a few flowers in a more detailed manner. The flowers of Papilionaceae are specially adapted for cross-fertilization. At the base of the ovary there is usually a disc, which

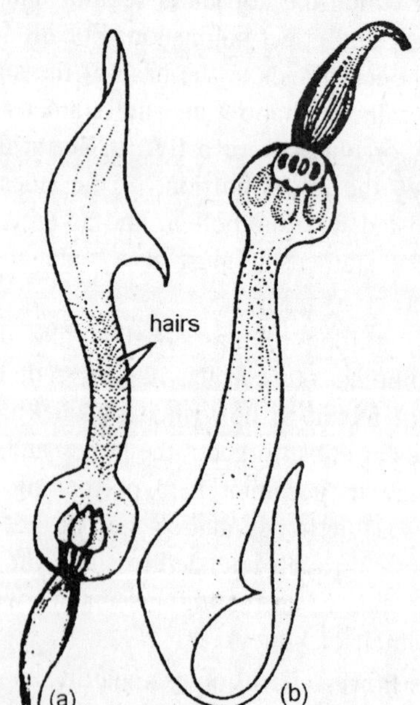

Fig. 8.8. Aristolochia showing pitfall mechanism.

secretes plenty of honey. As the stamens are united by their filaments the honey finds its way into the staminal tube. Of the five petals, the standard is the chief attractive portion. It stands erect and a very conspicuous; in some cases besides being conspicuous it also bears some special marks which are supposed to serve as guides to the place where honey is secreted. The wing-petals invariably constitute a platform for the insects to alight and move about. The insect always sits on the wing-petals with its head directed towards the standard, whether there are special marks or not in it to direct the insect to the honey. Getting at the honey in these flowers is not at all an easy affair. It lies hidden at the base of the ovary and in the trough or cavity formed by the filaments. So it is only very intelligent insects that are likely to get at the honey.

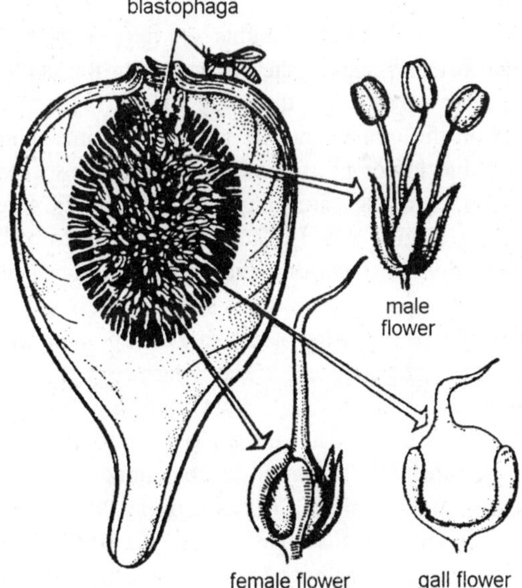

Fig. 8.9. L.S. of Ficus showing orific and blastophaga.

When an insect settles on the flower and moves about, either the stamens or the stigma come out and touch the body of the insect. In some cases, as in *Crotalaria verrucosa* and *Tephrostia maxima*, when insects alight on the wing-petals and move about, pollen- dust is rejected from the pointed tips of the keel-petals first and then the stigmas come out when the insects visits the flower later.

In the flowers of *Vigna Catiang* the filaments of nine stamens are united, one stamen alone being free. At the base of the ovary and around it there is a disc secreting honey. The petals are all connected at the base by means of outgrowths, dents and foldings in such a manner that the standards stands erect, the wing-petals spread themselves out horizontally so as to serve as a platform and the keel-petal remains below. The margins of the keel-petals are united, both above and below, except at the free end where there is a small opening just enough for the emergence of the stigma. When the wing-petals are pressed down, the keel gets depressed and the stigma pops out, and when the pressure is removed, it resumes its original position. In this flower the anthers shed their pollen, before the stigma becomes receipt. Although the stigma is close to the anthers, the pollen does not reach it, because of the hairs found on the style a little below it. Even if a few grains fall on it they will not germinate, as the stigma is not receptive.

When a bee or butterfly alights on the wing-petals the stigma comes out and brushes against the lower part of the body of the insect. If there is pollen already on the body of the insect the stigma gets pollinated. If on the other hand the visit is at a time when the anthers are dehiscing, the lower part of the body of the insect will be dusted with the pollen, and the same part of the body is sure to come in contact with the stigma when it goes to another flower. In the plant *Indigofera enneaphylla* the floral mechanism is of a peculiar sort. In the flower the keel-petals have short spurs at their sides and they are intended to support the wing petals and keep them in a horizontal position. A very slight pressure on the wing-petals is enough to depress the keel-petals and separate their upper margins. As soon as the keels get depressed, the stamens and the style seem to come up with a jerk and remain outside. The essential organs cannot regain their original position, because the petals fall off as soon as the flower has received a single visit. So in this case one single visit of the insect is enough for cross pollination. Instances of the same kind of explosive arrangement are afforded by the flowers of *Abrus precatorius* and *Alysicarpus rugosus*.

The flowers of Phaseolus are very interesting in their structure and behaviour. Like other papilionaceous flowers these also depend on insects for pollination; at any rate the arrangement of the petals and the position of the essential organs are such that self-pollination cannot take place. The keel-petals are in this flower prolonged into a beak and the beak is in the form of a spiral. The end of the spiral in the flower of *Phaseolus trilobus* and *P. mungo* is towards th right, looked at from the front. The right keel-petal possess a spur which supports the right wing-petal and helps it is retaining a horizontal position, so that it may serve as a platform for insects visiting this flower. There is a distinct passage between the right wing petal and the end of the keel-spiral, leading to the base of the standard where the honey is found. The left wing-petal lies higher than the right over the keel on the left side. An insect can get the honey only from the right side. On the left side the wing-petal, the keel and the standard are all close together and there is no opening. An insect coming to this flower for the sake of honey will, of course, alight on the lower wing-petal on the right hand side. As soon as it alights on the wing and begins to search for honey there will be some pressure exerted on the wing-petal. The keel will also be depressed on account of the spur of the keel on the right side. In as much as the insect is on the platform, the stigma touches the back part of its body. If the stigma is receptive and if the back of the insect's body is already dusted with pollen, pollination takes place. If on the other hand the insect visits a flower for the first time to start with, it will get dusted with the pollen, and the next flower visited will have its stigma pollinated.

In *Leucas aspera* and *L. linifolia* the corolla is bilabiate and the stamens are epipetalous and didynamous. The stamens and the style are enclosed within the upper lip of the corolla. Honey is secreted at the base of the ovary and when the insect alights on the lower lip of the corolla to such the honey, the stamens and the stigma are released from the upper hood of the corolla. As both the anthers and the stigma are turned downwards they will touch the back of the insect; if the insect is already dusted with the pollen then the stigma will be pollinated, and in case the visit is for the first time the back of the insect gets dusted with pollen.

The flowers of acanthaceae have also special devices for pollination. In many plants of this family the stamens lie within the corolla in such a way that they cannot help coming in contact with the back of the insect when it sucks honey. Even small inconspicuous flowers are regularly visited by butterflies. On one occasion in the month of October while engaged in collecting plants, the tiny flowers of *Justicia procumbens* were constantly visited by the small pretty violet butterfly, Zizera lysimon. At first the flowers of *Justicia procumbens* were not noticed; this small butterfly was seen hovering about and settling on this plant. On close inspection it was found to suck honey from the tiny flowers of the Justicia. These plants were not at all numerous and there were stray plants scattered all over the place. The violet butterfly continued to visit these flowers persistently for over twenty minutes. The insect proved a most satisfactory guide to lead to the places where this species of Justicia was growing. Similarly another butterfly, a white one with a red border on the front wings, was seen visiting the flowers of *Spermacoce hispida* with great assiduity. The flowers of *Tephrosia purpurea* were visited by a butterfly with golden yellow wings. The flowers of Tridax were watched to see what insects visit them for honey and pollen. Seven different species of insects were found visiting these flowers and they were Zizera lysimon, Colotis amata, Catopsila pyranthe, Terias hecabe, Parnara mathias and Ceratina viridissima.

There are flowers that are exclusively pollinated by the visits of flies. The flowers of Aristolochia and Aroideae are of this kind. A very foetid odour is usually emitted by some of the Aristolochias and in one species the smell is so strong as to attract flies from very long distances (fifty to hundred yards or more). In this flower the anthers are situated on the style below the stigma and they dehisce after the withering of the stigma. Inside the tubular perianth, when it opens there are found a number of hairs all directed inwards. The flies get into the perianth tube easily. But they cannot get out of it with the same ease, on account of the hairs. This flower is protogynous and therefore it has to be pollinated by pollen from some other flower older than itself. When the flies get inside the flower they pollinate the stigma if they have already visited other flowers; if on the other hand the visit of the insect is its first visit, it gets dusted with the pollen. When the flies get into the flower, the anthers are usually immature and the flies cannot get out of the flower, until the anthers dehisce, because the hairs dry only then. Until that time the flies will be wandering all over inside, in search of a way to escape; and in their wanderings they get dusted with pollen. By the time the pollen is liberated the hairs disappear and stigmas fade, and the way becomes clear for the flies to escape.

The inflorescence of Aroids are particularly interesting on account of the arrangements existing in it for pollination. The spadix bears the unisexual flowers at its lower portion only, those at the very base being female and those above male. Above or between these are a number of reduced flowers in the form of hairs directed downwards. The whole inflorescence is covered by a large spathe, the lower part of which forms a tube constricted a little above the region of anthers, or the hairs, whilst the upper portion is expanded exposing the upper free end of the spadix. Small flies attracted by the bad smell emitted by the flowers and also by the spathe, crawl down into the tubular part of the spathe. Once they are in, they cannot easily get out from the tubular part, because the neutral flowers are all directed downwards and the spathe is constructed just above these flowers, or the anthers. The flowers are protogynous as in the case of Aristolochia, and so the insect pollinates the stigma if it bears pollen from another plant. If the flower happens to be the first one that is visited by the insect, the insect is forced to stay within the spathe until the way is open for it to escape.

The withering of the downward directed hairs and the dehiscence of the anthers take place together and therefore the flies escape with a coating of pollen. They cannot avoid this as the anthers are at the top of the inflorescence just at the level of the constriction or a little below it. In the flowers of orchids we have a most perfect mechanism for securing cross-pollination although it is very complicated. As examples we shall select two species of orchids commonly met with in the plains.

The orchid *Eulophia virens* grows amidst scrubs and its flowers are greenish with red streeks. There are three sepals and three petals; the sepals are all alike, but one of the petals, the one lying on the lower side of the flower when it is open, is modified, and it is called the lip. In this flower the lip is slightly saccate at its back and the free front part is broad and in the flower it stands out as a platform for the insects to sit on. The short shallow sac secretes honey and the flowers are visited by butterflies. The anther is single and it is on the top of a column rising from the top of the ovary. The pollen in this and all orchids is collected in masses called *Pollinia*, and in this flower there are two such masses in the anther. Just below the anther there is a disc-like gland to which the two pollen masses are attached by means of strap-shaped stalks. The anther in the open flower lies just above the opening leading into the honey-sac. When the butterfly sucks honey the pollen masses stick on to its head, and so the insect carries away with it the pollen masses. The next flower that is visited by this insect is pollinated by the pollen masses sticking on to this head. The stigma lies just below the anther on the front side of the column. When the insect rushes into the flower to such honey the pollinia cannot help touching the stigma because the pollinia assume a direction which will coincide more or less, with the position of the stigma.

In Habenaria we have another very common orchid of the plains. The flowers in this orchid are all pure white and the raceme springs from the middle of two or three elliptic leaves laying flat on the ground. They are very conspicuous by reason of the recemes. Both in the morning just before sunrise and in the evenings the flowers are visited by moths. The lip is prominent below and it is prolonged at the back into a very distinct spur varying in length from quarter of an inch to one inch. The two lateral petals and the sepal lying above are united so as to form a hood.

There is a narrow passage leading into the interior of the flower and the anther is situated on a column just above the passage leading into the spur. The pollinia have long stalks and the basal portions of the stalk protrude a little. When the moth gets in, the two pollinia stick on to the two eyes of the insect and when it flies to another flower the pollinia are rubbed against the stigma lying below the anthers and the masses adhere to the stigma as its surface is very sticky. In *Calotropis gigantea* (as also in all Asclepiadeae), the pollen grains are held together in masses and there are ten pollinia. When an insect settles down on the top of the staminal column in the centre of the flower and moves about round the stigma, the pollinia adhere to the legs of the insects. When it flies to another flower the pollinium gets on to the stigma to which it will stick if it is receptive. There are many plants whose flowers are usually-pollinated by moths. As moths

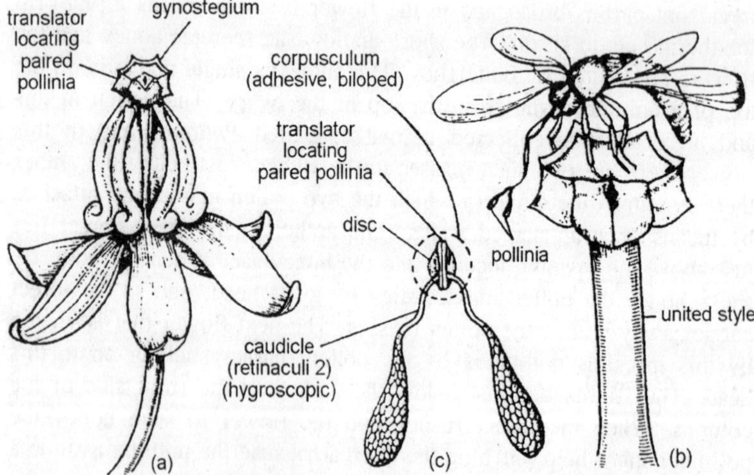

Fig. 8.10. Pollination in Calotropis. (a) A flower of Calotropic; (b) Bee removing part of pollinia; (c) A pair of pollinia of Calotropis.

move about only during the night or in the dusk, these flowers have white corollas, open in the dusk and also emit a strong scent at this time.

The flowers need not be irregular as a platform is not needed, because moths do not alight and they only hover in front of the flower. We may mention as examples Ipomoea, Tobacco, Mirabilis and Jasminum. In these flowers the anthers are generally loose and are well adapted to shed pollen on to the body of a hovering moth. The hawk moths, *Herse Convolvuli* and *Cephonodes picus* visit the flowers of many of the large flowered ipomoeas and the flowers of *Mirabilis jalapa*. The former is a very constant visitor, but the other one comes very rarely and it is extremely active and so rapid in its movements that it is impossible even to see it. We have also plants that depend on water for pollination and they are all aquatic plants.

The common water plant, Vallisneria may be selected as a type of plants fertilized by the agency of water. The flowers of this plant are unisexual and the plants are dioecious. Both the staminate and the pistillate flowers develop under water, and so, unless there is some special adaptation, fertilization cannot take place. The male flowers are borne on short stalks almost at the base of the plant. At the time of flowering, or when the flowering season approaches, these get separated from their stalks and rise to the surface of water to float there. Simultaneously, the female flowers lying under water with spirally coiled stalks come up to the surface, in consequence of the uncoiling and growth of the stalk.

The male flowers are most numerous and they float amongst the female flowers. The anthers open and the pollen is shed on the stigmas. In the case of flowers that are hermaphrodite, the flowers are raised above the water level, as in Nymphaea, so that they might be pollinated either by insects or by wind. It is only when flowers are unisexual and also submerged, pollination is effected by water currents. In all plants that are pollinated by currents of water the pollen grains are smooth, and pollination also is not a matter of certainty. So in these cases there is an abundance of pollen. During hot weather when water is low in ponds and tanks we generally see masses of small white flowers floating freely on the surface. Sometimes the acquatics which ordinarily raise their flowers above the water, do not do so when rain is heavy. Then the flower buds do not open and are then cleistogamic.

Protection of Pollen against Rain

Microspores are much less resistant to extremes of temperature and to drying when they have been moistened and in consequence have begun to germinate. Pollen may be protected from rain in various ways. In some flowers, especially those whose pollen is exposed to rain when the flower opens, the microspores are not readily wetted, having a covering of wax or of spines, etc.

Many flowers protect the pollen by their horizontal or drooping position *e.g.,* Ericaceae, Liliaceae. In some cases the flower closes up at night or in bed weather, *e.g.*, *Oxalis*, tulip, crocus, some Ranunculaceae; and the same kind of closing is effected in the capitula of many Compositae by the movement of the flowers and bracts. In iris the large petaloid stigmas cover the stamens, and in many flowers the stamens are protected by a hood formed by the sepals or petals, or by both.

Germination of Microspore

Process leading up to and ending in Fertilization. At first the microspore is unicelllular but later, even before it leaves the anther, its nucleus divides into two. The larger one of those in the vegetative nucleus; the smaller one the generative. Both are free in the cytoplasm of the microspore. Either before or after pollination the generative nucleus divides into two male gametes.

Germination and further development take place on the stigma, which secretes a sugary nutritive fluid. From one of the pores in the exine a slender pollen-tube protrudes, and grows down through the tissue of stigma and style and finally enters the ovary. After entering the ovary the pollen-tube grows towards and ovule, which it enters usually by the micropyle. It penetrates the apex of the nucellus and comes in contact with the megaspore near to the oosphere and synergidae.

During its growth the vegetative nucleus is found near the tip of the pollen-tube. The male gametes also pass down to the apex of the pollen-tube, but the vegetative nucleus is by this time disorganised. *One male gamete only* is concerned in the actual process of fertilization. It passes from the pollen-tube into the megaspore and fuses with the oosphere, hence their names synergidae or "help-cells" (Gr,*ouv*, with *epyov*, work). The tip of the pollen-tube swells and bursts, thus setting the male gametes free in the embryo-sac. The fusion of the male gamete, which appears to be entirely nuclear, with the nucleus of the oosphere constitute fertilization in the strict sense. The fertilized oosphere secretes a cellulose wall and is then called the oospore. Its nucleus is diploid.

The second male gamete fuses with the secondary nucleus of the megaspore. The resulting nucleus is called the *endosperm nucleus*. The significance of this process, which resembles fertilization, and which, together with the actual fertilization of the oosphere, constitutes what has been called "double fertilization," is considered in § 10. In a few Dicotyledons, *e.g.*, *Corylus* and *Betula*, the pollen-tube does not enter the ovule by the micropyle, but by piercing the chalaza. This is known as chalazogamic fertilization as distinguished from the usual porogamic method.

9

Fertilization

Fertilization involves the fusion of a male gamete with a female gamete. In angiosperms the female gametophyte is seated deep in the ovarian cavity, quite away from the stigma. The pollen (male gametophyte) are, normally, held at the Stigma, and there is no device for them to reach the egg inside the female gametophyte. To effect fertilization in this group of plants the pollen grains germinate on the stigma by putting forth tubes (pollen tubes) which grow through the style and find their way into the ovules, where they discharge the sperms in the vicinity of the egg. One of the sperms fuses with the egg (forming zygote) while the other fuses with the polars or the secondary nucleus (forming primary endosperm nucleus). The distance a pollen tube has to travel in order to reach the egg depends on the length of the style which is quite variable in different species. For example, in sugar-beet it has to grow only a few millimetres whereas in corn it grows as much as 450 mm.

Structure and Development of a Stamen

A very young stamen in a flowers bud is small, four angled, upgrowth from the receptacle. This upgrowth will four the anther, the filament being delayed in development. In each of the four angles a pollen sac containing pollen grains will be elaborated as development proceeds. These developments as seen in transverse sections of anthers of various ages, but it must be realised that logitudinal series of cells are involved, running the whole length of the anther. The left-hand figures represent early stages. The anther consists at first of undifferentiated parenchyma but soon cells in the four corners, lying just beneath the epidermis, become active. Divisions take place giving

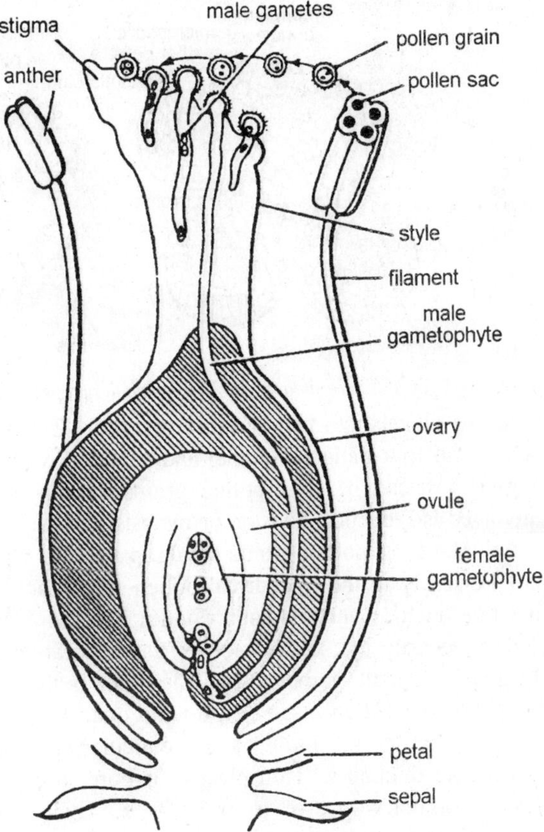

Fig. 9.1. L.S. of flower showing fertilization.

a group of inner cells (shaded) surrounded by flattened, actively dividing cells. The inner cells ultimately give rise to the pollen grains while the outer cells form the walls of the pollen sacs.

Division continue in both the inner and outer cell groups and the condition seen in the top right hand figure is attained, where each corner of the anther is occupied by a young pollen sac. Each pollen sac has a wall several layers thick, the innermost being a layer of cells known as the tapetum, which later provides food for the developing pollen grains. The cells in the centre of the sac are pollen mother cells with dense cytoplasm and large nuclei. These, at first joined closely together, soon round themselves off and float freely in a nutritive liquid derived from the tapetum. Each pollen mother cell now gives rise to four pollen grains by two successive divisions.

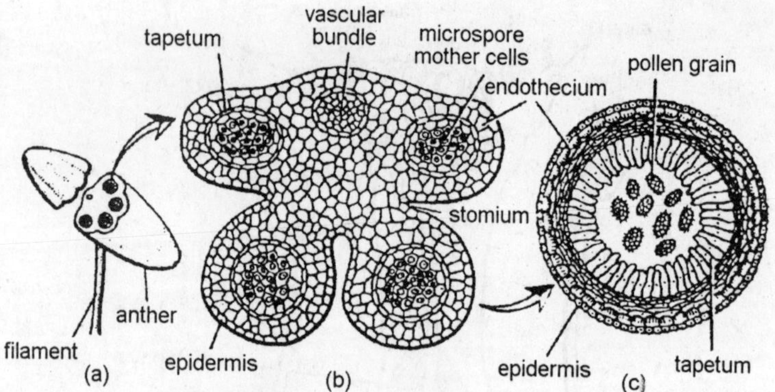

Fig. 9.2. T.S. of a mature anther, showing stomium and pollen grains.

The nucleus divides into two and then into four. Cytoplasm collects round each of the four daughter nuclei and partition walls are formed so as to give a tetrad of four pollen grains. The type of nuclear division involved is reduction division or meiosis. As the anther reaches maturity, the tetrads of pollen grains break up and the separate pollen grains now lie freely in the cylindrical pollen sacs. Each young grain has at first one nucleus but this soon divides into two. One of these, surrounded by denser cytoplasm, forms the generative cell (which ultimately gives the male gametes) and the other is the tube nucleus. The wall of the ripe pollen grain is a double one. There is dedicated inner wall of cellulose (the intine) and a cuticularised outer one (the exine) of variable thickness. Thin places, or pore, are present in the exine. The grains vary in size from 3-300 μ. Their shape may be ellipsoidal, spherical crystal-like with a varying number of facts, or many other shapes. Further variation given by characteristic sculpturing of the outer wall which may have spines, papillae, a network of ridges and so on.

Many plants can, indeed, be identified merely on the basis of their characteristic pollen. It has proved possible to learn something about the changes which have occurred in our vegetation since the Ice Age by the identification of pollen grains preserved at various depths in peat deposits. It may also be mentioned that the earliest known trace of Angiosperms is in the form of pollen-grains found in coal of Jurassic age in Scotland. As a result of the various developments described above the anther now has the structure. As the left hand figure indicates, the pollen sacs are long cylindrical structures. There are two of them in each lobe, the lobes themselves being joined by a connective containing a vascular bundle.

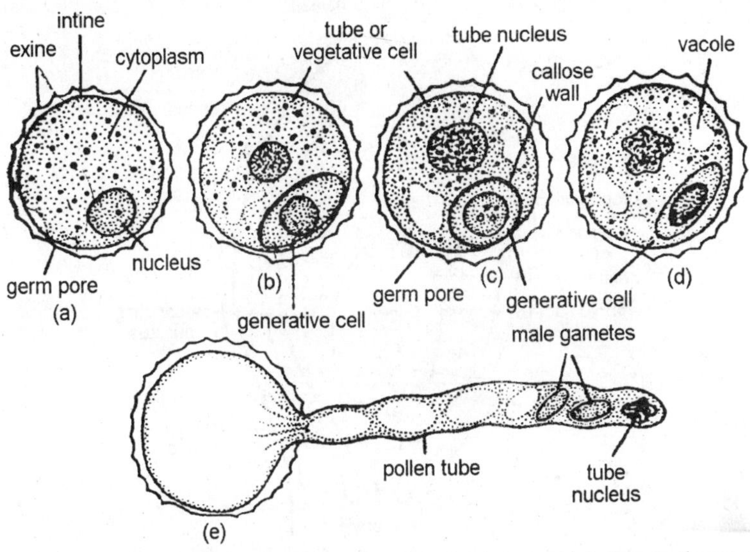

Fig. 9.3. Germination of pollen grain and formation of male gametophyte in an angiosperm.

The wall of each sac has now a highly differentiated structure. The cells lying just below the epidermis have enlarged and their walls have been modified by the deposition of lignin. This characteristic fibrous thickening is laid down on all the walls except the outer ones. In some anthers several layers of the wall may show this type of thickening. The thin outer walls of the cells of the fibrous layer shrink on drying and so cause a longitudinal rupture of each anther lobe along a line of specialised cells called the stomium. This rupture is accompanied by a breaking down of the wall between each pair of sacs. The pollen grains are thus liberated and pollination can now take place.

Structure and Development of an Ovule

The ovule when it is ready for fertilization is more or less egg-shaped. It consists essentially of an ovoid mass of parenchymatous cells called the nucellus which is borne on a short stalk or funicle by means of which it is attached to the placenta in the ovary. The nucellus is invested by one, or more frequently two, integuments which are protective coats growing up from its base. These cover over the nucellus except at the extreme tip, where a narrow channel is left open as the micropyle leading down to the nucellus. Embedded in the nucellus there is a large ovoid sac bounded by a thin cell-wall. This is called the embryo-sac, since, after fertilization, it will contain the embryonic

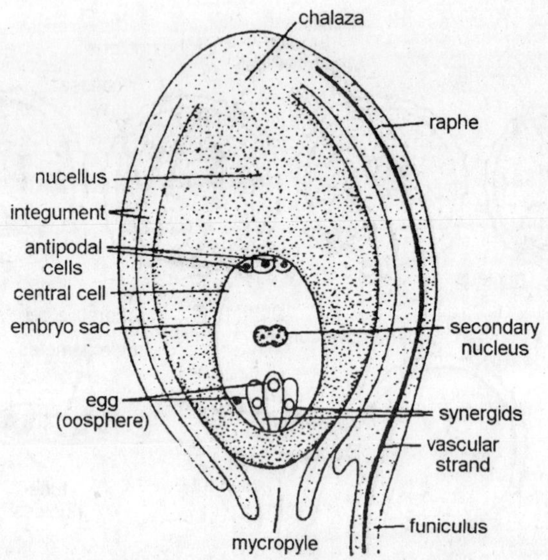

Fig. 9.4. Structure of a typical ovule (anatropous ovule) prior to fertilization.

plant. In some plants, for example, rhubarb, the ovule is straight and the micropyle is at the end opposite to the stalk. Such ovules are said to be orthotropous. In other examples, for example, shepherd's purse, the nucellus and embryo-sac are curved so that the micropyle is placed near to the stalk. This is the campylotropous type of ovule.

In the majority of ovules, however, the nucellus is straight but the entire ovule is inverted by a sharp curvature at the top of the stalk so that the micropyle lies near to the base of the stalk and also near to the carpellary wall. This is the common anatropous type of ovule. The embryo-sac at the time of fertilization contains vacuolated cytoplasm in which a number of prominent nuclei are embedded. At the end furthest from the micropyle there are three large nuclei, each surrounded by granular cytoplasm and a gel membrane; these are called the antipodal cells and often appear to play a part in the nutrition of the embryo-sac. At the micropylar end there are three other large nuclei and these too are each surrounded by cytoplasm and a membrane. This micropylar group constitutes the important egg apparatus. The central cell is the female gamete called the egg cell or ovum. The two other cells, which may correspond to non-functional ova, are called the synergids.

In the centre of the embryo-sac there is a conspicuous nucleus which is called the central fusion nucleus or the primary endosperm nucleus. When the ovule is in the condition just described it is ready for fertilization but before considering this process it is necessary to examine the way in which this structure has developed. An ovule arises on the placenta as a small upgrowth of parenchymatous tissue which is the young nucellus. Then integuments appear as ring-like upgrowths from its base and these gradually invest the growing nucellus until only the micropyle is left at its tip.

Meanwhile, if the ovule is of the anatropous type, the stalk has elongated and curved sharply at its top so as to bring the micropyle near the insertion of the stalk on the placenta. It is during these developments that the embryo-sac is formed. A single cell of the nucellus, situated just below its tip, becomes conspicuous by reason of its larger size and dense protoplasmic contents. This is the embryo-sac mother cell which then divides first into two cells and then into a row of four cells. As in the formation of four pollen grains from a

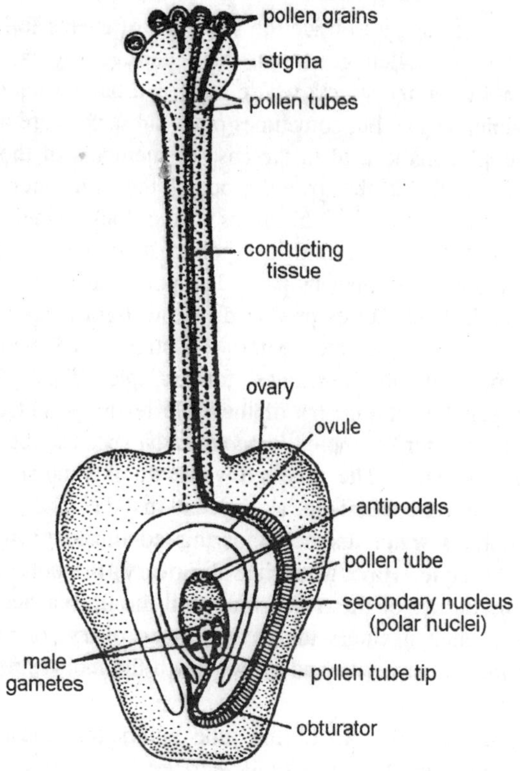

Fig. 9.5. Fertilization in an angiosperm through porogamy.

pollen mother cell, the nucleus of the embryo-sac mother cell divides by the process of meiosis to give the four potential embryo-sacs.

Usually, however, it is only the innermost of these which develops further as the functional embryo-sac. The other three collapse and are crushed as the surviving embryo-sac enlarges. When first formed, the embryo-sac has a single nucleus. This nucleus divides by mitosis and the daughter nuclei move to the two poles of the sac. Each of the two nuclei divides again twice so the four nuclei occupy the micropylar end and four the opposite (chalazal) end of the sac. One nucleus from each group of four now moves to a central fusion nucleus. The three at the micropyle end form the egg-apparatus already described and the other three form the antipodal cells. The embryo-sac thus reaches the condition which is found in practically all Angiosperms at the time of fertilization.

Processes of Fertilization

It is now necessary to trace the sequence of events following upon the deposition of pollen grains on the receptive stigma. The pollen grains germinate on the stigma where there is usually a liquid secretion, often containing sugar, but sometimes other substances are also present, as, for example, malic acid in the case of members of the Ericaceae. Germination results in the growing out of the thin inner wall of the pollen grain through one of the pores in the thick exine. This results in the production of a cylindrical pollen tube into which the tube nucleus and generative nucleus pass. The pollen tube, tending to grow towards chemical substances produced by the stigma, towards moisture and away from oxygen, then enters the stigma and begins to grow down the style. In some examples, for example, *Viola* species, there is an open canal in the centre of the style leading right down to the ovary; in others, for example, *Rhododendron* species, there is a canal filled with mucilage. The tube grows down the moist sides of the canal or through the mucilage, as the case may be, and so reaches the ovary. It obtains water and food for this continued growth from the tissues of the style. Having reached the ovary, the pollen tube either grows in the tissues of the ovary wall until the tip reaches the vicinity of an ovule when it enters the cavity of the ovary, or else it enters the top of the ovary cavity and grows down the moist inner surface in an ovule.

In either case the tip of the tube enters the micropyle of the ovule, possibly directed by a fluid secreted by the synergids. It thus reaches the nucellus, and by penetrating the few overlying layers of

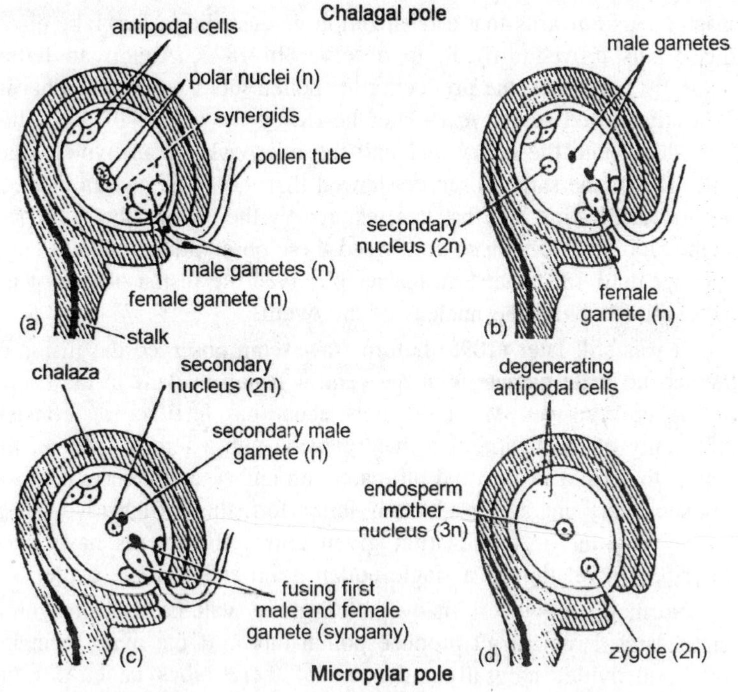

Fig. 9.6. L.S. of ovule showing different stages of fertilization.

this tissue, it comes into contact with the embryo-sac in the vicinity of the egg-apparatus. During the downward growth of the pollen tube the generative cell has divided to form the two male gametes. These occupy the tip of the tube, the tube nucleus having disintegrated. Fertilization now takes place.

The tip of the pollen tube becomes ruptured and the two male gametes, now spirally coiled, thread-like bodies, enter the embryo-sac. One of the gametes enters the egg and fuses with its nucleus. The egg, so fertilized, is called the zygote and it is from this that the embryo plant develops. The second male gamete moves deeper into the embryo-sac and fuses with the central fusion nucleus. The result of this second fusion is the production of a nutritive tissue, known as the endosperm; this is used by the developing embryo. The time elapsing between pollination and the occurrence of these fusions varies considerably. In rye it is seven hours; in maize, twenty-four hours; in some trees it may be a year or more.

The elucidation of the sequence of the events just outlined occupied botanists for many years. Although it was known from the time of

Camerarius onwards that a fertilization process did in fact take place, the details proved difficult to observe. In 1823, Amici, an Italian naturalist, observed the production of pollen tubes by pollen adhering to a stigma and seven years later he traced the course of the pollen tube down into the ovary and into the micropyle of an ovule. Later still (1846), the same observer showed that the ovule had an egg cell before fertilization and that this, excited by the pollen tube, gave rise to the embryo. Hofmeister confirmed these observations in 1849 but it was not until 1884 that Strasburger observed the fusion of one of the male gametes with the nucleus of the ovum.

It was still later (1898) before Nawaschin observed the fusion of the second male gamete with the central fusion nucleus in the centre of the embryo-sac. We have now seen that fertilization consists essentially of the fusion of a male gamete with a female gamete, the ovum, to form a zygote and ultimately an embryo. The second fusion is a subsidiary one and results only in the formation of nutritive tissue. In the account of fertilization given above the events have been described in relation to a single pollen grain and a single ovule.

Normally, however, many pollen grains will be deposited on a stigma and they will all produce pollen tubes. If the ovary contains only one ovule, naturally only one of these tubes penetrates the micropyle and liberates its male gametes into the embryo-sac. If, however, as in the majority of ovaries, numerous ovules are present, then the production of numerous pollen tubes is a necessity if all the ovules are to be fertilized. In a flower like that of *Rhododendron*, if a transverse section is cut through a style some time after pollination has occurred, the section will show a large number of pollen tube sections embedded in the mucilage of the stylar canal.

Meiosis

An essential feature of fertilization is the fusion of a male gamete with the nucleus of the female gamete. This results in the zygote or fertilized egg the nucleus of which contains the nuclear material of both the male and female gametes. If the male gamete has n chromosomes (a number varying with the species) and the female has n chromosomes the zygote will obviously possess $2n$ chromosomes. The chromosome complements in the vegetative cells of flowering plants consist of homologous pairs, one of each pair being maternal and the other paternal in origin. It is clear that these pairs came together in the act of fertilization which gave rise to the plant. As the zygote develops into the embryo, and then into the new plant, all the cell divisions which take place are mitotic and thus the $2n$ number of chromosomes is maintained. If, however, this type of division occurred throught out the life history, then the gametes would each have $2n$ chromosomes and, when fertilization occurred, the zygote would have $4n$ chromosomes. There is, however, a compensating process in the form of another type of nuclear division known as meiosis or reduction division, by which the number of chromosomes is halved.

Meiosis always occurs in the formation of the gametes or in some cell division prior to such gamete formation. The result is that the gametes themselves always have the haploid or n number of chromosomes and the zygote formed as a result of fertilization will have the diploid or $2n$ number. In flowering plants, meiosis occurs in the formation of the four pollen grains from each pollen mother cell and also in the formation of the four potential embryo-sacs from an embryo-sac mother cell. As the subsequent nuclear divisions which take place both in the pollen grain and in the functional embryo-sac are all mitotic, it follows that the make gametes and the female gamete will have the reduced or haploid number of chromosomes.

All plants which reproduce sexually show the occurence of meiosis at some point in their life-history between successive acts of fertilization but this point varies in the different big groups of plants. Meiosis consists of two very much modified mitotic divisions, normally giving rise to four cells, but it is essential that it should be considered as a single process with two stages. Cells which are about to undergo this type of division are usually filled with dense cytoplasm and have a large nucleus. The first indication that meiosis is in progress is the appearance of the chromosome threads just as in the prophase of mitosis, except that they are single and show the chromomeres more obviously along their length. The stage where the strands are obvious as separate entities is called leptotene and this is followed by zygotene where the homologous chromosome strands come to lie together, so precisely paired that corresponding segments and even chromomeres are in juxtaposition. These paired chromosome structures are called bivalents. In each bivalent both of the chromosomes now split longitudinally (except in the region of the centromere) giving a four-stranded structure which is characteristic of the pachytene stage. Pachytene is a very short stage and is seldom seen in preparations showing meiosis; but it is nevertheless important.

In each bivalent the chromatids now contract and twist around one another but the members of each pair repulse the opposite members except at points which are called chiasmata, (sing., chiasma). These chiasmata explain cytologically the genetic problem of 'crossing over'. This stage is diplotene and it is followed by diakinesis, which is characterized simply by a greater shortening and thickening of bivalents. The latter usually arrange themselves around the periphery of the nucleus and this stage also the nuclear membrane and the nucleolus disappear.

Metaphase I follows and is similar to the metaphase of a mitosis in that a spindle has now been formed and that the bivalents arrange themselves on the equatorial plate in exactly the same way as do the chromosomes in mitosis. The bivalents are placed with their two unsplit centromeres above and below the equatorial plate. Anaphase I now follows and the two centromeres of each bivalent move to the opposite poles of the cell, each pulling its pair of chromatids with it. Telophase I can be a very transient stage, and can frequently be regarded as non-existent since the daughter nuclei pass straight into the prophase of the second division. Metaphase II follows, each centromere (of which there are only half as many as in the original cell) moves onto the equatorial plate, taking with it the two chromatids which are attached to it.

The centromeres then divide and at anaphase II the two chromatids separate. Four daughter cells are thus produced, each with half the number of chromosomes which were present in the parent cell. One feature requires fuller treatment. At diplotene there is actual breakage and interchange of parts of chromatids, the position of the breakages usually being seen as chiasmata. Chromosome which has one chiasma and the result of this chiasma as it effects the constittution of the segregating chromatids at anaphase I and anaphase II. The interchange of segments extends from the chiasma to the ends of the chromatids. This means that two of the chromatids are actually made up of both maternal and paternal material while the other two are either wholly maternal or wholly paternal in their make-up. More than one chiasma can be present in a bivalent and the interchange can take place between any two chromatids provided that one is of maternal and the other of paternal origin. Extremely complicated segregations can thus occur.

The Seed

After fertilization has occurred, changes take place in all parts of the ovule. The structure resulting from these further developments in the ovule is the characteristic reproductive body of the flowering plants, the seed. Changes in the embryo-sac itself may be considered first. The fertilized egg forms a wall around itself and proceeds to divide so as to form a short chain of cells which is known as the pro-embryo. The cell nearest to the micropyle grows to a large size, while the cell at the tip of pro-embryo begins to divide in various planes, these divisions following a regular sequence. This terminal cell in fact gives rise to most of the embryo plant, the rest of the pro-embryo forming the suspensor. The large basal cell of the suspensor serves as an organ of attachment to the wall of the embryo-sac; the filamentous region continues to elongate and pushes the embryo into the nutritive tissue, or endosperm, which is developing in the embryo-sac at the same time. Continued cell division in the embryo soon results in the appearance of two cotyledons (or of one lobe if the plant is a Monocotyledon).

The stem apex is formed between the two cotyledons (or laterally at the base of the single cotyledon in a Monocotyledon). The lower

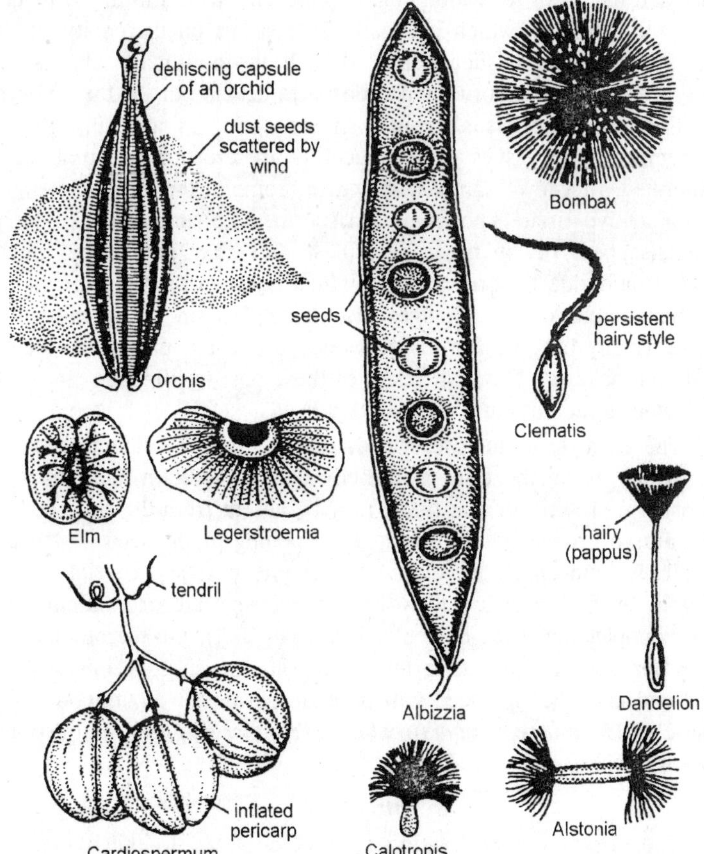

Fig. 9.7. Some examples of anemchorus fruits and seeds.

part of the embryo in both Dicotyledons and monocotyledons forms the bulk of the first root or radicle. The tip of the latter is, however, formed by divisions in the top cell of the suspensor. The tip of the root is thus attached to the suspensor and points towards the micropyle. Simultaneously with the development of the embryo, or even preceding this, endosperm is formed in the embryo-sac. This results from the active division of the central nucleus (which, it will be remembered, is the product of the fusion of the second male gamete with the central fusion nucleus). Repeated divisions of this nucleus give rise to numerous daughter nuclei which are not, at first, separated by cell walls (a type of divisions known as free nuclear division). These nuclei take up a peripheral position in the embryo-sac. Continued unclear division takes place and then wall formation commences. This results in the formation of a cellular tissue which gradually encroaches on the cavity of the embryo-sac. This tissue, which is rich in food materials, is the endosperm. As the embryo and endosperm develop inside the embryo-sac the latter increases rapidly in size and, as a result of this enlargement, the tissues of the nucellus are crushed and practically obliterated. In a few examples, however, some of the nucellus persists as a nutritive tissue known as perisperm. The antipodal cells may soon disappear or, in other examples, they may persist and either enlarge or divide to form a tissue which helps in the nutrition of the enlarging embryo-sac. Changes also take place in the integuments. These usually become fibrous or woody and constitute the protective seed coat or testa. The total result of these post-fertilization chages in the ovule is the structure known as a seed.

The testa is, as just described, derived from the integuments of the ovule. Inside the testa is the embryo. In addition there may be endosperm present, or this tissue may be absent from the ripe seed. If the embryo grows rapidly during the ripening of the seed it will use up all the endosperm to obtain the requisite food material for its growth. Such a seed is said to be non-endospermic or exalbuminous (for example, the seeds of apple, bean, pea etc.). On the other hand, the embryo may cease to grow before all the endosperm has been used and then the ripe seed will be endospermic or albuminous as in castor oil (*Ricinus communis*), wheat (*Triticum vulgare*), and coconut (*Cocos nucifera*).

The Fruit

The effects of fertilization are not confined to the ovules but extend to the other floral parts and, in particular, to the carpels in

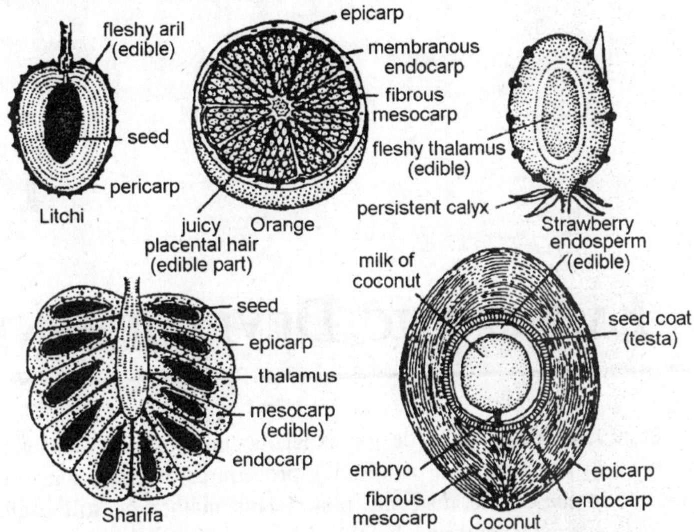

Fig. 9.8. Section of some common fruits to show edible parts.

which the ovules are borne. The carpellary or ovary wall is stimulated to further development, possibly by growth substances secreted by the developing ovules. It may become dry and membranous, or it may thicken considerably and become either woody or fleshy. This modified ovary wall, together with the contained seed or seeds, constitutes a fruit, the modified wall being the fruit coat or pericarp. It serves to emphasize the fact that the ovary wall becomes the pericarp (in this case, the pea pod), and that the ovules become the seeds. It may be noted that in a few cases, for example, banana (*Musa sapientum*), the fruit normally develops without fertilization having taken place. This phenomenon is known as parthenocarpy and naturally gives rise to a seedless fruit.

The development of seedless tomato fruits may be induced by spraying the flowers with a growth substance such as b-naphthoxyacetic acid. In this case the growth substance artificially supplied seems to act in a similar way to the growth substance produced by ovules developing after normal fertilization. After fertilization the sepals, petals and stamens usually wither, although their dead remains may often still be seen, for example, at the top of an apple or gooseberry. In some examples, however, the sepals may be persistent (for example, pea, tomato). In the mulberry (*Morus* species) the perianth becomes pulpy and embeds the true fruits.

10

EMBRYONIC DEVELOPMENT

Until about 1960 plant embryos for experimental work in vitro were obtainable only by somewhat painstaking procedures of dissection from the ovular tissues of the maternal plant. This method is still useful and necessary and is outlined below. With the discovery that tissue culture manipulation will lead in a number of predictable cases to the initiation and development of large numbers of embryos in a somewhat synchronized developmental sequence, new approaches have been opened to experimentation with embryos. In a few special cases, that is, the culture of whole anthers of certain dicot genera, embryos develop quite predictably and are of particular interest since they are haploid plants, having been derived from the haploid pollen cells produced by meiosis.

DISSECTION AND CULTURE OF PLANT EMBRYOS INITIATED IN OVULO

The fertilized egg or zygote is the single-celled stage with which one would like to begin to study plant embryogenesis. It would be useful if one could obtain easily and in large numbers unfertilized eggs, fertilize them *in vitro* at time zero, and follow their development from embryos into complex multicellular organisms. This type of study is possible in the brown alga, *Fucus*, growing in sea water in the light. No such accessibility to embryos is possible among the vascular plants where typically the eggs develop encompassed by multiple layers of tissues of the parent plant (the archegonium in the ferns, the ovule in the seed plants) and fertilization is achieved by complicated mechanisms which allow the fertilized egg to develop within the protective tissues of the mother plant.

To obtain the immature stages of developing embryos, one must dissect them from the protective surrounding tissues of the maternal plant. It has been proved impractical to dissect out single-celled zygotes in the case of flowering plants although this has been done for ferns. In the flowering plants, one must achieve dissection of young flowers soon after pollination.

Embryos from Dicotyledonous Plants

One of the most studied dicot embryos is the common weed, shepherd's purse *Capsella bursa-pastoris* L. which flowers readily and profusely; in the inflorescence, the embryonic stages are arranged along the axis with the younger stages at the top and the older stages toward the base. Rijven described stages in detail, methods of isolation and culture, and presented a "how-to-do-it" account for this species. The following description of the isolation of embryos is his:

The first thing to be done was to arrange all implements and appliances in working order on the table. Amongst these was a glass of water in which were the cut inflorescences of *Capsella*. A number of silicles, containing embryos in the desired stage, was selected and opened successively. Some practice was required for this operation, as the walls of the silicles had to be removed without severing the ovules from the placenta, in order to prevent their touching any unsterile parts. This was achieved by tearing the walls down from the ribs by means of a pair of coverglass tweezers after Kuhne. The remainder of the silicle, including the ovules, was then placed in a sterilized watch glass; then the ovules were pulled off from the placenta with sterilized needles under a dissecting microscope. Another watch glass with 5 ml sterile medium, covered by a larger watch glass, was, ready for the receipt of the ovules. The excision of the embryos followed by cutting a gap in the top of the ovule and exerting a slight pressure on its base near the micropyle. To prevent infection during these manipulations, the operator's head, except the eyes, was covered by a sterile cloth, as is usual in surgery.

About 20 embryos could be excised within ten minutes. By means of a braking pipette we then brought them to a second, and from this to a third covered watch glass with medium in order to clean them from adhering remains of endosperm and from eventual contaminations.

These operations having been repeated for a number of silicles, the culture was started.

The medium for successful culture of young heart-stage embryos of *Capsella* was described by Rijven and improved media were developed

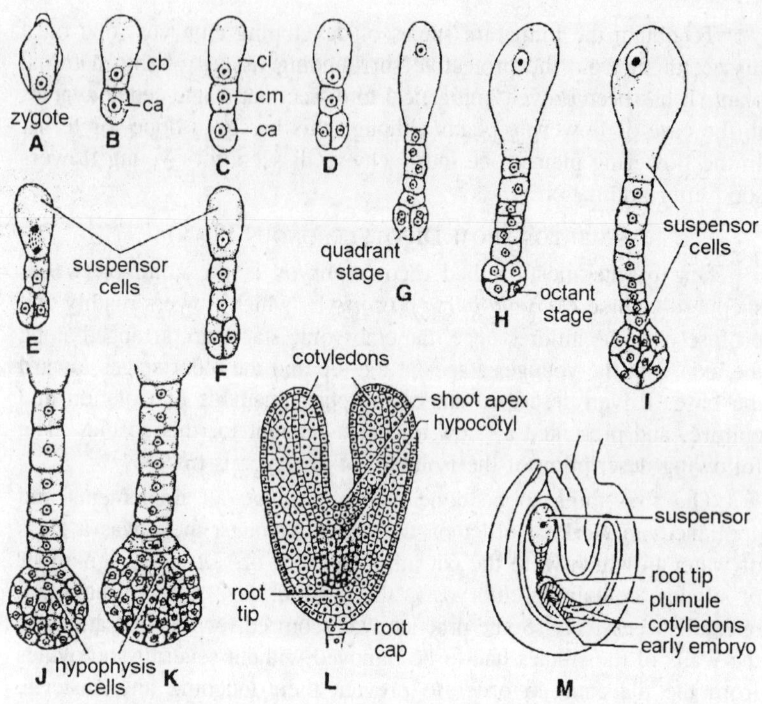

Fig. 10.1. Stages in the development of embryo in dicotyledons.

by Raghavan and Torrey for culturing *Capsella* embryos at the globular stage and as small as 50 mm in diameter. Although less well developed embryos, even down to 4 or 8-celled stage could be isolated, no success was achieved in their culture. Similar studies on embryos of *Datura stramonium* and hybrid species were described in some detail by Rietsema and Blondel.

Embryos from Monocotyledonous Plants

Methods of isolation, culture, and nutrition of monocot embryos are not very different from those of dicots. A carefully studied genus is barley, *Hordeum vulgare* L. Norstog presented details of isolation and successful culture of embryos down to 100 mm in size. He described his method as follows:

The exposed caryopses were placed on a flamed slide under a dissection microscope at 25-50X magnification. Using watchmaker's forceps and bacteriological inoculating needles ground to fine points, embryos as small as 0.2 mm were readily excised and transferred directly to the medium. Smaller embryos required different treatment

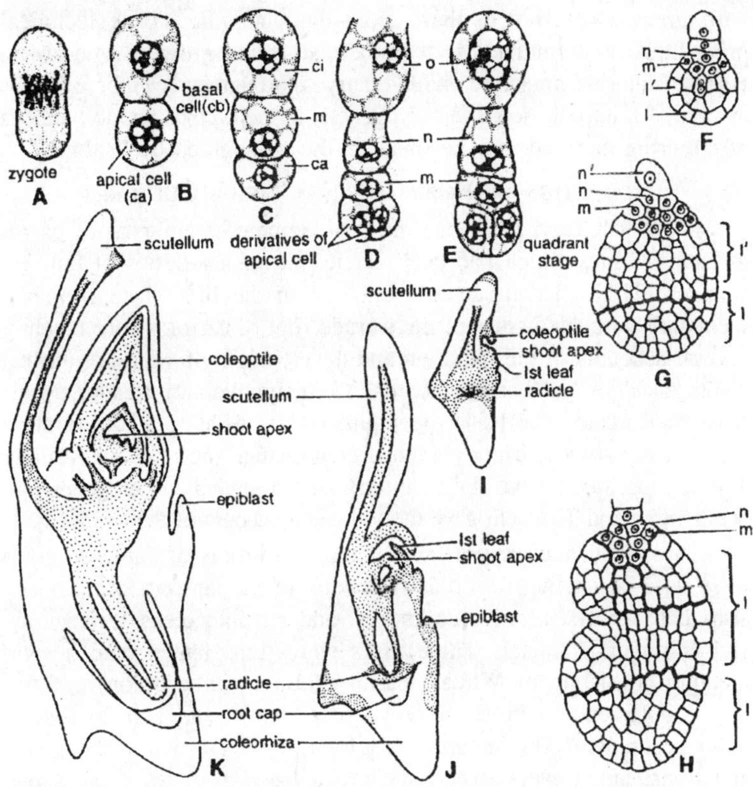

Fig. 10.2. Stages in the development of embryo in monocotyledons.

because they tended to dry out in transit. The region of the ovule that contains the embryo is beaklike in barley. The beak was excised and transferred to a small drop of sterile paraffin oil. The embryo was then teased apart from the beak, lifted out in a film of oil using a microspatula, and transferred to the medium. The oil appeared to float free, and it was possible to push the embryo to an oil-free area. The oil did not appear to interfere with the embryonic growth.

The synthetic medium used in the cultures was a White's agar medium modified by greatly increasing the phosphate concentration, raising the sucrose level to 9%, adjusting pH to precisely 4.9 using malic acid as a buffer, and adding an amino acid mixture.

Orchid embryos have been as much studied as any monocots. In many orchid species, the mature seed is released from the mother plant when the embryo is still not fully developed as, for example, still in the globular stage. Orchid seeds must therefore be nurtured with great care. Hence, there exist the elaborate sterile technical procedures used routinely by commercial orchid growers who are in essence culturing immature orchid embryos through early embryogenesis in vitro. An introduction to embryogenesis in the orchids and to methods of culturing the seed may be found in the monograph by Withner.

Production of Embryos from Tissue Cultures

In 1959 Reinert described the development of embryos of carrot in callus tissues which had been carried through a series of nutrient changes. The callus tissue was initiated in the first place from the secondary vascular tissues of the storage root of carrot. More recently several accounts of the initiation and development of what are termed "embryoids" or "adventive embryos" from cultured carrot callus tissues have been made. The basic procedure was to develop a proliferating callus tissue on a nutrient medium, then change the medium (usually withholding auxin from the medium), and allowing organogenesis to begin. Kato and Takeuchi gave the following account of their procedure:

Throughout the present investigation, tap-roots of *Daucus carota* were used as starting material. A portion of the tap-root was excised aseptically by means of a corkborer, and cut into disks 1 mm thick and 6 mm in diameter. These disks were transplanted onto a solid medium consisting of White's basic solution with addition of 0.5% agar supplemented with 0.1% Difco yeast extract and 1 or 10 ppm β-indoleacetic acid. The culture was grown in a dark room at 27 ± 1°, and transplanted every twenty days to a fresh medium of the above mentioned composition. The explants showed vigorous growth to produce a firm callus tissue, orange-yellow in colour.

After four months of culturing, single cells or small cell clumps were separated from the surface of the friable callus tissue, some of them floating on the wet surface of the agar and others penetrating into the agar medium. These cell colonies continued to grow on the agar surface and underwent a series of successive differentiation apparently similar to that of normal embryogenesis, finally to develop into a small but complete plantlet. Several stages of development were distinguished; single cell, globular, heart-shaped, torpedo-shaped bodies, and finally, young plantlet.

From callus tissue grown in liquid culture, cell suspensions could be separated by a mechanical filter and the small multicellular colonies isolated could be subcultured in synthetic medium to allow embryo development to occur. Embryoids developed singly from suspensions sieved at 45 μm and clumps of embryoids developed from the fraction

45-75 mm. Although initial cultivation was facilitated with complex addenda to the media such as coconut milk or powdered yeast extract, the entire cultivation could be carried out in defined synthetic media. Removal of high concentrations of auxin was critical for the conversion from proliferation of unorganized callus to organized embryos. Normal embryonic stages were observed although no real synchrony in this type of development has yet been achieved.

Embryogenesis from cultured callus tissues has been observed in a large number of species. Callus initiated from immature or mature embryos appears to form embryoids more readily when exposed to sequential treatment on different media than callus derived from mature tissues. No explanation for this responsiveness is known. Embryoids arise from callus tissues cultured for long periods of time provided the proper nutrient medium is provided. Reinert et al. have conclusively demonstrated with photographic evidence that embryoids can arise from single isolated cells grown in culture. This conclusion had been reached earlier by Steward et al. on indirect evidence based on the percentage embryoid formation from plated cell suspensions of carrot cells.

To date the use of embryos available in large numbers and at selected stages of development from cultured callus tissues or cell suspension cultures has been limited. Some abnormalities may be observed in embryonic development and must be selected out and discarded. Also there has been some debate as to the identity of embryos formed in *ovulo* with those formed *in vitro*. Yet here is a new source of embryo-like structures for analysis and further study. "Perhaps further experimental study of these induced embryoids will contribute to a greater knowledge of the factors involved in normal embryogenesis."

11

GROWTH HORMONES

Among the substances which markedly influence the reactions and metabolism of plants are those internally synthesized compounds called *hormones*. In general, the term "hormone" is used to designate certain organic compounds which exert important regulatory effects upon the metabolism of an organism when present in only minute quantities. In the animal body it is generally considered that a further characteristic of a hormone is that it exerts its effects at a site remote from the locus of its synthesis. Adrenalin, for example, secreted in higher animals by the adrenal gland, has pronounced effects upon the heart and vascular system. Many, but not all, plant hormones similarly exert their effects in cells at some distance from those in which they are synthesized, after translocation from the latter to the former.

Included among the plant hormones are certain substances usually classified as vitamins in considerations of animal physiology. In the higher plants those vitamins which are essential exhibit essentially the same general type of behaviour as hormones and may be regarded as falling into the same general category of substances. In addition to the naturally occurring hormones in plants, a number of organic compounds are known which, when introduced into plants in relatively small quantities, induce effects which are similar to, and often apparently indentical with, those induced by naturally occurring hormones.

By an extension of the original concept, such substances are also often called plant hormones, although the more rigorous definition of the term would strict it to naturally occurring compounds. Other terms commonly used to designate plant hormones are *phyto-hormones*, *growth hormones*, *growth substances*, and *growth regulators* (a term which includes both *growth activators* and *growth inhibitors*).

Emergence of the Hormone Concept

Soding (1923), after Paal's deduction that specific substances produced in the coleoptile tip were responsible for phototropism, established that these very substances were capable of stimulating straight growth as well. Among the workers attracted by the demonstration of a correlation carrier in oat tips were Cholodny (1927) in Russia and Went (1928) at Utrecht, who independently extended the correlation carrier theory to both phototropism and geotropism. They concluded that all tropisms were mediated by a growth hormone system which was essential to all plant growth.

Went, while working on the role of auxin in plant growth discovered that hormone could be collected in an agar block by diffusion, and also presented a technique for obtaining the hormone from a great variety of plant materials. Using oat coleoptile he established a test so accurate and reproducible that it still stands as the best auxin assay technique, the *Avena* test. The sound basis which Went gave to auxin physiology resulted into a great deal of very productive work in subsequent years, and in a short eight-year period, from 1928 to 1936, three auxins were isolated characterized and identified, the quantitative relationships of auxin to tropisms of roots and shoots were established, and at the end of this period half of the significant and major functions of auxin in growth and development had also been discovered.

Kogl (1933) and his co-workers found two materials, strongly active in the *Avena* test, which they named auxin *a* and auxin *b*. Auxin *a* has a molecular weight of 328, which is very close to Went's figure for diffused auxin from *Avena*, i.e. 372. These compounds, today are only of historical interest since they have never been positively isolated from growing plant tissue. Kogl group (1934), as a result of further research, discovered another auxin compound which was identical to indole 3-acetic acid. The presence of this auxin was demonstrated in *Rhizopus* cultures by Thimann (1935). It is now generally accepted that indole acetic acid is the common growth hormone in higher plants.

Since the time of Went several physiological roles of auxins have been clarified. Went (1934) himself discovered that auxins stimulated the formation of adventitious roots (throwing light on another correlative effect). The developmental importance of auxin in morphological differentiation came to a full realization when Skoog and Tsui (1948) found that relative auxin levels in plant tissues play a crucial role in determining growth pattern. La Rue (1936) found that auxins applied to leaves could retard leaf abscission. Later researches have proved that abscission of all plant organs (leaves, flowers, fruits, etc.) is correlated with low auxin content. The development of knowledge of the auxins has had a remarkable effect on the agricultural sciences as well. A historical outline of the early and recent contributions to our knowledge of plant growth hormones has been given by Boysen-Jensen (1936).

Definitions and Consideration of Nomenclature

It will be convenient at this point to turn to a consideration of nomenclature, since a wide range of terms have been used to characterize plant growth regulating substances. It is generally agreed that an ideal system of nomenclature must be based on their biochemical and physiological attributes, irrespective of their mode and site of production and processes involved in transporting them to the places where they act. Such an ideal nomenclature must therefore embrace not only naturally occurring compounds, but also all artificially made substances having the same action in the cell. A recent treatise by van Overbeek (1950) has given a very broad definition of plant hormones as "organic compounds which regulate plant-physiological processes regardless of whether these compounds are naturally occurring and/or synthetic, stimulating and/or inhibitory, local activators or substances which act at a distance from the place where they are formed.

Similarly, the term auxin is made to include all synthetic compounds having the specific auxin action. Before entering into an extensive discussion of these compounds, it will be well to define these terms. Out of the recent definitions of a plant hormone is given by Thimann (Pincus and Thimann, 1948) as "An organic substance produced naturally in higher plants, controlling growth or other physiological functions at a site remote from its place of production and active in minute amounts "Thimann favours the term "Phytohormone" (Greek : Phyton = a plant) which literally means a plant hormone. *Growth hormone* is the phytohormone involved in growth. The term auxin was originally suggested to refer to substances which were capable of promoting growth in the manner of the growth hormone. The term *growth regulator* refers to organic compounds other than nutrients, small amounts of which are capable of modifying growth. Thimann Pincus and Thimann, (1948) has defined auxin as "an organic substance which promotes growth (*i.e.,* irreversible increase in volume) along the longitudinal axis when applied in low concentrations to shoots of plants freed as far as practicable from their own inherent growth-promoting substances. Auxins may, and generally do , have other properties, but this one is critical." This definition is widely accepted among plant physiologists today.

Extraction, Detection, and Estimation by Bioassay of Auxins

Although a detailed account of extraction and estimation techniques of auxin is beyond the scope of this text, a brief account may however be given. All procedures for the determination of auxin content of plant materials do not measure the same constituents. There auxin concepts are, however, not entirely simple. There are many examples were bound auxin is released in free form during extraction. Consequently it appears that the free and bound forms are in a dynamic stage and their strictly separate measurement is often difficult. There are two well defined methods for the extraction of auxins from material.

Diffusion method

Diffusion method, the simplest of all, consists of obtaining the growth hormone from plant material by diffusion into agar. The procedure consists of severing the growing tip or other organ to be tested under conditions which discourage transpiration and placing the cut surface for a period of an hour or so on a block of agar, usually of 1.5 per cent concentration. Three major difficulties may arise in the operation of diffusion techniques :

(a) The excessive loss of water, or a negative tension in the vascular system can prevent the accumulation of the diffusate in the agar block.

(b) The destruction of the auxin at the cut surface frequently interferes with the quantitative yield. Such destruction is enzymatic and is attributed in some cases, to polyphenol oxidase and in other cases to peroxidase.

(c) Growth inhibitors, whose existence is common in many green plants may prevent the effective use of diffusion techniques.

Solvent extraction method

Several solvents have been employed for the extraction of auxins from plant material. Among the solvent used are, chloroform, diethylether, ethyl alcohol and even water. A serious drawback to the use of chloroform, however, is the slow accumulation of a toxic substance, perhaps an auxin in activator, thought to be chlorine Thimann and Skoog (1940). Boysen-Jensen(1936) demonstrated that diethylether may serve as the most satisfactory solvent. But before use the ether should be redistilled over ferrous sulphate and calcium oxide in a small amount of water. This is done in order to avoid an oxidation of easily oxidizable auxin by the presence of spontaneously formed peroxide. It has been amply demonstrated that the formation of new auxin during extraction may be a source of serious error. This can be successfully avoided by using Gustafson's (1941) technique which consists essentially of boiling the plant material a short time prior to solvent extraction. The main features of his technique are as under:

1. Freezing the tissue rapidly on carbon dioxide ice.
2. Grinding the tissue with mortar and pestle.
3. Dropping the tissue into boiling water and allowing one minute of active boiling.
4. Collecting the plant material on a filter paper and extracting with ether for 16 hours, using 3 changes of ether.

Gustafson's technique has some limitations, since as pointed out by Thimann, Skoog and Bayer (1942), certain amount of the free auxin must be destroyed during heating, and by Van Overbeek, *et al.* (1945) that heating may cause the release of inhibitors which interfere with auxin assay. The formation of new auxin during extraction is also avoided by the use of freezing and lyophilization technique first described by Wildman and Muir in 1949. Their technique may be summarized as follows:

1. Plunging the plant material into liquid air or dry ice and acetone for rapid freezing.
2. Drying by lyophilization.
3. Grinding to 40 mesh in Wiley mill.
4. Storing in vacuo over phosphorus penta-oxide, in darkness, until use.
5. Extracting with peroxide-free ether (95 percent) at 0°C for four half-hour intervals.
6. Combining ether extracts and reducing in volume to a few ml.
7. Transferring qualitatively to agar for *Avena* assay. Some plant materials may not require either boiling or lyophilization for solvent extraction of free auxin.

Van Overbbeek *et .al* (1945) have developed a technique for obtaining free auxin using short term extraction. It may be epitomized as below:

1. Freeze plant material on CO_2 ice.
2. Slice bulky tissues into 2-5 mm slices.
3. Extract with peroxide-free ether at 0°C for two half-hour intervals

4. Combine the ether extracts and reduce volume by evaporation to a few ml.
5. Transfer quantitatively to agar for *Avena* assay.

All the above techniques have been designed for the extraction of free auxin. Bound auxins can be extracted by using either of the latter two methods by carrying on extraction over a period of time.

Relation of Auxins to Growth of the Oat Coleoptile

The *auxins* have been the most comprehensively investigated group of plant hormones. Their action was first clearly demonstrated in the leaf sheath or *coleoptile* of the oat plant (*Avena sativa*). This is a tubular, leaf-like structure, closed at the top, which is the first part of the plant to emerge from the soil. Similar coleoptiles develop during early seedling growth of other members of the grass family. The coleoptile encloses the initial leaf and is eventually pierced at the tip as a result of the growth of this leaf, soon after which all growth in length of the coleoptile ceases. Oat coleoptiles are approximately 1.5 mm. in diameter, and when illuminated seldom attain lengths of more than 2 cm. In the dark they may attain height ranging up to 6 cm. Cell divisions cease relatively early in the life history of an oat coleoptile, and during approximately the last three- fourths of its growth period all increase in its length results from cell elongation. If the tip of a coleoptile is removed by a clean cut made several millimeteres below the apex, the rate of elongation of the stump is immediately retarded.

If, however, the cut-off tip of the coleoptile or a similar tip from another coleoptile is affixed on the stump, its elongation will be resumed, and may nearly regain the original rate. Retipping the

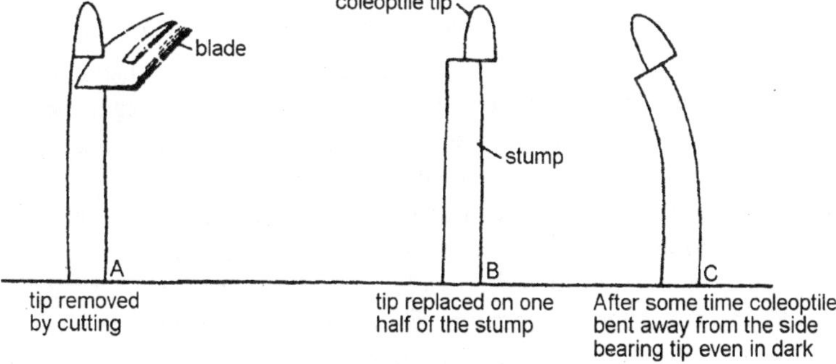

Fig. 11.1. Discovery of auxins. Experiment of Paal-eccentric placement of tip caused curvature.

coleoptile with a short segment cut out of another coleoptile somewhat below the apex results in little or no increase in elongation rate. Such experiments indicate that the elongation of a coleoptile, which occurs in the more basal regions, is maintained only under the influence of some sort of a "stimulus": orginating in the tip, whence it is transmitted basipetally (apex to base) through the coleoptile. Went (1928, 1935) placed the cut-off tips of oat coleoptiles on a thin layer of 3 percent agar and after 1 hr, removed them and sliced the agar into a number of equal-sized small blocks. If one of these blocks was placed upon the stump of a detipped coleoptile, the rate of elongation was accelerated just as if the stump had been capped with a fresh coleoptile tip. On the other hand, retipping a coleoptile with a block of pure agar had no appreciable accelerating effect on elongation.

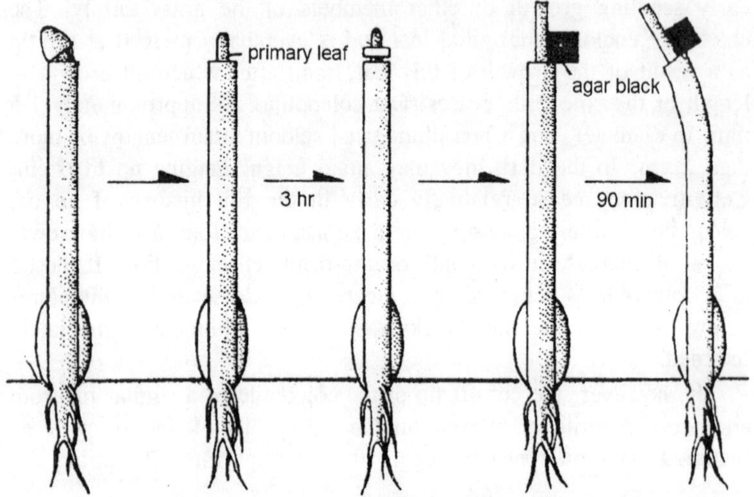

Fig. 11.2. Discovery of auxins. Experiment of F.W. Went-Avena Curvature test.

It seems evident from these results that some substance or substances were transported out of the cut-off tip into the agar block, and subsequently out of the block into the coleoptile stump, whence they were translocated downward to the elongating region of the coleoptile. The substances which induce such a reaction now are classed as auxins. Many other plant organs such as stems, petioles, flower stalks, and coleoptiles of other species behave similarly upon removal of the apical region. Elongation is stopped or retarded by such a treatment but will be resumed if the excised apex of the organ is carefully relocated on the cut surface of the sump.

Biological Tests for Auxins

Auxins are known to be of widespread distribution in plants. They occur in such small quantities, however, that detection of their presence in an organic material by chemical methods is usually impossible. Recourse is had, therefore, to sensitive biological tests in order to demonstrate the presence of these substances. Several such tests have been used rather widely. The oat coleoptile test has been the most extensively employed method of determining the relative quantities of auxins present in plant tissues or other materials. If an agar block containing auxin from one source or another is affixed onesidedly on a detipped oat coleoptile elongation is found to be more rapid on the side of the coeloptile below the portion of the tip on which the block is perched, resulting in curvature of the coleoptile.

Translocation of the hormone is almost strictly longitudinal, the elongating cells on the side of the coleoptile under the block receiving much more auxin than cells on the opposite side, with a corresponding differential effect on growth. When the block is centered on the coleoptile stump, as in the experiment described in the preceding section, all sides of the coleoptile receive approximately equal quantities of auxin, and growth proceeds in a vertical direction. Furthermore, it has been found that the curvature resulting from the eccentric attachment of agar blocks to detipped oat coleoptiles is proportional, within the range of about 0 to 20 degrees, to the concentration of the auxin in the agar block. It is this proportionality between hormone concentration and curvature that makes possible the use of oat coleoptiles as living

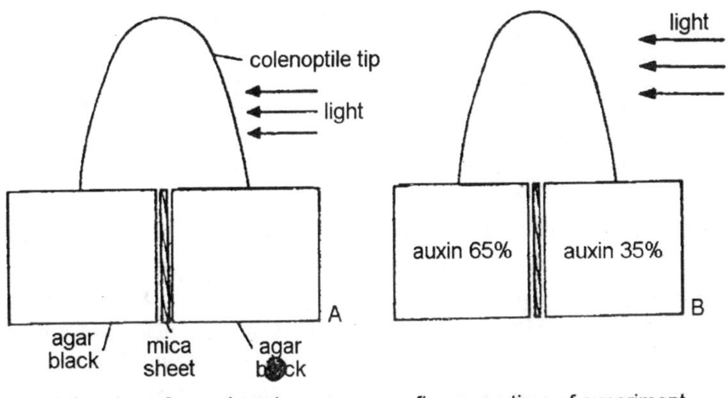

Fig. 11.3. Differential distribution of auxin in coleoptile tip under the influence of unilateral light.

test objects in the quantitative estimation of the auxin content of plant tissues or other materials.

Quantitative measurements of auxins by the oat coleoptile technique must be carried out under carefully standardized conditions. The oat seedlings (usually from a genetically uniform variety) are grown in a dark room at a temperature of 25°C, and a relative humidity of 90 percent. All manipulations are performed under phototropically inactive orange or red light. The Coleoptiles are used when about 2.3 to 4cm in length. The extreme tip of the coleoptile is first cut off, and after 3 hr, the topmost 4mm of the stump is removed. For reasons which cannot be considered in a brief discussion, the coleoptiles are more sensitive when this method of double decaptitation is employed than when the tip is cut off in one operation. The primary leaf, which is enclosed by the coleoptile, is then pulled loose so it will not interfere with the determination by its continued growth. If guttation water exudes at the cut surface it is carefully blotted off. An agar block (2 x 2 x 1 mm is a commonly used size), continuing the substance to be tested, is then affixed unilaterally to the cut tip. After a standard length of time (usually 90 min), the resulting degree of curvature of the coleoptile is determined. The greater the degree of curvature, within limits, the greater the hormone concentration in the agar block.

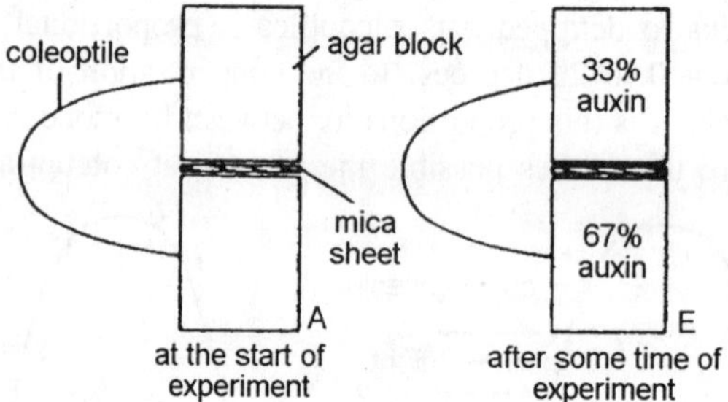

Fig. 11.4. Differential distribution of auxin from coleptile under the influence of gravitational force.

Various methods of applying the material to be tested for auxins to detipped coleoptiles have been employed. Sometimes small plant organs or pieces of plant organs are affixed directly to the cut surface of the coleoptile. More commonly plant tissues are placed in contact with 3 percent agar into which the hormone will move. The tissue is generally left in contact with the agar for about 2 hr. The agar is then cut into block of standard size each of which is then affixed unilaterally to a detipped coleoptile. The effects of pure chemicals or extracts can be tested by first dispersing them in agar, and them, after solidification, determining the influence of standard sized blocks of this agar on curvature of the coleoptiles. Or agar blocks can be soaked in a solution of the substances and then used in the coleoptile test for auxins.

Another commonly used biological test for auxins is to immerse sections of young oat coleoptiles in the solution to be tested and measure their increase in length over a certain period of time (commonly 6=25 hr.) as compared with increase in length of similar section immersed in water or an auxin free solution.

Chemical Constitution of the Naturally-occurring Auxins

Kogl *et al* (1934) isolated from biological sources three chemically pure crystalline substances which give the reactions of auxins when tested by the oat coleoptile technique. These substances have been called auxin a ($C_{18}H_{32}O_5$), auxin b ($C_{18}H_{30}O_4$), and heteroauxin ($C_{10}H_3O_2N$). The chemical names of these substances are auxentriolic acid, auxenylonic acid and indole-3-acetic acid, respectively. Auxin *a* was isolated from urine, and both auxins *a* and *b* from malt and various vegetable oils, indoleacetic acid was isolated from urine and from certain yeasts and molds. At one time it was considered possible that indoleacetic acid did not occur in the tissues of higher plants, but more recently it has been isolated from corn grains and there are numerous indications that it occurs in many other tissues of higher plants including oat coleoptiles. It seems probable that this will prove to be the principal naturally-occurring auxin.

The Occurrence and Synthesis of Naturally-occurring Auxins in Plants

Auxins appear to be universally present in plants, and their occurrence has actually been demonstrated in a wide variety of species. Furthermore, the auxins are nonspecific in their action, i.e., the same auxin, chemically speaking, which influences growth phenomena in one species usually also influences the same or similar phenomena in other species. Auxins are present in plant cells in several different forms: free auxins, auxin precursors, and bound auxins. Various methods of extracting the "total" auxins (all forms) from plant tissues have been devised and more or less successfully employed. Other investigators have devised methods which they believe extract only the free auxins from plant tissues.

Only in the free form is an auxin readily diffusable, and only in this form is it effective in the oat coleoptile tests. Since, however, free auxins may be continuously formed from bound or precursor auxins, considerably more free auxin than originally present may diffuse into agar blocks from plant tissues. In most tissues thus far investigated the auxins present in inactive forms are many times greater than the free auxins present; the later seldom constituting more than 10 percent of the potentially available auxins.

The amino acid tryptophane has been shown to be a precursor of indoleacetic acid in plants. Conversion of the former compound into the latter apparently takes place through the intermediate stop of indoleacetaldehyde, which is therefore an even more immediate precursor of indoleacetic acid. The transformation of tryptophane to indoleacetic acid is catalyzed by a specific enzyme system which has been found in a number of plant tissues. The presence of zinc is necessary for tryptophane synthesis, and one of the indirect effects of zinc deficiency is a reduction in the quantity of auxin present. Following are the structural formulas for tryptophane and indoleacetic acids.

Many, but not all, of the bound auxins are auxin-protein complexes. Since, by suitable treatments, active auxins can be released from bound auxins, the latter are sometimes referred to as "auxin precursors," although they would not be so regarded in the usual sense of the term.

The auxins naturally present in plants are synthetic products of plant metabolism. The principal centers of auxin synthesis are apical meristematic tissues of aerial organs such as opening buds, young leaves, and flowers or inflorescences on growing flower stalks. Small quantities of auxins are also synthesized in apural root meristems although much of the auxin present in roots probably comes from aerial organs of the plants. The auxin synthesized in one tissue is frequently translocated to other organs of the plants. The concentration of auxin may vary greatly from one tissue to another; in general auxin is found in greatest concentration in the tissues in which it is synthesized or stored. Temperature is a factor in auxin synthesis, but the optimum for this process probably is not the same in all plants and tissues. In coleoptile tips the auxin is apparently synthesized from a precursor which is translocated atropetally (base to apex) through the coleoptile from the grain.

Auxins are not only synthesized in plant cells but are also inactivated in them. Inactivation may be brought about in various ways. Among other inactivation agents is a specific enzyme which breaks down indoleacetic acid; this enzyme has been isolated from the epicotyls of etiolated pea seedlings.

The Role of Auxins in Cell Elongation

Auxins play a role in the elongation phase of growth in many other plant organs similar to that described for the oat coleoptile. It is generally considered that cell elongation occurs only in the presence of auxins, and that with increase in auxin concentration there is an increase in the rate of elongation if no other factors are limiting. The optimum range of concentration for cell elongation varies greatly with different tissues, and relatively high concentrations usually exert an inhibiting, effect upon this phase of growth.

If the extreme tip of a maize or lupine root is cut off, its rate of elongation increases, although not greatly. Replacement of the root tip in maize plants results in a retandation in elongation rate at compared with detipped roots. Furthermore, attachment of coleoptile tips of maize to detipped root tips of the same plant results in a retardation in the elongation rate of the root tip. These results suggest that the same concentrations of auxin which accelerate elongation in coleoptiles and other aerial organs retard elongation in roots.

This supposition has been confirmed by experiments in which the roots of oat seedlings were immersed in pure solutions of auxins. The growth of the roots was found to be retarded in proportion to the concentration of auxin used. However, when roots which contain either no auxin at all or virtually none, are treated with auxin solutions of very low concentration, acceleration of growth as compared with similar but untreated roots often results.

The apparently contrasting effects of auxins upon elongation of roots and aerial organs may be explained by assuming that roots, buds, and stems all react in a comparable way to auxins their growth being inhibited by relatively high, and promoted by relatively low, auxin concentrations. Elongation of roots is favoured only at very low concentrations; at all higher concentrations their growth is checked. Stems and coleoptiles show a similar behaviour except that the optimum range of concentrations for elongation is much higher than for roots. The same concentrations of auxins which favour stem elongation result in retardation of root elongation. Briefly, therefore, whether an auxin will exert an accelerating or an inhibiting effect upon growth seems to depend in part upon its concentration and in part upon the specific tissue involved.

Shortly after the discovery of the naturally-occurring auxins various investigators showed that certain compounds, not known to occur naturally in plants, induce reactions in plants similar to those evoked by the naturally-occurring auxins. The list of such "synthetic" auxins has become quite extensive. The best known of these substances are α-naphthalene acetic acid, indolebutyric acid, 2,4-dichlorophenoxyacetic acid, and α-naphthoxyacetic acid. Most of these compounds induce curvature of oat coleoptiles when tested by the standard technique, although many of them are not as effective in causing this reaction as the naturally occurring auxins.

The term "auxin" has been used in different senses by different authorities. Most commonly, however, an auxin is considered to be any organic compound that promotes growth along a longitudinal axis when applied in low concentrations to organs which are initially low in their content of such growth-promoting substances but are under conditions which are otherwise favourable for elongation growth. The phrase "low concentrations" is a somewhat vague one, but in general can be taken to refer to concentrations of less than 10^{-3} molar. In spite of the apparent diversity of the compounds which act as auxins, certain similarities in molecular structure are common to all of them. These are: a ring system with a side chain containing at least one carbon atom between a terminal carboxyl or potential carboxyl group and the ring, a double bond in the ring adjacent to the side chain, and a definite space relationship between the carboxyl group and the ring system. *Cf.* the structural formula for indoleacetic acid given earlier.

Translocation of Auxins

If a block of agar containing auxin is affixed to the morphologically upper end of a segment of oat coleoptile, and a block of pure agar to the lower end, auxin will move into and accumulate in the lower block. The final concentration of auxin in the basally attached block may greatly exceed that in the one affixed to the apex. If the agar block containing auxin is affixed to the morphologically basal end, no translocation of auxin will occur. Translocation of auxin in oat coleoptiles apparently takes place through the paraenchyma tissues.

The results of such experiments show that transport of auxin in the oat coleoptile is *polar* i.e., occurs only basipetally, and that it can occur against a concentration gradient since the auxin accumulates in the lower block. There is evidence that a similar basipetal translocation of auxin, either naturally-occurring or introduced, occurs in many other plant tissues or organs. Among these are coleoptiles of other species than oat, the veins and petioles of leaves, hypocotyls, herbaceous stems, and woody stems. In such organs the polarized downward movement occurs in parenchyma or phloem tissues. In roots on the other hand,

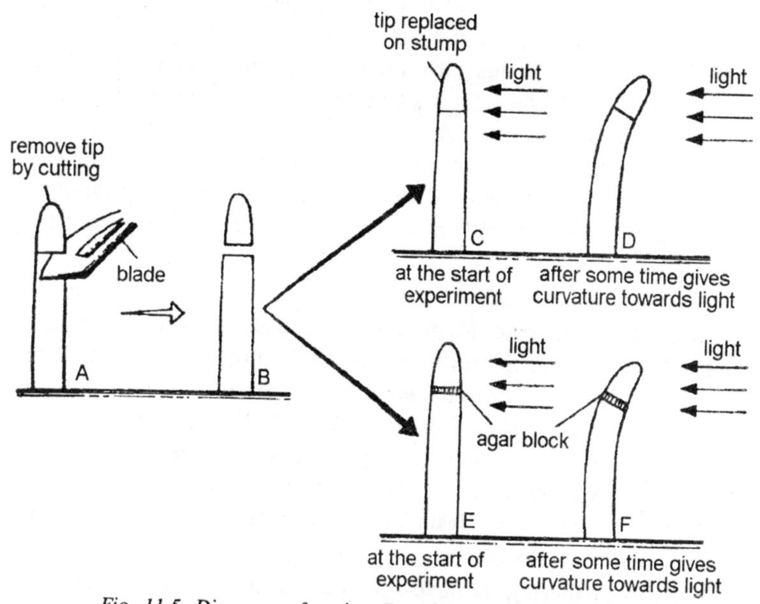

Fig. 11.5. Discovery of auxins. Experiments of Boysen-Jensen.

movement of auxins appears to be nonpolar and there are undoubtedly other tissues in which this is also true. The mechanism of the polar movement of auxins is unknown. Etherization stops the transport of auxin, except insofar as it can be accounted for by diffusion, and destroys its polarity. This indicates that living cells are involved in the process, but tells nothing of the manner in which they operate.

It has been suggested that the polarity in the movement of auxins may result from differences of electrical potential in the tissues, but experiments designed to test this hypothesis have not yielded evidence in its support. Upward translocation of auxins can occur in plants, at least under certain conditions. If an auxin is applied to the soil or to the basal parts of entire plants or to cuttings in adequate concentrations, their absorption and upward movement through the plant can be demonstrated. Such upward transport apparently takes place only when the auxin molecules pass into the transpiration stream. As soon as the auxin molecules move back into the living tissues of the stem or leaf their polar basipetal movement is resumed.

Role of Auxins in Root Formation

It has been known for many years that the presence of buds on a cutting favours development of roots when the basal portion of the cutting is introduced into a suitable rooting medium. Developing buds are more effective in promoting root formation than quiescent buds. Leaves, especially if young, also often favour the production of roots on cuttings. These observations suggest that root initiation on cuttings is favoured by hormones which are synthesized in the buds and young leaves and are subsequently translocated to the basal part of the cutting. Soon after the identification of them as naturally occurring auxins it was found that auxin *b* and indolesacetic acid are active in inducing root formation.

There is good evidence that other hormones besides auxins are also necessary for root formation or atleast for their continued development, whether the roots are initiated on other roots, on stems, or on leaves. The effect of auxins on root *formation* should be clearly distinguished from their effect on root *elongation*. In general, the concentrations required for the former process are much greater than for the latter. A number of the "auxins" not known to occur naturally in plants have also been found to be effective in promoting root formation in many species.

Extensive experiments have been carried out on the suitability of treatments with various auxins as a practical method of aiding in the rooting of cuttings. Such treatments are not effective with all kinds of plants, but with cuttings of many species they lead to a speeding up of the process of root formation and to the development of a greater number of roots per cutting. Hormones do not induce root formation, however, on cuttings of species on which at least some roots do not develop without their application. Various techniques are used to introduce hormones into cuttings. Formerly the most favoured procedure was to immense the basal end of the cuttings in a dilute (10-200 p.p.m) solution of the hormone for periods ranging up to 24 hr, before setting them in the rooting medium. Laterally this method has been largely superseded by two less time-consuming procedures. In one of these the hormone is applied in a day form, being first mixed with an inert powder such as talc, most commonly in proportion of 500-2000 parts of the hormones to 1,000,000 parts of talc.

The basal end of the cutting is first dipped in water, and then in the powder before insertion into the rooting medium. In the "quick dip" method the basal ends of the cutting are dipped momentarily (for about 5 sec) into a relatively concentrated solution of the hormone (4,000-10,000 p.p.m, in water or 50 percent ethyl alcohol) before being a set in the cutting bench. Auxins many also be applied to stems or cuttings in lanolin or an vapours. The compounds most commonly employed in all of these methods, either singly or in mixtures, are α-napthaleneacetic acid, napthalene acetamide, and indolebutyric acid. The most effective treatment varies according to species; extensive tabulations of the effects of various compounds and methods of treatment on numerous species are given by Avery and Johnson (1947) and Mitchell and Marth (1947).

Other Effects of Auxins

One of the most remarkable facts about the auxins is the multiplicity of the growth reactions in which they participate. Only a few of their roles are discussed in this chapter; other important growth phenomena in which they play a part include the development of fruits, abcission of leaves and fruits, activation of cambial cells, apical dominance, flower initiation, geotropism and phototropism. These various roles of the auxins will be discussed in subsequent chapters.

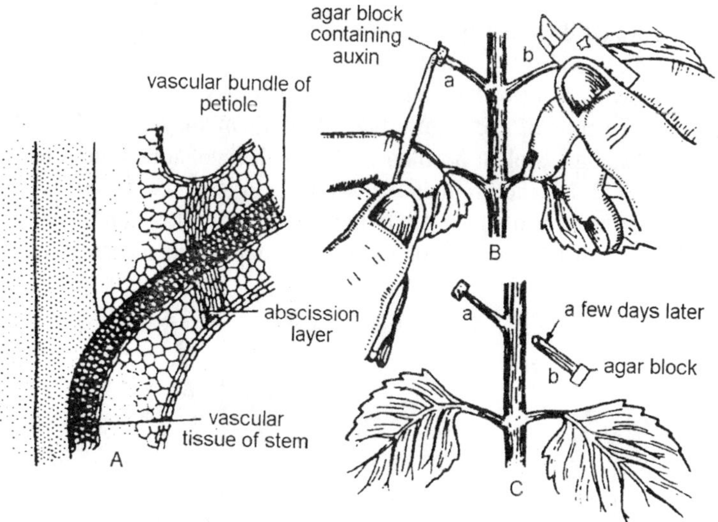

Fig. 11.6. Effect of auxins on abscission. A–A normal abscission layer at the base of petiole. B–(a) agar block contain auxin is fixed on debladed petiole (b) agar block without auxin is being fixed on debladed petiole. C–(a) There is retardation of abscission of petiole (b) petiole abscised.

Toxic Effects of Auxins

Reference has already been made to the inhibitory effect of relatively high concentrations of auxins on the process of cell elongation. Applications of auxins in relatively high concentrations also result in various kinds of growth malformations in plants such as distortions of leaves, stems and roots, discolourations of leaves, inhibitions of stem or root elongation or flower opening, and the formation of tumors. It should be emphasized that the term "relatively high concentration" as used in this discussion refers to concentrations which, in absolute terms, are very low, of the general order of magnitude of 1000 p.p.m. In somewhat higher concentrations, but in absolute terms still very low, these compounds often result in death of the plant. Realization that auxins, when applied in relatively high but actually very low concentrations, exert toxic or lethal effects on plants led to the suggestion that they could be employed for the purpose of killing weeds or other noxious plants.

The phenoxyacetic acids have proved especially effective as herbicides. The most widely used of these has been 2,4 - dichlorophenoxyacetic acid ("2,4-D"), although numerous other organic compounds with hormone-like effects or plants also show promise as herbicides. The results of tests on the growth-inhibiting activity of over a thousand different organic compounds are listed by Thompson *et al.* (1946),who also summarize previous work on the chemical control of plant growth. Most of the compounds which they list are not auxins in the usual sense of the word, but all of them may be classified, broadly speaking, as plant hormones or growth regulators. The effects on plants of 2,4-dicholorophenoxy acetic acid may be taken as an example of the action of an auxin-like herbicide. This compound is readily absorbed from sprays or dusts when applied to leaves.

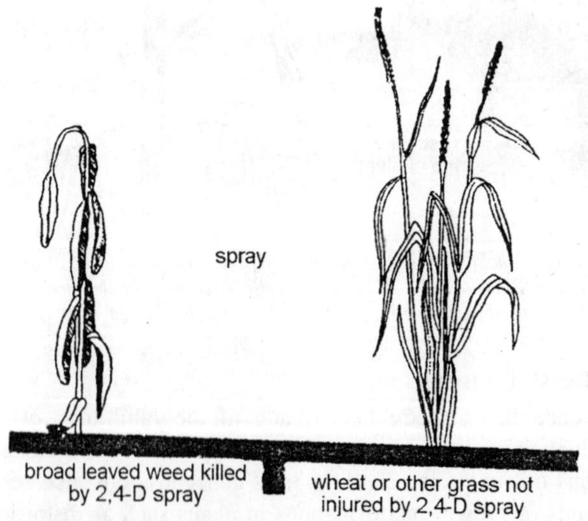

Fig. 11.7. Destruction of weeds by 2,4-D.

It is quickly translocated to other parts of the plant and affects especially the meristems. The rapid distribution of this compound throughout the plant contributes greatly to its effectiveness as a toxicant. Death results from demagements of metabolism, especially in the meristems. Different kinds of plants differ markedly in their reactions to applications of 2,4 -dichlophenoxyacetic acid. Cereal grains and most other grasses are less susceptible, for exmple, than most broad-leaved annuals, and most woody plants are less susceptible than most herbaceous species. This very selectivity of effect is one of the advantages of this compound, and of many similar ones, as herbicides. Broad-leaved weeds can be elinimated from sugar cane fields or from lawns, for example, by application of a spray in the proper concentration and at the proper volume per square foot. Besides its selectivity of effect, 2,4-dichloro-phenoxyacetic acid has certain other advantages when used as herbicide. The absolute concentrations required are very low.

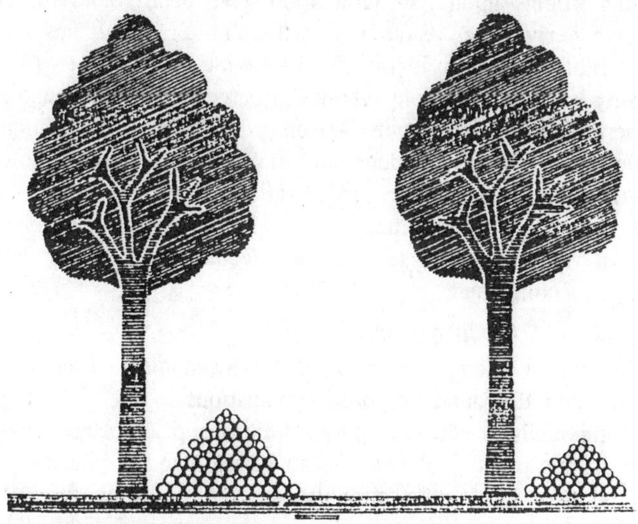

Fig. 11.8. Auxin spray on a plant prevents prematures fruit abscission and increases the yield. A–Unsprayed, B–Sprayed.

Many plants can be killed, for example, by spraying with an 0.1 percent solution at the rate of 5 gal.per 100 ft^2. In the concentrations generally employed this compound is harmless to men and animals. Under most conditions, 2,4-dichlorophenoxyacetic acid disintegrates rapidly in soils. The possibility of detrimental effects on plants which subsequently grow on soils in which this compound was once present thus disappears rapidly. Great care must be exercised, however, in the use of this herbicide, that the spray does not drift to plants other than those being treated. Accidental damage or destruction of valuable plants as a result of careless application has been the chief disadvantage in the use of 2,4-dichlorophenoxyacetic acid as an herbicide.

The differential effects on various species of plants of some of the other compounds used as herbicides is unlike that of 2,4-dichlorophenoxyacetic acid. Isopropylpheny learbamate, for example, in contrast with 2,4-dichlorophenoxyacetic acid is much more effective in killing certain grasses than broad-leaved annuals

It is convenient to mention several other growth inhibitors at this point, although whether or not they would be classed as hormones is a matter of definition. Coumarin favours cell enlargement in such plant tissue as oat coleoptiles and leaf blades at very low concentrations, but checks cell enlargement at all higher concentrations. Similar checking effects upon root elongation have been found for certian coumarin derivatives. Another growth inhibitor which has attracted considerable attention is maleic hydrazide. Applied to plants in relatively low concentrations (about 0.4 percent) this compound results in general cessation of growth. At somewhat lower concentrations loss of apical dominance is evident, and axillary buds start to grow soon after treatment. At certain concentrations flowering appears to be largely suppressed without much suppression of vegetative development. Plants of various species seem to be affected in essentially the same way by this compound.

Mechanism of Auxin Action

The earlier attempts to elucidate the mechanism of auxin section mostly centered around proposed explanations of the part played by such compounds in cell elongation. Auxins appear to have two main effects in this process: they cause an increase in the plasticity of the wall and they participate, directly and indirectly, in the reactions whereby additional cellulose molecules are deposited within the wall. With the growing relization, however, of the large number of growth reactions conditioned by auxins, it has become obvious that these compounds must play a role in some pivotal metabolic process. The apparent necessity of specific chemical structure for a compound to act as an auxin, mentioned earlier, also suggests a particular metabolic role. The effect of auxins on cell wall development is, therefore, now generally considered to be, not a direct one, but only one possible end expression of fundamental auxin-conditioned or regulated metabolic processes.

There is considerable evidence that the auxins act primarily in a catalytic or regulatory capacity in some phase of the carbohydrate metabolism of plants. A suggestive finding in this connection is that introduction of auxins into leaves or cuttings induces marked hydrolysis of starch. Auxin also appears to participate in some part of the respiratory process but the exact nature of this relationship has not yet been traced. A significant fact in this connection is that auxins exert their effects only under aerobic conditions. The discovery by Wildman and Bonner (1947), that certain auxin protein complexes from spinach leaves possess phosphatase activity, may prove to be a significant one in allocating a specific role to the auxins. Although the question of the metabolic role of the naturally-occurring auxins as yet cludes a definite answer, it seems practically certain that they operate as carriers, coenzymes, or prosthetic groups in come fundamental enzyme system which plays a part in carbohydrate or organic acid metabolism.

The inhibiting as well as the accelerating effects of the auxins must be accounted for in any hypothesis of the mechanism of their action. If we accept the likely assumption that an auxin is active when it operates as the prosthetic group of an enzyme, it is reasonable to postulate that two fundamental properties of its molecules would be: (1) a specific group which reacts with the substrate molecules, and (2) the necessary structural configuration to combine in some manner with the protein portion of the enzyme.

Viewed in the light to this hypothesis (which incidentally is also applicable to other enzyme systems), relatively high concentrations of an active auxin may result in inhibitory effects as a result of some of the auxin molecules preempting all free positions on the protein component of the enzyme, while others become chemically attached to substrate molecules. This effectively blocks the reaction which can occur only when the protein and auxin operate as a catalytic team, so that substrate molecules become linked temporarily to the protein through auxin bridges

Inhibition of auxin-controlled reactions may also result from the presence in the metabolic system of growth-inhibitors with an auxin-like structure which possess strongly only one of the two properties listed above and the other one only weakly or not at all. If such a compound possesses only the capacity of combining with the protein, it may act as an inhibitor by occupying positions in the protein complex which would otherwise be taken by more active auxins. On the other hand, if the auxin like compound possesses only the property of reacting with the substrate, it may block the overall reaction which can only take place if the compound can act as a chemical bridge between the protein and substrate molecules.

Certain compounds, often called *antiauxins*, are known which offset or counteract the usual growth-enhancing effect of auxin in plants. Among these are coumarin and maleic hydrazide both mentioned earlier in this chapter as growth inhibitors. Another antiauxin is *trans* -cinnamic acid. The effect to this compound is of especial interest in view of the fact that its isomer *cis* -cinnamic acid has the properties of an auxin.

Other Plant Hormones

The auxins are only one kind of a number of hormones occurring in plants. Some of the other compounds in this category have been isolated from plant tissues ; the existence of others is inferred from the occurrence of various physiological reactions; other such substances doubtless are as yet undiscovered or unsuspected.

Traumatic acid

Haberlandt (1921) showed that if freshly cut plant tissue is immediately rinsed with water, very few cell divisions occur in the cells adjacent to the would. However, if the wounded area is smeared with finely ground tissue of the same species cell division takes place. This result led him to postulate the existence of substances which he called "wound hormones" in injured tissues, which are required if cell division is to be engendered in the cells bordering a wound.

More recently English et al. (1939) have succeeded in extracting from bean pods and purifying a compound called traumatic acid which acts like a "wound hormone", This compound has the following formula:

$$HOOC.CH = CH.(CH_2)_8.COOH$$

Traumatic acid induces extensive wound periderm formation in washed disks of potato tuber. It is probable that there are also other "wound hormones" present in plants.

Calines

Went (1938) has postulated the existence in plants of a group of hormones which he calls the *calines* : (1) rhizocaline, made in the leaves and necessary for root formation; (2) canlocaline, synthesized in roots, but necessary for elongation of stems; and (3) phyllocaline, made or at least stored in cotyledons, and necessary for leaf growth. It is also considered that rhizocaline and caulocaline may be stored in seeds. Most of the evidence for the existence of such hormones in plants is indirect and the effects attributed to these hypothetical hormones may actually turn out to result from the activity of substances already well known to have important influences on the growth or metabolism of plants. Glaston and Hand (1949), for example, have obtained evidence that adenine has effects on plants analogous to those of the postulated calines. The calines are discussed further in the following chapter.

Hormones of reproduction

Several hormones are known or believed to play a role in the reproductive process of plants. Among these are the ubiquitous auxins, the "embryo growth factor" and the postulated "florigen".

Vitamins

From the standpoint of human physiology the vitamins constitute a group of specific organic substances which must be supplied in diet, but which are required in relatively small, often only minute, quantities compared with carbohydrates, fats, and proteins. From the standpoint of living organisms in general, for reasons for discussed later, vitamins must be regarded simply as one rather arbitrarily delimited group of growth and metabolism regulators which cannot be sharply distinguished from the hormones. The principal substances recognized as vitamins in human and animal nutrition constitute a very heterogeneous group of compounds.

All of the vitamins, or at least their immediate precursors, are sythesized in green plants. The human body, on the other hand is dependent on sources outside its own metabolism for most essential vitamins and obtains a large proportion of them in green plants used as food. One partial exception is vitamin D which can be synthesized in the human body under irradiation from appropriate precursor which come from foods. Absence of deficiency of any one of the necessary vitamins in the human body results in physiological malfunctioning often evidenced as a specific disease. Some of the vitamin-deficiency diseases of man, such as scurvy, resulting from ascorbic acid deficiency, and beri-beri, resulting from thiamine deficiency, have been known for centuries, although only a comparatively recent years have their causes been recognized. Other higher animals appear to have vitamin requirements very similar to those of man.

The latest addition to the group of B vitamins, is vitamin B_{12}. This vitamin is of especial interest because cobalt is a constituent of the molecule. Whether of not this vitamin plays any role in plant metabolism is not known. Vitamin requirements differ from one kind of living organism to another, but no plant or animal is known for which at least some of them are not essential. The first fundamental question to be answered regarding the vitamin physiology of any organism is: Does the organism require this specific vitamin in its metabolism? Certain of the vitamins appear to be necessary in the metabolism of all plants and animals. This is true of many, if not all, of the vitamins of the so-called B complex. On the other hand, certain vitamins seem to be essential in the metabolism of only certain kinds of organism.

Table 11.1. The Vitamins.

"Alphabetical" Designation	*Name*	*Molecular Formula*
Vitamin A	Hydrolytic product of carotene	$C_{20}H_{29}OH$
Vitamin B (Complex)	Thiamine chloride hydrochloride (B_1)	$C_{12}H_{18}N_4SOCl_2$
	Riboflavin (B_{12} Vitamin G)	$C_{17}H_{20}N_4O_6$
	Nicotinic acid (niacin)	C_5H_4N-COOH
	Pyridoxine(B_6)	$C_8H_{11}NO_3$
	Pantothenic acid	$C_9H_{17}NO_5$
	Inositol	$C_6H_{12}NO_6$
	Biotin(vitamin H)	$C_{10}H_{16}O_2N_2S$
	Folic acid	$C_{19}H_{19}N_7O_6$
	p-amino benzoic acid	$NH_2C_6H_4COOH$
Vitamin C	Ascorbic acid	$C_6H_8O_6$
Vitamin D	Derivatives of ergosterol, cholesterol and other sterols	$C_{28}H_{43}OH$ (activated dehydrocholesterol)
Vitamin E	α-tocopherol (and others)	$C_{29}H_{50}O_2$
Vitamin K	K_1 : 2-methyl, 3 phytyl, 1,4-naphthoquinone	$C_{31}H_{46}O_2$
	K_2 : 2-methyl, 3-difarnesyl, 1,4-naphthoquinone.	

A second fundamental question to be answered regarding any essential vitamin for a given organism is: Does the organism synthesize this vitamin in quantities adequate to meet its own metabolic requirements? The answer to this question for the human organism is essentially "no" for all of the corresponding question for green plants is "yes". For bacteria and fungi no categorical answer is possible since the vitamin- synthesizing capacities of such organisms vary greatly from one species to another, and even from one variety of a given species to another. For many years it has been known that, in the culturing of bacteria or fungi on artificial media, it is necessary to introduce some organic material such as potatoes, peptone, oat or corn meal, yeast extract, dung, or wood into the medium in addition to sugar and other pure chemicals if growth of the organism is to occur. Only in comparatively recent years has it been recognized that these organic materials are sources of essential growth substances, some of which, at least, are identical with the known vitamins.

Direct experimentation has demonstrated that many bacteria and fungi cannot synthesize certain of the vitamins which they require, or at least cannot synthesize them in sufficient quantities to permit optimum growth even when all other growth conditions are favourable. If the substrate on which they are growing is deficient or lacking in one or more of the necessary vitamins, development of the organism will be retarded and may cease entirely. By systematic addition of the various vitamins to a vitamin-free medium on which an organism is cultured it is possible to ascertain which of the essential vitamins that organism must obtain from its substrate.

It is probable that the vitamin requirements of all fungi are very similar; but different species differ greatly in their vitamin-synthesizing capacity. Many species, for example, cannot synthesize thiamine in adequate quantities. Hence, unless this compound is present in the substrate, the fungus will be retarded in development as a result of the thiamine deficiency. In capacity to synthesize adequate quantities of biotin, pyridoxine, pantothenic acid, have also been demonstrated for many species of the fungi.

It has already been mentioned that all of the known vitamins, or at least their immediate precursors, are synthesized in higher green plants. Whether or not all such compounds are essential in the metabolism of green plants is an open question. The evidence regarding this point must of necessity be somewhat indirect. There are no good reasons, however, for believing this to be true of vitamins A, D, E and K. On the other hand, thiamine, nicotinic acid, riboflavin and pyridoxine are known to be constituents of the prosthetic groups or coenzymes of important enzymes found in vascular green plants and are probably necessary in the metabolism of all living cells in such organisms. It is highly probable that some, and perhaps all, of the other B vitamins are required by green plants and ascorbic acid may also be an essential green plant vitamin.

Although the higher green plants appear to be self-sufficing with regard to necessary vitamins, and such compounds are widely distributed through the organs of such plants, this does not necessarily mean that all cells of all tissues synthesize these compounds in adequate quantities. Some parts of a plant are dependent upon other parts for certain necessary vitamins. Experiments on excised roots of certain plants growing in sterile culture show, for example, that thiamine must be added to the culture medium if normal growth is to continue. Obviously roots, at least of some species, do not synthesize enough thiamine to meet their own needs, and irract plants are presumably dependent upon down-ward translocation of this substance from leaves in which it is synthesized. Such downward translocation of thiamine, and also of pantothenic acid and pyridoxine, has been demonstrated in the tomato. This is probably also true of nicotinic acid. Upward translocation of thiamine from older to younger leaves also occurs. There is also evidence for a similar downward translocation of thiamine from older to younger leaves also occurs. There is also evidence for a similar downward translocation of ascorbic acid in plants. On the other had, roots of at least some species appear to synthesize certain other vitamins in such quantities as not to be dependent upon the tops for a supply of these compounds.

The growing embryo and endosperm in the developing seed of at least some kinds of plants appear, like roots, to be dependent upon translocation from other parts of the plant for necessary thiamine. In wheat, for example, as the content of this hormone in the developing grains increases, there is a corresponding diminution in the thiamine content of vegetative parts. It is possible that young developing embryos of some species may similarly be dependent upon vegetative tissues for other essential vitamins.

From the foregoing discussion it should be evident that no sharp distinction can be drawn between "vitamins" and "hormones" in considerations of the metabolism of higher plants. Some of the so-called hormones, such as traumatic acid, operate in or close to the cells in which they are synthesized;' others, such as the auxins, are frequently translocated to other, often distant cells, in which they influence metabolic processes. Similarly, some of the so-called vitamins, such as riboflavin, appear to operate principally in cells in which they are synthesized, whereas others, such as thiamine, are often present in some tissues largely or entirely as a result of translocation from other organs of the plant. From the standpoint of plan metabolism, all such compounds fall into the one comprehensive category of "growth-regulating substances" or "hormones".

The Effect of External Factors on Auxin Content

It is difficult to make generalizations of aid to plant physiologists owing to sparse literature on this aspect of auxin physiology. Nevertheless several such external factors may be listed, which influence the auxin content of plants:

Temperature

Few, if any, effects of temperature are interpretable in terms of auxins. Several workers in the past have attempted to study the relation between auxin content of the plant and temperature prevailing at the time of experimentation, but only a few of the recent ones are mentioned. Burton (1956) found no consistent relationship between storage temperature and ether - extractable auxin content in potato tubers. Blommaert (1955) and Hendershott and Bailey (1955) reported a decrease or total absence of auxin in winter-dormant buds of peach and marked resurgence in auxin content immediately prior to and during the onset of growth in thc spring.

Mineral Nutrition

The relation between auxin content of intact plants and mineral nutrition has been studied in detail, only for nitrogen and zinc; deficiencies of either of the element lead to a lowered auxin content. The effect of nitrogen is considered to be an indirect one, since its effects appear after the appearance of visible deficiency symptoms or a decline in growth. Zinc probably affects auxin content possibly by reducing tryptophan synthesis.

Like nitrogen, effects of copper and manganese on auxin content of the plant appears to be indirect, because in copper and manganese deficient plants decreased auxin content is found only after the appearance of visible deficiency of these elements. Eaton (1940) suggested that boron deficiency reduced auxin level in cotton plants but MacVicar and Tottingham (1947) failed to confirm these results with cotton, tomato, sunflower, soybean and tobacco plants. The effect of other mineral elements on the endogenous auxin level is little studied and the facts thus, are incoherent.

Hydrogen-ion Concentration

Rufelt and Fransson (1956) studied the effect of pH on the auxin content of wheat roots, with solutions at pH 5.0-7.5. They noticed a short-term increase in auxin content, with a maximum at about six hours after transfer, and a subsequent restoration of the original level after 24 hours in the new solution. The mechanism of this effect is, however, obscure.

Ionizing Radiations and Ultraviolet

The publications on this aspect clearly indicate that X-irradiation can markedly and rapidly lower auxin content probably by interfering with auxin synthesis.

Skoog (1935) reported that moderate X-ray doses immediately reduced the amount of diffusible auxin obtainable from apices of *Pisum*, *Vicia* and *Avena* plants. Gordon's work (1956, 1957) has confirmed Skoog's observations of immediately decreased auxin content following X-irradiation but stresses the significance of reduced auxin synthesis. Spencer and Cabanillas (1956) reported that exposure of *Indigofera endecaphylla* seeds to either X-rays (80,000r) or thermal neutrons, both significantly reduce the auxin content of plants emerging from the treated seeds. The effect of ultraviolet irradiation has also been found to decrease endogenous auxin level.

Visible Light

A considerable work on the effects of visible radiations on the auxin content of plants had been undertaken. High light intensity, length of photoperiod and effects on etiolated plants, all have been investigated in detail. The photoinactivation of auxins has already been discussed in this chapter. It may be concluded that visible light has the effect of inactivating the auxin present in the plants.

Chemicals

Certain externally applied chemicals, such as ethylene, maleic hydrazide, and 2, 4-dichlorophenoxyacetic acid have been found to exet influence on the auxin content of intact plants. Loçkhart and Weintraub (1957) showed that 2,4-D decreases the free auxin content of terminal shoot of *Phaseolus* seedlings. It is unanimously but unusually concluded that growth inhibitory properties of maleic hydrazided are not due to any effect on auxin content. Exposure of *Avena* coleoptile tips to ethylene has been found to decrease the diffusible auxin content by van der Laan (1934).

Gibberellic Acid

Nitsch (1957) reported that application of gibberellic acid to certain woody plants results in an increase in extractable auxin, Galston's observation that feeding of gibberellic acid (GA) to pea plants raises the level of an auxin inhibitor of the enzyme IAA oxidase leads us to believe that the overall effect of GA is that it has an auxin sparing action. Similar view was expressed by Stutz and Watenabe (1957) with *Lupinus albus*. Both gibberellic acid and long photoperiods were found to depress overall initial IAA oxidase activity, thus probably leading to a "sparing" of auxin by gibberellic acid.

Miscellaneous

Several other factors, in addition to those discussed above may be responsible for altering both the level and metabolism of the endogenous auxin in the plant. Among these may be mentioned: (i) abnormal growth and pathology (ii) root-nodule bacteria, (iii) crown gall, (iv) virus diseases, and (v) other pathogens. All these, in some way or the other, are known to alter auxin level of intact plants and plant parts.

Theories of the Mechanism of Auxin Action

It would appear to be over-simplication if we ascribe the full responsibility for growth to any one function in the plant. This is so because the action of auxins in the control of growth is a complex of many functions. Although the mechanism of these functions it may be concluded that none of them known till today can entirely account for the effects of auxin on growth.

The numerous extremely interesting physiological and biological responses to plant hormones, observed in the last 25 years account for the intricate bearing on their mechanism. Gordon (1952) enumerated some of the many responses which may be briefly summarized.

1. increase in plasticity of the shoot and elasticity of root cell walls,
2. increased permeability of the cell to water,
3. enhanced capacity to retain water taken up,
4. "active"; uptake of water and solutes,
5. decreased photoplasmic viscosity,
6. increased respiratory rate,
7. more rapid synthesis of proteins with lowered levels of free amino acids in the free amino acid pool,
8. increased accumulation of monosaccharides at the expense of polysaccharides, and
9. a stimulation of the activity of many enzymes, such as alcohol and malic dehydrogenase, catalase, phosphatase and ascorbic acid oxidase, and also several other responses.

Several theories which have been put forward to explain the mechanism of auxin action consider one of the above effects as the basic response on which other phenomena rest. For the sake of convenience, discussions of the hypotheses concerning the mechanism of auxin action will be grouped into five heads.

Molecular Reaction Theories

A molecular reaction into which auxin might enter in causing growth was first suggested by Skoog et.al (1942) who postulated that auxins may act as coenzymes, serving as a point of attachment for some substrate onto an enzyme controlling growth. A different suggestion for the role of auxins was forwarded by Veldstra (1955). He opined that the degree of fat solubility as influenced by the ring structure and water solubility as influenced by the side chain structure could be correlated with auxin activity. His conception was that the action of auxin was something of a physical binding of some fatty material to some more aqueous phase.

Muir *et al*. (1949) gave a third suggestion that hormones of the phenoxy acid type may combine with some material (presumably proteinaceous) at the ortho position of the ring. They conceived that hormones react with some material in the cell at two positions. viz (i) at some position in the ring (ortho position in the phenoxy acids), and (ii) at the acid group of the side chain. On the basis of these Foster *et al* (1952) advanced a theory of hormone activity by two-point attachment and brought forward variety of kinetic evidences to support their hypothesis.

Theories of Enzyme Effects

It has been observed that growing tissues when treated with auxin show an increased activity, either directly or indirectly, of a number of enzymes. This fact has given rise to a theory of auxin action through enzyme mechanism. Northen (1942) found that auxins cause decrease in cytoplasmic viscosity and suggested that they bring about dissociation of the proteins constituents of the cytoplasm. This dissociation effect would increase water permeability, increase the osmotic value of the cytoplasm, and possibly also bring about increased enzymatic dissociation can sometimes activate enzymes and such dissociation effect would increase water permeability, increase the osmotic value of the cytoplasm, and possibly also bring about increased enzymatic activity. It has been shown by Hand (1939) that gentle protein dissociation can some times activate enzymes and such dissociation might increase the availability of substrates for the enzymes as well. As a consequence of this an increased respiratory activity and growth might follow.

Thimann (1951) postulated that auxins may act, not as enzyme activating agents, but as agents protecting growth enzymes from inactivation. He points out that organic acid metabolism is primarily responsible for growth. One of the enzymes (succinic dehydrogenase) in this system, which has a sulfhydril structure, is a critical link and may be very intimately involved in growth. Poisons which attack sulfhydril enzymes also antagonize auxin action and growth.

Bonner (1949) and Bonner and Bandurski (1952) have suggested that auxins may serve in some way to couple or mesh together the respiratory process with growth processes, and thus they act in a manner which would make the energy formed in respiration available to growth processes.

Theories of Osmotic Effects

Water uptake, serves as the basis of growth through increase in cell volume. The uptake of water could be due to changes in the cytoplasm itself, specially changes in osmotic value; or it could be due to changes in the properties of the wall and the cell membranes, particularly with respect to extensibility and permeability. Each of these two factors in water uptake has been defended as a possible mechanism through which auxins may bring about growth.

Czaza (1935) suggested that auxins may increase the osmotic value of the cell sap which would result directly in water uptake and growth. A basic limitation to Czaza's concept lies in the fact that growth is not necessarily associated with an increase in osmotic value. Actually van Overbeek (1944) and Hackett (1951) have been able to obtain growth with an associated decrease in osmotic value.

Commoner et al. (1942,1943) have proposed that auxin may influence the respiratory uptake of salt and the resultant increase in the osmotic value of the cell sap would cause water uptake and hence growth. Reinders (1942), however, has shown that auxin induced growth can occur in pure water and in the absence of salt uptake.

Reinders (1942) and Mackett and Thimann (1952) have collected evidence that water uptake in response to auxin treatment is dependent upon oxidative metabolism. Bonner et al, (1953) suggest that phosphorylation reactions provide energy for water uptake phenomenon.

Theories of Cell Wall Effects

Direct measurements of the effect of auxins upon the stretching properties of the cell walls have been made by Heyn (1932, 1933). He found that auxin application causes an increase in the flexibility and extensibility of cell walls. According to this, increased extensibility would result in a drop of wall pressure around the cell and would allow water uptake due to this simple drop in turgor pressure. This concept attributes growth primarily to the dynamic function of the cell wall.

Burstrom (1953) after a critical study of water uptake concluded that cell wall attains a plastic quality during growth and that water uptake only follows the changes in the cell wall. Thus water uptake is a consequence and not the cause of growth.

Toxic Metabolism

It is known that auxin, besides being growth promoters, can also cause inhibition of elongation. In shoots this inhibition requires high concentrations of auxin and is not prominent. In roots the regular response to exogenous auxin is an inhibition of elongation even at relatively low auxin concentrations. Very little is known concerning the mechanisms of this specific inhibition. According to one view it is conceived that the inhibition is due to excess auxin molecules inactivating the sites of auxin action and thus preventing maximum growth response. This mechanism although plausible, is supported by limited decisive evidences.

It may be concluded that the mechanism of auxin action remains yet unsolved, but a variety of promising lines of evidence seem to be emerging. The different angles from which the problem is being tackled may provide valuable lines of approach.

Synthetic Growth Hormone

A natural consequence of the discovery of auxin activity was the isolation and characterization of the auxin molecule. As soon as this was accomplished, an intensive search began for compounds chemically similar to IAA and with similar activity. Before long, the results of this search brought forth other indole derivatives, such as indole-3-propionic acid, indole-3-butyric acid and indolepyruvic acid all of which demonstrate physiological activity similar to that of IAA. Other compounds, similar in activity but not in chemical structure of IAA were also discovered. Of these, the more important ones are α- and β-naphthylacetic acids, phenylacetic acid naphthoxyacetic acid and phenoxyacetic acid. The structures of the above-mentioned compounds are given.

Molecular Structure and Auxin Activity

The chemical characterization of physiologically active compounds never fails to generate interest in the relationship between the structure of the compound and its physiological activity. It was interest such as this that led to the listing of certain minimal requirements needed by a compound for auxin activity. These requirements are:

1. An unsaturated ring system.
2. An acid side chain.
3. Separation of the carboxyl group (—COOH) from the ring (several exceptions).
4. A particular spatial arrangement between the ring system and the acid side chain.

The above requirements are minimal for auxin activity. However, the degree of substitution in the ring and side chain, nature of the ring (indole, phenyl, anthracene, etc.), and length of the side chain all are factors that will influence auxin activity.

Nature of the Ring System

After IAA had been isolated and characterized, it was soon found that the nitrogen of the indole ring was not essential for auxin activity. When either a carbon or an oxygen atom was substituted for nitrogen activity, although considerably diminished, was still observed. One might have anticipated this due to the fact that ring sizes ranging from the small phenyl ring to the relatively lare anthracene ring have been found in compounds having auxin activity. Nitrogen is not found in the phenyl or anthracene ring. There seems to be considerable evidence supporting the requirements that the ring be unsaturated. Activity decrease with hydrogenation of the double bonds of the ring, with complete cessation of activity occurring in the saturated ring.

It was not until the auxin activity of the phenoxyacetic acid series was discovered that the profound effect of the substitution of various groups onto the ring or side chain was truly appreciated. The nature of the group substituted and the location of the substitution was found to influence the activity of the compound. A striking example of this may be seen in the substitution of the chlorine atom at various positions on the phenyl ring of phenoxyacetic acid.

This was clearly demonstrated by Muir *et al.* (1949) when they experimented with the substitution of halogens and methyl groups in the 2, 4, and 6 positions of the phenyl ring. They found that substitution of both the 2 and the 6 positions with chlorine atoms resulted in complete loss of activity. However, substitution of the 3 or 4 position alone increased activity. Chlorine atoms attached to the 2 and 4 positions of the phenyl ring of the phenoxyacetic acid molecule gave the greatest auxin activity. Instead, 2, 4 - dichlorophenoxyacetic acid (2,4-D) is one of the most widely used synthetic auxins at the present time. The fact that there is a complete loss of activity when both the 2 and the 6 positions are chlorinated, led these investigators to hypothesize that the position on the phenyl ring adjacent to the point of attachment of the side chain is involved in the growth reaction.

Nature of the Acid Side Chain

According to the work of Koepfli et al. (1938) and others, the position and length of the acid side chain has a striking influence on auxin acitivity. Side chains that have the carboxyl group separated from the ring by a carbon or a carbon and oxygen given optimal activity. For example, the acid side chains of IAA and 2,4-D, two highly active auxins, fulfill these requirements.

As the length of the side chain in the phenoxyacetic acid series in increased, there is a falling off of activity. This drop is erratic, activity falling much lower when the side chain contains an odd number of carbons. That is, 4-dichlorophenoxybutyric acid (4 carbons) is more active than 2, 4-dichlorophenoxy propionic acid (3 carbons). A possible explanation for the above phenomenon may be found in the work of Synerholm and Zimmerman (1947) and Fawcett et al. (1952). Apparently, side chains containing an odd number of carbons are metabolized in living tissues to the inactive phenol, where as the even-numbered chams are broken down to the active phenoxyacetic acid.

Substitution of different groups on to the side chain also affects activity. Thus, substitution of a methyl group on the carbon of the side chain of phenylacetic acid does not take away auxin activity. However, substitution of two methyl groups on the carbon eliminates auxin activity entirely. Later, when we discuss the mechanism of auxin action, we will learn why the substitution of "bulky methyl" groups on the acid side chain inhibits auxin activity.

Hydorxyl substitution in the side chain also can eliminate auxin activity. For example, substitution of a hydroxyl group or an alcohol group on the carbon of phenyl acetic acid produces two inactive derivatives. Earlier, it was thought that separation of the carboxyl group from the side chain was essential for auxin activity. However, many exceptions to this rule have been found. For example 2,3, 6-trichlorobenzoic acid exhibits a strong auxin activity.

Spatial Arrangement

The spatial relationship between the ring and side chain is an important factor in the activity of an auxin molecule. For example, cis-cinnamic acid demonstrates good auxin activity in the *Avena* straight growth test, and its *trans* isomer does not. Veldstra (1944) suggested, after a study of the relation between structure and activity, that in order for a molecule to have auxin activity the —COOH group and the ring should lie in different planes. This theory was supported by observation of the activity of *cis* and *trans* forms of tetrahydronaphtylideneacetic acid and the above *cis* and *trans* forms of cinamic acid.

Antiauxins

If one assumes that the chemical configuration of a compound is responsible for its effect on physiological processes, then we must also recognize that there can be an interference with such action by similar, but not identical, compounds . Many antiauxins have been discovered and, generally, these combination with auxin, inhibit its acitivity.

Actually, the term antiauxin should define only those compounds that will complete with auxin for a reactive site in the growing cell. What do we mean by a reactive site? Because of the relationship of molecular structure and configuration with degree of physiological activity, most theories on auxin action are based on the attachment of the auxin molecule to some substance in the cell (e.g. protein). This complex (bound auxin)can then induce auxin activity. True antiauxins, then, are compounds which, because of the molecular similarity to auxin, would become attached to reactive site, thus neutralizing them for action in growth . However, if true competition for reactive sites is involved here, increasing applications of auxin should eventually swamp the reactive sites with auxin molecules and overcome the antiauxin effect.

There is general agreement that in order for an auxin molecule to be active, it must make a *two -point* attachment at a reactive site. In addition, it is thought that the two points of attachment are made through a position on the unsaturated ring and by the carboxyl group of the side chain. In the phenoxyacetic acids, the position on the ring through which attachment is made is the *ortho* position.

Based on the two-point attachment theory, McRae and Bonner (1953) have drawn up a rigorous classification for true, antiauxins. Using 2, 4-D, a synthetic auxin, as representative molecule, they have shown where "analogs" of the 2, 4-D moleucle containing some, but not all, of the structural properties of the auxin are capable of competing for reactive sites. The antiauxin makes a cone-point instead of the two-point attachment necessary for growth action. McRae and Bonner have listed three ways by which a modification of the 2,4-D molecule can lead to antiauxin activity.

1. Elimination of the essential carboxyl group.
2. Elimination of the essential reactive *ortho* group.
3. Elimination of proper spatial relationships between the ring and the carboxyl group as by introduction of bulky groups in the side chain.

Although not as popular as the two-point attachment theory, a three-point attachment theory has been proposed as necessary for auxin activity. According to this theory, an auxin molecule in order to be active must contain the following necessary structural, properties; an unsaturated ring, a carboxyl group, and at least one α-hydrogen. A further stipulation is that all three must be correctly oriented in space with each other. Of the isomers of 2, 4- dichlorophenoxy-α-propionic acid, only the "+" form is active. The "—" form is not properly oriented, thus failing to accomplish the three -point attachment necessary for auxin activity.

Contact is made by the auxin with the reactive site simultaneously at three positions on the auxin molecules. If only one site or even two positions are occupied, no activity ensues. In fact, molecules that occupy only one or two of the positions on the reactive site can be considered antiauxins.

A type of antiauxin which has not, as yet, been considered is the compound having weak auxin activity. A weak auxin can make the necessary two-point (or three-point) attachment and initiate a stimulation of growth. However, this stimulation is small, and at the same time active sites involved with the weak auxin cannot be occupied by a strong auxin. An example of a weak auxin having antiauxin characteristics is phenylbutyric acid.

Kinetics of Auxin Activity

A valuable contribution to the study of auxin-induced growth reactions has been the application of the Lineweaver-Burk kinetic analysis of competitive inhibition. McRae and Bonner (1953) demonstrated that auxin-induced growth reactions could be treated by the methods of classical enzyme kinetics.

It is generally accepted that in enzyme reactions, an intermediate complex is formed between the substrate and enzyme and that this complex is formed at an active site on the enzyme. The complex is converted to the enzyme and reaction products.

$$E + S = ES \rightarrow E + P$$

Using the above scheme, McRae and Bonner demonstrated that stimulation of straight growth of *Avena* coleoptile sections by auxin could be mathematically analyzed. In their scheme, enzyme (E) is the auxin receptor, substrate (S) is the auxin applied, complex (ES) is the receptor-auxin attachment, and the product in this case is growth. Let us rewrite the above equation using A for auxin, R for receptor, RA for the intermediate complex, and G for growth.

$$R + A = RA \rightarrow R + G$$

Now, in classical enzyme study, a competitive inhibitor is thought of as a compound that will compete with the normal substrate of an enzyme for active sites on that enzyme. The formation of an enzyme-inhibitor complex may be illustrated in the following manner.

$$E + I = EI$$

The fact that the formation of EI is reversible is important since this allows for competition by the substrate with the inhibitor for active sites. Therefore, by increasing the substrate, inhibition by a competitive inhibitor may be overcome.

The effect of a competitive inhibitor may be observed in a decrease in the rate of an enzyme reaction. However, if the substrate concentration is increased until all active sites on the enzyme are "swamped," then maximum velocity (V_{max}) or rate will be obtained. This maximum velocity will be identical to that of the same reaction without a competitive inhibitor. In other words, increasing the concentration of a substrate decreases the amount of inhibition, and conversely, decreasing the substrate concentration increases inhibition.

We have mentioned that antiauxins compete with auxins for active sites on an auxin receptor or growth center. This situation,of course, is analogous to the concept of competitive inhibition in enzyme study.

Now, using the Lineweaver-Burk plotting method, one can measure the velocity of an auxin reaction (in this case, rate of growth) and, at the same time, calculate the effect of an antiauxin on this velocity. By plotting the reciprocal of the velocity (I/V) of the auxin reaction against the reciprocal of the concentration of auxin (I/[A]) applied, one obtains a straight line relationship. Maximum velocity (V_{max}) may be obtained by extending this line to the ordinate, the intercept being I/V_{max}. Note that the concentration of inhibitor will affect the slope of the line, but not the intercept. A mathematical analysis of the interaction of 2,4-D and the antiauxins 4-chlorophenoxyisobutyric acid, 2,6-dichlorophenoxyacetic acid, and 2, 4- dichloroanisole has been under taken. The compound 4-chlorophenoxyisobutyric acid is an antiauxin because of bulky methyl groups in the side chain interfering with attachment of the carboxyl group to the auxin receptor. 2,6-Dichlorophenoxyacetic acid owes its antiauxin properties to block age of the reactive *ortho* positions on the ring by chlorineatomes. 2, 4-Dichloroanisole has to carboxyl group and therefore cannot make the necessary two-point attachment.

Inactivation of Auxin

Just as the production and subsequent physiological effects of auxin have a profound influence on plant development, the inactivation of auxin appears also to be of significance in this respect. For example, the inactivation of auxin is important in phototropisms, control of cell elongation, and in the aging of plant tissues. We will discuss the mechanisms involved in the destruction of auxin and the influence of its destruction on cell elongation and aging.

Mechanisms of Auxin Inactivation

A preponderance of literature has developed on the mechanisms of auxin inactivation since the isolation in 1947 by Tang and Bonner (1947) of an enzyme capable of oxidizing IAA. This enzyme is now called *IAA oxidase*. Recently an IAA oxidase was extracted from tobacco roots and partially purified. Although IAA oxidase represents one way for a plant to destroy auxin, other natural means of auxin inactivation have been discovered. However, two systems for the destruction of auxin in the plant appear to dominate, and these are (a) enzymatic oxidation and (b) photo-oxidation.

Enzymatic Oxidation

Enzyme systems that oxidize IAA have been found in several plant tissues. However, as is generally true, one system is usually studied in much more detail than the others, and in this case it is the enzyme system present in extracts of etiolated pea epicotyls. It appears that in this system a flavoprotein must be present, which gives rise to hydrogen peroxide. The oxidation of IAA by hydrogen peroxide is catalyzed by a peroxidase to yield some inactive product, probably indolealdehyde. In the inactivation of IAA by this system, 1 mole of O_2 is consumed for every mole of IAA inactivated and CO_2 released.

In addition to indolealdehyde, other breakdown products have been suggested. However, it is generally accepted that the logical end product of IAA oxidation is indolealdehyde. As mentioned before, IAA oxidase systems have been found in many plants, and in several cases these have differed from the original IAA oxidase system found in the pea plant. Perhaps in these, different end products of IAA oxidation are obtained.

An inverse relationship between IAA oxidase activity and IAA content in the plant has been found. That is, where IAA content is high, IAA oxidase activity is low and vice versa. Meristematic regions that have a high auxin content have been found to below in IAA oxidase activity. The root, which is generally thought to below in auxin content, has been found to be generally thought to be low in auxin content, has been found to be high in IAA oxidase activity. In fact, Galston (1956) has found (at least in the pea plant) that as cells age, their IAA oxidase activity increases, and their auxin content drops.

Increased capacity to inactivate IAA has been demonstrated by young plant tissues treated with synthetic IAA or analogs of the IAA molecule. It appears, then, that IAA is capable of inducing the formation of the enzyme that destroys it. This is particularly interesting since IAA, which initiates growth, also puts into action the mechanisms leading to the termination of growth. Galston (1956), a leading figure in research on plant growth, has this to say: It seems possible that the decreased sensitivity to auxin of older cells is a consequence of their higher IAA oxidase activity, which in turn is a consequence of prior induction by IAA. According to this scheme,. the administration of IAA to a young cell not only initiates growth, but also sets in motion a chain of events leading to the diminution and eventual culmination of growth.

Photooxidation

It has long been known that IAA can be inactivated by ionizing radiation. Skoog (1934; 1935) demonstrated that rapid inactivation of pure IAA takes place when it is subjected to x-and gamma-radiation. He also noted that little, if any, inactivation takes place in a nitrogen atmosphere, suggesting that inactivation is due to oxidation by peroxides formed during irradiation. There is some evidence that only a small amount of IAA is inactivated or oxidized in this manner, most of the detrimental effect of this type of irradiation to IAA being of an indirect nature. For example, Gordon (1956) has claimed that the major effect of ionizing radiation on auxin metabolism may be found in the destructive effect of the radiation on the enzyme system converting tryptophan to IAA.

Ultraviolet light also inactivates IAA. This might have been predicted because of the ring structure of the IAA molecule, which absorbs to some extent in ultraviolet (maximum absorption at about 280 mμ). Here, there is a direct effect on the IAA molecule due to the absorption of ultraviolet light. Determinations of auxin content before and after irradiation with ultraviolet light have shown that this type of irradiation reduces auxin levels in plants.

GIBBERELLINS

The gibberellins are tetracarbocyclic compounds whose small amounts profoundly stimulate the growth of many plants. Gibberellins were originally regarded as unusual and interesting fungal metabolites, but their importance in the regulation of plant growth has recently been emphasized by the widespread occurrence of gibberellin-like substances in the plant kingdom. The chemical identification of some of these has been established. The discovery of gibberellins is very interesting and rather accidental. These growth regulating substances were discovered as a direct consequence of interest in the "bakanae" disease of *Oryza sativa*, a disease which had serious economic effects on the rice industry in Japan. The disease has two important symptoms:

1. seedlings assumed long, thin, and pale green appearance than those of healthy plants, and
2. mature plants, sometimes taller than their healthy counterparts often failed to set fruit.

The "bakanae"symptoms were first described by the plant pathologist S.Hori in 1898, although its technical account appeared in the literature much later. Early in the twentieth century, extensive studies by Japanese plant pathologists conclusively showed the "bakanae"disease to be resulting due to certain strains of a species of fungus now known as *Fusarium monilliforme* Sheld (*Gibberella fujikuroi*). Sawada (1912) suggested that the seedling symptoms of the disease could be due to a "substance" secreted by the fungus. This was

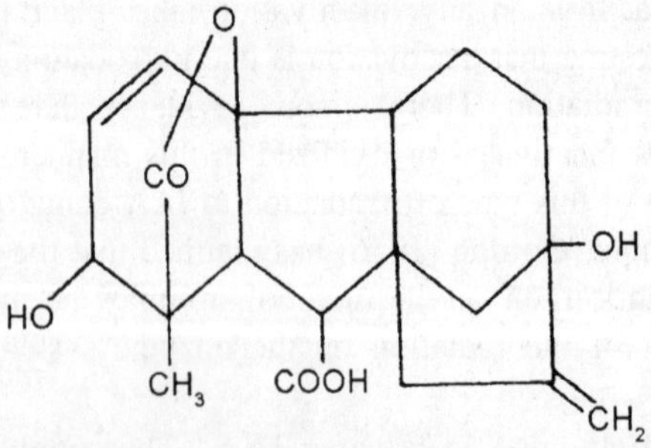

Fig. 11.9. Gibberellic acid.

experimentally proved by Kurosawa in 1926. He demonstrated the appearance of bakanae symptoms in *Oryza sativa* fungus. This observation attracted little attention outside Japan, but the work on isolation and purification of the growth-promoter was initiated. Progress was slow but eventually, in 1939, Yabuta and Hayashi isolated a crystalline 'A'.

More recently Japanese chemists have suggested that this substance is mixture of several different growth promoters collectively known as gibberellins. Pure gibberellin was first obtained in England. Many years after the description of gibberellin 'A' in Japan, interest developed in other countries. All the Japanese work, from Kurosawa's observations of 1926 to the isolation of an active material by Yabuta and Hayashi in 1939 was promptly abstracted in "Chemical Abstracts" and the "Review of Applied Mycology". In attempting to repeat Japanese work, Curtis and Cross isolated, in 1954, a substance obviously chemically and physiologically similar to the Japanese gibberellin 'A', but nevertheless distinct, they called this substance gibberellic acid. Shortly afterwards Stodola, in United States, described a new gibberllin which he called gibberellin 'X', this was found to be identical with gibberellic acid. Several pure gibberellins are now known. They are probably fairly closely related chemically and all have similar effects on plant growth.

Terminology

Following the suggestions of Phinney and West (1960), two terms, gibberellin and gibberellin-like are maintained. The former term is restricted to substances defined both by biological and chemical properties whereas the latter term defined by biological properties only. The term, gibberellins will therefore be reserved for substances biologically active in stimulating an increase in the size of a plant organ or parts thereof and known to consist chemically of a carbon skeleton identical with,or closely related to, that of gibberellin 'A_3' (gibberellic acid). The five gibberellins identified are : gibberellin 'A_1' (GA_1), gibberellin 'A_2' (GA_2) gibberellin 'A_3' (GA_3), gibberellin 'A_4' (GA_4), and gibberellin 'A_5' (GA_5).

Assays

Depending on the physical or chemical properties of the gibberellins rather than on their physiological activities, a number of qualitative and quantitative assays have been developed.

Physico-chemical assays

With the use of filter paper chromatography a variety of detection methods have been employed to locate gibberellins. Gibberellin A_3 is

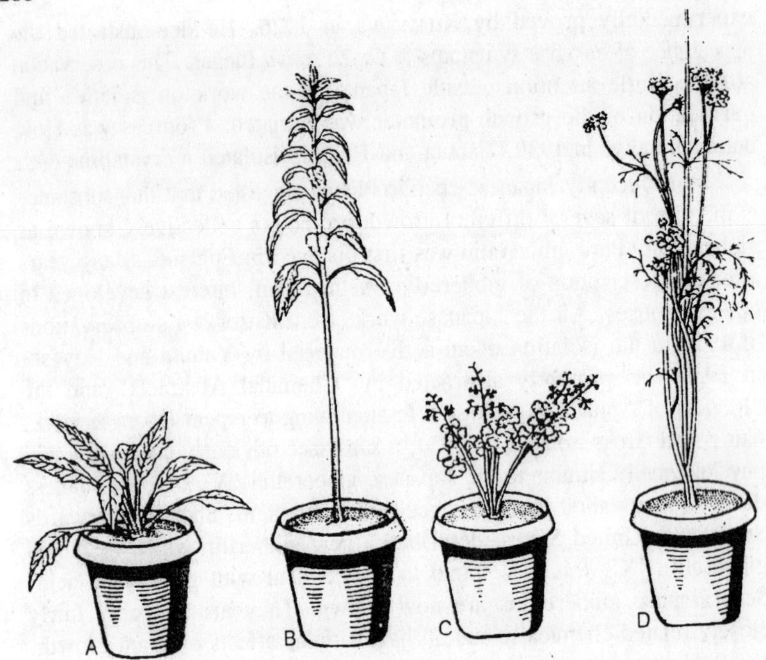

Fig. 11.10. A-B–Henbane plants which usually require a period of cold treatment and long days for flowering-flowered when they were treated with Gibberellic acid as in B (no low temp. or long day were required), C-D–Carrot plants require low temperature for flowering, C–Plant without low temperature but with gibberellin spray flowered, D–Plant provided with low temperature.

defected by a characteristic fluorescence developed in sulfuric acid. The substance, by this method, could be detected in amounts as low as one microgram. The fluorescence of the fluorogen formed from gibberellin 'A_3' in sulfuric acid solution has been used as the basis for a quantitative analysis. A linear calibration curve is obtained for gibberellin 'A_3' concentrations in the range of 0.00625 to 3.2 micrograms per ml. The amount of fluorescene formed from a sample is subject to a number of variables which must be controlled to get reproducible gibberellins, GA_1, GA_2, GA_4 and GA_5. Other spray reagents used include 0.5 percent potassium permanganate reagent and an acidic periodate-permanganate reagent.

A number of useful isotopic labelling methods, for the assay of small amounts of gibberellins present in relatively crude mixtures have been developed by Baumgartner (1958) and Banumgratner *et al.* (1959). Selected absorption bands in the infrared region has been used for the quantitative determination of gibberellins and a polarographic method.

Biological assays

Angiospermous plants in which the dimensional change of the shoot, or parts thereof occurs, serve as a measure of response in these assays. Floral induction and hastening of flowering have also been used to a limited extent for the detection of gibberellin-like substances. Generally, the assays which employ intact plants are more specific than those which employ the growth responses of plant sections in culture. The various bioassays used for the determination of gibberellins and gibberellin-like substances can be summarized.

Table 11.2. Species of plants used as assays for gibberellins and gibberellins-like substances.

Plant species	Plant part	Specificity
1. *Avena sativa* L.	leaf section	non-specific
2. *Perilla ocymoides* L.	intact seedling	specific
3. *Pharbitis Nil chois*	intact seedling	specific
4. *Phaseolus vulgaris* L.	intact seedling	non-specific
5. *Pisum sativum* L.	intact seedling	specific
6. *Oryza sativa* L.	intact seedling	specific
	leaf section	non-specific
7. *Rudbeckla bicolo* Nutt	rosetted plants	specific
8. *Triticum vulgare* Vill	leaf sections	non-specific
	excised coleoptile	non-specific
9. *Zea mays* L.	intact seedling	specific

Gibberellin-Like Substances from Flowering Plants

The presence of the giberellins in *Fusarium* has already been discussed. The first definitive evidence for the presence of gibberellin-like substances in organisms other than *Fusarium moniliforme*, came as a result of the use of gibberellin-type of growth response in bioassays, assays that could be shown to be specific for gibberellins only. Several worker groups have reported the widespread occurrence of gibberellins in flowering plants.

Gibberellin-like substances have been reported from 64 genera reporting 15 different families of angiosperms, from one member of the mosses, from two genera of fungi and also from two members of Actinomyces. These gibberellin-like materials have been reported from the root and all organs of the shoot, and, from both young and old tissues of flowering plants. Macmillan and Suter (1958) have isolated gibberellin A_1 in small quantities from immature seed of *Phaseolus vulgaris*. West and Phinney (1959) extracted a substance, bean factor I, from immature seed of *Phaseolous vulgaris* and which subsequently was shown to be identical with gibberellin A_1, Kawarada and Sumiki (1959) have isolated gibberellin A_1 from "water sprouts" of *Citrus unshuii*. West and Phinney (1959) obtained a second substance, bean factor II, form extracts of immature seed of *Phaseolus vulgaris*, which had gibberellin like biological properties but differed in chemical and physical properties from the reported fungal gibberellin. Macmillan, Seaton and Suter (1959) also obtained a second gibberellin, which they name gibberellin A_5, from their extracts of *Phaseolus multiflorus* seed. A comparison of the infrared spectra of gibberellin A_5 and bean factor II, and their methyulesters, has shown that these substances are identical. The name gibberellin A_5 has been accepted by both groups. gibberellin A_3, the gibberellin produced in largest amounts in most fermentations has not been isolated from flowering plants.

Chemistry of Gibberellins

Structural Studies on the Fungal Gibberellins

The two fungal gibberellins, gibberellin A_3 and gibberellin A_1 are structurally known as reported by the British group at Akers Research :Laboratories of ICI. The results of more recent investigations of the Tokyo group on gibberellin A_1 and gibberellin A_2 fractionated from the gibberellin A mixture, have led to proposals IB and IIB for gibberellin A_3 and gibberellin A_1 respectively. These differ from the above proposal only in the positions of attachment of the lactone ring in A.

The relationship between gibberellin A_1 and gibberellin A_3 has been established. Grove *et al.* (1958) could partially hydrogenate methyl gibberellate ($C_{20}H_{24}O_6$) and separate from the mixture of products two isomeric methyl ester ($C_{20}H_{26}O_6$). One of these methyl-α-dihydrogibberellate, was identical with the methyl ester of gibberellin A_1. Since gibberellin A_1 still possesses an exocyclic methylene group as indicated by ozonization studies the two hydrogens must have added to saturate the A ring. A few of the products which have been derived by chemical treatment of gibberellin A_2 and gibberellin A_1 can be summarized.

Stodola et.al (1957) and Cross (1954) indicated the molecular formula $C_{19}H_{22}O_6$ for gibberellin A_3. The functional groups in this were identified as a carboxyl, two ethylenic double bonds, two alcoholic hydroxyl groups (one secondary and one presumably tertiary), a saturated lactone, and probably one methyl group. This indicated a compound with four carbocyclic rings. Acid hydrolysis yielded a number of products, such as allogibberic acid (identical with gibberellin B of Japanese) and gibberic acid.

Cross et al. (1956 ,1958) assigned the structure 'V' to gibberic acid. The Japanese group obtained the hydrocarbon, gibberene, as a product of the selenium catalyzed hydrogenation of gibberellin A or gibberellin B or gibberic acid. Yabuta et al. (1941) identified this hydrocarbon as a substituted fluorene. Mulholand and Ward (1954) also isolated gibberene as a hydrogenation product of giberric acid and showed it to be 1,7 dimethyl-fluorene. These probable presence of a substituted, perhydrofuorene nucleus is gibberic acid. Gibberic acid was also converted by Cross et al (1958) to methyl -1, 7-dimethyl fluorene-9-carboxylate by appropriate series of reactions. This has established the position of the carboxyl group. By a step-wise degradation procedure gibberic acid was converted to the methyl ester of a tetracarboxylic acid by Cross et. al.(1958).

Cross et al. (1956), and Mulholand (1958) assigned the structure IV to allogibberic acid. Like gibberellin A_2, it gave formaldehyde of ozonolysis indicating the presence of a terminal methylene group. Allogibberic acid was converted to 7-hydroxyl-1-methylfluorene by a series of reactions including a selenium dehydrogenation. This located the hydroxyl group substitution on the nucleus.

Gerzon, Bird and Woolf (1957) assigned structure IIIa or IIIb to gibberellenic acid—another product obtain from gibberellin A_3. Gibberellenic acid is readily converted in acidic solution to allogibberic acid, which in turn is readily converted to gibberic acid, an end product of the acid hydrolysis.

The establishment of structure of allogibberic acid and gibberic acid also fixed the structure in the B, C and D rings of gibberellin A_2. It still remained to be established how the lactone, secondary hydroxyl and ethylenic double bonds were accommodated in the ring A. The position of the secondary hydroxyl was indicated by the conversion of the methyl ester of gibberellin A_1 through a series of intermediates to 2- hydroxyl 1, 7-dimethyl fluorene or 2-hydroxyl-1-methylfluorene. There seems at present no satisfactory way, however, of reconciling all the reported degradation products with one structure of gibberellin A_2 and gibberellin A_1. Structure has been proposed by Kitamura et al. (1958, 1959) for gibberellin A_2 and structure for gibberellin A_4. There structures are similar to that proposed for gibberellin A_1 (ring A is shown in the form proposed by the Japanese) except for the position of substitution of the tertiary hydroxyl and the absence of unsaturation in A_2 and the absence of the tertiary hydroxyl in A_4.

Structural Studies on Gibberellins from Angiosperms

The chemical nature of the active principles in angiosperms has been determined in only a few instances. Some of the most important sources from which the gibberellins have been isolated in angiosperms has already been mentioned. Structure has been assigned to gibberellin A_5 by MacMillan *et al.* (1959). Thus, gibberellin A_5 is dehydrogibberellin A_1 in which the secondary hydroxyl grop is eliminated from the ring A. A key compound in the structural proof was the keto-acid formed from gibberellin A_5 on acid treatment. Thus at least two gibberellins, one identical to a fungus-produced gibberellin and the other very closely related to the fungal gibberellins chemically, have been found to occur naturally in flowering plants.

The Relation of Chemical Structure to Biological Activity of Gibberellins

In an assessment of the relation of chemical structure to biological activity of gibberellins many factors influence the interpretation of results. These include (i) the types of assay methods used; (ii) the method of application of the test material, and (iii) accompanying permeability problems and the range of concentration of the test material. Studies with the naturally occurring gibberellins have shown gibberellin A_3 to be the most active followed by gibberellin A_1, gibberellin A_4 and gibberellin A_2 in decreasing order of activity in most assay used. But this is not true always because the activity of gibberellin A_4 stimulating growth of some cucurbits at levels at which the other gibberellins are inactive, has been found. Also depending on the particular dwarf mutant used for assay, gibberellin A_5 is as effective as gibberellin A_2 or less than 10 percent as active as gibberellin A_1.

Gerzon et al. (1957) showed that gibberellenic acid formed from gibberellin A_3 in acid solution, is devoid of biological activity. Allogibberic acid and gibberic acid which are formed from gibberellin A_3 on more vigorous acid treatment are likewise devoid of biological activity. Besides, gibberellin C, formed on acid catalyzed rearrangement of gibberellin A_1, retains some activity. The isomeric products formed from gibberellin A_1 and gibberellin A_2 by mild alkaline treatment are biologically inactive. Under some condition which do not open the fact one ring, gibberellin A_1 is inactivated; this is believed to be due to the formation of an primer (pseudogibberellin A_1) in which the secondary hydroxyl group in the ring A is inverted from an axial to a more stable equatorial configuration. On mild alkaline hydrolysis of gibberellin A_3, the diacid results by an allylic rearrangement of the hydroxyl group formed on opening the lactone ring.

The free acid and salts both, of gibberellin A_3 are biologically active. It has been found that conversion of the carboxyl group of gibberellin A_3 to the methyl, ethyl, butyl, or acetyl esters results in a complete loss of biological activity. Generally, those products derived from the gibberellins which involve modification of the A or B ring structures are inactive. Sumike and J Kawarada (1941) found the derivative of gibberellin A_2 in which the alcohol is oxidized to a Keto Group, to be inactive. Many of the products derived from the gibberellins which involve structural modification only in the C or D rings, such as gibberellin C, are active.

Biosynthesis of Gibberellins

The broad outlines of the gibberellin biosynthesis have been indicated but very little detailed knowledge has been gained. Cross et al. (1958) advanced "biogenetic grounds" as one of their reasons for favouring the carbon skeleton they proposed for gibberellin A_3, since it could be considered as an "isoprenoid" (isopentane) derivative. Birch et al. (1958), and Birch and Smith (1959) have proposed a general route from acetate and mevalonate (β-δ-dihydroxy-β- methyl-valerate) to gibberellin A_2 *via* diterpenoid intermediates. Some key features of this proposal may be summarized. Mevalonate (B) which can be biosynthesized from acetate, has been shown to be a precursor of sterols and terpenes.

Condensation of four molecules of a mevalonate derivative in a "head- to-tail" fashion leads to an acyclic diterpene with the carbon skeleton on C. The cyclization of the acyclic precursor leads to a tricyclic diterpene of carbon skeleton D.Subsequent modification of the skeleton to that of gibberellin A_3 (E) would occur by (1) elimination of the C_{17} methyl group, (2) a ring contraction of the B ring, and (3) a rearrangement involving the C ring and its attached vinyl group to produce the phyllocladene type C-D rings of gibberellin A_3.

This general proposal has been supported by the labelling studies. The previous figure shows one of the ways in which gibberellin A_3 would become labelled from acetate-1-C^{14} or mevalonate -2-C^{14}. Zweig and Cosens (1959) have also presented C^{14} labelling evidence for the incorporation of both the methyl and carboxyl carbons of acetate into gibberellin A_3 by the fungus. Little, direct information bearing on the biosysnthesis of gibberellins in flowering plants is available at the present time. It is presumed that the route in the fungus and in flowering plants will be very similar.

Anatomical Effects of Gibberellins

It is now well established that changes in size and form of plants take place due to gibberellin treatment. Hence it raises the problem of whether these effects are the result of changes in the net cell number, net cell size (including form of the cell) or combinations of the two. In general, it was showed by Japanese that increased cell length rice seedlings. Nevertheless since some of the early studies showed increased cell elongation to be insufficient to account for all of the elongation observed at the organ level, increased cell number was also implicated but only by inference and only to a minor degree. The discovery by yabuta and Hayashi (1939) that gibberellin increased the "reproductive rate"of *Lemna paucicstata* gave a signal that the effect must have been associated with increases in cell number.

It is now realized that gibberellins may markedly increase both number and length of cells, the effect, however, depending on the nature of the plant material and the conditions under which the material is grown. Lang (1956) pointed out that stem elongation in gibberellin treated *Hyoscyamus niger* must be due to an appreciable increase in cell number since the internodes are essentially absent in the non-treated iosetted forms. In 1956 Lona reported that cell length increases would account only for about 13 percent of the elongation of *Perilla ocymoides* stems following gibberellin application. He thus concluded that gibberellin treatement must result in an appreciable increase in cell number in the stem of this plant. Sachs and Lang (1957) and Sachs, Breitz and Lang (1959) have shown a very marked increase in the frequency of dividing cells in gibberellin induced elongation, of *Hyoscyamus niger* and *Samolus parviflorus*. Bradley and Crane (1957) showed an increase in cell number in the meristems of spur shoots of gibberellin treated *Prunus armeniaca*. Gundersen (1958) has observed increase in both cell number and cell lengths in certain of the internodes of *Begonia*, and both cell number and cell lengths are factors in the gibberellin induced shoot growth of *Phaseolus vulgaris*. This is also true for petiole elongation of *Fragaria* sp and seedling elongation of *Zea mays* and *Pharbitis nil*.

Increased cell number is indeed a reflection of an increase in mitotic activity. In angiosperms this increase due to gibberellin treatment is most marked in meristems. Differential growth is also a predominant feature of the gibberellin response at cellular level. The planes of mistoses are such that cell progenies are almost exclusively formed in one direction, followed by cell elongation in the same direction. The response in cell number and cell length would suggest that the effect of gibberellins may be to control a physiological mechanism common to both. While it appears that mitotic activity can precede cell elongation there are cases of gibberellin-induced elongation of pollen tubes which occur without any preceding flush of mitotic activity. Haber and Luippold (1960) have shown that the gibberellin-induced growth of *Triticum vulgare* seedlings, which come from irradiated grains, must be due to increases in cell lengths only, since the irradiation completely inhibits mitosis. Thus it appears that the two types of responses at the cellular level can occur independently of one another. It is possible that the response of cell to the application of gibberellin will depend on the physiological age of the cell, i.e., enhanced cell division (mitotic activity) in meristems, primarily cell elongation in regions of elongation, and no response or very limited response in regions which consist of differentiated cells.

Gibberellin-Induced Growth

A number of types of growth responses now known to be associated with the gibberellins have been reported. Some of the "bakanae" symptoms have already been described. Here an attempt will be made describe some of the general growth responses induced by gibberellins.

Among the various growth responses induced by gibberellins shoot growth is the most apparent response of flowering plants. At low dosage level the plant size is generally increased, while little or no changes in form take place. At higher dosage levels the response may become one of growth, primarily, in the dimension of normal elongation of the plant. excessive treatment with gibberellins may result in marked differential growth to produce plants with leaves and long and thin stems. The ability to respond is dependent on the genotype of the plant and the environment in which the plant is grown. Field grown plants are often more responsive to gibberellin treatment when grown under environmental stresses. Gibberellin treatment may result in inhibition of lateral buds and thus lateral branching. Abscission has also been reported to be affected by gibberellin treatment. The increased stem thickness often seen is indeed a reflection of the stimulation of the cambium and its immediate cell progeny.

The type of leaf response is also associated with the developmental pattern of the leaf. Thus leaves of grasses with intercalary meristems respond mainly by elongation. Leaves of dicotyledons may respond by increases in area of the blade. Both acceleration and retardation of abscission have been reported.

Generally roots of intact plants show inhibition or no response as a result of gibberellin treatment, although exceptions are found in seedlings where elongation of the radicle has been reported, for example, among the gymnosperms, *Pseudotsuga menziesii* and *Pinus lambertiana*. Rooting of cuttings has been observed to be inhibited and certain cases of modulation of roots are inhibited of a consequence of gibberellin treatment.

Physiological Role of Gibberellins

The specificity of response of many flowering plants to exogenous gibberellin, and the widespread occurrence in flowering plants of gibberellin-like substances of which some have been isolated and chemically identified as true gibberellins, establishes the fact that gibberellins may be regarded as native plant growth regulators. Critical evidence for a causal relationship between endogenous gibberellin and growth has come from the positive correlation of certain types of growth with the level of endogenous gibberellin-like substances. Although synergism between gibberellins and auxins have been demonstrated for a number of cases, nevertheless the mechanistic interpretations of these data are questionable beyond the idea that numerous growth regulators must be present in optimum amounts for maximum growth of an organism. At present, however, the more convincing examples of growth which may be dependent on a gibberellin mechanism are those which exhibit a specified response, i.e. they respond to gibberellins but not to auxin, other known growth regulators.

Shoot Growth

Many cases of appreciable shoot growth resulting specifically from gibberellin treatment are now known. These include; the bolting and flowering responses of numerous photoperiodic and cold-requiring plants, normal growth of certain single gene dwarf mutants, elongation of red-light-inhibited plants, and possibly the breaking of certain types of dormancy and shortening of the after-ripening time required by certain seeds. Generally the effects seem to be not of differentiation of tissues but more of enhanced growth of preexisting cell types, with changes in form being consequences of differential growth. Whenever examples of primordial initiation are recorded, they are apparently indirect consequences of a gibberellin-induced general growth stimulation.

Bolting and flowering

Most rosetted long-day plants and rosetted cold-requiring winter biennials bolt and flower in response to exogenous gibberellin,.and these effects can be brought about under an environment which would normally maintain the rosetted habit of growth. With appropriate gibberellin dosages the bolted and flowering plants appear very similar to those induced by photo induction or cold treatment. At limiting dosages of gibberellin, however, it is possible to separate shoot elongation (bolting) from floral differentiation so that bolting will occur without flowering. Such experiments lead us to the view that the flowering response is only an indirect effect of the gibberellin treatment, as a consequence of increased growth of the shoot; the endogenous factors than gibberellins are elaborated and ultimately result in the differentiation of floral primordia. That the action of gibberellins in flowering is an indirect one is also evidenced by the fact that short-day plants do not flower even though the gibberellin treatment may cause appreciable stem elongation. It has been reported that the flowering response can be enhanced by gibberellin treatment in *Xanthium pennsylvanicum* under marginal day lengths which by themselves will produce some flowering, there are, nevertheless, no examples of short-day plants grown under long-day conditions, shown floral induction following gibberellin application, and in some cases gibberellin treatment has been found to reduce flowering in short-day plants under short-day conditions. Thus it is apparent that gibberellin will replace the long-day requirement for flowering but not the short-day conditions. Thus it is apparent that gibberellin will replace the long-day requirement for flowering but not the short-day requirement, and the gibberellin-treated plants show appreciable stem elongation just as do those plants growing under long-day conditions.

Studies of Lang (1956,1957) that there exists a correlation between levels of native gibberellin-like substances and the presence or absence of bolting in biennial *Hyoscyamus niger*, have also been extended to other plants. By use of *Zea mays* bioassay, several gibberellin-like components are found in appreciably higher amounts than in non-bolting plants. Harada and Nitsch (1959) and Nitsch (1959) have also found a positive correlation between amounts of gibberellin-like substances and bolting in the cold-requiring plant *Chrysanthemum morifolium. Ram* cv. *Shuoka*, and the long-day plant *Rudbeckia speciosa* Wenderoth. They have also demonstrated increases in auxin-like substances as a result of photoinduction and cold treatment. However, since only exogenously applied gibberellins, and not auxins, induce bolting without photoperiodic or temperature induction, it may be inferred that the increase in endogenous auxin area consequence of the increased level of the native gibberellins. The accumulated evidence indicates that gibberellin may be the primary limiting factor in the bolting of at least some long-day and cold-requiring rosetted plants.

Dwarfism

It has been found that gibberellin treatment does not always lead to stem elongation, since many cases have been recorded where the process is actually reversed by gibberellin treatment. Reduced growth results from a shortening of the internodes rather than a decrease in number of internodes. As a result, the gibberellin treated dwarfs become essentially indistinguishable from the tall or non-treated forms, by the elongation of internodes rather than by the increase in the number of internodes. In considering possible mechanisms to explain genetic dwarfism, a clear distinction should be made between the use of the general term "genetic dwarf: and the specific term "single gene dwarf". In cases of single gene dwarfism, the gene responsible for dwarfism, may in someway block a single step in a metabolic pathway. The theoritical unitary control in a single gene mutant suggests that a unitary limiting factor may be responsible for the dwarf habit of the growth. In contrast genetic dwarfs can also include cases which result from several mutant genes (multiple factors). A multiple phenomenon may have a multiple control at the physiological or biochemical level.

It has been reported by Brian and Hemming (1955) that certain dwarf cultivars of *Pisum sativum*, *Vicia faba* and *Phaseolus multiflorus* respond to gibberellin A_3 to become practically indistinguishable from the tall cultivars. At the same time the tall cultivars showed little or no response to exogenously applied gibberellin. It is now known that the ability of a genetic dwarf to respond to gibberellin can be under the control of a single gene. Such a unitary control of the gibberellin response has been demonstrated for the gene in *Pisum sativum* the *d* gene in *Lolium perenne* and d_1, d_2, d_3, d_5 and an_1 genes in *Zea mays*. The dwarf mutants of *Zea mays* have been usefully used for physiological studies of gibberellin action. Out of the ten mutants studied, nine were simple recessives and one a simple dominant. Five have been found to respond to gibberellin treatment by normal growth, other five showing little or no growth response. None of these mutants respond to other growth regulators or to variations in the nutrient medium. The specificity of response of the responding mutants suggests that each gene is in some way controlling a different step in a native gibberellin pathway leading to a product necessary for normal growth. The non-responsive nature of the other five mutants to all known gibberellins suggests that there are other reasons for dwarfism than merely a gibberellin treatment. There is at present no evidence, however, for inhibitor accumulation to explain the dwarf habit of growth, at least for the gibberellin-responding dwarf mutants of *Zea mays*.

Light inhibition

Many plants exhibit inhibited growth following exposure to low intensity red radiation (540-695 mμ), and this inhibition is reversed by subsequent exposure to far-red radiation (695-800 mμ). Lockhard (1956) reported that the red light induced inhibition of epicotyl elongation in etiolated seedlings of *Pisum sativum* could be specifically reversed by gibberellin treatment. In subsequent years significance has been given to the fact that the growth of irradiated and fully etiolated plants converged to a common maximum at identical saturating dosages of gibberellin, thus the ability of the plant to respond to gibberellin is dependent on its exposure to red light. These observations have led to the interpretation that the red light-induced inhibition of stem elongation is a direct consequence of a lowered availability of gibberelline-like substances but today no determinations have been reported of the amounts of gibberellin like substance from such system. This interpretation has, however, not met universal acceptance, since gibberellin and red light appear to act independently in certain other stem growth systems. In at least one plant, *Brassica alba* (*Sinapis alba*), stem elongation inhibited by red light has not been reversed by gibberellin A_3 treatment Gibberellin and red light both promote the germination of seeds of *Lactuca sativa*.

Seed and fruit growth

Parthenocarpy, induced by gibberellin has been reported in *Lycopersicum esculentum*, *Cucumis sativus* and *Solanum melongena*. In case of *Zephyranthes* the parthenocarpic fruit contained normal appearing seeds which were devoid of embryos. The growth of ovary and integuments were specific for gibberellins. Reduced grain yield has often been reported in bakanae disease as well as with exogenous gibberellin treatments. Hayashi *et al.* (1953) found that 2 mg/i GA reduced rice grain production 32 percent, although the yield of straw increased by 14 percent. Wittwer and Bukovac (1957) found gibberellin to be approximately 500 times more effective than IAA in inducing parthenocarpy of tomatoes. It appears from several examples that native gibberellins of the seed are one of the controlling factors for seed growth. Most direct information is available on the apparent level of native gibberellins in growing seed. Corcoran (1959) has shown that increases in extractable gibberellin-like substances from the seed occur during the growth of the seed and after the virtual completion of pericarp growth.

Detached plant parts

The use of detached plant parts is often advantageous in the study of gibberellin responses. Under such conditions the investigator is able to define more precisely the environment under which the material is grown. This has, however, the disadvantage in that the limiting growth requirements must be determined before the system can be studied.

Among the detached plant parts,(i) stem sections (ii) leaf sections and leaf disks, and (iii) tissue explants and tissue cultures are used. Gibberellin affects the growth of such plant parts in various ways and these studies have the obvious advantage of being able to demonstrate and analyze the interaction of the several growth factors which may be involved.

Chlorosis

Yellowing symptoms, typical of the bakanae disease are also produced by gibberellins. Fewer chloroplasts are present in diseased tissue and the chlorophyll decreases Gibberellin treatments also decrease the percent chlorophyll. It has been shown by the I.C.I group (1954) that increase nutrients markedly reduced gibberellin chlorosis. It would be really interesting to know which of the nutrients are most important.

Metabolism

It has often been reported that when gibberellins promote elongation, they do not always cause a parallel increase in dry weight. The I.C.I group has showed that the total dry weight of wheat and peas is increased by gibberellic acid treatment, provided that sufficient nutrients are available and the experiments cover a long enough period. They also emphasized that redistribution of material from the root to the shoot must be taken into account. The increased dry weight was, however, traced to more carbon fixation and the largest carbon changes involved carbohydrates. The nature of the dry weight changes as effected by gibberellins is as yet a complex one.

The Tokyo group has indicated a decrease in total sugars, dextrin, reducing sugar, and sucrose intreated rice plants. On the other hand, the British group reported marked increase in sucrose, fructose, and glucose in wheat; in peas only glucose was affected. No starch was found and it was suggested that protein or cellulose must increase.

Recently Hayashi et al. (1956) have examined changes of enzymatic activity with time during the development of the seventh leaf of rice. Phosphatase, alkaline, pyrophosphatase, acetylesterase, maltose, β-glucosidase, α-galactosidase amylase, urease dipeptidase, ascorbidc acid oxidase, and catalase decreased on a fresh weight basis more rapidly than in non-treated controls, but peroxidase and invertase increased more rapidly than controls and gibberellin was shown to have no effect on their action. However, these enzymatic changes did not differ in any other way from the controls except for the fact that the changes were more rapid and more marked.

The effect of gibberellin on plant respiration has been little studied. Hayashi (1940) found no effect of gibberellin on yeast fermentation . Kato (1956) recorded a 15 percent increase in oxygen consumption in growing pea stem sections, the promotion was not found in non-growing tissue. He (1957) also found that cyanide, arsenite, and p-chloromercuribenzoate inhibited gibberellin-induced pea stem elongation in low concentrations whereas copper enzyme poisons did not. He thus concluded that gibberellin did not change the terminal oxidase of the tissue.

Relationship of Gibberellin to Auxin

Although gibberellins are similar to auxins in that both promote cell elongation, it is apparent that they differ from previously known auxins in several ways. They do not in short term experiments inhibit root growth, they inhibit rather than promote root initiation, they do not cause typical epinasty nor callus formation, their action on leaf growth or dwarfism is not paralleled by auxin, and they are more potent than auxin in inducing parthenocarpy. Several other properties of auxins have been compared with gibberellin. Brian et al. (1955) could find no effect of gibberellic acid on water uptake by potato tuber disks, nor did it cause any delay of leaf abscission, also it broke potato dormancy. Perhaps the most striking of all the differences is the evident indifference to light of the gibberellin effect. So there is good reason to believe that gibberellins are not auxins in the true sense of the term.

KINETIN AND CYTOKININS

Up to now, we have been concerned with growth hormones, synthetic and natural, whose primary function is to promote cell elongation. We have mentioned that IAA and gibberellin do promote an increase in the number of cells in certain circumstances, but this is the exception rather than the rule. The only growth regulator we have discussed so far, concerned primarily with cell division, was traumatic acid (wound harmone). However, in addition to traumatic acid, there exists in plants several compounds capable of promoting cell division. For example, coconut milk was found to be very active as a stimulation of cell division by the van Overbeek et al. (1941).

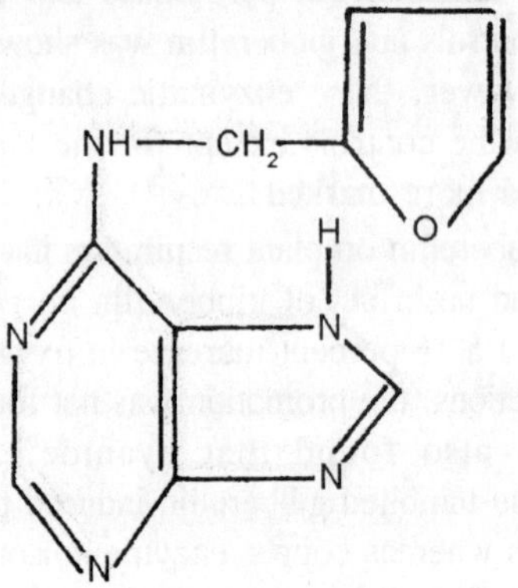

Fig. 11.11. Kinetin (6-furfuryl aminopurine).

Subsequently, this finding was supported by several investigations on a variety of plant tissues, confirming that coconut milk is, indeed an active promoter of cell division. Perhaps the most exciting discovery in the search for compounds that will induce cells to multiply is *kinetin* (6- furfury-laminopurine), a compound isolated from yeast DNA by Miller et al. (1955). Actually, kinetin is formed from deoxyadenosine, a degradation product of DNA and, as such, cannot be considered natural product of plant biosynthesis. Subsequent to its discovery, many analogs of kinetin, active in promoting cell division, were synthesized. In order to group this type of substance under one title, the generic term *cytokinin* has been given to all compounds with biological activity similar to that of kinetin. As might be expected cytokinins have widerspread occurrence in the plant world.

Substances having cytokinin activity have been extracted from about 40 species of higher plants, and in most cases, the actively dividing tissues of the plants have proven to be the best sources. Evidence is also mounting for the presence of cytokinins in micro-organisms. Despite the fact that many, if not all, plants contain cytokinins, it was almost 10years after discovery of kinetin before the chemical composition and properties of a natural cytokinin were described. Miller (1961) managed to extract and bring to a high state of purity a cytokinin from immature maize seeds. Attempts to crystalize and characterize the compound were unsuccessful. However, Letham (1963 : 1967) successfully extracted and purified to crystalline form a cytokinin from sweet corn. The naturally occurring cytokinin was named *zeatin*. Later, in a joint study, Letham and Miller (1965) were able to isolate in crystalline form the cytokinin that Miller had earlier isolated (in noncrystalline form) from immature maize seeds. The cytokinin proved to be zeatin. In assays for cytokinin activtty such as carrot root tissue and soybean callus cultures, zeatin proved to be much more active than kinetin.

Physiological Effects

Shortly after the discovery of kinetin, there followed a great number of papers describing its effects on many different plant growth systems. Most of these were concerned, directly, or indirectly, with kinetin's ability to pomote cell division and cell enlargement. We will discuss the effect of kinetin on cell division, cell enlargement, root initiation and growth, shoot initiation and growth, and breaking of dormancy.

Cell division

The stimulation of cell division in plant tissue cultures was the first effect of kinetin to be observed. In the tobacco pith cultures used by most investigators, it was noted that, in addition to kinetin. IAA is also needed for continuous growth. Although either growth regulator, when used one, produces a small response. It has been suggested that the small response invoked by kinetin or IAA used alone on tobacco pith cultures is due to small amounts of endogenous kinetin-like substances and IAA already present. however, when IAA and kinetin are applied together in the right ratio of concentrations, the results are striking and growth of the culture can be maintained indefinitely. This property, the stimulation of cell division, appears to be characteristics of all cytokinnis. The ability of kinetin in the presence of IAA to promote cell division.

In order that cell division may take place, an ordered sequence (DNA synthesis, mitosis, and cytokinesis) must take place. Is there a specific influence of IAA or cytokinin alone on any step in this sequence? The answer is apparently, yes Das *et al* (1956) found that both IAA and kinetin, when used alone, stimulate DNA synthesis in tobacco pith cultures. The above authors also found that both growth regulators are needed for mitosis, although IAA appears to dominate in this step.

In addition, they suggested that when either kinetin or IAA is present in high concentration, the other may become limiting for at least one of the three steps needed to complete cell division. In a later paper, these authors stated that of the three steps in cell division, IAA is involved in the first two (DNA duplication and mistosis), but that the last step (cytokinesis) is controlled by kinetin. Here again, as with our discussions on gibberellins and IAA, we are presented with the importance of balance between growth hormones in plant growth and development.

How a cytokinin induces cell division is still an unsolved question. The adenine moiety of the cytokinin molecule appears essential for this process, many different substituted side chains being applicable. Strong (1958) has suggested that the side chain may influence some physical property (such as solubility) bearing on the efficiency of the growth regulator to induce cell division.

Cell enlargement

Not only do cytokinins promote cell division, but they also induce cell enlargement, an effect usually associated with IAA and gibberellin. Treatment of leaf discs cut from etiolated leaves of *Phaselous vulgaris* (bean) with kinetin causes sigificant cell enlargements. This effect of kinetin can occur in the absence of IAA. Cell enlargement after kinetin treatment has also been observed in tobacco pith cultures, tobacco roots, and in excised artichoke tissue. Stimulation of cell enlargement by cytokinins other than kinetin has also been observed. Since cytokinin-induced cell enlargement has been clearly shown, cytokinins should not be considered solely as cell division factors.

Root initiation and growth

Although relatively few studies have been made of cytokinin effects on the root system, it appears that cytokinins are able both to stimulate and to inhibit root initiation and development. Kinetin in the presence of casein hydrolysate and IAA stimulates root initiation and development in tobacco stem callus cultures. Increases in dry weight and elongation of the roots of lupin seedling were found by Frics (1960) to be promoted by kinetin. It can be seen that all concentrations of kinetin increase the dry weight of the root system even though at the higher concentration root elongation is inhibited.

In excised pea root segments, lateral root development is slightly stimulated by low concentrations of kinetin (5×10^{-5} M). At higher concentrations, however, kinetin is inhibitory. There is some evidence that interaction between cytokinins and auxin may influence the site of lateral root initiation. Bonnett and Torrey (1965), for example, demonstrated that by applying auxin and cytokinin at different concentrations to the opposite ends of excised root segments of the common bind weed (*Convolvulus*) they could alter the site of lateral root formation.

Shoot initiation and growth

In the original work with tobacco callus cultures and kinetin, it was found that callus tissue can be kept in an undifferentiated state as the proper balance of IAA and kinetin is maintained. However, if the ratio of kinetin to IAA is increased, either by the addition of more kinetin or the use of less IAA, leafy shoots are initiated. Torrey (1958) observed that kinetin initiated bud primodia on root segments of *Convolvulus arvensis* (bindweed), this effect being much more marked when the segments were grown in the dark.

Five day old bean seedlings soaked in kinetin solutions and then allowed to grow for an additional 46 hours respond with an increase in fresh weight of the epicotyl, increase in leaf expansion, and increase in the elongation of stems and petioles. In a recent study by Skoog et al (1967), auxin-cytokinin interaction in regulating growth and organ formation in tobacco callus cultres has been remarkably illustrated. The natural cytokinin, 6 (γ-γ-dimehthylallyamino) purine, is much more active than kinetin. This natural cytokinin has been found as a constituent of sRNA in yeast, corn, pea, and spinach. There have been several additional demonstrations of cytokinin induced promotions of shoot initiation and growth. However, the above studies serve to illustrate that cytokinins are active in the initiation and development of the aerial portions of the plants.

Breaking of dormancy

Earlier, we discussed apical dominance, the inhibition of lateral bud growth by auxin emanating from the apical bud. The controlling features of this phonomenon are not clearly understood and may involve not only IAA but other factors, which may interact with the auxin. This has been suggested in a study by Wickson and Thimann (1958) on the interaction of IAA and kinetin in apical dominance. They found that the growth of the lateral buds of pea stem sections in culture solutions containing IAA is inhibited, as might be expected. The growth of lateral buds on stem sections in nutrient solutions not contain in IAA, of course, is unihibited. However, the addition of kinetin along with IAA stimulates the growth of these buds. Kinetin alone has little effect. These investigators also demonstrated that the effect of kinetin on apical dominance can also be observed in entire shoots; that is, the apical bud is present. They found, as in the classical studies of apical dominance, that removal of the apical bud. stimulates the growth of the lateral buds. On the other hand, if the apical bud remains, the lateral buds are completely inhibited. However, if the instance shoot is soaked in a kinetin solution, inhibition of the lateral buds by the apical bud is overcome to a large extent. In addition to the above study, there have been several other investigations demonstrating the stimulatory influence of cytokinins on lateral bud growth. It appears that apical dominance may be controlled by a balance of concentrations between endogenous kinetin-like substance and IAA.

Other Physiological Effects

It is a well-known fact that the germination of lettuce seeds (*Lactuca sativa*) may be stimulated by red light and inhibited by infrared (far red) light. Also, the growth of bean leaf discs is sensitive to red and far red light treatment, being stimulated by red light and inhibited by far-red light treatment. In both of the above situations, the effect of kinetin treatment is similar to that of red light treatment. Only in one respect, does it differ. The stimulatory effects of kinetin are in no way inhibited by subsequent far-red treatment as in the case of red light treatment germination of seeds of white clover and carpet grass has also been observed to respond positively to kinetin treatment.

Table 11.3. Effect of kinetin and red and far-red irradiation on growth of bean leaf discs during a 48-hour growth period.

Conc.of kinetin M	*Light treatment*	*Increase in diam., mm*
0	none	1.05 ± 0.04 3
5×10^{-5}	none	2.48 ± 0.03
0	5 min red	2.48 ± 0.08
0	5 min far red	1.01 ± 0.06
0	5 min red and then 5 min far red	1.17 ± 0.07
5×10^{-5}	5 min far red	2.49 ± 0.08

Cytokinins are not only necessary factors in the growth and development of higher plants but they also markedly influence the growth of certain microorganisms. Kinetin, for example, can influence the growth of viruses, bacteria, fungi and algae all of which suggests that cytokinins are also present as natural components of lower plants. Indeed, crude extracts of natural cytokinins have been prepared from

Table 11.4. Effect of kinetin and red and far- red irradiation on germination of Grand Rapids lettuce seeds during a 72-hour period.

Cone of kinetin, M	*Light treatment*	*Germination %* *Expt. 1*	*Expt. 2*
0	none	8	7
5×10^{-5}	none	84	86
0	8 min red	96	96
0	5 min red and then 8 min far red	5	7
5×10^{-5}	8 min far red	86	83

at least two micro-organisms. It is also quite evident that natural cytokinins interact with endogenous IAA to affect the growth and development of the plant. Again, we are presented with evidence supporting the concept that the growth and development of a plant is under the influence of delicate chemical balances maintained by the presence or absence of interaction between growth regulators.

12

Seed Germination

A seed consists of an embryo and its stored food supply, surrounded by protective seed coverings. When the seed separates from the plant on which it was produced, the seed is *quiescent*; that is, there is no external evidence of activity within the seed. The resumption of active growth by the embryo, resulting in the rupture of seed coverings and the emergence of a new seedling plant capable of independent existence, is known as *germination*. In order for germination to occur, three conditions must be fulfilled. *First* the seed must be *viable*; that is, the embryo must be alive and capable of germination. *Second*, *internal conditions* within the seed must be favourable for germination; that is, any physical or chemical barriers to germination must have disappeared. *Third*, the seed must be subjected to favourable *environmental* conditions, the essential factors being available water, proper temperature, a supply of oxygen and sometimes light. Although in any one seed each of these conditions may have an effect distinct from the others, the beginning of germination may be more often determined by the interactions among them.

The Germination Process

The germination process involves a complex sequence of biochemical, physiological, and morphological changes in which certain stages can be recognized. The *first* stage begins with the inhibition of water by the dry seed, the softening of the seed coverings, and the hydration of the protoplasm. This process is largely physical and occurs even in a non-viable seed. As a result of water absorption the seed swells, and the seed coats may break. The *second stage* begins with the initiation of cellular activity and includes the appearance of specific

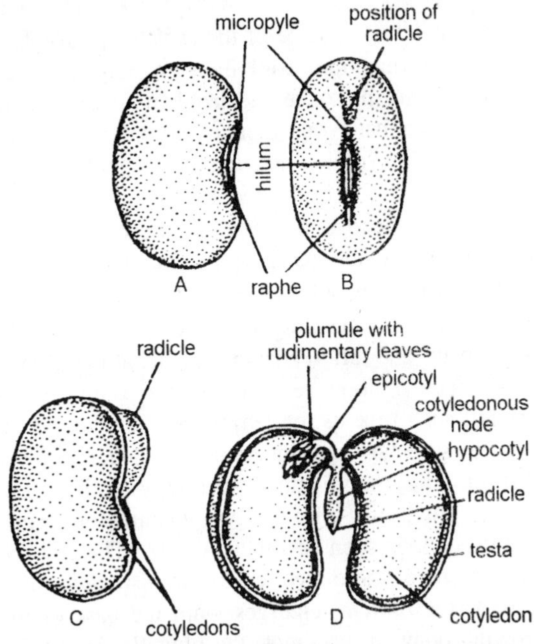

Fig. 12.1. Structure of bean seed. A-B-External structure. C-Seed coats removed. D-Seed cut open to show various parts.

enzymes and a rise in respiratory rate. A plant growth hormone—gibberellin—is believed to play a key role in the initiation of germination. This effect has been demonstrated most clearly in seeds of cereal grains, such as wheat and barley. In these seeds the important structures are the *embryo*, *endosperm* (nonliving storage tissue containing mostly starch), and the *aleurone* (the outer layer of endosperm one or two cells thick). When the dry seed imbibes moisture, gibberellin appears in the embryo and is translocated to the aleurone layer where it activates enzymes. On of these enzymes, alpha-amylase, moves to the endosperm, causing the starch to be converted to sugar. Other enzymes appear in the aleurone, weakening the seed coats and allowing the root tip to burst through.

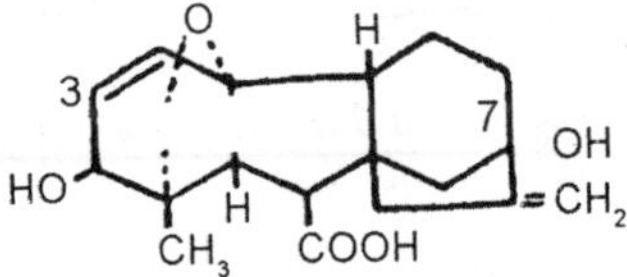

Fig. 12.2. Chemical structure of gibberllic acid (GA_3), a plant growth hormone associated with seed germination.

Cell elongation and emergence of the radicle are events associated with the onset of germination. Cell division may also occur at an early stage, but this seems to be independent of cell elongation. A *third stage* is the enzymatic digestion of complex insoluble reserve materials, mostly carbohydrates and fats but sometimes proteins, to soluable forms which are translocated to the active growing areas. The *fourth stage* is the assimilation of these substances at the meristematic areas to provide energy for cellular activity and growth and for conversion into new cell components.

In the *fifth stage,* the seedling grows by the usual processes of division, enlargement, and differentiation of cells at the growing points. The seedlings depends upon reserves in the seed for continuing development until such time as the leaves can function adequately for photosynthesis. In summary, germination takes place in the following steps: inhibition, enzymatic and respiratory activity, digestion, translocation, assimilation, growth. As germination proceeds, the structure of the seedlings soon becomes evident. The embryo consists of an axis bearing one or more seed leaves, or *cotyledons*. The growing point of the root, the *radicle*, emerges from the base of the embryo axis. The growing point of the shoot, the *plumule*, is at the other end of the embryo axis, above the cotyledons. The seedling stem is divided into the section below the cotyledons—the *hypocotyl*—and the section above the cotyledons—the *epicotyl*. The initial growth of the seedling follows two patterns. In one type—*epigeous* germination—the hypocotyl elongates and raises the cotyledons above the ground. In the other type—*hypogeous* germination—the lengthening of the hypocotyl does not raise the cotyledons above the ground, and only the epicotyl emerges.

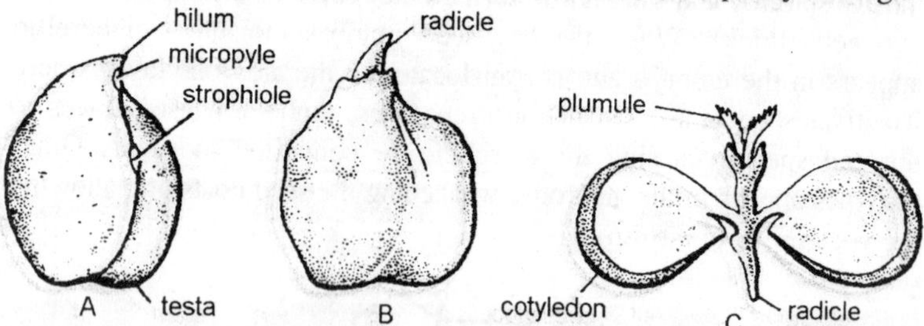

Fig. 12.3. Germ seed: A–Whole seed, B–The kernel after removal of seed coat, C–The two opened cotyledons with tigellum.

Viability of Seeds

A supply of viable seed is essential in successful propagation from seed. However, the distinction between a live and a dead seed is not

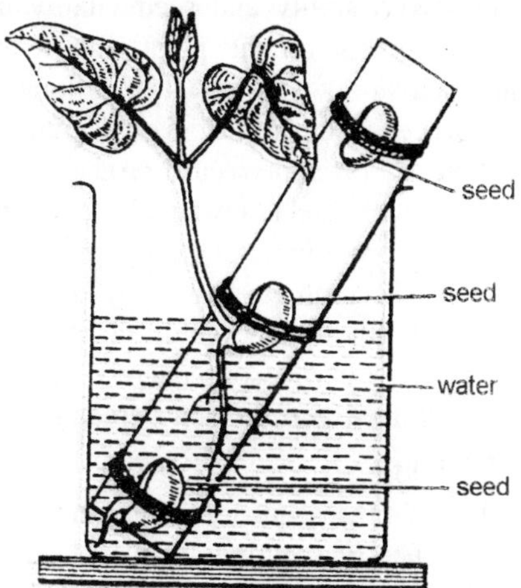

Fig. 12.4. Experiment to demonstrate conditions necessary for germination of seeds.

necessarily sharp, and is often characterized by necrosis or injuries in localized areas of the seed. Viability is represented by the *germination percentage*, which expresses the number of seedlings which can be produced by a given number of seed. Germination should be prompt, and growth of the seedling vigorous. This is the seed vitality, or germinating power, and may be represented by *germination rate*. In seeds of low viability, a low germination percentage and a low rate of germination are often associated.

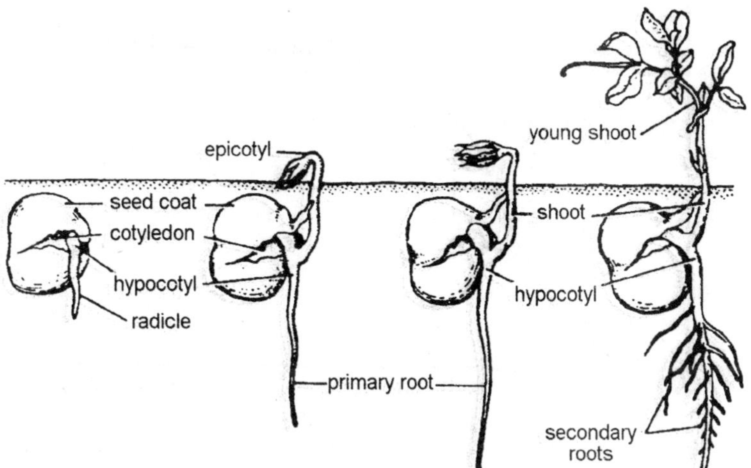

Fig. 12.5. Successive stages of hypogeal germination of dicotyledonous exalbuminous seed of pea.

A reduction in seed viability and seed vitality may result from incomplete seed development on the plant, injuries during harvest, improper processing and storage, or aging. With long storage, reduced viability is usually preceded by a period of declining vitality. Seeds with a low germination rate or embryos that produce weak and abnormal seedlings are less able to withstand unfavourable environmental conditions in the seed bed than more vigorous seedlings. Weak and injured seedlings are likely to succumb to attacks by disease organisms, or they may lack the strength to emerge if planted too deeply or if adverse seed bed conditions exist. Consequently field survival is apt to be less than a predetermined germination percentage would indicate.

Measurement of Viability

If one measures the time sequence of germination of a given lot of seeds or the emergence of seedlings from a seed bed, one usually finds a pattern that is the germination curve. There is an initial delay in the start of germination, then a rapid increase in the number of seeds that germinate, followed by a decrease in the rate of appearance. When viability is less than 100 percent, the exact end point may be difficult to ascertain. Measurement of germination involves two factors—the *germination percentage* and the *germination rate*. Germination percentage should involve a time element, indicating the number of seedlings produced within a specified length of time. Germination rate can be measured by several methods. One determines the number of

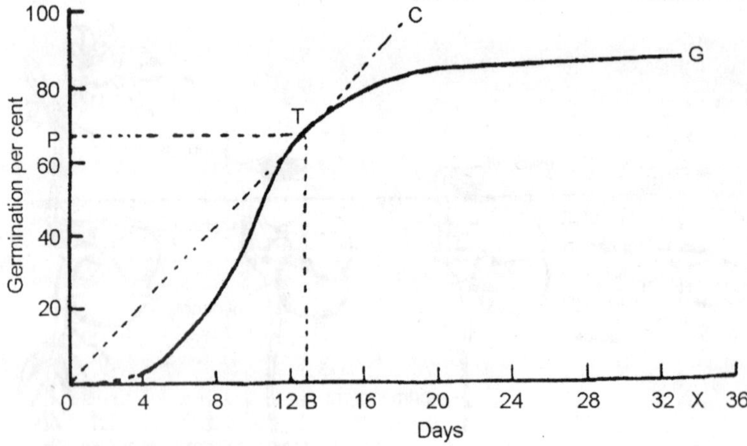

Fig. 12.6. Typical germination curve of a seed sample. After an initial delay, the number of seeds germinating increases, then decrease. Such a curve can be used to measure germination.

days required to produce a given germination percentage. A better method, that has been used for many years, calculates the average number of days required for radicle or plumule emergence as follows:

$$\text{Mean days} = \frac{N_1T_1 + N_2T_2 + \ldots N_xT_x}{\text{total number of seeds germination}}$$

N values are the numbers of seeds germinating within consecutive intervals of time; T values indicate the time between the beginning of the test and the end of the particular interval of measurement. Kotowski has used the reciprocal of this formula multiplied by 100 to determine a *coefficient of velocity*.

Czabator has suggested another measurement that includes both rate and percentage- *germination value* (GV). To be obtained by periodic counts of radicle or plumule emergence. The important values on the curve are T—the point at which the germination rate begins to slow down—and G—the final germination percentage. These points divide the curve into two parts—a rapid phase and a slow phase. Peak value (PV) is the germination percentage at T divided by the days to reach that point. Mean daily germination (MDG) is the final germination percentage divided by number of days in the test. Then GV = PV × MDG.

Regulation of Germination

A seed enclosed within the fruit normally will not germinate while still attached to the plant on which it is produced. Certain highly specialized plants—for example, the mangrove, a swamp-growing tree—are exceptions in that they produce *viviparous* embryos that germinate on the tree. These grow into massive seedlings, with a foot-long, javelin-shaped root; such seedlings eventually fall and become embedded in the mud below. Also, wet weather during harvest in certain seasons may result in premature sprouting in some grain crops, such as wheat.

The tendency toward *vivipary* is inherited as a defective characteristic and is automatically selected against. Ripening of seeds involves the development of internal mechanisms that function to regulate the time of germination so it will coincide with periods having environmental conditions most likely to favour survival of the seedlings. During maturation most seeds lose moisture to a level below that required for germination. The seed can remain in this dry state for long periods of time and can be handled with relative economy, ease, and safety. If the embryo is merely quiescent and no other germination block exists, the seed can germinate immediately whenever sufficient

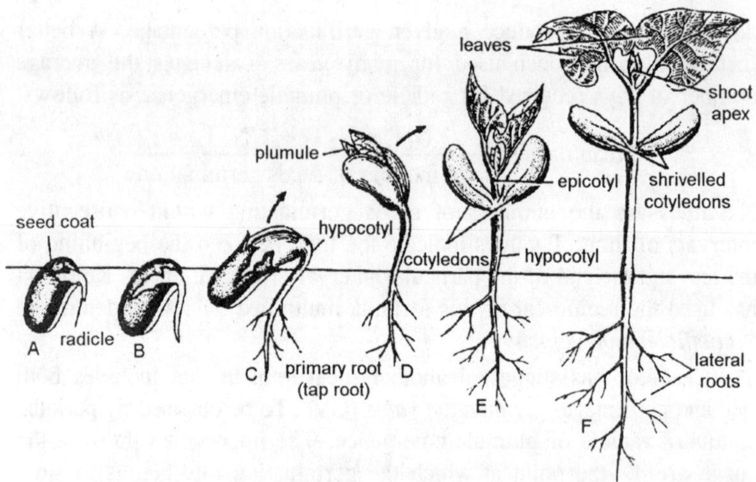

Fig. 12.7. Successive stages of the germination of bean seed.

water is absorbed and suitable temperature and aeration conditions prevail. On the other hand, most freshly harvested seeds have additional germination regulating mechanisms that exist within the seed, and germination may fail to take place even under seemingly favourable environmental conditions.

Propagators of cultivated plants have long recognized these germination delaying phenomena and have learned to cope with them through the adoption of appropriate pre-germination and handling procedures arrived at through trial and error. Furthermore the domestication of many seed-propagated cultivars has undoubtedly included selection for easier propagation. Terminology based on these empirical methods has depended to a large extent upon the particular group of propagators. On the other hand, investigations of the fundamental nature of these phenomena have been carried out only in comparatively recent times, and an understanding is still far from complete. Such investigations have been extended from the cultivated plants to their relatives in nature, where such phenomena are not only much more prevalent and complex but play an important role in ecological adaptation.

Seeds may be grouped into the following broad categories on the basis of their response to particular environmental conditions and to methods of handling.

Group—I. Seeds in which the covering is hard and moisture-impermeable and in which the embryo thus cannot absorb water. The group also includes seeds with coats so hard as to resist embryo expansion.

Group—II. Seeds which have a dormant embryo that responds to pre-germination chilling.

A. Seeds requiring a single chilling period.

B. Seeds requiring a warm period (for root or embryo development) prior to the chilling period.

C. Seeds requiring two consecutive chilling periods, separated by a warm period.

Group—III. Seeds which combine an impermeable seed coat with a dormant embryo.

Group—IV. Seeds that contain chemical inhibitors that can be removed by leaching.

Group—V. Seeds that are dormant when freshly harvested but become germinable upon dry storage (post-harvested dormancy).

A. Seeds in which germination is promoted by light.

B. Seeds in which germination is inhibited by light.

C. Seeds in which germination is inhibited by high temperatures.

The term *dormancy* has broad applications in plant physiology to refer to lack of growth in any plant part due either to internally or externally induced factors. Seed technologists, on the other hand, have used the term in a somewhat narrower sense to refer to nongermination resulting from conditions within the seed (other than nonavailability). The Association of Official Seed Analysis, in the "Rules for Testing Seeds," further distinguishes between "hard seeds" and "dormant seeds". *Hard seeds* include those (groups I and III, above) which cannot absorb moisture because of the impermeable seed coat. *Dormant seeds* include those (Groups II, IV, and V, above) which are able to absorb moisture but fail to germinate because of restrictive influences within the seed that block some physiological reaction in the embryo and prevent the initiation of germination.

Conditions that exist within the seed at the time it matures on the plant to prevent germination have been called *primary dormancy*. The physiological changes that occur within the seed so that germination can take place are referred to in horticultural literature as *after-ripening*. Dormancy may be transitory, lasting only for a few days, disappearing with dry storage (in the case of seeds in group V, above); on the other hand, dormancy removal may require complex and time consuming treatments. Once a seed has passed through an after-ripening period it may again become dormant if the imbibed seed is subjected to particular unfavourable environmental conditions. This is referred to as *secondary dormancy*.

Germination controlling mechanisms are important in nature because they contribute to natural survival and to the dissemination of plants to different areas. Such mechanisms are particularly important in plants growing in desert or cold regions where environmental conditions may not be favourable for germination immediately following dissemination of the seed. For instance, in the temperate zone, spring-ripening seed on such trees as elm, maple, or willow germinates immediately, and the seedling establishes itself the same season.

If fall-ripening seeds of trees growing in the same region germinated immediately, the seedlings would probably be killed during the winter. Seeds of many plants of the latter type require winter chilling for germination, and consequently do not germinate until the following spring. Variation among individual seeds of a given lot within a particular species may distribute germination over a period of years. If those which germinate at a certain time are lost, other seeds remain to germinate at a later and perhaps more favourable time. With cultivated plants, prevention of premature germination on the plant or during seed harvesting is beneficial. On the other hand, expensive and time-consuming pre-germination seed treatments required to obtain good, uniform germination are undesirable.

If reliable pre-germination treatments are unknown, germination may be unsatisfactory and reduced stands may result. Consequently the development of cultivated crop plants has involved the selection of cultivars which do not have complex germination problems. Most difficulty in germination regulation in propagation is found in seeds of trees and shrubs of native plants or those recently introduced into cultivation. Particular difficulty is experienced in getting quick and reliable results in testing seed for viability, especially when this is attempted shortly after the seed is harvested.

Internal Conditions Affecting Germination

Seed Coverings

Impermeability to Water. The maturation of seeds of many species results not only in reduced water content but also in deposition of particular substances in the seed coverings to produce impermeability to water. This is a genetic characteristic of certain plant families, but it can also be modified by particular environmental conditions and methods of handling. A hard, impervious seed coat has value in prolonging storage life, since the internal parts of such seeds, once dry, are held in sealed storage until the seed coverings become modified. The effective seed covering may be only the hardened outer seed coat, or it may include various parts of the pericarp which either are attached to the seed or surround it.

A number of plant families contain species whose seeds have hard coats; these include the Leguminosae, Malvaceae, Cannaceae, Geraniaceae, Chenopodiaceae, Convolvulaceae, and Solanaceae. The plant group most commonly associated with harseededness is the legumes, in which are found clover, alfalfa, and similar agricultural plants, as well as locust (*Robinia*), *Acacia*, and other woody legumes.

Seed coats can sometimes be modified during seed development or by the treatment the seed receives at harvest or during storage. For instance, white clover seeds are hard when ripened in hot, dry weather but are soft when ripened during rainy weather. If seeds are harvested before they are completely ripe and before the covering has become hard, and then kept from drying out, hareededness may never develop. Further changes in the degree of hardness can take place during storage. For instance, in studies with *Symphoricarpos*, as the length of time after harvest increased, the length of the sulfuric acid treatment required to soften the coats also increased.

In some cases, seeds which normally do not have hard seed coats, such as beans, develop hareededness with dry storage and when planted, fail to germinate unless they are pretreated. Seeds with hard coverings may be germinated by any method which artificially breaks or modifies the seed coat, provided that another type of dormancy is not also present. In nature, softening of the seed coat comes about through agencies of the environment: mechanical abrasion, alternate freezing and thawing, attack by micro-organisms in the soil, or passage through the digestive tract of birds or other animals. Fungus activity takes place at moderate temperatures—50°F (10°C) or higher—but does not occur to any appreciable extent at lower temperatures. For effective seed coat decomposition, the seeds must be held moist at warm temperatures in the soil. Addition of nitrates to the medium has increased seed softening, presumably because it stimulates fungus activity.

Mechanical Resistance to Embryo Expansion. In most seeds, once water is absorbed, the expanding pressure of the embryo during germination is sufficient to rupture the seed coats. However, the seed coverings can be so hard as to offer mechanical resistance to embryo expansion. In the olive, for instance, the seed is surrounded by a thick, bony, indehiscent endocarp which is both mechanically hard and water-impermeable. The hard seed covering of *Symphoricarpos* is indehiscent, but water can be absorbed through the micropyle. Other seed structures, such as the "pits" of stone fruits or the shells of walnuts and other nuts, are extremely hard and may produce temporary resistance to germination. These structures are dehiscent, however, and water can be absorbed through the layer separating the two halves. Seeds of certain weeds, e.g. *Amaranthus retroflexus* and *Alisma plantago*, also have hard coats of this type.

The force required to overcome resistance of freshly harvested seeds of black walnut (*Juglans nigra*) and hickory (*Carya* sp.) was shown to be considerably greater than that of the calculated breaking force of the embryo during germination. However, shell resistance decreased markedly during moist, warm storage, provided that the medium was unsterilized. Some structures within the seed, such as the endosperm, are believed to mechanically restrict embryo expansion in some kinds of dormant seeds. Germination occurs when the expanding force of the embryo increases or when the restrictive force of the covering decreases, or both.

Restriction of Gaseous Exchange. Physical restriction of the movement of oxygen to the imbibed embryo by the inner membranous seed coat or an enclosing nucellus or endosperm layer has frequently been cited as a factor in seed dormancy. Evidence for this is that freshly harvested dormant seed, which are light-sensitive or temperature-sensitive, can be made to germinate promptly by excising the embryo or by physically or chemically altering the seed coat. Increasing the oxygen content of the surrounding atmosphere will stimulate germination of the intact seed in many cases. The benefits of after-ripening in dry storage have been attributed to increase in permeability. The regulatory function of these seed coverings in dormancy may be real, but the mechanism does not seem to be simple.

Other factors, in addition to physical restriction, may be involved. For instance, differences in oxygen requirements of different parts of the seed or at different stages of after ripening may be involved. Cocklebur (*Xanthium*) seed illustrates this phenomenon. Two seeds are present in the bur, one germinating readily, the other delayed for one or two years. This difference was first attributed to a difference in inner seed coat permeability to oxygen uptake. It has since been found that the embryos contain two water-soluble chemical inhibitors that will not pass through the seed covering. However, the inhibitors can be removed by leaching the excised embryo with water or by subjecting the seed to an increased concentration of oxygen.

Dormant Embryos

Seed with a Single, Low-Temperature Requirement for Germination. Plant propagators have known since early times that moist seeds of certain fall-ripening tree and shrub species of the temperate zone must be chilled as they overwinter in the ground before they will germinate in the spring. This requirement led to the horticultural practice termed *stratification*, in which seeds are placed between layers of moist sand or soil in boxes (or in the ground) and exposed to chilling temperatures either out-of-doors or in refrigerators. A more accurate term for this procedure, used by some propagators, is *moist-chilling*.

Conditions required for after-ripening changes to take place within these dormant seeds include : (a) temperatures just above or slightly below freezing; (*b*) imbibition of moisture by the seed; (*c*) aeration; and (*d*) a certain length of time. After ripening is considered to be most effective at approximately 35°to 45°F (2° to 7°C), although changes also occur at higher and lower temperatures. De Haas and Schander have shown that the lowest temperature at which such changes occur in apple seeds is about 23°F (–5°C). Moist, dormant seeds of many species that are exposed to a high temperature (greater than the effective chilling range) before after-ripening is complete not only fail to germinate but also develop secondary dormancy. Abbott has shown that in apple seed at 62°F (17°C) the processes leading to after-ripening and those resulting in secondary dormancy are in equilibrium. He suggested that this *compensation temperature* should be used to test germination of dormant seeds. Compensation temperatures occur in dormant seeds of other plants, but the exact temperature probably varies with different species and possibly with the stage of after-ripening.

If the seeds are placed at relatively low temperatures, the germination rate is slow but the germination percentage high. At higher temperatures germination rates are faster, but the germination percentage decreases in proportion to the increase in temperature; nongerminating seeds revert to secondary dormancy. The temperature conditions most effective for germination may be similar to those in natural environment in which soil temperatures gradually increase with

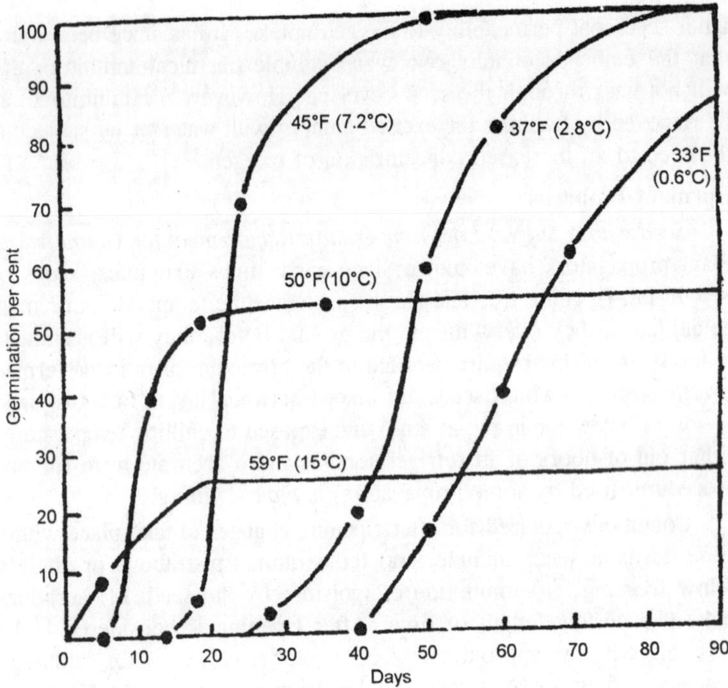

Fig. 12.8. The effect of temperature on germination of apple seeds previously stratified for 65 days at 37°F (3°C). The abscissa represents the days following stratification.

the advance of spring. Late planting or an early hot period can inhibit germination and produce secondary dormancy.

Moisture in the seed is necessary during pregermination chilling. Drying will stop after-ripening causing secondary dormancy, or it can injure the seeds. Reduced aeration will slow or stop after-ripening and has been used experimentally to induce secondary dormancy.

The time required for moist-chilling (stratification) varies among species, among clones within a species, among different seed lots of the same kind which were grown in different areas or in different years, and even among individual seeds of a single lot. Individual differences in this requirement probably account for the temperature response. It is apparent that the time requirement for after-ripening is a genetic characteristic that can be modified by environment and conditions of production. The time required to after-ripen seeds of most woody perennial species is from 1 to 3 months, although for certain species 5 to 6 months is necessary.

Removal of the seed coverings permits germination of the excised embryo, although the response of the excised embryo tends to be sluggish and the resulting seedling dwarfed and abnormal. The basis for this germination-regulating role of the seed covering is not clear. It has been explained, on the one hand, as being due to a restriction in oxygen uptake, the level of which becomes limiting to the dormant embryo at high temperatures. It has also been explained as being due to the action of germination inhibitors which are found in the seed coverings.

Flemion showed that incompletely after-ripened peach seedlings remain dwarfed for many years if held at high temperatures but will resume normal growth after being subjected to 6 weeks of chilling. Later, Pollock demonstrated that peach seedlings were dwarfed when the apical meristem of the excised embryo was exposed to germination temperatures between 73°and 81°F (23° and 27°C) but normal when exposed to higher or lower temperatures. Dwarfing can be offset by exposure of the seedlings to long photoperiods or continuous light (provided that this action is taken before the apical meristem becomes fully dormant) or by repeated application of gibberellic acid. Treatment of nonchilled seeds of some peach varieties with thiourea will produce prompt germination, but the resulting seedlings will be dwarfed.

The biological mechanism whereby embryo dormancy is overcome within the seed is not well understood. Many changes that occur within the embryo during after-ripening appear to indicate merely the increasing ability of the seeds to germinate. Such changes include increasing water-absorbing power, increasing enzyme activity, increased acidity, and gradual changes of the insoluble complex storage materials into soluble simpler substances. Pollock has measured the increase in fresh weight, number of cells, and respiratory activity in the embryo axis of cherry seeds held for 16 weeks at 50°F At this temperature, phosphorus was increasingly found in the energy-rich compounds (nucleotides) involved in the metabolic activities of the cell, whereas in seeds held at higher temperatures, the phosphorus accumulates as inorganic phosphate.

Growth inhibiting and growth-promoting substances occur within various parts of the seed. Luckwill found inhibitors in dormant apple seeds in the endosperm, integuments and embryo in the ratio of 30 : 13 : 1, respectively. The inhibitors disappeared during chilling, and growth-promoting substances appeared. Inhibiting substances have likewise been shown to be produced in the cotyledons of *Fraxinus* seeds during the period in which the dry seeds imbibed water. Lipe and Crane identified an inhibitor extracted from the integuments of peach seed as dormin (or a compound similar to it). Dormin is a dormancy-inducing substance which has been extracted from Sycamore buds and leaves; this is also known as abcisin II or as *abscisic acid.* Similarly, an inhibitor occurs in the integuments of nonchilled birch (*Betula*) seeds. Dormin and abscisin II have been shown to induce dormancy in seeds. In each of these cases the effect of this inhibitor is decreased by gibberellic acid and, to some extent, by leaching with water. Although these inhibitors tend to diminish during chilling, there is also an increase in the content of growth-promoting substances prior to and during germination. Consequently it is difficult to ascertain specific cause-and-effect relationships. Nevertheless, there is considerable belief among plant physiologists that dormancy of the kind represented in these seeds is controlled through a balance among naturally occurring inhibitors and promoters, interacting with environmental factors such as temperature and possibly oxygen supply. Gibberellin has been cited as a major part of the promoter complex, and dormin as a part of the inhibitor complex.

Seeds with a High-Temperature, Followed by a Low-Temperature, Requirement. Several cases exist in which a single low-temperature treatment is inadequate to produce germination unless the moist seed is previously subjected to warm temperatures. In nature, ripe seeds fall to the ground, are exposed to warmth and moisture in late summer and fall, and are then subjected to chilling in winter. With this sequence, germination may be delayed until the second spring. In one group of plants—wild ginger (*Asarum canadense*), several lily species (*Lilium auratum*, *canadense*, *japonicum*, *rubellum*, *superbum*, and *szovitsianum*), herbaceous and tree peony (*Paeonia*), and a number of *Viburnum* species—only the radicle grows at high temperatures. Low temperatures must follow to after-ripen the epicotyl and cause the shoot to grow. Two to 6 months (in some *Viburnums*, 17 months) at high temperatures are required for root growth before a chilling period—of 1 to 4 months—is provided.

Another group of plants with similar requirements include those in which the embryo at the time of fruit ripening is incompletely developed; it increases in size during the warm period, then after-ripens during the chilling period. Ash (*Fraxinus excelsior*) seeds have this requirement. Holly (*Ilex* sp.) seeds consist mostly of endosperm—the embryo being small and hardly differentiated—and require a warm period for the embryo to develop. In both ash and holly, however, the problem is complicated by seed coat dormancy conditions as well.

Seeds with a Low-Temperature, Followed by a High-Temperature, Followed by a Low-Temperature, Requirement. Still more complex requirements occur in a number of other plants, mostly wild species of the temperature zone—blue cohosh (*Caulophyllum*), lily-of-the-valley (*Convallaria*), Solomon's seal (*Polygonatum communtatum*), bloodroot (*Sanguinaria canadensis*), false Solomon's seal (*Smilacina racemosa*), and *Trillium erectum* and *T. grandiflorum*. Their requirements are as follows : a cold period of 1 to 6 months to after-ripen the radicle, a warm period of 1 to 6 months for the radicle to grow, and then a second cold period of 1 to 6 months to after-ripen the epicotyl.

Combinations of Two or more Types of Seed Dormancy

Seed germination in a number of species is complicated by the presence of more than one type of dormancy the usual combination being that of seed coat dormancy combined with a dormant embryo. Such seeds have been recognized by nurserymen as being among the most difficult to handle because of the long period of time required to produce germination. This group has been referred to as "two-year" seeds, because seeds planted in the spring remain dormant and will not germinate until the next spring. If planted in the fall, they will not emerge until the second spring following planting.

Treatment of seeds with double dormancy involves the combination of procedures which overcome each type of dormancy present. In nature, decomposition of the seed coverings takes place by various agencies of the environment, as has been previously discussed. Warm stratification for several months, during which time micro-organisms act upon the seed covering, followed by cold stratification, is an effective method of handling. This explains the fact that seeds planted in spring or summer fail to germinate until the following spring. The period of handling can be shortened by treating the seed coats artificially and then stratifying. In some cases giving the seeds a short, warm stratification period between the time of seed coat treatment and cold stratification will assist considerably in the elimination of dormancy. If seeds of some woody plant species are dried following harvest, a hard seed coat develops, and germination does not take place until the second spring following harvest. If, on the other hand, the seeds are fall planted without drying, germination takes place the following spring.

Chemical Inhibitors

Substances which inhibit germination can be extracted from a variety of plant parts, including seeds, fruits, leaf sap, bulbs, and roots. Some of these naturally occurring germination inhibitors have been identified as specific chemical substances : ammonia (from beet seed), hydrogen cyanide (from amygdalin), ethylene (from ripe fruits), essential oils, unsaturated organic acids, alkaloids, (nicotine, cocaine, caffein), unsaturated lactones—coumarin and others. The existence of such substances in plants does not necessarily mean they have an essential role in controlling seed germination. Nevertheless, there is increasing emphasis on the biological role that naturally occurring inhibitors play.

During fruit and seed development many different chemical materials accumulate in the fruit, seed coverings and embryo. It is not surprising then that most fleshy fruits, or juices from them, strongly inhibit germination. This occurs, for instance, in citrus, cucurbits, stone fruits, apples, pears, grapes and tomatoes. Likewise many dry fruits and fruit coverings, such as the hulls of guayule, *Pennisetum cilirare*, and wheat (*Triticum*), and the capsules of mustard (*Brassica*), and others produce inhibition. Undoubtedly these substances play an important biological role in preventing premature germination while the seeds are present on the parent plant. Where the fruit covering remains with the seed, the inhibiting effect can persist for a considerable period even after the seed is separated from the plant.

Inhibitors in seeds appear to play a direct germination controlling role in some plants. For instance, seed inhibitors are important in the ecology of certain desert plants. Such substances have been referred to as chemical rain gauges in that a heavy rain (which would insure survival of the seedling) is necessary to leach out enough of the inhibitor to allow germination to take place. A light soaking is insufficient.

Inhibitors appear to the involved in germination control of many freshly harvested seeds, although their exact role is difficult to assess. Part of the evidence is that removal of the seed coat makes germination possible. Inhibitors have been repeatedly demonstrated to occur in various seeds when freshly harvested. Such materials either disappear in dry storage or leach out at germination. Dormancy has been induced experimentally in lettuce seed by treating it with an inhibitor—coumarin—and subsequently overcome by the same treatments required for naturally dormant seed. A probable role of inhibitors was described in the discussions or gas-restricting seed coats and dormant embryos.

Environmental Conditions Affecting Germination

Water

Inhibition of water by the seed is the first stop in the germination process. The two most important factors which affect water uptake by seeds are : (a) the nature of the seed and its coverings and (b) the amount of available water in the surrounding medium. Seeds have great absorbing power, owing to their colloidal nature. In storage, seeds can absorb water from the surrounding air. Different kinds of seeds vary greatly in the amount and rate of water absorbed, either in storage or during germination. The rate of water uptake is also influenced by temperature, a higher temperature favouring an increased rate. The seed covering also plays an important role in water uptake. In some seeds, it is so impermeable to water that germination will not occur until the seed covering has been altered in some manner.

The moisture supplied to the germinating seed may affect both the germination percentage and the germination rate. Germination percentage tends to be equal over most of the range of available soil moisture from field capacity (FC) to permanent wilting percentage (PWP). Differences between species become evident as the moisture content of the soil approaches dryness (PWP). Some seeds germinate only above PWP; others can germinate below PWP. For instance, vegetable plants can be grouped according to their moisture requirements for germination as follows :

Group—1. Seeds that will germinate in soils with moisture from permanent wilting percentage (or a little above) to moisture content above field capacity.

cabbage	sweet corn	muskmelon	pepper
turnip	squash	cucumber	onion
radish	watermelon	tomato	carrot

Group—2. Seeds that will germinate in soils from intermediate moisture content to above field capacity.

snap bean	pea	endive	beet
lima bean	lettuce		

Group—3. Seeds that will germinate only in soils near field capacity.

celery

Group—4. Seeds that germinate well at lower moisture contents but show reduced germination near field capacity.

spinach New Zealand spinach

Rate of emergence from a seed bed is influenced particularly by the available moisture supply. From a point approximately halfway through the range from FC to PWP there is a decline in rate. Excess soluble salts in the germination medium may inhibit germination and reduce seedling stands. Such excess soluble salts may originate from the soil and other materials used in the germination medium, the irrigation water, or excessive fertilization. Since the effects of salinity become more acute when the moisture supply is low and the concentration of salts thereby increased, it is particularly important to maintain a salinity exists.

Surface evaporation from subirrigated beds can result in the accumulation of salts at the soil surface even under conditions in which salinity would not be expected. Planting seeds several inches below the crown of a sloping seed-bed can minimize this hazard. Maintaining an adequate continuous moisture supply can be difficult, because germination takes place in the upper surface of the germination medium, which is subject to fluctuations in temperature and in moisture supply. The problem is greater with the necessarily shallow planting of small seeds or where the rate of germination is slow. Careful watering, deeper planting, and the application of a mulch are ways to maintain a more uniform water supply. On the other hand, excess watering accompanied by poor drainage can be deleterious, because it reduces aeration in the germination medium and favours "damping-off". Soaking seeds before planting is sometimes utilized to initiate the germination process and to shorten the time required for seedlings to emerge from the soil.

Such a treatment may be advantageous with seeds normally slow to germinate, with seeds which are hard and dry, or when certain dormancy conditions exist. However, if the seeds ordinarily germinate without difficulty, there is little need for soaking. Seeds which have imbibed water are easily injured and more difficult to plant. Prolonged soaking can result in injury to the seed, and reduce germination. The harmful effect has been attributed principally to the presence of microorganisms and to poor aeration, although there seem to be other effects as well that are not understood. If soaking is to be prolonged, the water should be changed at least every 24 hours.

Temperature

A favourable temperature is a second requirement for germination. Plants in general can be classified into the following groups according to temperature requirements : (a) those whose seeds germinate only at relatively low temperatures; (b) those which germinate only at relatively high temperatures; and (c) those which are able to germinate over a range of temperatures from cool to warm. The temperature requirement is an important factor in the adaptation of a particular species to a particular environment. Seeds of alpine plants would be expected to germinate well at low temperatures. Indeed, studies have shown that some alpines, for instance *Camassia leichtlini* and *Lewisia rediviva*, germinate only below 41°F and 50°F, respectively. On the other hand, seeds of most tropical plants require high temperatures.

Temperature largely determines the time of year at which seeds will germinate out-of-doors. As a result, seedlings of many self-sown plants, particularly annual weeds, appear only at certain times of the year, depending upon whether they are warm-season or cool-season plants.

The temperature requirements for germination of seeds are generally considered in relation to three points: minimum, maximum, and optimum. The designation of these temperatures for any one species is somewhat difficult, because temperature affects both the germination percentage as well as the germination rate. Furthermore, temperature requirements of dormant seeds may change with the age of the seed and the progress of after-ripening. Germination percentage can be rather constant within the range of temperatures at which germination takes place. The rate of germination, on the other hand, is affected more; an increase in temperature invariably increases the germination rate. Above the optimum, rates decrease as injury occurs.

Minimum temperatures are those below which germination will not occur. For "cool-season" plants, this temperature is approximately 40°F (4.5°C) or less, although for some, such as endive, lettuce,onion, parsnip, and spinach, it approaches freezing. Germination rates are invariably very low at these low temperatures. Minimum temperatures for "warm season" plants are in the range of 50° to 60°F (10° to 15°C). Below these temperatures, either the seeds fail to germinate, or "chilling injury" can result in seedling abnormalities. In lima bean, Pollock has shown that there is a temperature-sensitive period during the initial imbibition in which injury to the embryo axis occurs if seeds are exposed to temperatures below 60°F (15°C).

The maximum temperatures are the highest at which germination will occur. The upper limits of soil temperature for the survival of most vegetable seeds is between 86°F (30°C) and 104°F (40°C). Seeds placed at 113°F (45°C) were killed within 24 hours. During hot weather, direct sunlight striking the soil surface may raise the temperature to a level injurious to plant tissue. Also, moisture is rapidly lost. This so-called "heat injury" affecting young seedlings resembles the "damping-off" caused by pathogenic organisms. For may plants shading is necessary.

Short exposures can be made to temperatures much higher than those which would be used for germination. In one study, exposure of seeds of a number of different species to 120°F (49°C) for 1 hour did not decrease the germination percentage even though the seeds had imbibed water. At higher temperatures, the amount of injury increased but depended upon the kind of seed, the duration of exposure, and the moisture content of seed. Dry seeds could withstand brief exposure to temperatures of 212°F (100°C), but above 250°(121°C) all were killed.

Such heat treatments are important in freeing planting material of harmful organisms. The temperature should be high enough to kill the organisms but not so high as to impair germination. Heat tolerance is greater with seeds of low moisture content and with those that are fresh, uninjured, and of high viability.

Seeds of some species—for instance, lettuce, celery, endive, delphinium, and numerous flower species—remain dormant at temperatures over 75°F (24°C). This temperature sensitivity is associated with freshly harvested seeds and tends to disappear with after ripening in dry storage. It has been called *thermodormancy*. Germination can be induced by subjecting the seeds to lower temperatures or to dry storage. In laboratory testing, chilling moist seeds at 41° to 50°F (5°to 10°C) for 5 days will induce prompt germination when the seeds are subsequently shifted to higher temperatures. Seed germination of some woody species is also inhibited by high temperatures. Optimum temperatures are those most favourable for germination. This should be the range wherein the highest percentage of seedlings will be produced at the highest rate of germination. On this basis, the optimum temperature for seeds of most plants is between 80°and 95°F (26.5° and 35°C).

Germination is often much better if the seeds are subjected to daily alternating temperatures rather than a constant temperature. Commonly used alternations are 59°F (15°C) or 68°F (20°C) for 18 hours and 86°F (30°C) for 6 hours. The effective temperature alternation has been shown to change as the seed after-ripens in dry storage, and the effect may disappear entirely. The above discussion refers to the effect of temperature on the initiation of germination itself. In addition, temperature affects other influencing factors in the seed-bed, such as the activity of pathogenic organisms. Temperature likewise affects seedling growth following germination. Usually a temperature somewhat lower than that which is optimum for germination is best for growing the seedlings.

Oxygen

Respiration may be summarized as follows:

sugar	+	oxygen	→	carbon dioxide	+	water	+	energy
$C_6H_{12}O_6$		$6O_2$		$6CO_2$		$6H_2O$		673kcal

This process takes place in seeds as long as the seed is alive. In a non germinating dry seed the respiration rate is low, and little oxygen is utilized. During germination the respiration rate increases, oxygen uptake increases, and carbon dioxide is given off at an increased rate. The biochemical mechanisms that control seed germination are not well known, but oxygen is utilized in separate metabolic processes that may change with the progress of germination.

Oxygen is involved in some way with the initial triggering reactions of germination, and aerobic conditions are necessary for after-ripening reactions. Consequently limitation in the oxygen supply at the initial stages can inhibit germination. In seeds, fats are transformed into sugars, in which form they are translocated. Since a fatty acid molecule contains less oxygen than a sugar molecule, additional oxygen must be supplied. Energy to drive the cellular mechanisms and to transform specific materials into growth processes is provided through the oxidation of the reserve substances in the seed. Metabolic pathways in seeds appear to be essentially the same as in other plant tissues. Part of the energy is evolved as heat and can be measured by appropriate instruments.

Reduced aeration can decrease germination. One of the effects of a hard crust in a seed-bed is to limit oxygen diffusion and thus inhibit seedling emergence. Limitation in oxygen supply in poorly drained seed-beds or after heavy rains or excessive irrigation can result in the pore spaces of the soil being filled with water.

Seeds of land plants vary considerably in their ability to germinate under water, but those of the following species germinate well: timothy, *Agrostis nebulosa*, *Axonopus compressus*, Canadian bluegrass, Bermuda grass, lettuce, wormwood, carrot, celery, portulaca, iceplant, snapdragon, *Melissa officinalis*, bittersweet, and petunia. Seeds of water plants and rice normally germinate under water. The ability of rice to germinate at low oxygen presseures has been attributed to the presence of an anaerobic, energy-liberating system within the seeds. Cattails (*Typha latifolia*) give poor or no germination in air but germinate promptly in water or when the oxygen supply is reduced.

LIGHT

Light can play an important role in seed propagation both because of its effect upon the initiation of germination and because of its controlling influence upon seedling growth.

Light and Germination

The fact that visible light can stimulate or inhibit germination of seeds of some plants has been recognized since the middle of the nineteenth century. Plants whose seeds have an absolute requirement for light, with viability being lost in a few weeks without it, include mistletoe (*Viscum album*), strangling fig (*Ficus aurea*), and *Areuthobium oxycedri*, all epiphytic plants. Seed germination of another group, including celery, lettuce, tobacco, most grasses, and many conifers is favoured by light. Seeds of another group, e.g., some species of *Phacelia*, *Nigella*, *Allium*, *Amaranthus*, and *Phlox*, are inhibited by light.

Germination control is exerted through a photochemically reversible reaction involving the response of a pigment, known as *phytochrome*, to light of particular wavelengths :

$$\text{phytochrome}_{\text{red}} \underset{\text{in far-red light}}{\overset{\text{in red light}}{\rightleftharpoons}} \text{phytochrome}_{\text{far-red}}$$

(inhibits germination) (instantaneous reaction) in darkness (slow reaction) (promotes germination)

Exposure of the imbibed seed to red light (6400Å to 6700Å) causes the phytochrome, in it to change to photochrome$_{fr}$ which is linked in some way to reactions inducing germination. Exposure to far-red light (7200Å to 7500Å) produces an instantaneous change to the alternate form, phytochromer, which inhibits germination. In the dark, in the presence of oxygen, and at favourably low temperatures, the latter change takes place slowly. In plants under natural light the red wavelengths dominate the far-red so that the phytochrome is converted to the active $P_{far\text{-}red}$ form.

Light-inhibited seeds are less common, but evidently their response is to the same phytochrome system. Blue light may also be involved, but the reactions are not known. Light control appears to involve the seed coats or the endosperm layer, and the light requirements disappear if the embryos are excised.

Knowledge of light effects has been obtained by experiments with particularly sensitive seeds under controlled conditions. The role of light as a germination-controlling mechanism in propagation and in nature is not always clear, since response varies with the kind of seed, the conditions of seed production, and accompanying environmental conditions. In general, a light requirement is found in freshly harvested seeds and disappears with dry storage; light stimulation will not occur if the temperature is too high. The light requirement can be partially replaced by alternating temperatures, by potassium nitrate, or by kinetin, as well as by gibberellic acid and thiourea.

In the soil, light penetration depends upon the lenght of the rays. Red light penetrates to a depth of about an inch in sandy soil. Most light-favoured seeds are small. Seed germination occurs with those situated close enough to the surface for seedlings to emerge but deep enough so that water supply will not be limiting. At greater depths there is complete darkness, or only far-red rays penetrate; in this case the seeds remain dormant until the soil is disturbed.

Photoperiod can affect germination of seeds of some species. Eastern hemlock (*Tsuga canadensis*) and birch (*Betula*) for instance, are "long-day" seeds, but germination is also promoted by low temperatures. Photoperiodic control can partially replace a seed-chilling requirement and vice versa. These light-temperature requirements for seed germination evidently are involved in the ecological adaptation of the species. Seeds of some other species, such as *Nemophila*, *Nigella*, *Veronica persica*, and *Eschscholtzia californica* are inhibited by long days.

Light and Seedling Growth

Light affects the growth processes in the seedling and has an important role in its emergence through the soil. In the darkness of the seed-bed, the hypocotyl or epicotyl is elongated and etiolated, and the leaves are unexpanded. There is a hook at the end of the plumule which pushes through the ground. When the seedling shoot emerges into the light, shoot elongation decreases, the plumular hook straightens out, leaves expand, and normal growth takes place.

In the early germination stages, the seedling utilizes the reserve supply of the seed. Later growth depends upon the production of carbohydrates and other materials resulting from photosynthesis in the leaves. Light of a relatively high intensity is necessary to produce sturdry, vigorous plants. An extremely high light intensity, on the other hand, can result in high temperatures which may produce heat injury to the seedling. Consequently excessively high as well as excessively low light intensities need to be avoided. Partial shading is necessary for many plants during their early seedling growth.

Supplementary artificial light to increase the length of the photoperiod is sometimes provided in growing seedlings, particularly during winter when the day length is short and cloudy weather often prevails. Artificial light has been used as the sole illumination in indoor propagating structures for germinating seeds. The principal problems in artificial lighting in relation to plant growth are to get a sufficiently high intensity without heating and to obtain a proper balance of light quality.

Light intensities of 700 to 1200 foot candles are satisfactory, although lower intensities can be used for some shade plants. The length of the photoperiod should be 12 to 18 hours ; below 12 hours the amount of photosynthesis becomes limiting, while photoperiods longer than 18 hours may produce poor results with some plants. Where low light intensities are used, lower temperatures should also be used. With higher light intensities, higher temperatures are permissible. A certain amount of blue light is necessary to produce stocky seedlings; red light alone produces tall, "leggy" plants. Satisfactory artificial light sources are fluorescent lamps of the daylight type, 3500°K, or 4500°K white types, or a mixture of the two, or the "cool-white" alone.

Seedling Production Indoors

The production of seedlings within some type of indoor shelter is an important method of propagating plants. Seeds are sown in special germinating media and the seedlings transferred to pots, flats, or special beds and later transplanted into their permanent location. Seeds may also be sown directly into pots or other containers. This technique is used, when outdoor growing conditions are unfavourable, to produce plants for pot plants or benching in greenhouses or to start plants for transplanting later to out-of-door locations.

It is extensively used to raise vegetables for early production, to grow plants which might not otherwise be adapted to an area having a late spring and a short growing season, and to produce bedding plants for landscaping purposes. It may also be used in the nursery production of trees and shrubs. Starting seedlings indoors for outdoor growing may enable the propagator to obtain higher germination percentages because he can control environmental conditions and reduce loss from disease, insects, and other adverse conditions. To obtain these benefits certain facilities are required, and somewhat more labour may be necessary in the handling of seedlings through to the transplant stage than would be required with direct seeding. It also requires rather close attention to details and a certain degree of skill and experience. On the whole, growing seedling indoors is somewhat more expensive than direct seeding and would be justified only with valuable plant material or expensive seeds; or when seedlings are difficult to start under more vigorous outdoor conditions, or to obtain the benefits of early season production.

Facilities

The facilities required for starting seedlings indoors depends upon the number being grown. If only small lots of seedlings are to be grown, as might be done by an amateur gardener, a small box in a sunny window would be sufficient. When large numbers of seedlings such as greenhouses, cold frames, or hotbeds are necessary. Any container that will hold the germination medium and provide drainage could be adapted for germinating seeds. Useful containers are wood, plastic, or metal flats; individual flower pots; bulb pans; or plastic freezer boxes. Seeds of plants which are difficult to transplant bare-root—for instance, cucumber or melon—could be planted individually in plant bands. Polyethylene plastic bags can also be used for germinating seeds.

Seedling Production

Germinating Media

There are a number of materials and mixtures of materials which are satisfactory for seed germination. Clean sterilized containers should be used. The container is completely filled with the germination medium, which is worked carefully into the corners to eliminate air pockets. Excess soil is removed with a straight board drawn across the top of the flat. The soil is then tamped firmly with a flat block of wood to a level approximately ½ in below the rim of the container. If fine seeds are to be sown, if may be desirable to water before planting.

Sowing

The method of sowing seeds depends on the size of seed. Containers with the germination medium may be presoaked, drained, and then enclosed in polyethylene to hold moisture until planted. Depth of covering varies with the kind of seed and the germinating conditions. Very fine seed may merely be dusted onto the surface. Larger seeds may be covered to one to two times their minimum diameter, assuming that good moisture conditions prevail in the medium during the first week after planting. During the initial germination period a uniform, but not excessive moisture supply is essential in the appear layers of the medium. Containers should be sprinkled lightly after sowing and then covered. A plastic or glass cover will prevent drying out, but it should be shaded from the direct rays of the sun. Some seeds, however, must be exposed to light. Placing the planted containers under intermittent mist controlled with a time clock is an excellent method of handling.

The temperature of which the flats are placed depends upon the germination requirements of the seeds. The best temperature for seeds of most plants is around 68°F (20°C). For some, 55°F (13°C) is better, and for seeds of warm-season and tropical plants temperatures up to 86°F (30°C) are preferable. Higher temperatures (over 86°F) result is rapid moisture loss and inhibition of germination in some seeds.

Handling of the Seedlings

The primary objectives from seedling emergence until the plant is placed in its permanent location are to control damping-off and to develop stocky, vigorous plants capable of being transplanted with little check in growth. After seedling emergence, the cover over the flat is removed and the seedlings subjected to increased but not intense light. Moderate to low temperatures produce stocky growth. High temperatures lead to undesirable succulent growth, excessive moisture loss, and development of damping-off organisms. General recommendations are a 60° to 65°F. (15° to 19°C) temperature during the day and 5° to 10°F lower at night for cool season plants, and 70° to 75°F (22° to 24°C) during the day, and 10° to 15°F lower at night for warm-season plants. Seedlings subjected to adequate light produce short, stocky plants rather than spindly, elongated plants, which result if they are grown in weak light. However, full sunlight during the early stages of growth should be avoided because of injury from high temperature.

The moisture supply should be constant but not excessive. Over-watering can result in poor aeration, and the resulting high humidity contributes to damping-off. When root growth is limited in the initial germination stages, frequent light waterings are necessary to keep the upper layer of the germination medium moist. As the root system develops the frequency of watering can be reduced, but the medium should be wetted completely. Watering early in the day so that plants dry before evening is desirable to reduce fungus development. Covers of closed frames should be opened at intervals to lower the humidity as the seedling become larger.

If damping-off becomes a problem, it can be controlled to a certain degree by watering at intervals with a commercial fungicidal solution, although the success with damping-off can be controlled by this means is variable.

Transplanting Seedlings

When planted closely in the medium, the seedlings soon become overcrowded and a check in growth will occur if they are not promptly transplanted. This operation comes as soon as the first two to four true leaves have developed and the seedlings are large enough to handle.

A seedling should be transplanted—with wider spacing—either into another flat or individually into pots, plant-bands, or similar containers.

A transplant flat is prepared as was done for the germination medium. Seedlings are lifted carefully and inserted 1 to 2 in apart into holes made with a wooden dibble in the transplant medium. The soil is then pressed firmly about the seedlings to eliminate any air pockets about it, and the flat is then thoroughly watered. For the first few days while the seedlings are becoming re-established, the flats should be shaded, held at low temperature, and kept from drying. When the seedlings have grown so that they are well developed and have begun to crowd, they are again transplanted either into their permanent location in the field or into pots or other containers.

Success in transplanting depends to a large extent upon the previous handling. When the permanent location is in the greenhouse, environmental conditions are controlled and are not different from those to which the seedling has been exposed during development. When movement is from a greenhouse or hotbed to the open field, the operation is somewhat more critical and requires that the plant be "hardened" prior to its shift to the open field "Hardening" involves a checking of growth resulting in the accumulation of carbohydrates which makes the plant better able to withstand adverse conditions. The process can be brought on by withholding the supply of moisture, reducing the temperature, and gradually shifting from the greenhouse or hotbed to the environment of the permanent location. A cold frame or lathhouse is useful for this purpose. Flats of seedlings can be moved into them and allowed to remain for 7 to 10 days prior to placing in the field.

Before being moved into the field, the plants should be watered thoroughly. Planting is done in the field by hand or, in some cases, by transplanting machines. During transplanting , it is desirable to retain as much soil about the roots as practical to avoid disturbing the root system. Afterward, the plants should be thoroughly watered, and if practical a temporary shade provided. For the first few days, until the plants have become established, they should be watched for wilting, and watered as necessary.

The use of "booster" or "starter" solutions containing nitrogen, phosphorus, and potassium shortly before or after transplanting is sometimes beneficial in established plants in the field. Such solution should be used with caution, since if the soil is low in moisture at transplanting time, high concentrations of fertilizer can be injurious. This effect may vary with the soil condition.

Direct Seeding

Direct sowing of seeds in permanent plant locations is a technique of seed propagation often preferred to the use of special seed-beds. In general, direct seeding is more economical, since it utilizes no special plant-growing facilities and involves no individual handling of seedlings. With many plants it is the only practical method to use. It is a standard method of growing field crop, and many commercially grown vegetables. Much forest regeneration is done through direct seeding practices. Aerial broadcasting is used for large acreages. Amateur vegetable and flower gardeners may find direct seeding preferable to other methods, since it is simple and does not make demands on time and facilities. The lower germination percentages often obtained with direct sowing can be offset by increasing the rate of sowing and thinning any excess plants after germination. This procedure is feasible where the cost of the individual seed is not a factor. Of course, if much thinning is necessary, the cost of production again increases. Direct seeding results in continuous and rapid development of the seedling, with no check in growth associated with transplanting. The total time between seeding and harvest is less than by the other methods. Some plants, such as corn, cucumbers, or beans, are difficult to transplant, and are almost always planted directly in the field.

Seed-Bed Preparation

Proper seed-bed preparation is the keynote for successful field sowing. The requirements of a good seed-bed are (a) to have an initial supply of moisture to carry the seeds through the germinating and early seedling period, (b) to have a physical condition that allows moisture to be supplied continuously to the seed, and (c) to have good aeration. A problem in seed-bed preparation is to obtain the proper balance between the extremes of low moisture-high aeration and high moisture low aeration. This can be best obtained by a medium-textured loam which can supply moisture continuously without excessive drying. A light sandy soil dries out rapidly, whereas a heavy clay soil gives poor drainage and inadequate aeration, and tends to form a hard surface crust as it dries.

Soil conditioning can be provided in the filed by plowing under a cover crop or animal manure, allowing sufficient time before sowing for decomposition to take place. Incorporating peat moss, leaf mold, or other organic material may be feasible on a small scale or for high value crops. The ideal seed-bed would be one in which the soil is moist but not wet, finely pulverized to a depth of 6 to 10 inch particularly in the upper 3 or 4 inch and firmed to eliminate large air spaces which would increase evaporation and water loss.

The method of preparation depends upon the size of the operation and upon the crop being grown. For large-scale operations, implements such as plows, disks, harrows, and land-levelers are necessary. For smaller operations, the rototiller type of implement is convenient, since it loosens and pulverizes the soil in one operation. For small plots, spading or forking is the time-honored system. The soil should be spaded to a depth of 6 to 10 inch and then vigorously raked. If it is dry, irrigation several days before preparation is necessary. Working the soil when it is too wet or too dry destroys its structure and leads to difficulty in aeration and water penetration later. Determining the optimum soil condition is often difficult, but as a rule of thumb, if the soil forms a tight ball when squeezed with the hand, it is too wet. It should crumble when squeezed.

Seed-bed preparation may involve soil treatments to destroy harmful insects, disease organisms, and weed seeds. The modern development of specific chemicals and effective methods of application has made this phase of operation important, if the crop has sufficient economic value to justify the cost. This cost is offset to some extent by reduction in later costs of cultivation and weed control.

Seed Planting

The time of planting is determined by the temperature requirement for germination. Cool-season crops are planted early in the spring when temperatures are low; conversely, seeds requiring higher temperatures should not be planted until after the soil warms up. The time of planting is also determined by the date at which production from the plant is desired. For instance, planting small numbers of vegetable seeds at consecutive time intervals throughout the early spring and summer to produce a continuous supply from a home garden would be more desirable than a single planting to produce the entire crop at one peak harvest.

One of the problems in field planting is to determine the rate of sowing to obtain a desired stand of plants. The final stand of the plant is determined in order to produce the maximum yield of a high-quality, plant product. Too low a stand will reduce yields ; too thick a stand will decrease size and quality. Once the desired final stand is determined, the required rate of sowing can be calculated if the germination percentage, the purity percentage, and the number of seeds per pound (or ounce) are known:

$$\text{Pounds (ounces) of seed required per unit area} = \frac{\text{Number of plants per unit are desired}}{\text{Number of seeds per pound (ounces)} \times \text{percentage germination} \times \text{percentage purity}}$$

This figure is the minimum number of seeds to use. In practice, it is often desirable to increase the rate of sowing to offset expected losses in the seed-bed. The seedlings are thinned to a desired spacing after emergence. The depth of planting depends upon the size of the seed, the conditions of the seed- bed, and the environment at the time of planting. With too-deep planting, germination may fail because the seedling is not able to emerge before the food reserves in the seed are exhausted. In addition, poor aeration may occur at lower depths. Proper depth is also related to moisture supply. Too-shallow planting will place the seed in the top soil layers, which are subject to drying. In light sandy soils, or during periods of warm weather, deeper planting is best, whereas in heavier soils and during periods of cool, cloudy weather, shallower planting is permissible. A general rule is to plant seeds three to four times their thickness, being sure this depth is well within the moist layer of the seed-bed.

Various mulching materials have been used on seed-beds. Paper of special manufacture, and clear or black polyethylene or polyvinyl plastic film have been used. These materials are laid over the surface and either removed at the time of seedling emergence or prepared with perforations for the seedling to grow through. A later innovation is a black asphalt emulsion nontoxic to plants and remains in place until disturbed through cultivation. Other materials include perlite or vermiculite treated with polyvinyl acetate. These materials benefit seedling stands by preventing crust formation, conserving moisture, controlling weeds (in some cases), and controlling seed-bed temperatures. Temperature control depends upon the type of material; clear plastic and asphalt emulsions increase day temperatures more than black plastic but lose heat more rapidly at night.

Growing Seedlings in the Nursery

Growing trees and shrubs by seeds is an important part of nursery production. Some nurseries propagate seedlings almost entirely, dealing very little in vegetative methods. This is true in the production of trees and shrubs for reforestation, roadside planting, erosion control, and similar purposes. Nurseries producing fruit trees or ornamental shrubs and trees use seedlings extensively as rootstocks upon which to bud or graft selected clones or varieties. The discussion which follows gives a general picture of the operations involved in the handling of seeds under nursery conditions. Details of operation vary from nursery to nursery, depending upon such factors as the kind of plant, the size of the operation, the purposes for growing, the inclinations of the operator, and the location of the nursery. Nursery management is a specialized field involving many more problems than the actual propagation of plant material.

Time of Planting

Seeds may be planted in the fall or in the spring depending upon their germination requirements and upon the management practices of the nursery. Most tree species can be placed into three general categories in regard to their seed-germiantion requirements.

Group I includes species (apple, pear, *Prunus*, *Rosa multiflora*, and yew) whose seeds require moist-chilling (stratification) and that, upon the completion of after-ripening, are sensitive to high germination temperatures. Germination temperatures of 50° to 62°F (10° to 17°C) would be optimum. High soil temperature results in damping off, seedling injury, and a tendency to revert to secondary dormancy. Such seeds could be effectively planted in the fall and sprouting would not take place until early in the spring. If they are kept in stratification storage overwinter, planting should take place as early in the spring as practical, but after frost danger is over.

Group II includes most fir, pine, and spruce species and many deciduous hardwood species whose seeds require varying amounts of moist-chilling (unless exposed to light) but that, after this is over, do not germinate in the spring until after the ground becomes warm. Optimum germination temperatures are 68°F to 86°F (20° to 30°C). Seeds of these species do not germinate in the cool fall season and not until late in the spring. Such seeds can be handled without difficulty either by fall planting or by moist winter storage and spring planting.

Group III includes those species (black locust, Colorado and Norway spruce, Chinese and Siberian elm, European larch, bristlecone pine, and Douglas fir) whose seeds are not temperature sensitive and are able to germinate over a range of 60° to 90°F (15° to 32°C). Some of these species require moist-chilling or have hard coats requiring special treatment. If fall-planted, seeds of this group will usually germinate prematurely and the seedling plants can be injured by winter cold. They are best planted in the spring, the actual time to plant not being as critical as that for the other two groups.

Other species with special requirements have been described earlier in this chapter. Planting schedules for these seeds should be geared to their particular requirements.

Fall planting is particularly useful where a large volume of seeds is to be handled and adequate cold storage facilities are not available. The seasonal labour requirements is distributed more uniformly throughout the year if some of the planting is done in the fall. As soon as the environmental conditions are favourable in the spring, germination takes place, and is not delayed by late planting, resulting in better stands and a longer growing season. On the other hand, losses sometimes result from unfavourable winter conditions, drying, disease, or rodents. Also, herbicidal weed control is necessary.

Seed-Bed Culture

Seedlings of many species are grown in special out-of-doors seed-beds during the first 1 or 2 years in the nursery. A common size is 3½ to 4 in width with a walkway between seed-beds, the length varying with the size of the operation. In some cases, sideboards are placed alongside the seed-bed after sowing to maintain the shape of the bed and to provide support for glass frames or lath shade. Seed may either be broadcast over the surface of the bed or drilled into closely spaced rows. Regulating the density of planting is one of the major problems in planting a seed-bed. For economical use of space, seeds should be planted as closely together as feasible. On the other hand, overcrowding leads to greater difficulty with damping-off and reduces vigor and size of the seedling resulting in thin, spindly trees and small root systems. Seedlings with these characteristics do not transplant well.

The optimum density depends on the species and on the purposes of propagation. In other words, if a high percentage of the seedlings are to reach a desired size for field planting or for use as rootstocks for grafting, lower densities might be desired. If the seedlings are to be transplanted into other beds for additional growth, higher densities (with smaller seedlings) might be more practical. Once the actual density is determined, the necessary rate of sowing can be calculated from certain data obtained from a germination test and from the experiences of the operator at that particular nursery. The following formula is used.

$$W = \frac{A \times S}{D \times P \times G \times L}$$

where W = weight of seeds in pounds to sow per given area.

A = area of seed-bed in square feet.

S = number of living seedlings desired per square foot.

D = average number of seeds per pound at the moisture content at which the seeds are sown.

P = average purity percentage of seeds (expressed as a decimal).

G = average effective germination percentage in the laboratory (expressed as a decimal).

L = average percentage of germinating seeds that will be living trees at the end of the season (expressed as a decimal). This is a correction factor which takes into account the expected losses which experience at that nursery indicates will occur with that species.

Seeds of a particular lot should be thoroughly mixed before planting to be sure that the density in the seed-bed will be uniform. Treatment with a fungicide for control of damping-off is desirable. Small conifer seeds may be pelleted for protection against disease, insects, birds, and rodents. Seeds are planted either by hand or by machine. Depth of planting varies with the size of the seed. In general, a depth of about two to four times the thickness of the seed is a fairly safe estimate, but this also varies with the kind of seed. During early stages of development, seedlings generally must be protected against drying, heat, or cold. In the case of tender plants, glass frames could be placed over the beds, although with most plants a lath shade is sufficient. With some plants, shade should be provided all through the first season, with others, shade is necessary only during the first part of the season. Sprinkling with water to reduce ground temperature during the hot part of the day is useful. A mulch applied to the seed-bed after planting helps to protect against drying, crusting, and cold, discourages weed-growth.

It is particularly desirable with fall-sown seeds, for seeds which are to remain for long-periods in the seed-bed before germination, or for seeds sown in cold areas. Materials which have been used include sawdust, burlap, pine litter, straw, hay, ground corncobs, wood shavings, sandpaper, canvas, shredded pine cones, sand, manure, and snow. One nurseryman reports the use of old rooting media of sand and peat as a seed-bed covering. The use of polyethylene film as a seed-bed cover has been described. In this case, the seed-bed was sown in the fall, covered lightly with sawdust, well watered, and then covered with a sheet of polythylene film, on top of which burlap was placed. The following spring the film was removed as soon as germination occurred.

During the first year in the nursery, it is important to keep the seedlings growing continuously without any check in development. A continuous moisture supply, cultivation to control weeds, and proper disease and insect control contribute to successful seedling growth. Fertilization with nitrogen is usually necessary, particularly when a mulch has been applied. Decomposition of organic material can produce nitrogen deficiency. Weed control can be facilitated by careful seed-bed preparation, cultivation, and chemical sprays. Three types of chemical controls are available.

Pre-planting fumigation with methyl bromide, chloropicrin, DD, Vapam, steam, or the like is effective and also kills disease organisms and nematodes. *Pre-emergence* weed sprays are applied to the soil before crop seeds emerge. *Post-emergence* weed sprays are applied after the crop or nursery seedlings have emerged and are growing. A wide range of selective and nonselective commercial products are available. However, such materials should be used with caution since improper use can cause injury to the young plants. Not only should directions of the manufacturer be followed, but preliminary trials should be made before largescale use.

The seedlings may remain in the seed-bed for 1 to 3 years, depending upon the kind of plant. Many plants are dug at the end of the first year and placed in *transplant beds* or "linedout" in the nursery bed for further development. Deciduous plants are planted 4 to 6 inch apart in nursery rows 18 inch to 4 ft. apart. Nursery plants in rows are often undercut at the end of one year to stimulate subsequent production of a more fibrous root system. Conifers usually go into transplant beds similar to the seed-bed but at wider spacing. Spacing may be several inches apart in rows 6 to 8 inch apart. Other cases involve field planting directly from the nursery. Seedlings produced in a nursery are often designated by numbers to indicate the length of time in a seed-bed and the length of time in a transplant bed. For instance, a designation of 1-2 means a seeding grown one year in a seed-bed and 2 years in a transplant bed or field. Similarly, a designation of 2-0 means a seedling produced in 2 years in a seed-bed and none in a transplant bed.

Direct Nursery Planting

Seeds of many deciduous trees are planted directly in nursery rows rather than in special seed-beds. This procedure is used to produce root-stocks for deciduous fruit and nut varieties. Where plants are to be budded or grafted in place, the width between rows is about 4ft and the seeds are planted 3 to 4 inch apart in the row. If the seeds show poor germinability, the seeds must be planted closer together to get the desired stand of seedlings. Large seed (walnut) are usually planted 4 to 6 inch deep, medium-sized seed (apricot, almond, peach, and pecan) about 3 inch and small (myrobalan plum)about 1½ inch. This may vary with soil type. Plants to be grown as seedlings without budding could be spaced at closer intervals and in rows closer together.

If germination is low, and a poor stand results, the surviving trees may, owing to the wide specing, grow too large to be suitable for budding. Usually, no shading is required by deciduous tree plants grown in the nursery row, although other cultural operations are similar to seed-bed culture. Plants generally remain in place in the nursery row until they are to be transplanted to their permanent location. A variation of this procedure is sometimes followed with species that germinate well but require some time to grow to budding size. Seeds are either planted close together to stand of 10 to 15 seedling per ft, or planted in a narrow band about 4 inch wide in the nursery row. The seedlings remain relatively small during the first season, after which they are lifted and lined-out in a nursery row. Cherry, apple, or pear seedlings are often produced in this manner.

INDEX